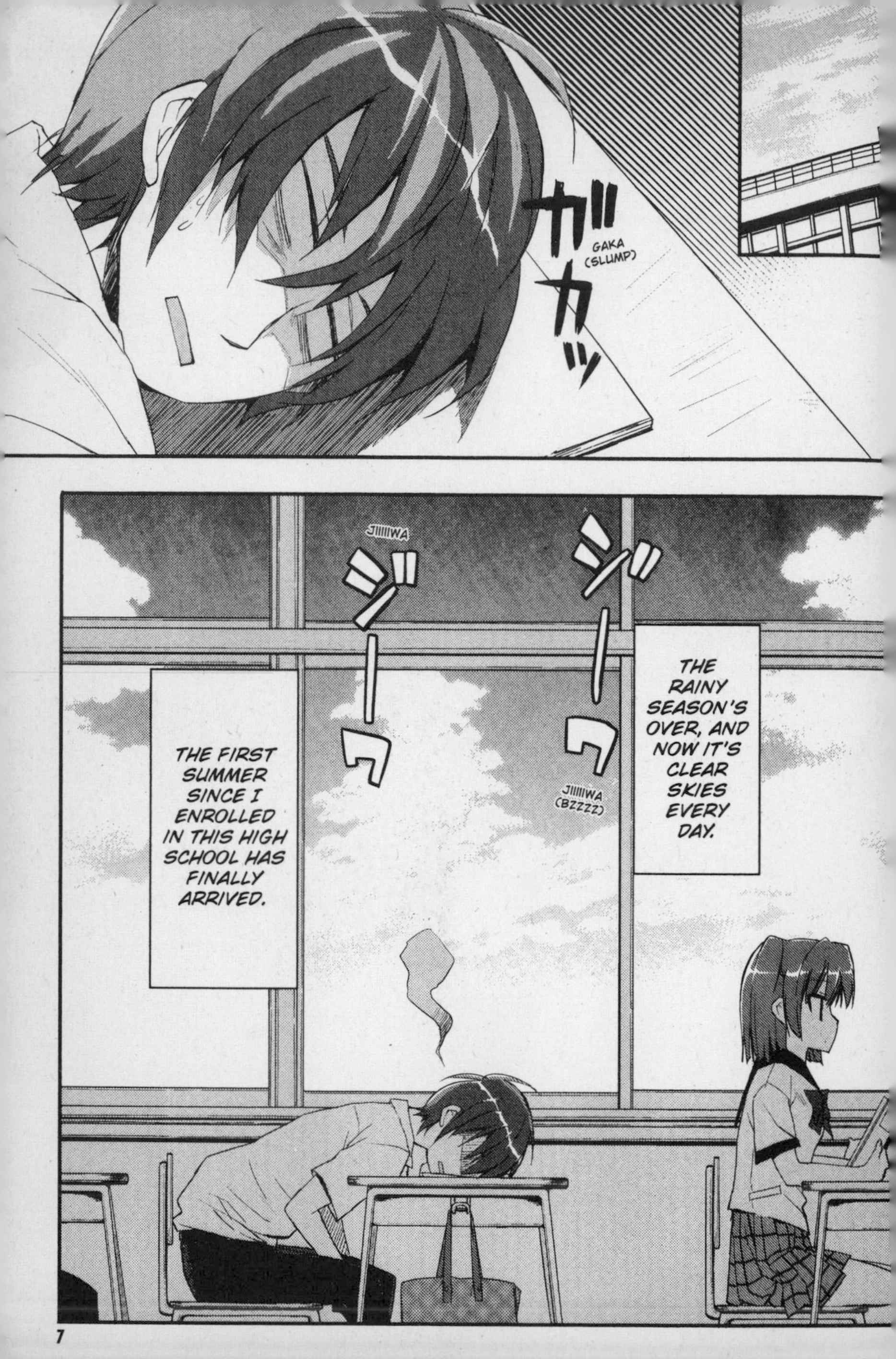
GAKA
(SLUMP)
THE RAINY SEASON'S OVER, AND NOW IT'S CLEAR SKIES EVERY DAY.
JIIIIWA
(BZZZZ)
JIIIIWA
THE FIRST SUMMER SINCE I ENROLLED IN THIS HIGH SCHOOL HAS FINALLY ARRIVED.

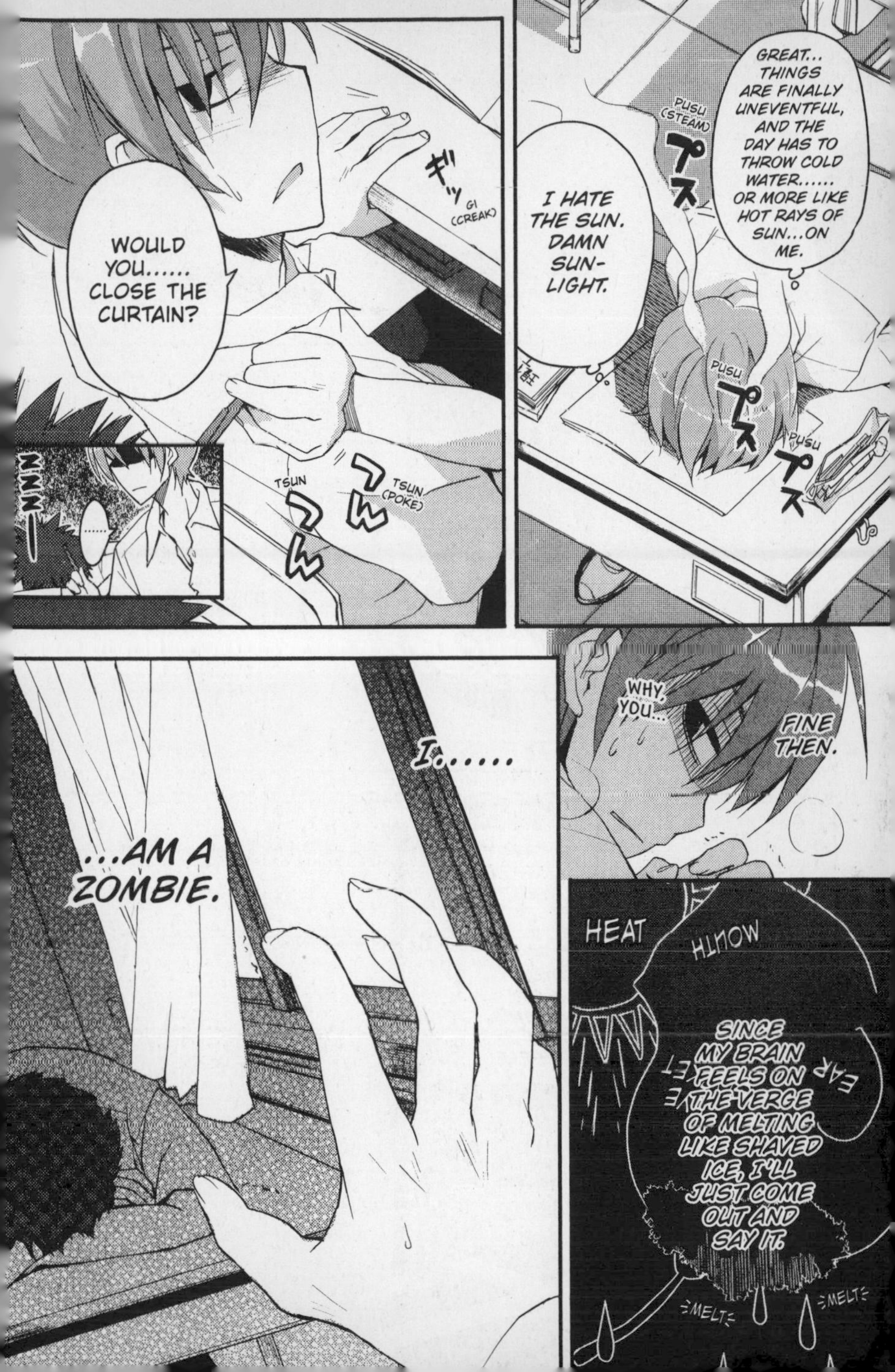
GREAT... THINGS ARE FINALLY UNEVENTFUL, AND THE DAY HAS TO THROW COLD WATER...... OR MORE LIKE HOT RAYS OF SUN...ON ME.
PUSU (STEAM)
I HATE THE SUN. DAMN SUN-LIGHT.
PUSU
PUSU
GI (CREAK)
WOULD YOU...... CLOSE THE CURTAIN?
TSUN (POKE)
TSUN
MNNN—
......
WHY, YOU...
FINE THEN.
HEAT
MOUTH
EAR
EYE
SINCE MY BRAIN FEELS ON THE VERGE OF MELTING LIKE SHAVED ICE, I'LL JUST COME OUT AND SAY IT.
MELT
MELT
I......
...AM A ZOMBIE.

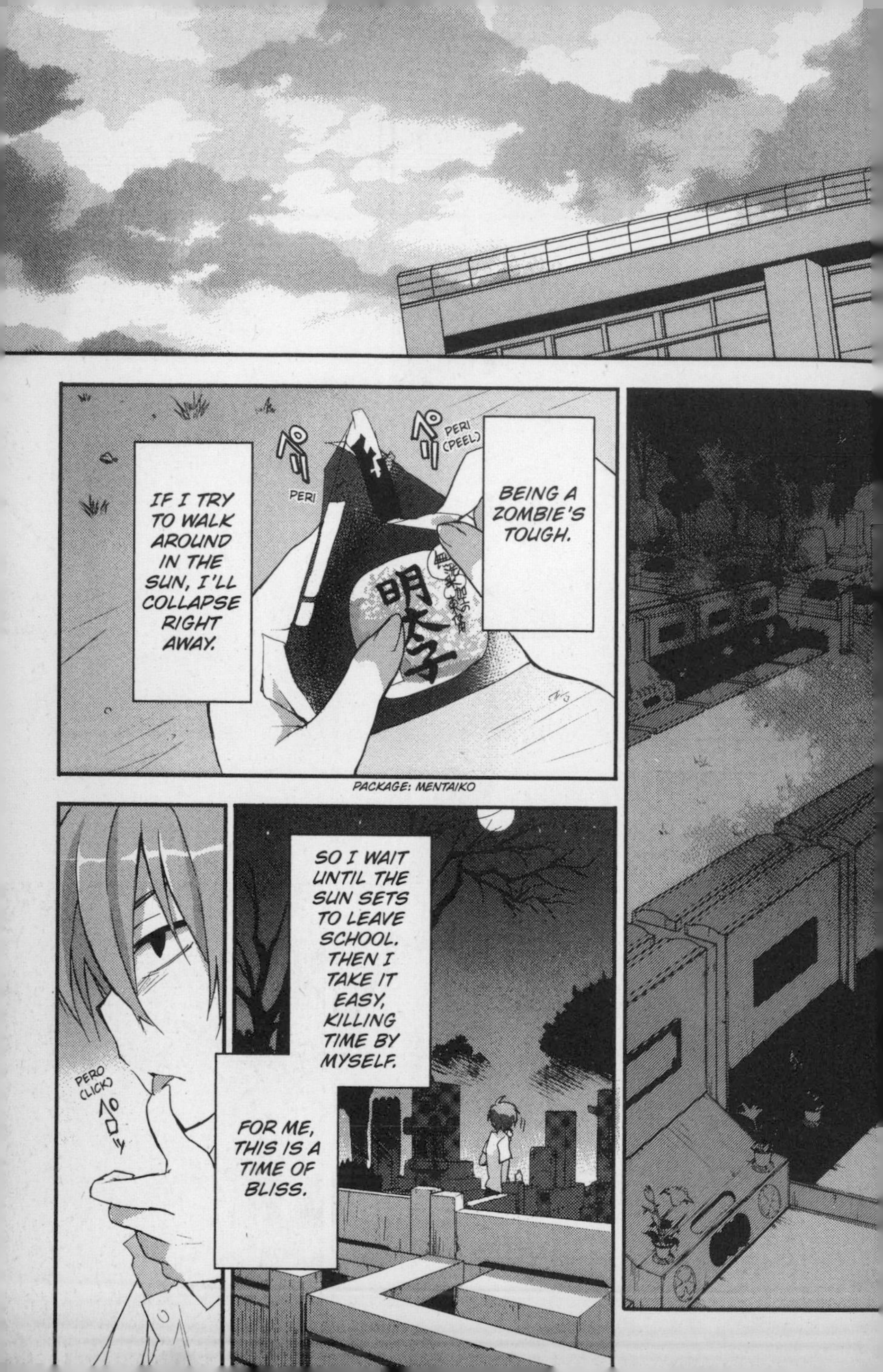
PERI (PEEL)
BEING A ZOMBIE'S TOUGH.
PERI
IF I TRY TO WALK AROUND IN THE SUN, I'LL COLLAPSE RIGHT AWAY.
明太子
PACKAGE: MENTAIKO
SO I WAIT UNTIL THE SUN SETS TO LEAVE SCHOOL. THEN I TAKE IT EASY, KILLING TIME BY MYSELF.
FOR ME, THIS IS A TIME OF BLISS.
PERO (LICK)

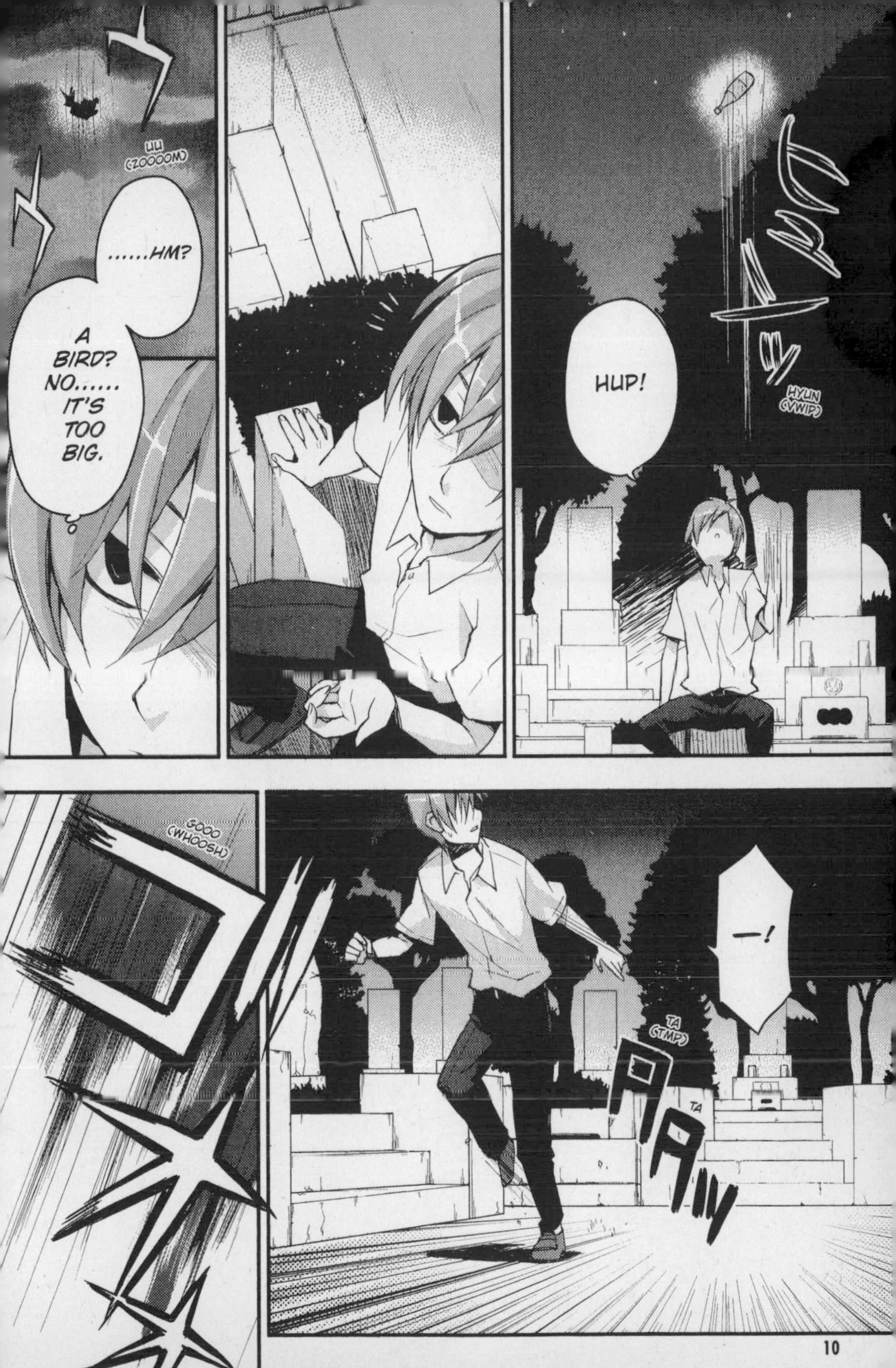
HYUN (VWIP)
HUP!
UU (ZOOOOM)
......HM?
A BIRD? NO...... IT'S TOO BIG.
—!
TA (TMP)
TA
GOOO (WHOOSH)

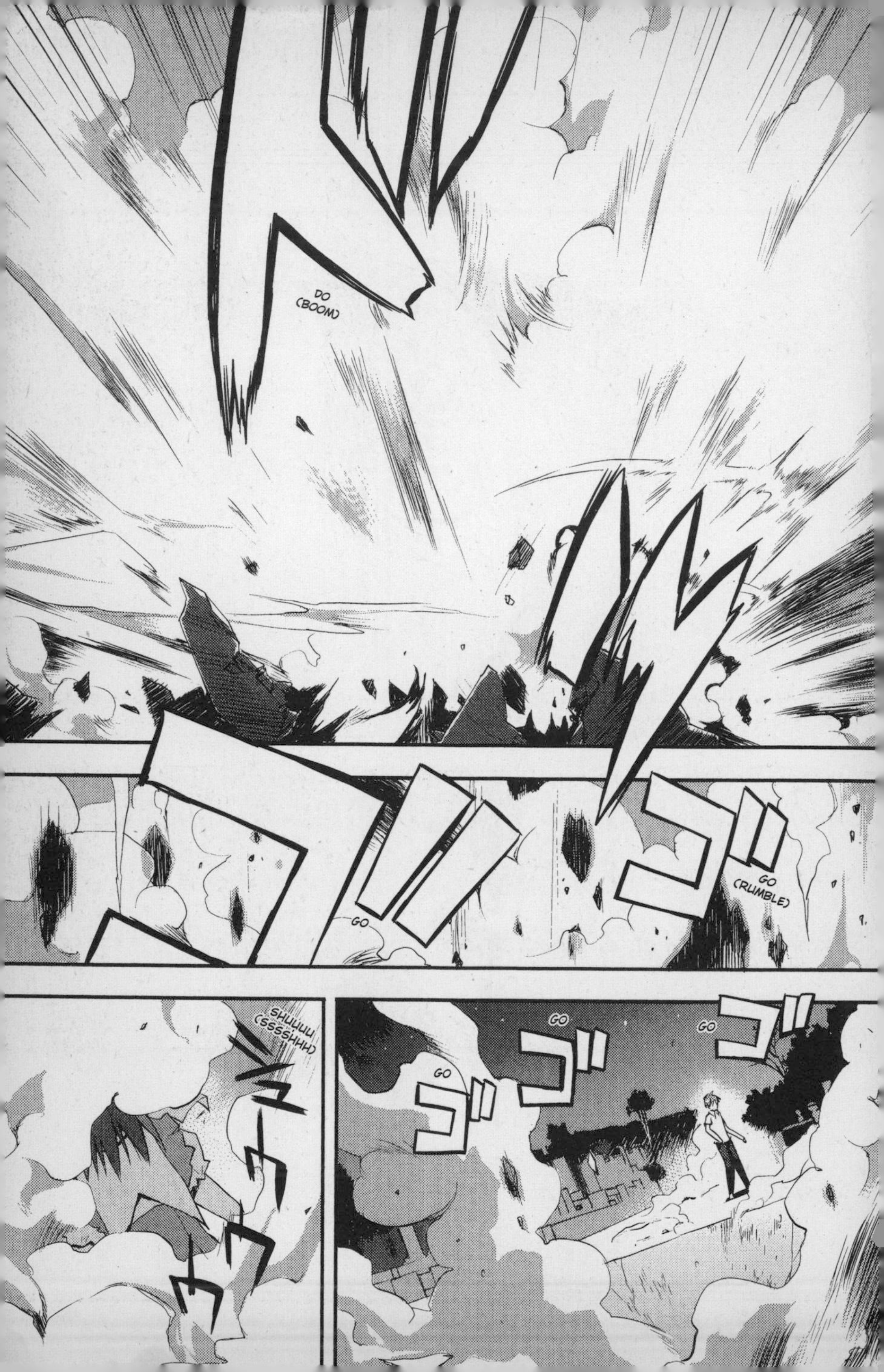
DO
(BOOM)
GO
(RUMBLE)
GO
GO
GO
GO
SHUUUU
(SSSSSHHH)

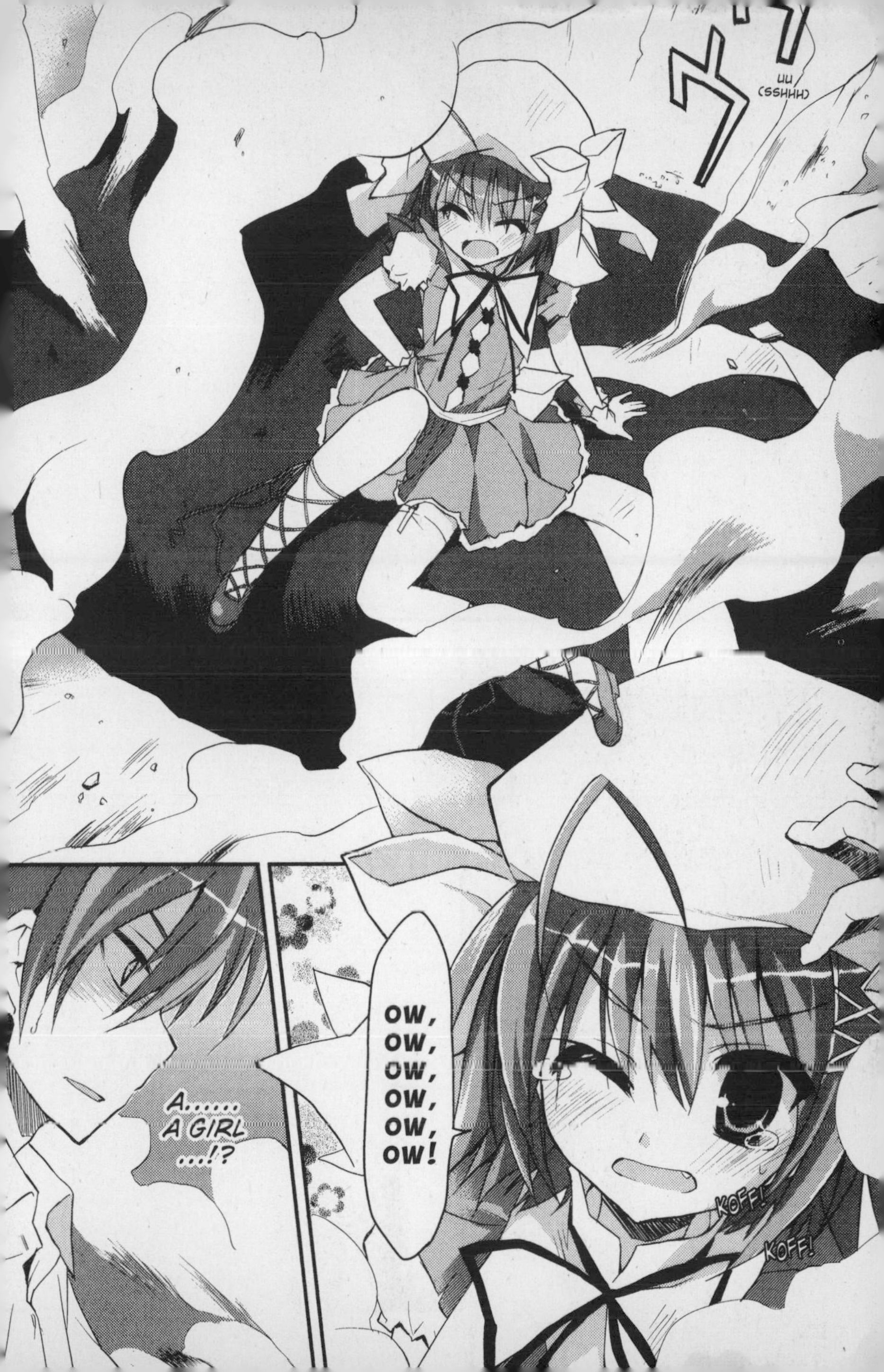
uu (SSHHH)
OW, OW, OW, OW, OW, OW!
KOFF!
KOFF!
A...... A GIRL ...!?

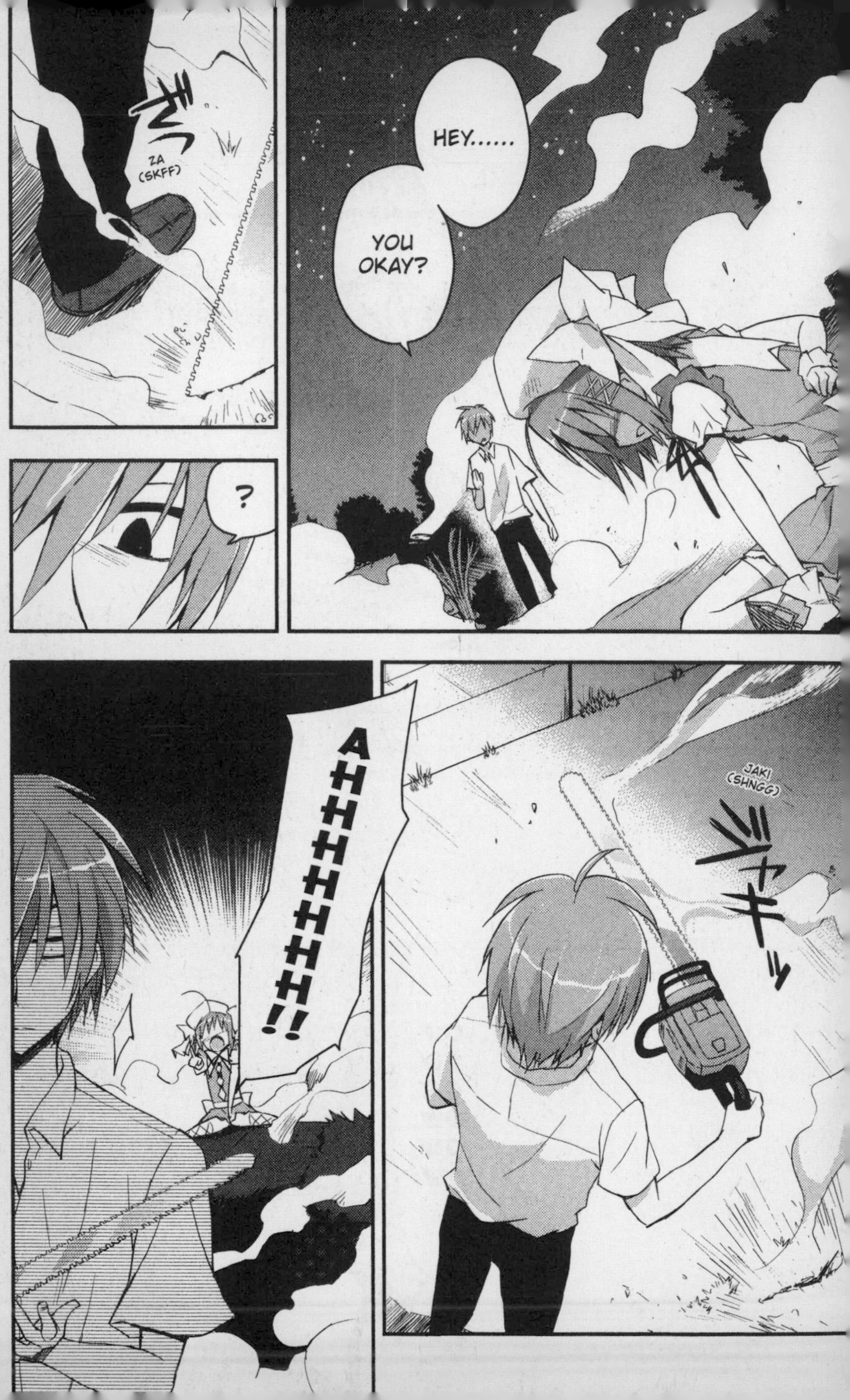
HEY......
YOU OKAY?
ZA (SKFF)
?
JAKI (SHNGG)
AHHHHHHH!!

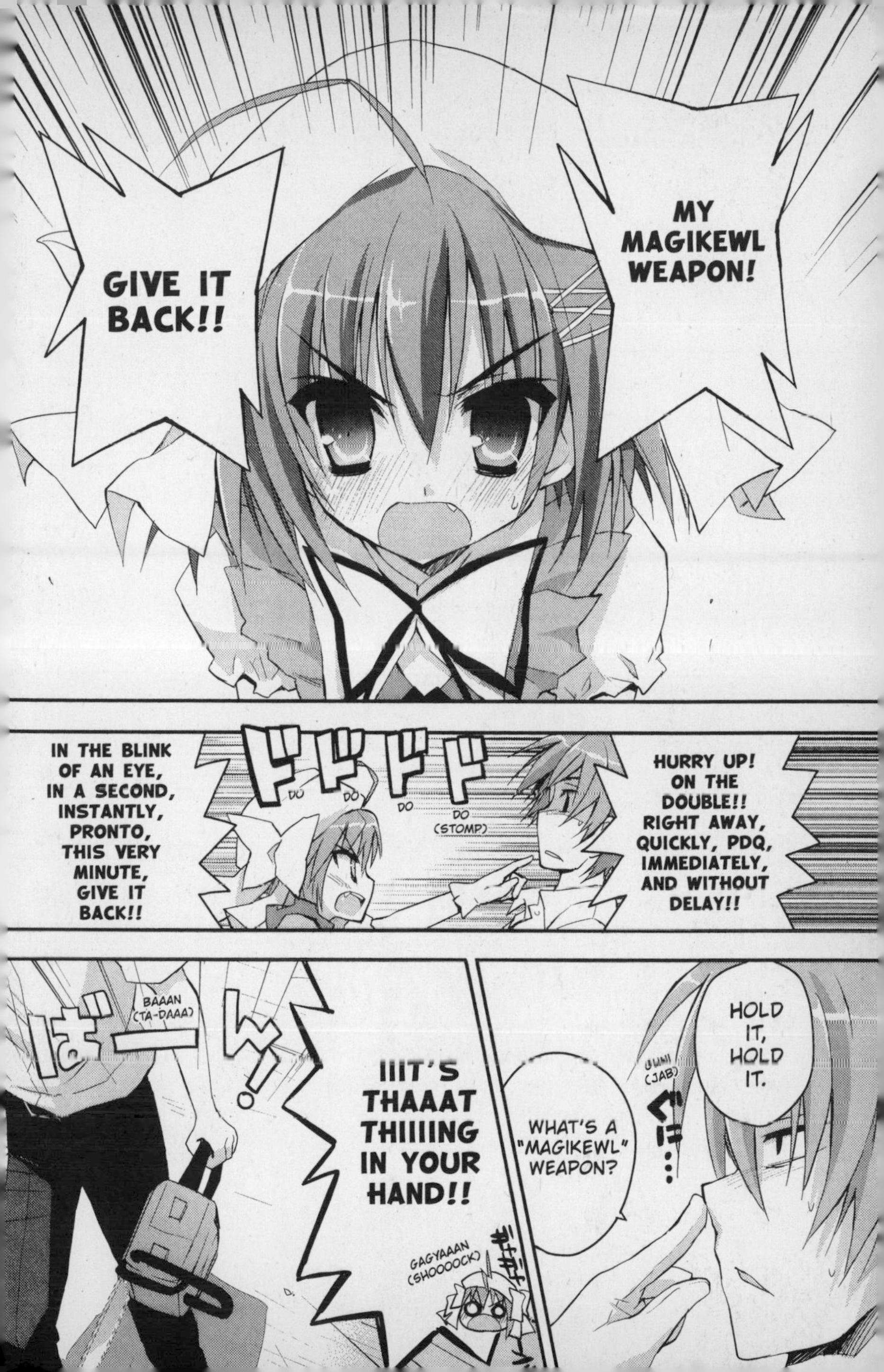
MY MAGIKEWL WEAPON!
GIVE IT BACK!!
HURRY UP! ON THE DOUBLE!! RIGHT AWAY, QUICKLY, PDQ, IMMEDIATELY, AND WITHOUT DELAY!!
ドドドド
DO DO DO DO (STOMP)
IN THE BLINK OF AN EYE, IN A SECOND, INSTANTLY, PRONTO, THIS VERY MINUTE, GIVE IT BACK!!
HOLD IT, HOLD IT.
ぐに…
UNNI (JAB)
WHAT'S A "MAGIKEWL" WEAPON?
IIIT'S THAAAT THIIIING IN YOUR HAND!!
ばーん!
BAAAN (TA-DAAA)
GAGYAAAN (SHOOOOCK)

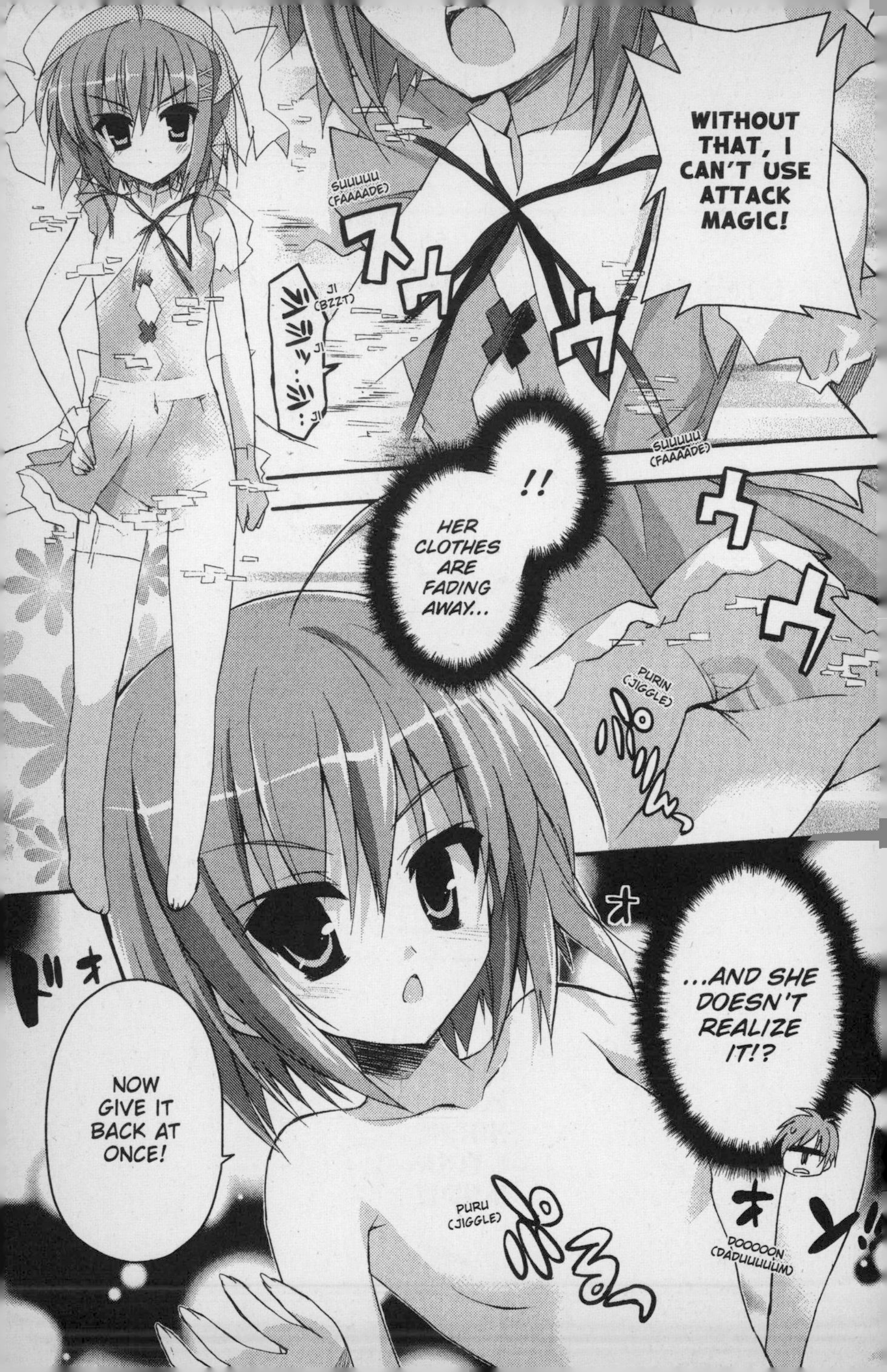
WITHOUT THAT, I CAN'T USE ATTACK MAGIC!
SUUUUU (FAAAADE)
!!
HER CLOTHES ARE FADING AWAY...
SUUUUU (FAAAADE)
PURIN (JIGGLE)
JI (BZZT)
JI
JI
...AND SHE DOESN'T REALIZE IT!?
NOW GIVE IT BACK AT ONCE!
PURU (JIGGLE)
DOOOOON (DADUUUUUM)

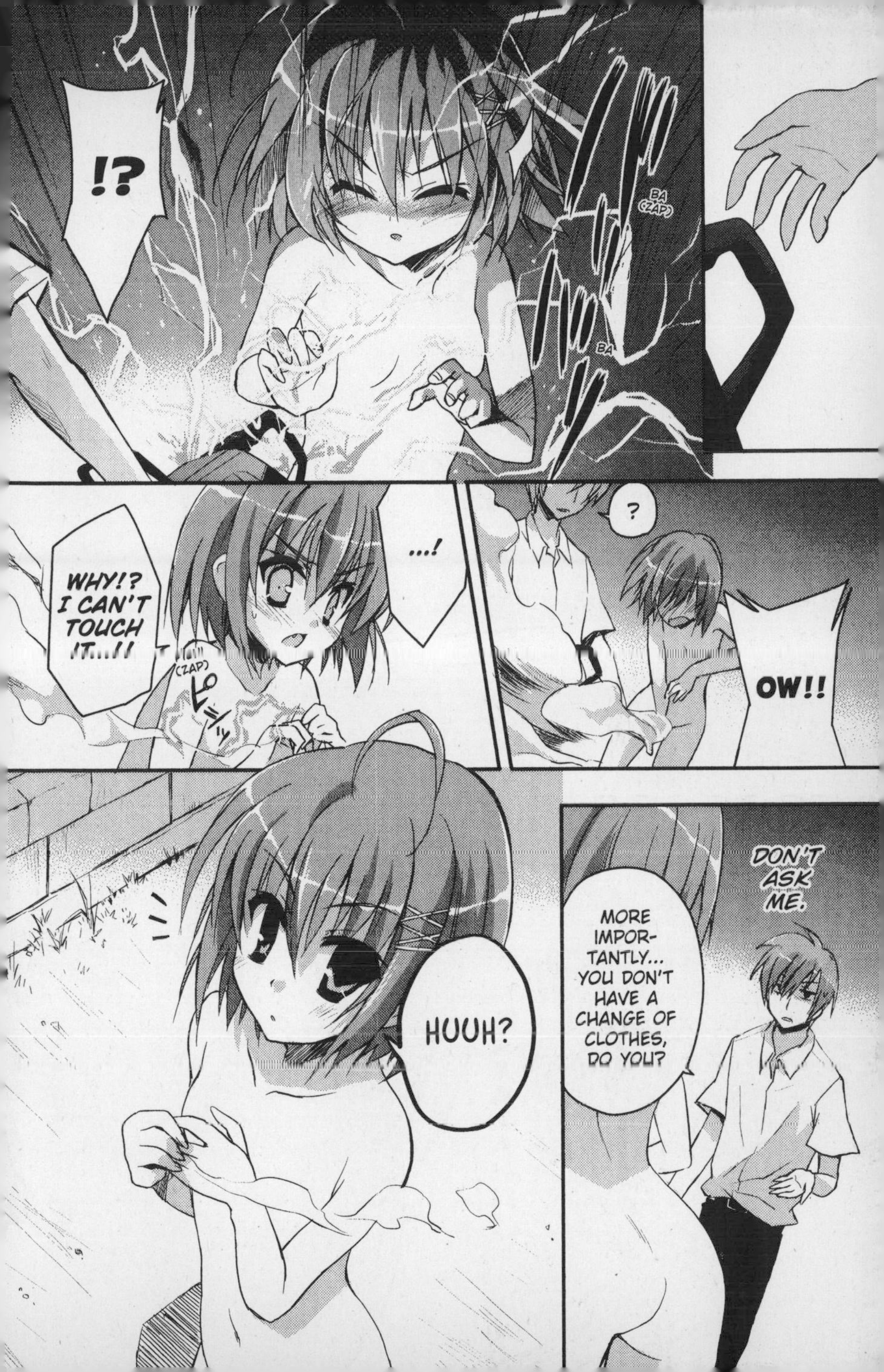
BA (ZAP)
BA
!?
?
OW!!
...!
WHY!? I CAN'T TOUCH IT...!!
(ZAP)
DON'T ASK ME.
MORE IMPORTANTLY... YOU DON'T HAVE A CHANGE OF CLOTHES, DO YOU?
HUUH?

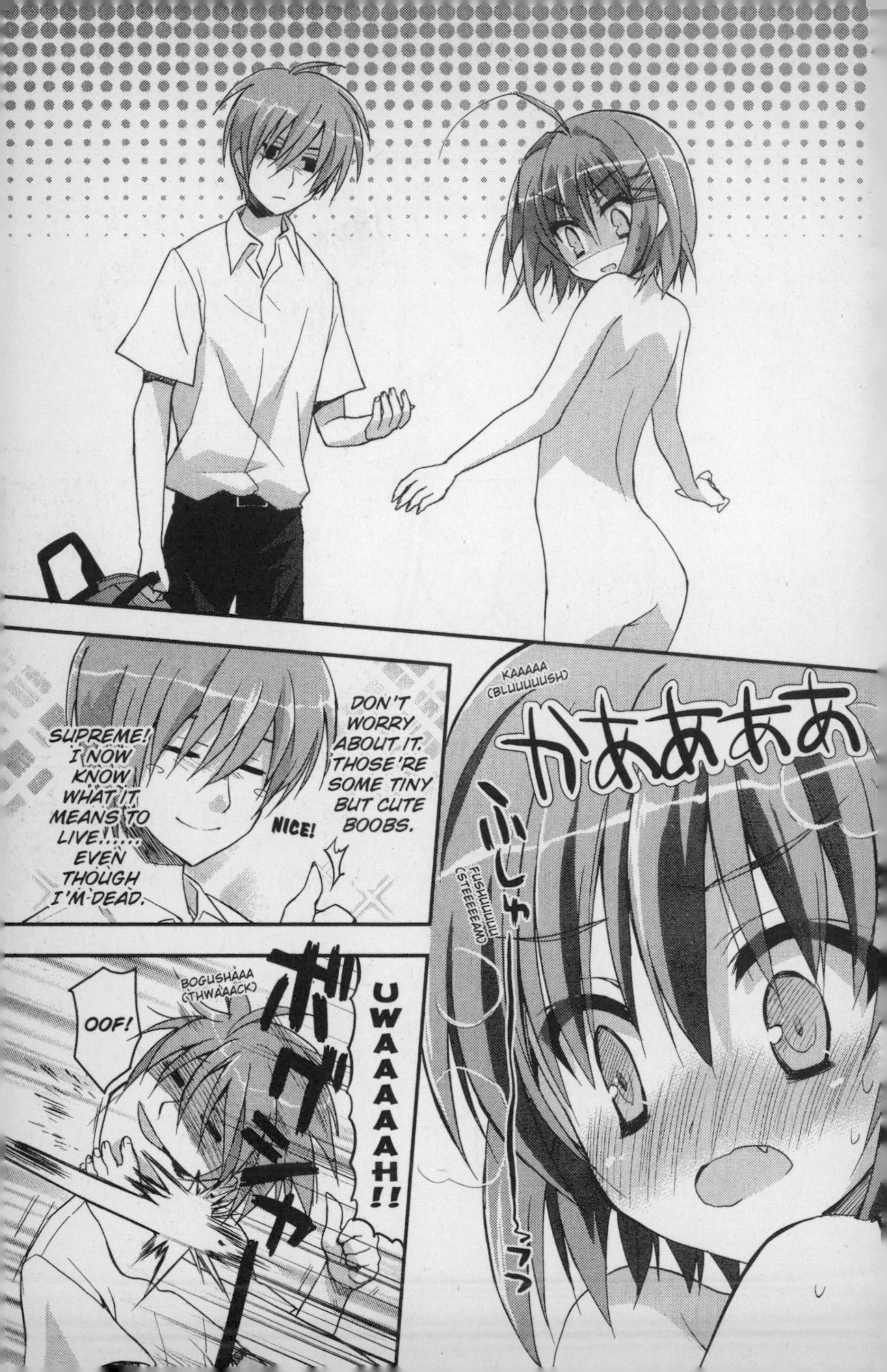
KAAAAA (BLUUUUUUSH)
かあああああ
ぷしゅ
FUSHUUUUU (STEEEEEAM)
DON'T WORRY ABOUT IT. THOSE'RE SOME TINY BUT CUTE BOOBS.
NICE!
SUPREME! I NOW KNOW WHAT IT MEANS TO LIVE!...... EVEN THOUGH I'M DEAD.
UWAAAAAAH!!
ボグシャ
BOGUSHAAA (THWAAACK)
OOF!

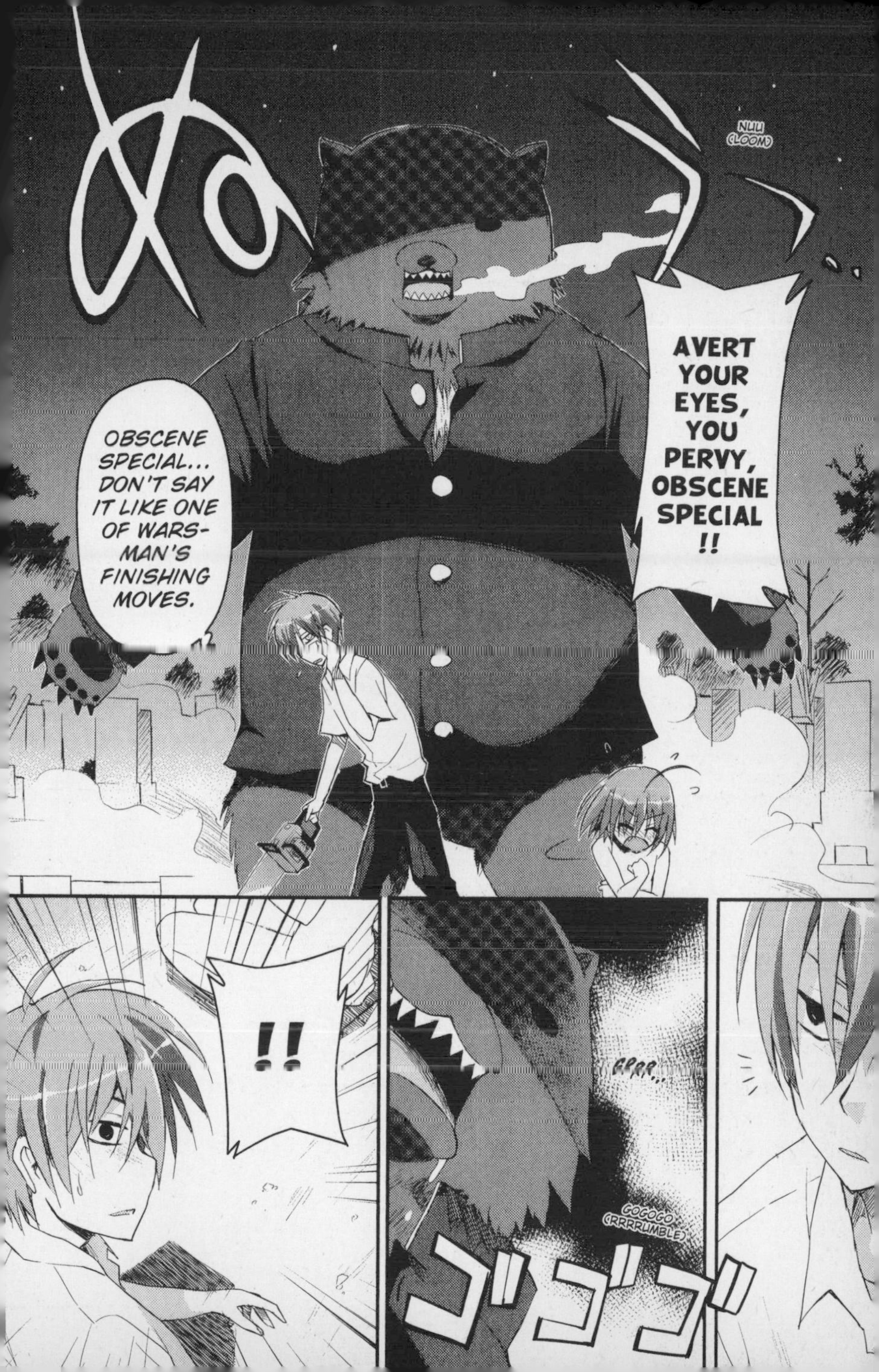
NUU (LOOM)
AVERT YOUR EYES, YOU PERVY, OBSCENE SPECIAL !!
OBSCENE SPECIAL... DON'T SAY IT LIKE ONE OF WARS-MAN'S FINISHING MOVES.
GRRR...
GOGOGO (RRRRUMBLE)
!!

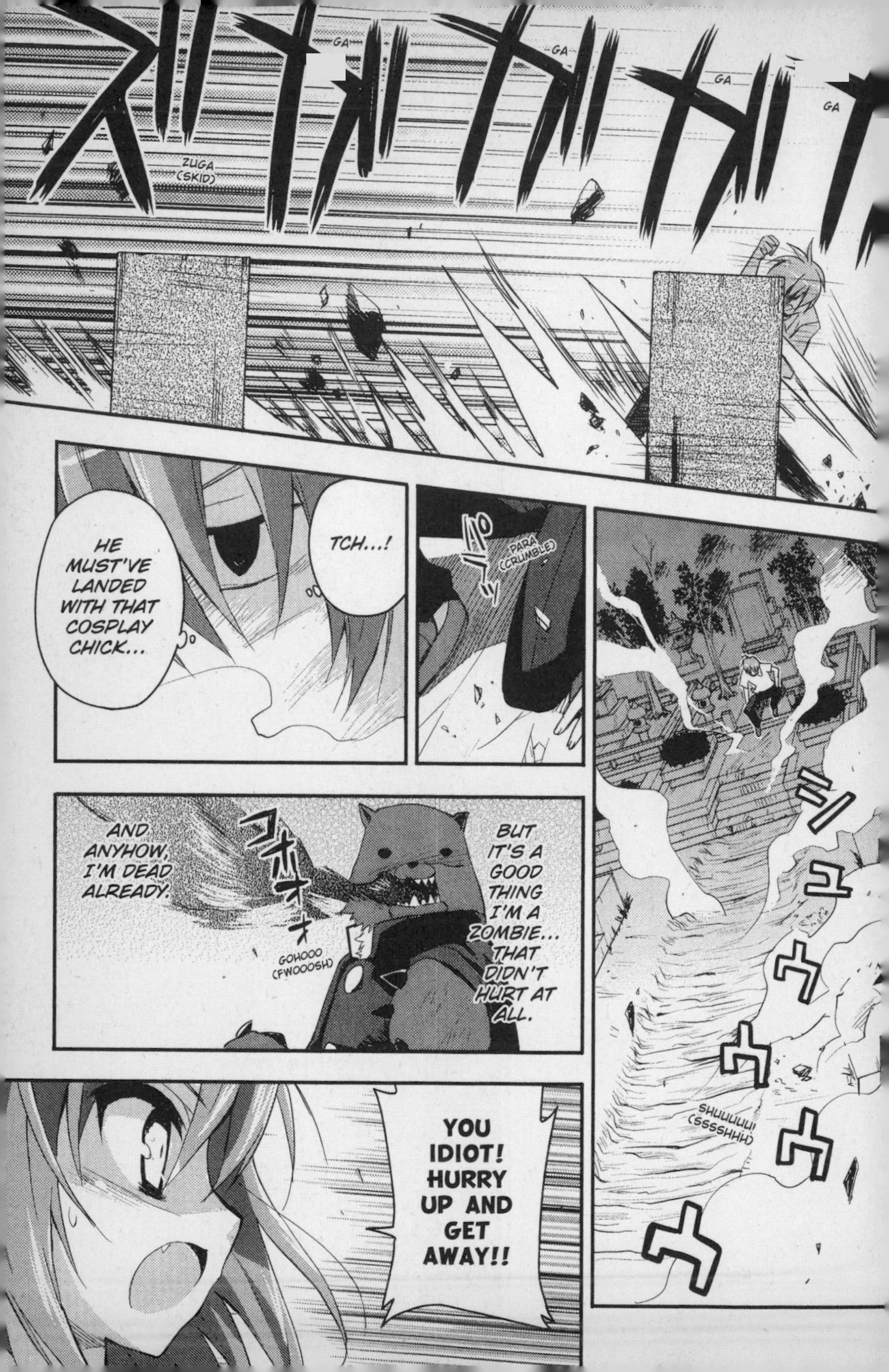
GA
GA
GA
GA
ZUGA (SKID)
SHUUUUU (SSSSHHH)
PARA (CRUMBLE)
TCH...!
HE MUST'VE LANDED WITH THAT COSPLAY CHICK...
BUT IT'S A GOOD THING I'M A ZOMBIE... THAT DIDN'T HURT AT ALL.
GOHOOO (FWOOOSH)
AND ANYHOW, I'M DEAD ALREADY.
YOU IDIOT! HURRY UP AND GET AWAY!!

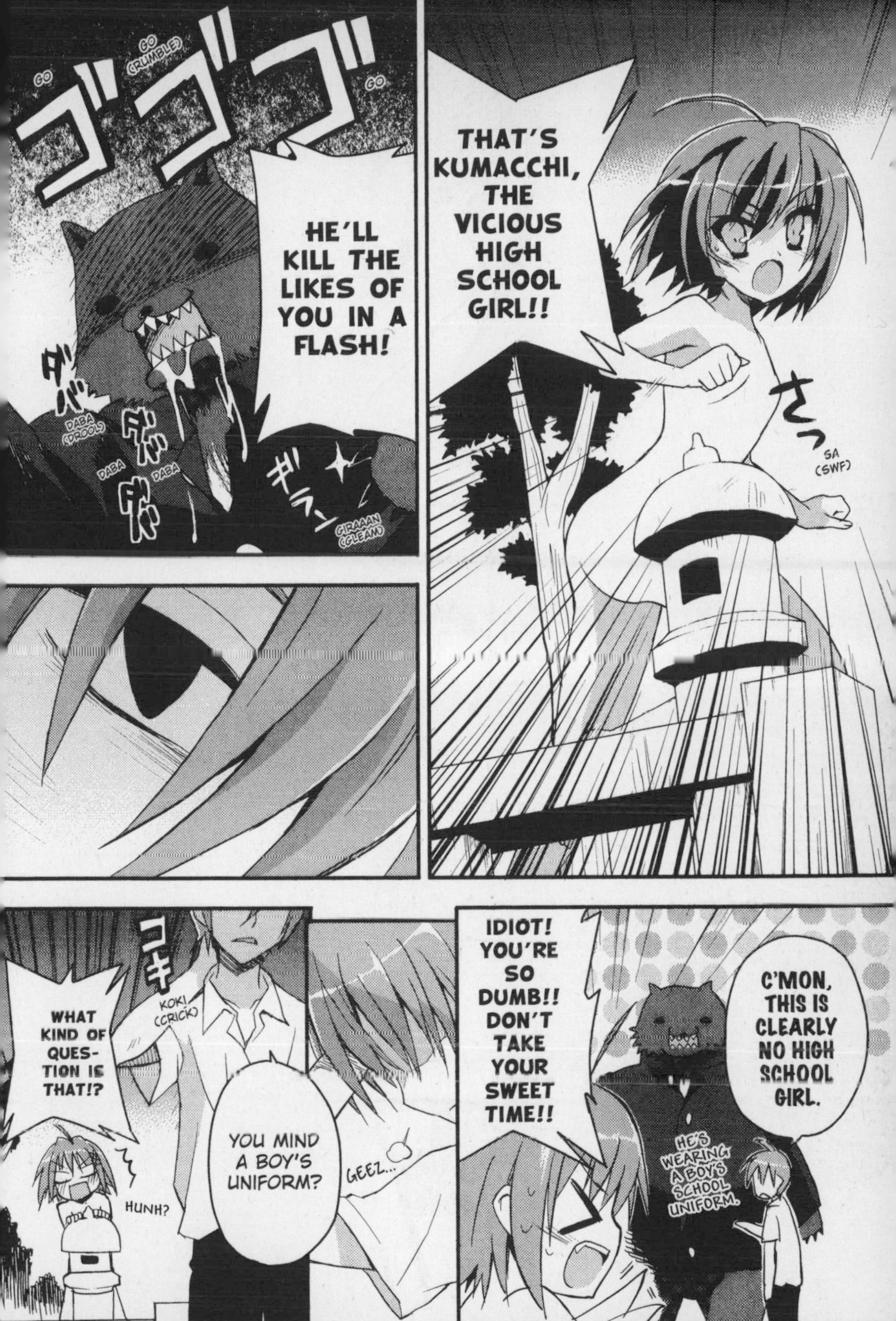
THAT'S KUMACCHI, THE VICIOUS HIGH SCHOOL GIRL!!
SA (SWF)
GO
GO (RUMBLE)
GO
HE'LL KILL THE LIKES OF YOU IN A FLASH!
DABA (DROOL)
DABA
DABA
GIRAAAN (GLEAM)
IDIOT! YOU'RE SO DUMB!! DON'T TAKE YOUR SWEET TIME!!
C'MON, THIS IS CLEARLY NO HIGH SCHOOL GIRL.
HE'S WEARING A BOY'S SCHOOL UNIFORM.
KOKI (CRICK)
GEEZ...
YOU MIND A BOY'S UNIFORM?
WHAT KIND OF QUES-TION IS THAT!?
HUNH?

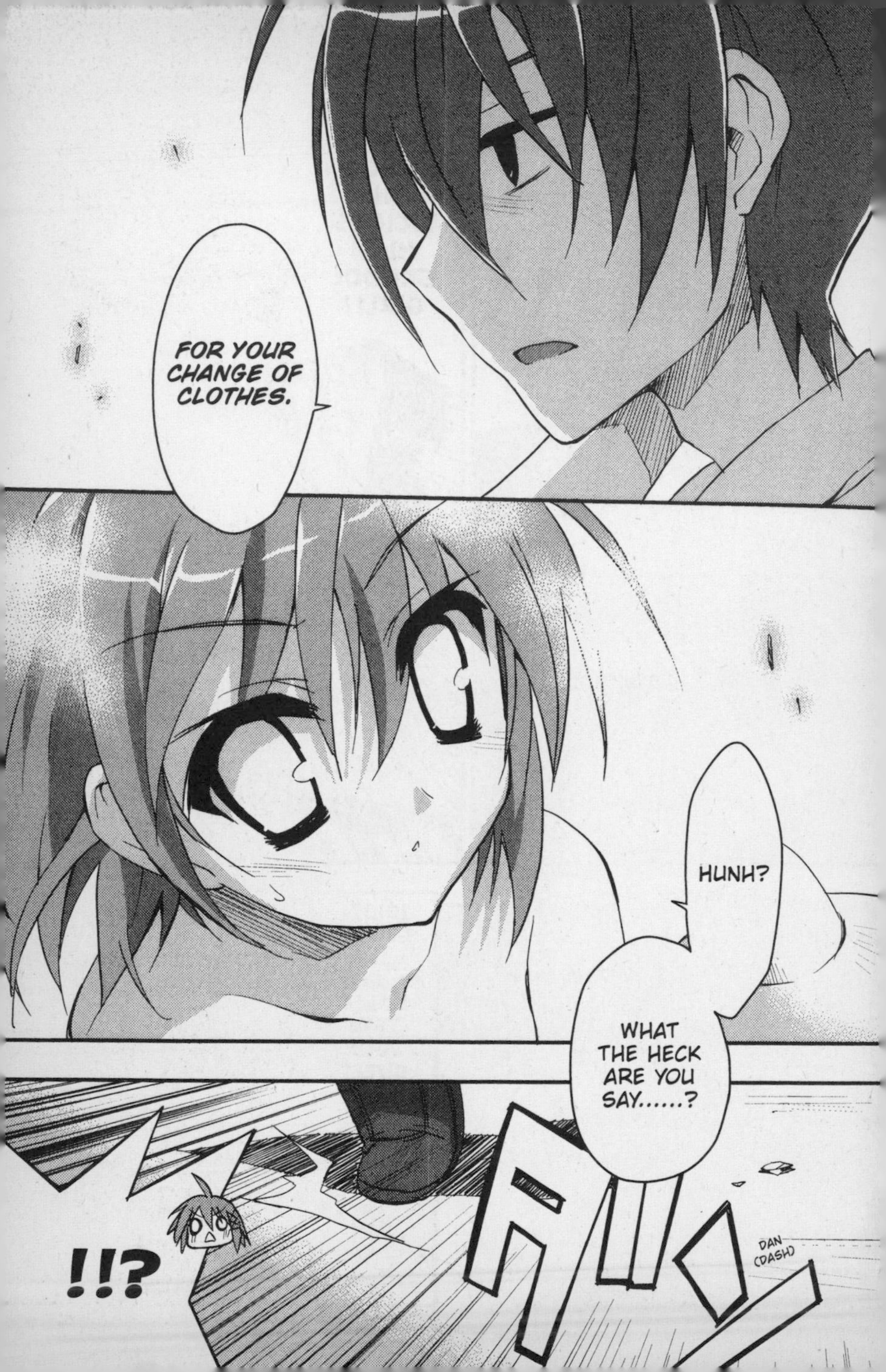
FOR YOUR CHANGE OF CLOTHES.
HUNH?
WHAT THE HECK ARE YOU SAY......?
DAN (DASH)
!!?

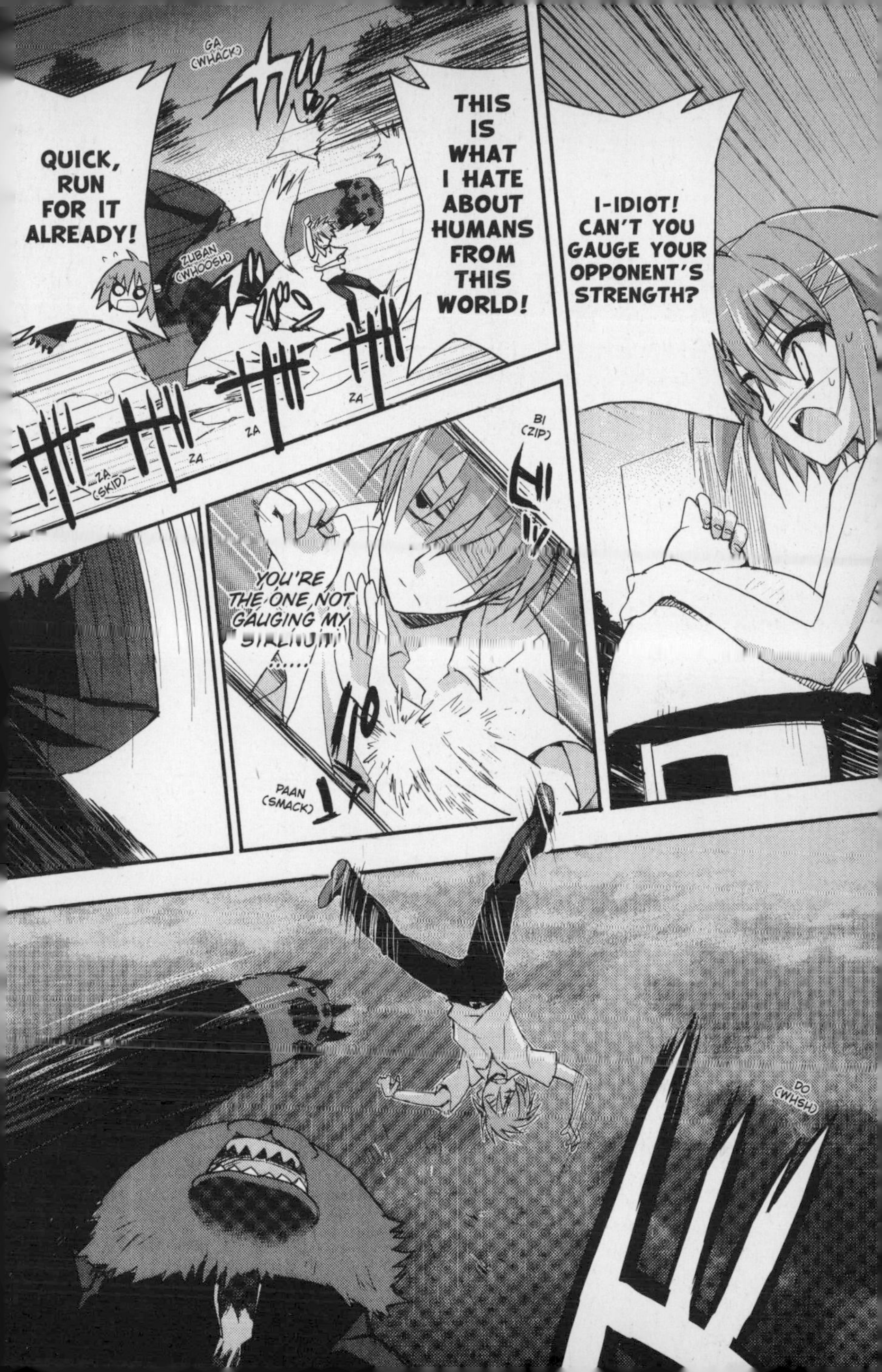
I-IDIOT! CAN'T YOU GAUGE YOUR OPPONENT'S STRENGTH?
THIS IS WHAT I HATE ABOUT HUMANS FROM THIS WORLD!
GA (WHACK)
QUICK, RUN FOR IT ALREADY!
ZUBAN (WHOOSH)
ZA
ZA
ZA
ZA (SKID)
BI (ZIP)
YOU'RE THE ONE NOT GAUGING MY
......
PAAN (SMACK)
DO (WHSH)

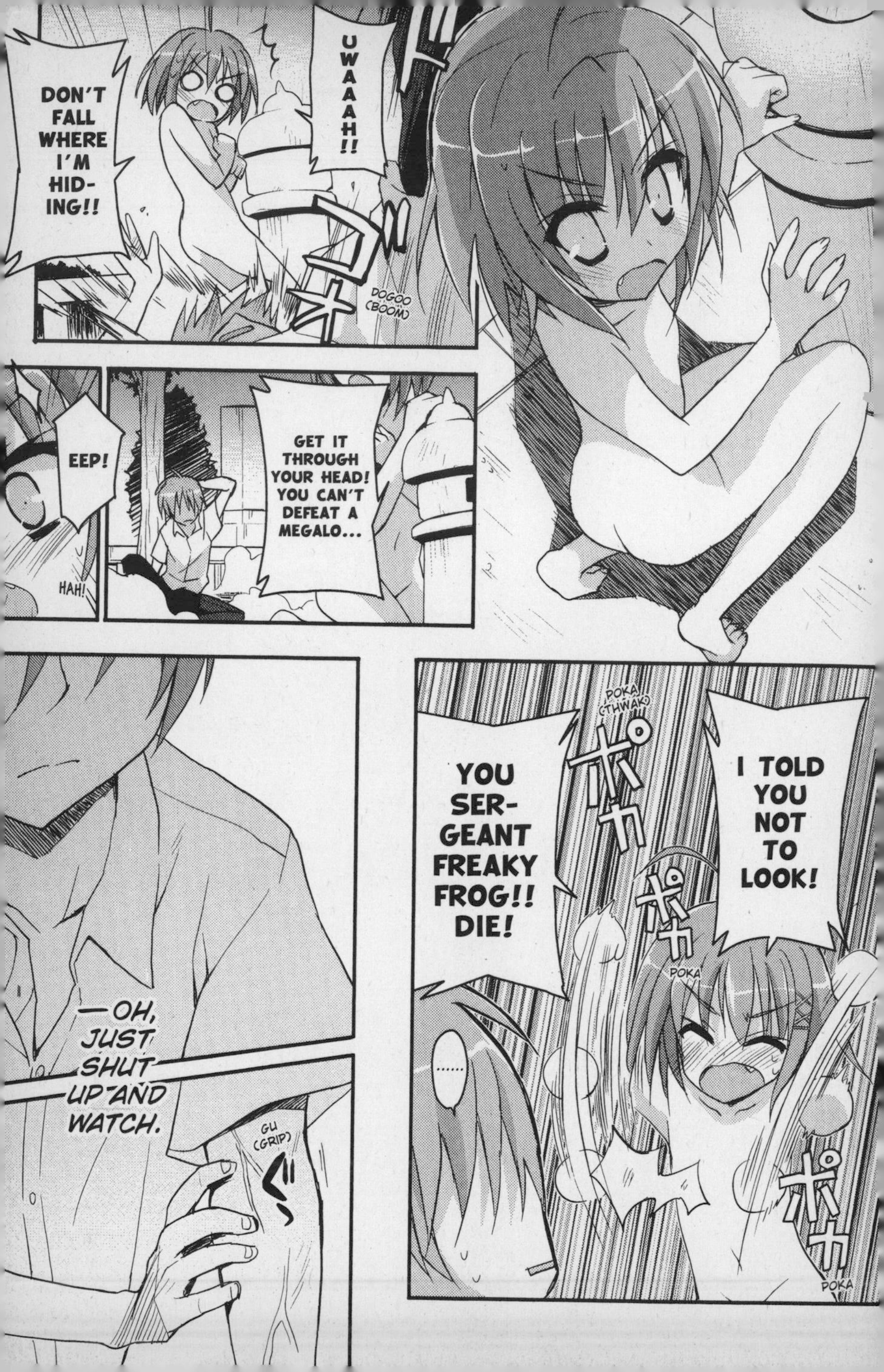
UWAAAH!!
DOGOO (BOOM)
DON'T FALL WHERE I'M HID-ING!!
GET IT THROUGH YOUR HEAD! YOU CAN'T DEFEAT A MEGALO...
EEP!
HAH!
I TOLD YOU NOT TO LOOK!
POKA (THWAK)
YOU SER-GEANT FREAKY FROG!! DIE!
POKA
......
POKA
—OH, JUST SHUT UP AND WATCH.
GU (GRIP)

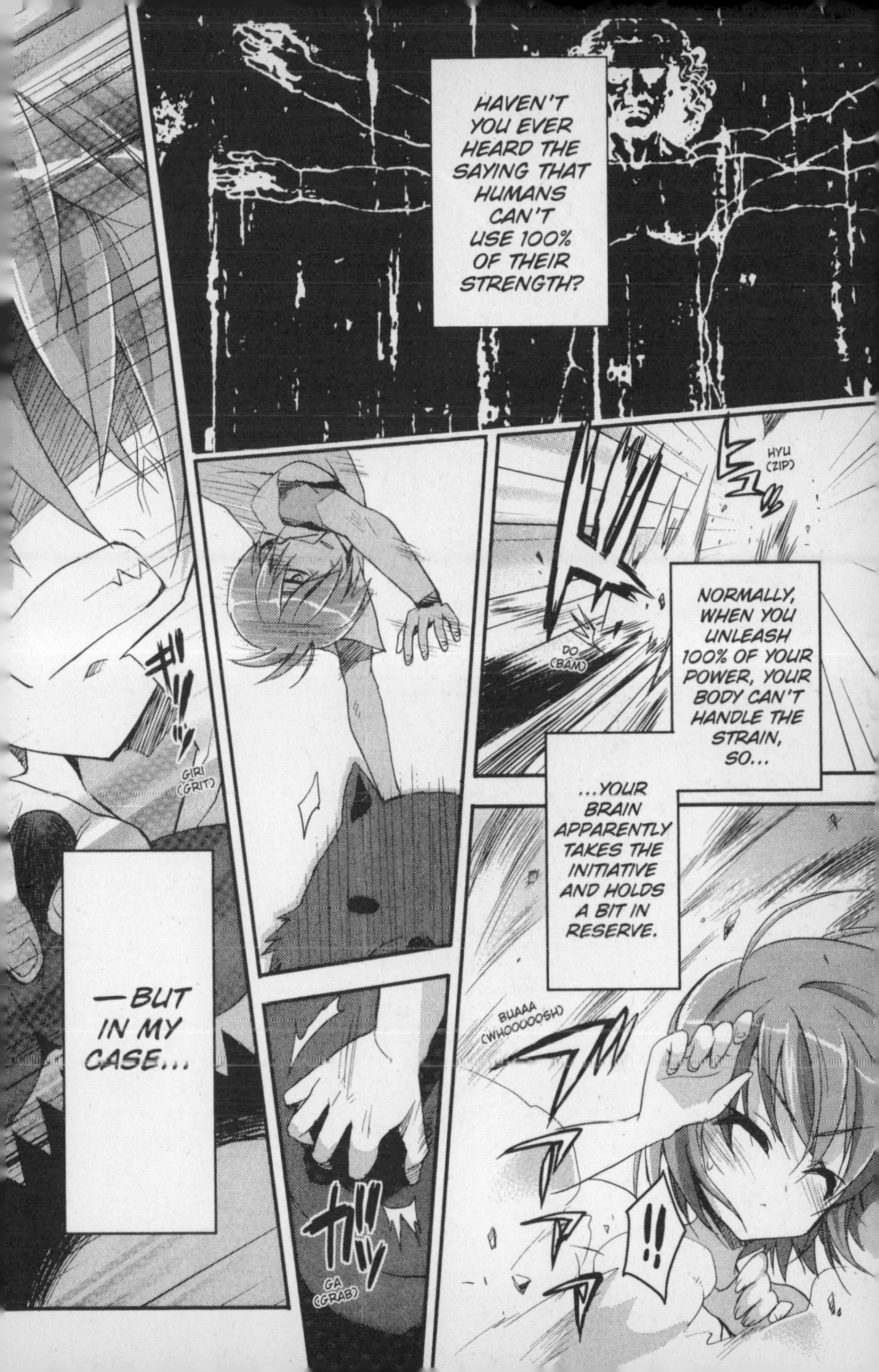
HAVEN'T YOU EVER HEARD THE SAYING THAT HUMANS CAN'T USE 100% OF THEIR STRENGTH?
HYU (ZIP)
DO (BAM)
NORMALLY, WHEN YOU UNLEASH 100% OF YOUR POWER, YOUR BODY CAN'T HANDLE THE STRAIN, SO...
...YOUR BRAIN APPARENTLY TAKES THE INITIATIVE AND HOLDS A BIT IN RESERVE.
BUAAA (WHOOOOOSH)
!!
GA (GRAB)
GIRI (GRIT)
—BUT IN MY CASE...

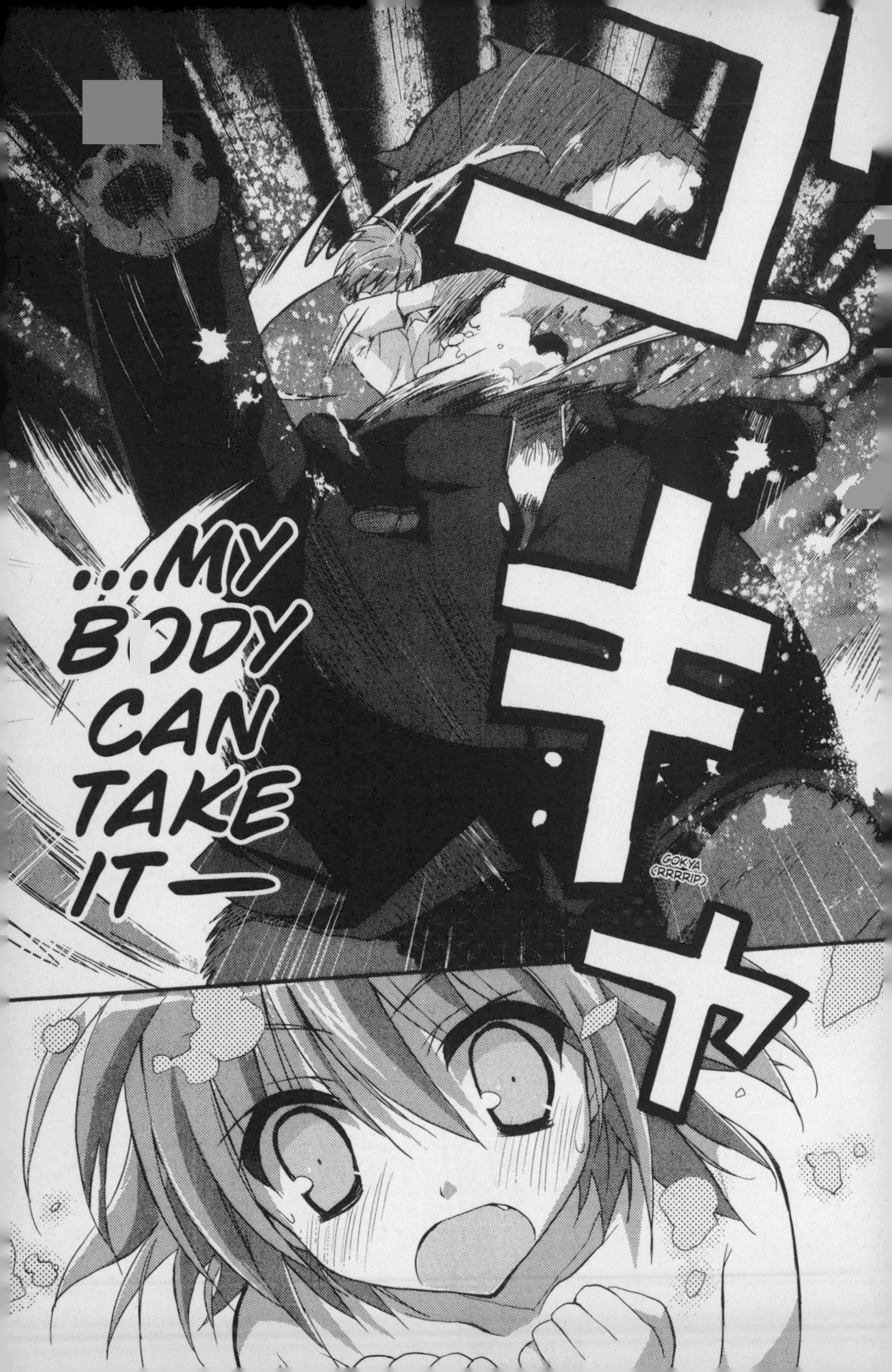
ゴキャ
GOKYA (RRRRIP)
...MY BODY CAN TAKE IT—

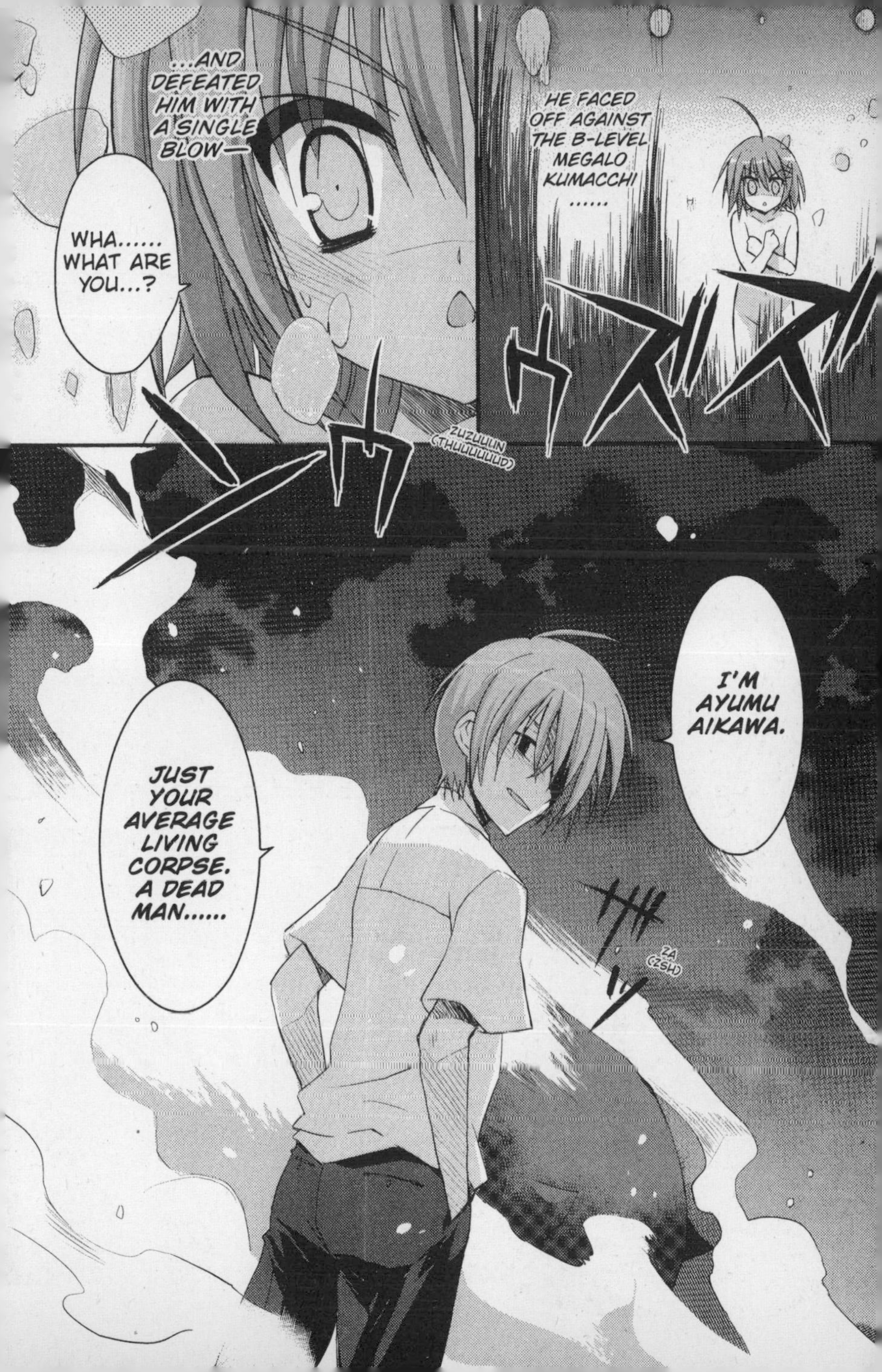
HE FACED OFF AGAINST THE B-LEVEL MEGALO KUMACCHI ......
...AND DEFEATED HIM WITH A SINGLE BLOW—
WHA...... WHAT ARE YOU...?
ZUZUUUN (THUUUUUUD)
I'M AYUMU AIKAWA.
ZA (ZSH)
JUST YOUR AVERAGE LIVING CORPSE. A DEAD MAN......

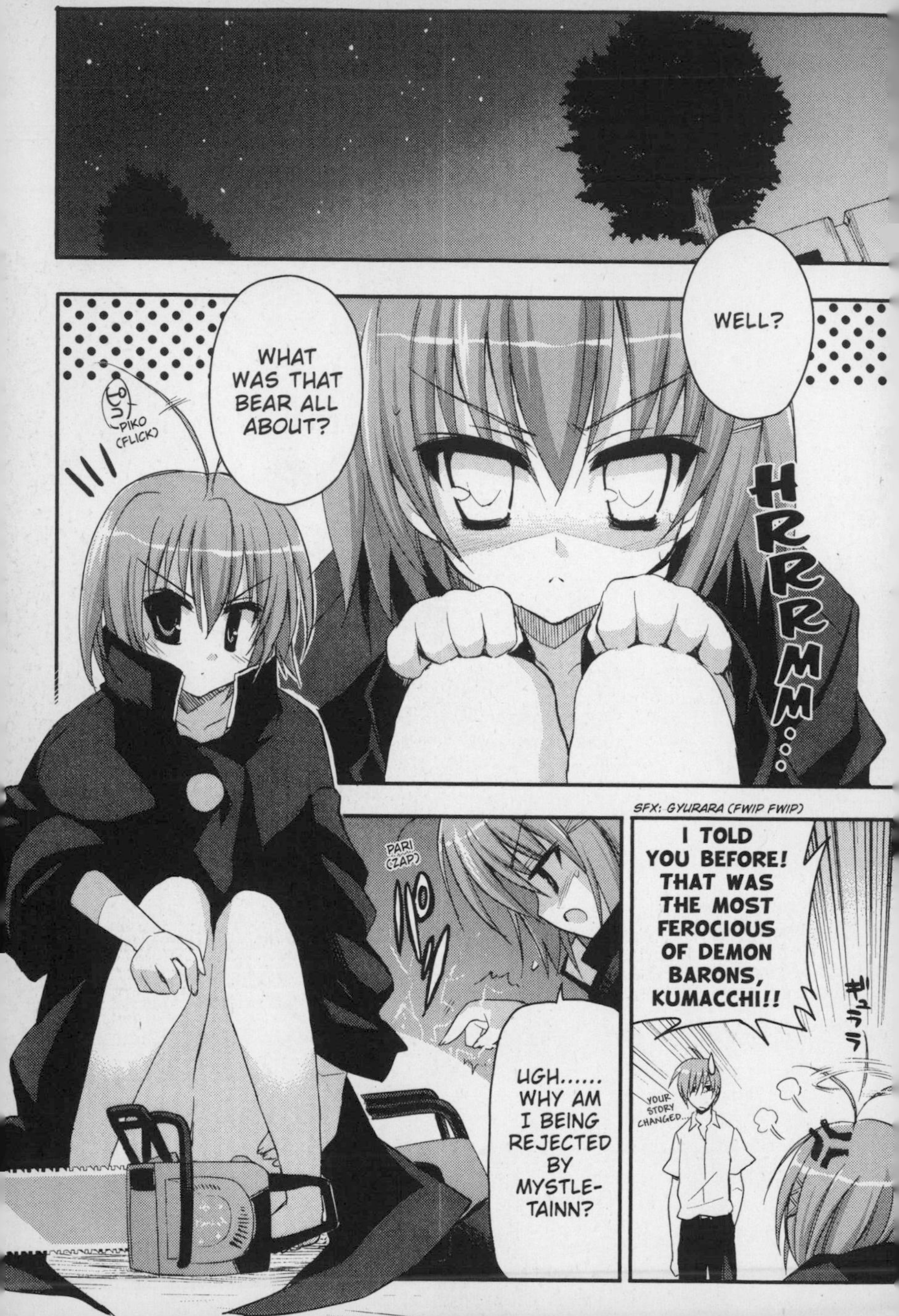
WELL?
HRRRMM...
WHAT WAS THAT BEAR ALL ABOUT?
PIKO (FLICK)
SFX: GYURARA (FWIP FWIP)
I TOLD YOU BEFORE! THAT WAS THE MOST FEROCIOUS OF DEMON BARONS, KUMACCHI!!
YOUR STORY CHANGED...
PARI (ZAP)
UGH...... WHY AM I BEING REJECTED BY MYSTLE-TAINN?

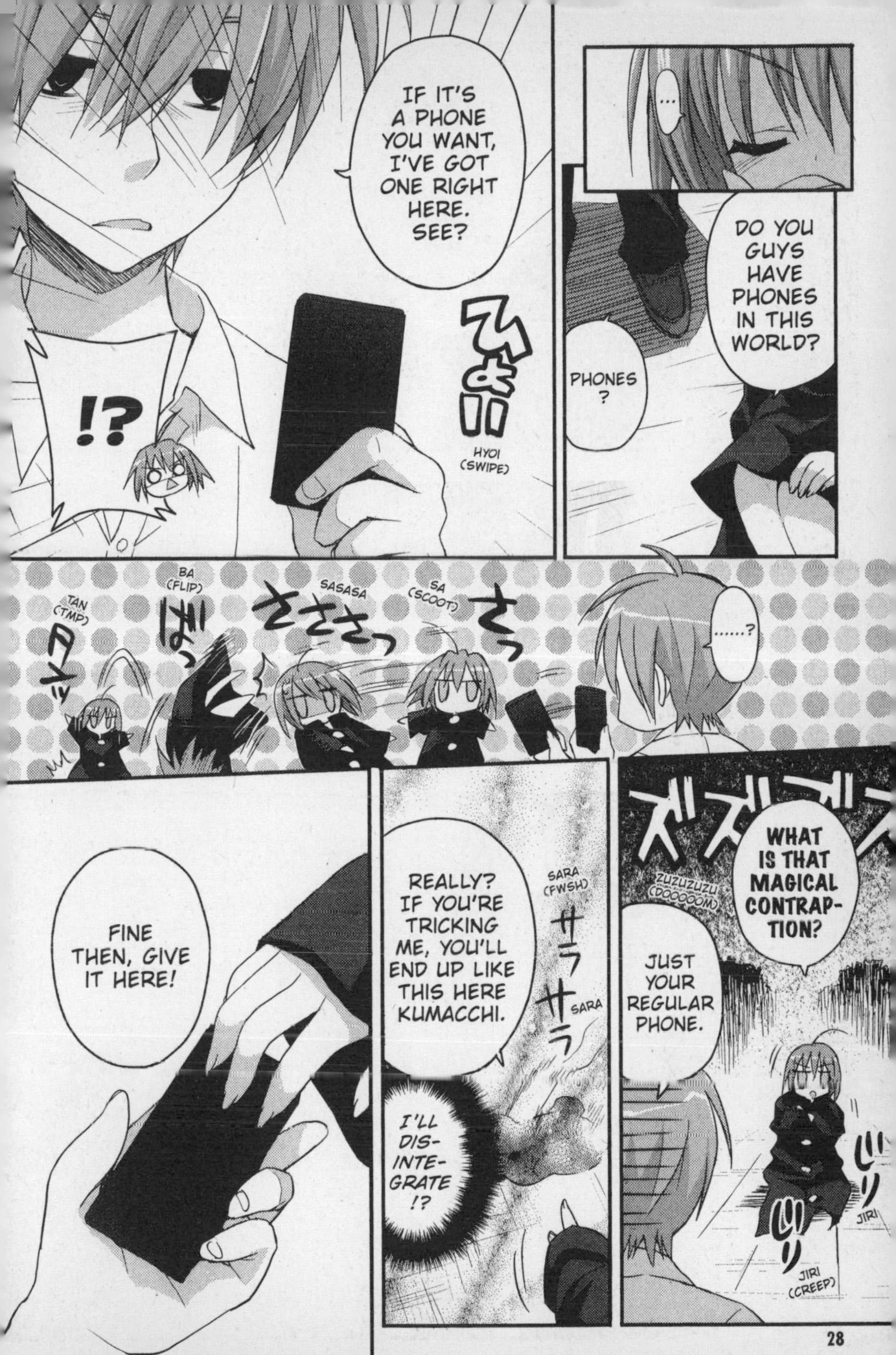
...
DO YOU GUYS HAVE PHONES IN THIS WORLD?
PHONES?
IF IT'S A PHONE YOU WANT, I'VE GOT ONE RIGHT HERE. SEE?
ひょい
HYOI (SWIPE)
!?
......?
さっ
SA (SCOOT)
さささっ
SASASA
ばっ
BA (FLIP)
タンッ
TAN (TMP)
WHAT IS THAT MAGICAL CONTRAP-TION?
ZUZUZUZU (DOOOOOM)
JUST YOUR REGULAR PHONE.
じり
JIRI
じり
JIRI (CREEP)
REALLY? IF YOU'RE TRICKING ME, YOU'LL END UP LIKE THIS HERE KUMACCHI.
サラ
SARA (FWSH)
サラ
SARA
I'LL DIS-INTE-GRATE !?
FINE THEN, GIVE IT HERE!

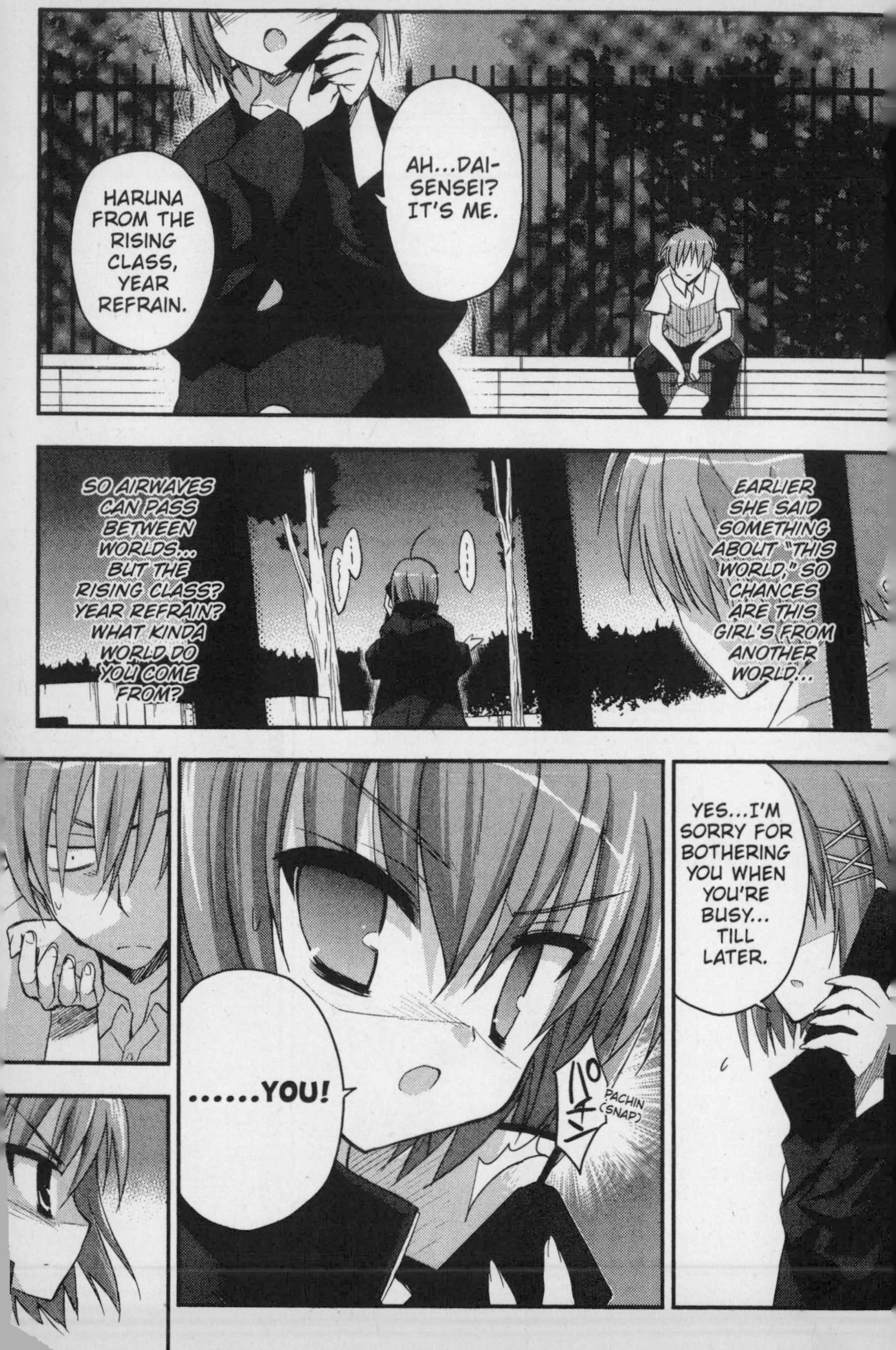
AH...DAI-SENSEI? IT'S ME.
HARUNA FROM THE RISING CLASS, YEAR REFRAIN.
EARLIER SHE SAID SOMETHING ABOUT "THIS WORLD," SO CHANCES ARE THIS GIRL'S FROM ANOTHER WORLD...
SO AIRWAVES CAN PASS BETWEEN WORLDS... BUT THE RISING CLASS? YEAR REFRAIN? WHAT KINDA WORLD DO YOU COME FROM?
YES...I'M SORRY FOR BOTHERING YOU WHEN YOU'RE BUSY... TILL LATER.
......YOU!
PACHIN (SNAP)

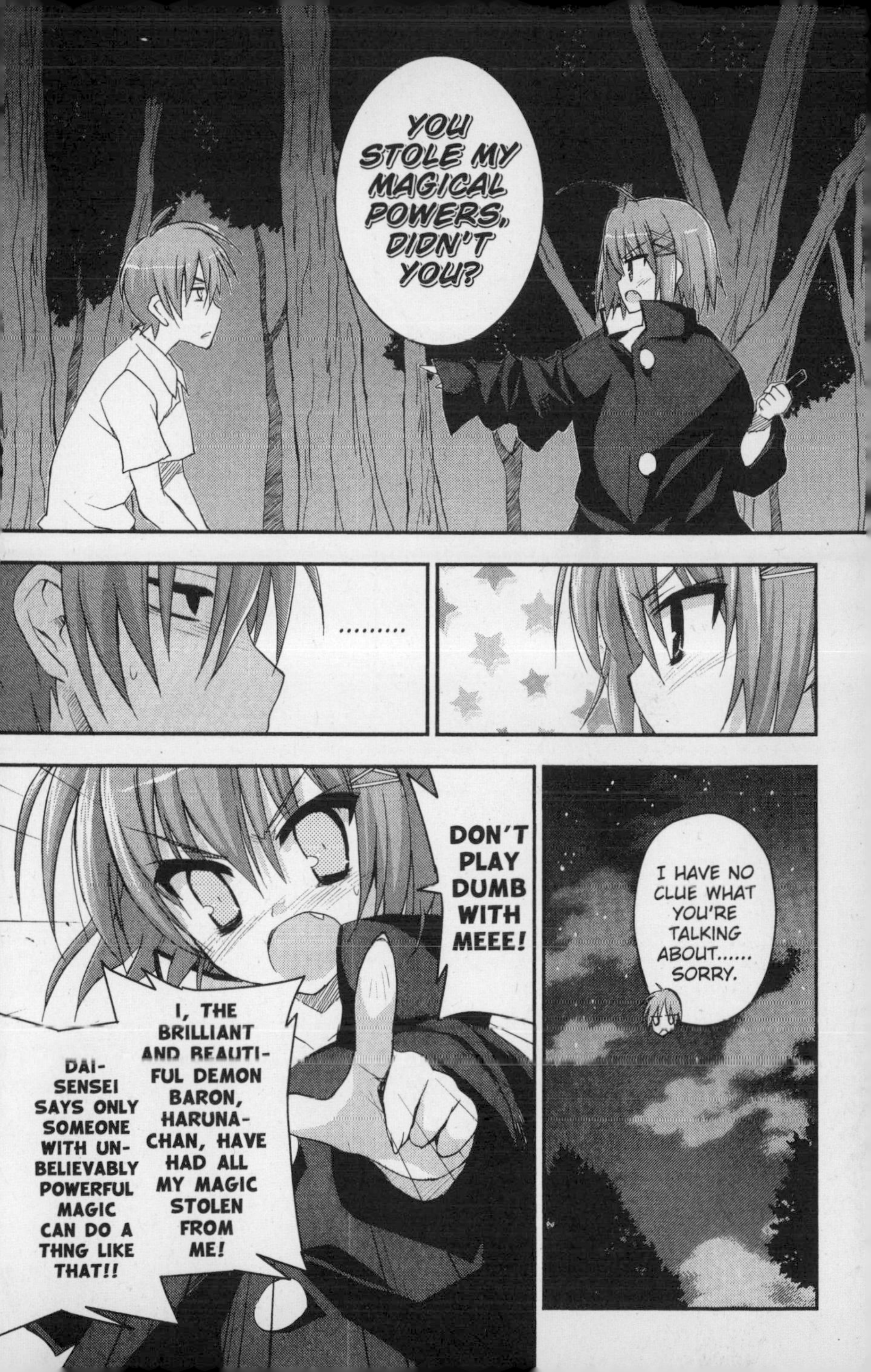
YOU STOLE MY MAGICAL POWERS, DIDN'T YOU?
....
I HAVE NO CLUE WHAT YOU'RE TALKING ABOUT...... SORRY.
DON'T PLAY DUMB WITH MEEE!
I, THE BRILLIANT AND BEAUTIFUL DEMON BARON, HARUNA-CHAN, HAVE HAD ALL MY MAGIC STOLEN FROM ME!
DAI-SENSEI SAYS ONLY SOMEONE WITH UNBELIEVABLY POWERFUL MAGIC CAN DO A THNG LIKE THAT!!

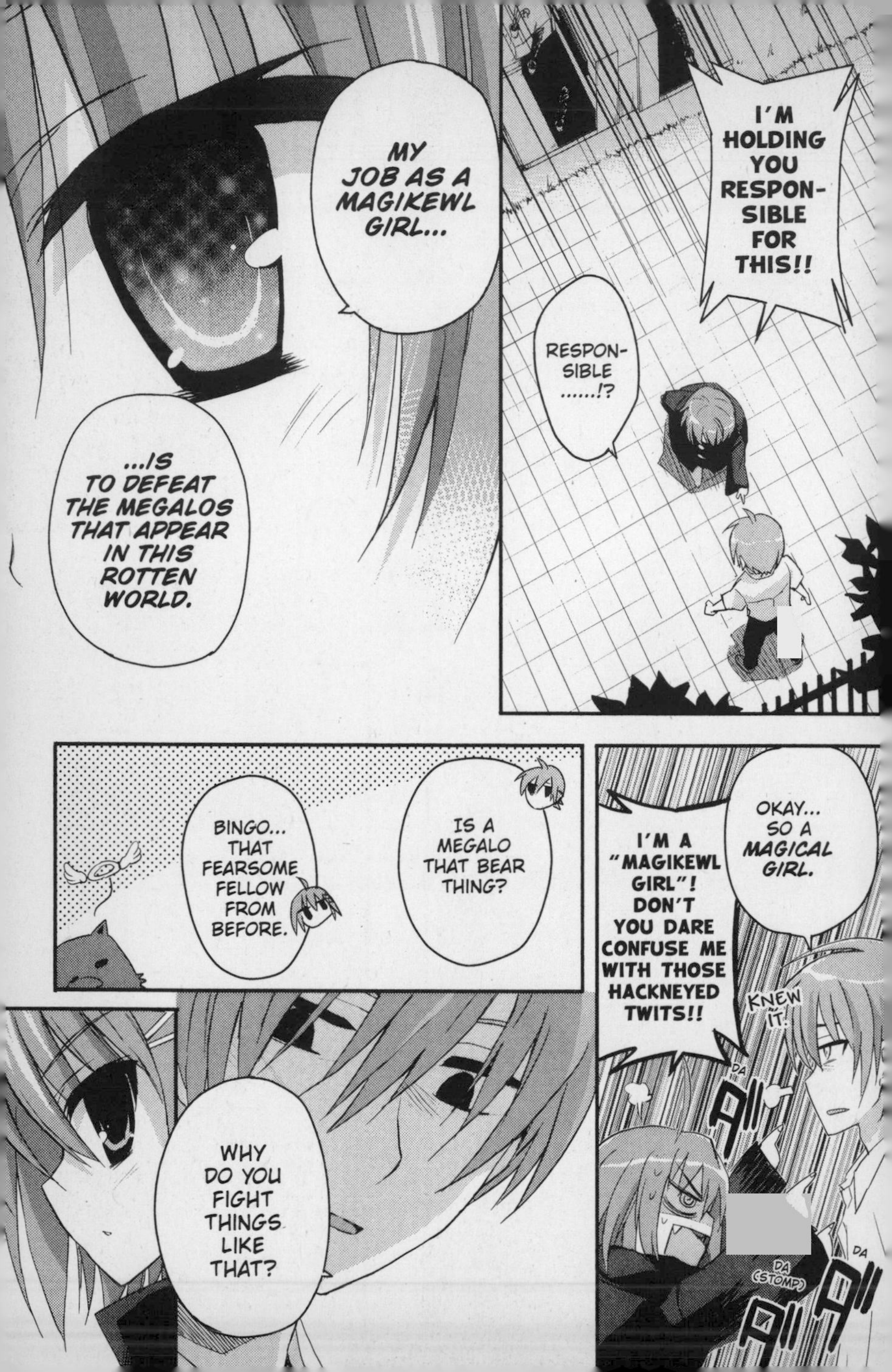
I'M HOLDING YOU RESPONSIBLE FOR THIS!!
RESPONSIBLE ......!?
MY JOB AS A MAGIKEWL GIRL...
...IS TO DEFEAT THE MEGALOS THAT APPEAR IN THIS ROTTEN WORLD.
OKAY... SO A MAGICAL GIRL.
I'M A "MAGIKEWL GIRL"! DON'T YOU DARE CONFUSE ME WITH THOSE HACKNEYED TWITS!!
KNEW IT.
DA
DA (STOMP)
DA
IS A MEGALO THAT BEAR THING?
BINGO... THAT FEARSOME FELLOW FROM BEFORE.
WHY DO YOU FIGHT THINGS LIKE THAT?

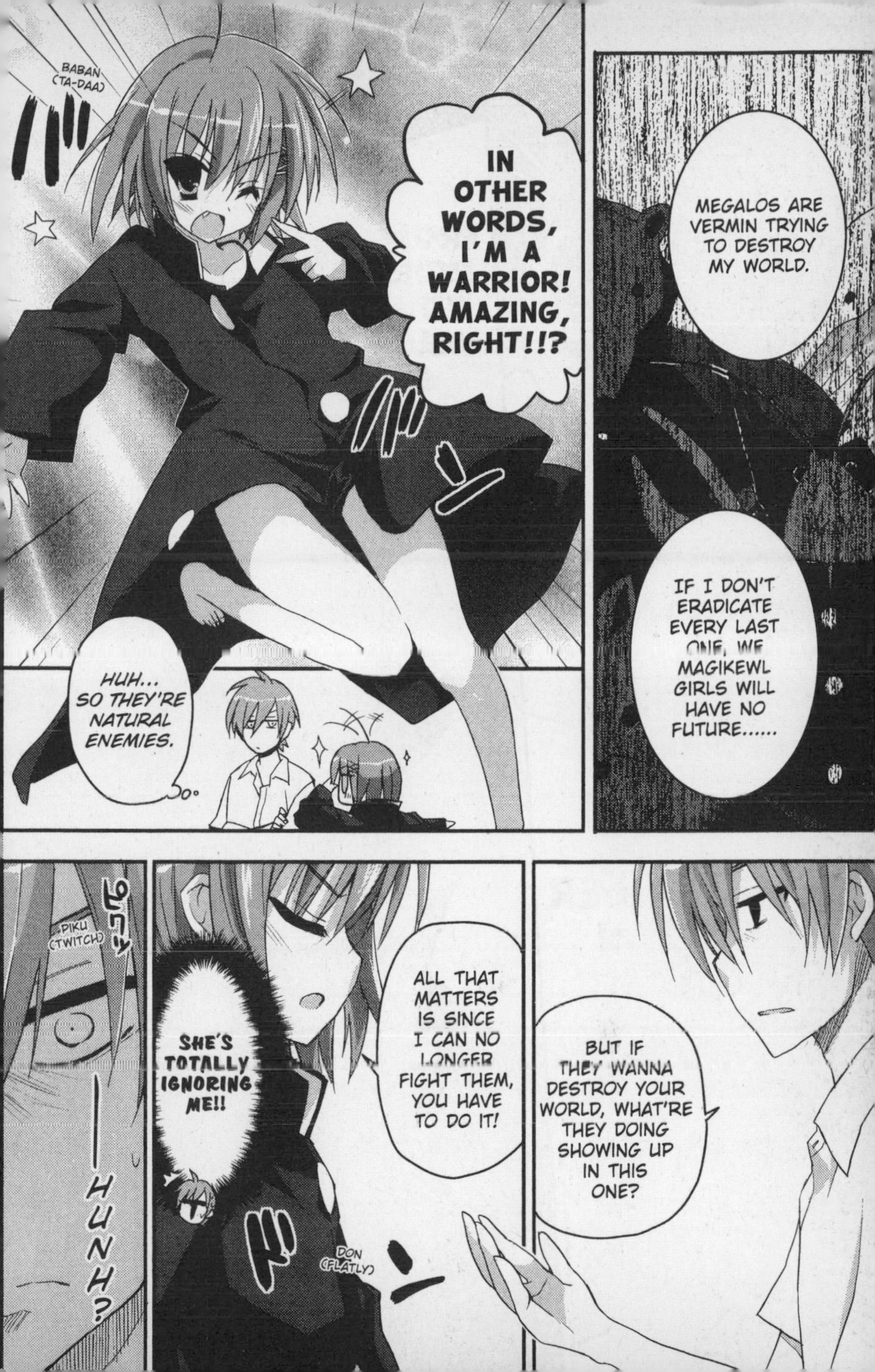
MEGALOS ARE VERMIN TRYING TO DESTROY MY WORLD.
IF I DON'T ERADICATE EVERY LAST ONE, WE MAGIKEWL GIRLS WILL HAVE NO FUTURE......
BABAN (TA-DAA)
IN OTHER WORDS, I'M A WARRIOR! AMAZING, RIGHT!!?
HUH... SO THEY'RE NATURAL ENEMIES.
BUT IF THEY WANNA DESTROY YOUR WORLD, WHAT'RE THEY DOING SHOWING UP IN THIS ONE?
ALL THAT MATTERS IS SINCE I CAN NO LONGER FIGHT THEM, YOU HAVE TO DO IT!
SHE'S TOTALLY IGNORING ME!!
DON (FLATLY)
PIKU (TWITCH)
——HUNH?

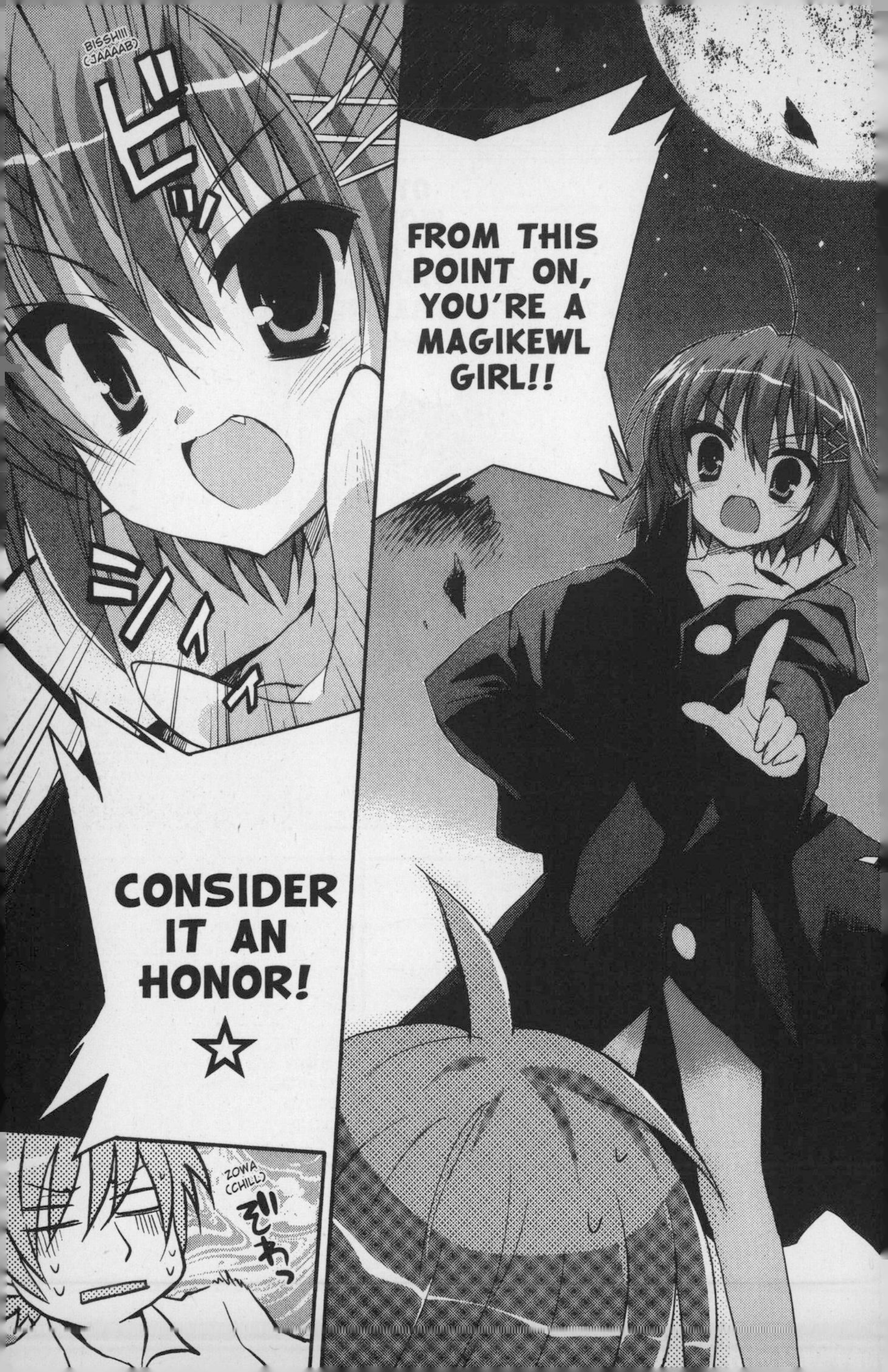
FROM THIS POINT ON, YOU'RE A MAGIKEWL GIRL!!
BISSHIII (JAAAAB)
CONSIDER IT AN HONOR! ☆
ZOWA (CHILL)
ぞわっ

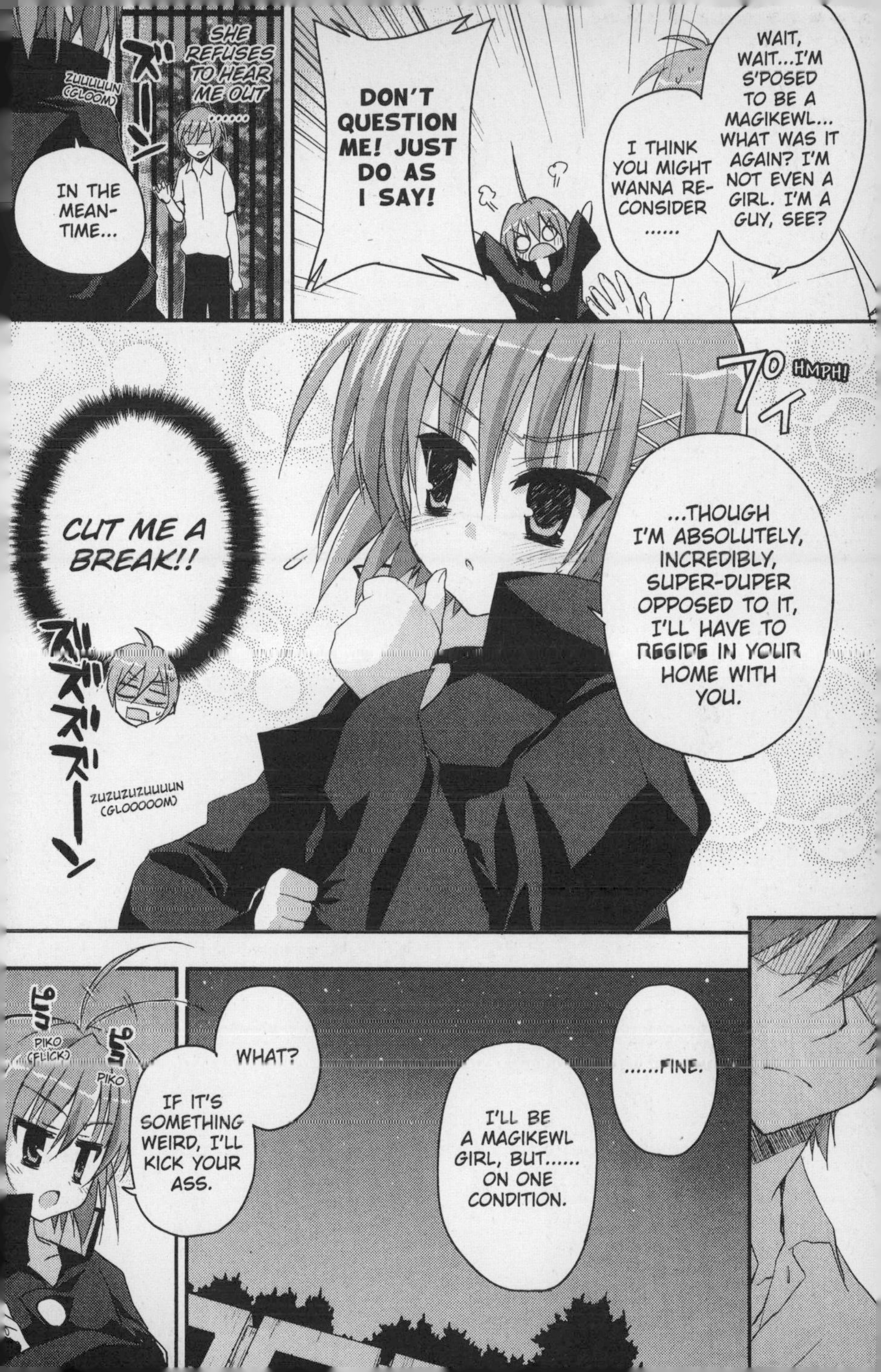
WAIT, WAIT...I'M S'POSED TO BE A MAGIKEWL... WHAT WAS IT AGAIN? I'M NOT EVEN A GIRL. I'M A GUY, SEE?
I THINK YOU MIGHT WANNA RE-CONSIDER ......
DON'T QUESTION ME! JUST DO AS I SAY!
SHE REFUSES TO HEAR ME OUT
....
ZUUUUUN (GLOOM)
IN THE MEAN-TIME...
HMPH!
...THOUGH I'M ABSOLUTELY, INCREDIBLY, SUPER-DUPER OPPOSED TO IT, I'LL HAVE TO RESIDE IN YOUR HOME WITH YOU.
CUT ME A BREAK!!
ZUZUZUZUUUUN (GLOOOOOM)
......FINE.
I'LL BE A MAGIKEWL GIRL, BUT...... ON ONE CONDITION.
WHAT?
IF IT'S SOMETHING WEIRD, I'LL KICK YOUR ASS.
PIKO (FLICK)
PIKO

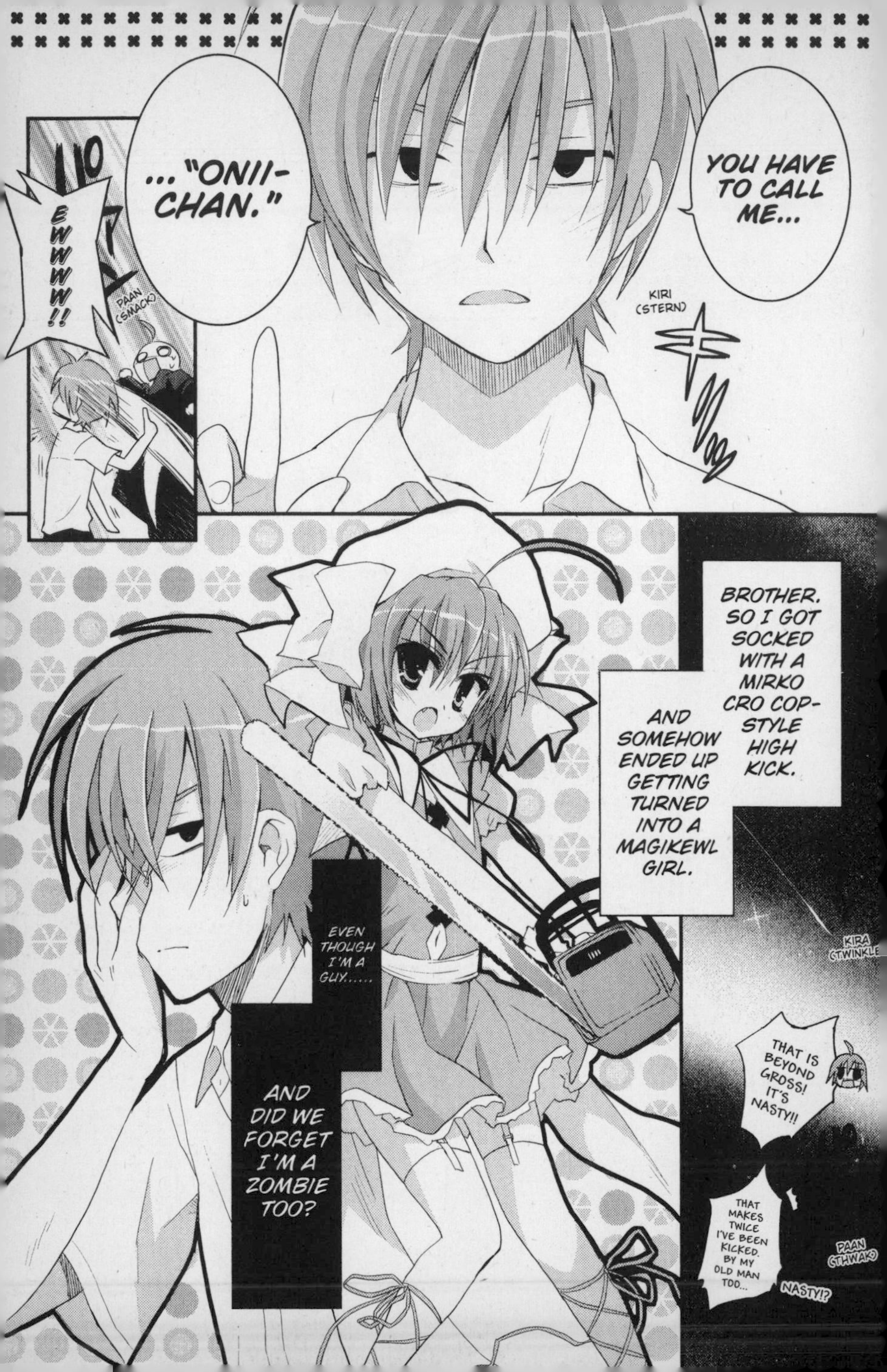
YOU HAVE TO CALL ME...
..."ONII-CHAN."
KIRI (STERN)
EWWWW!!
PAAN (SMACK)
BROTHER. SO I GOT SOCKED WITH A MIRKO CRO COP-STYLE HIGH KICK.
AND SOMEHOW ENDED UP GETTING TURNED INTO A MAGIKEWL GIRL.
KIRA (TWINKLE)
EVEN THOUGH I'M A GUY.....
AND DID WE FORGET I'M A ZOMBIE TOO?
THAT IS BEYOND GROSS! IT'S NASTY!!
THAT MAKES TWICE I'VE BEEN KICKED. BY MY OLD MAN TOO...
NASTY!?
PAAN (THWAK)

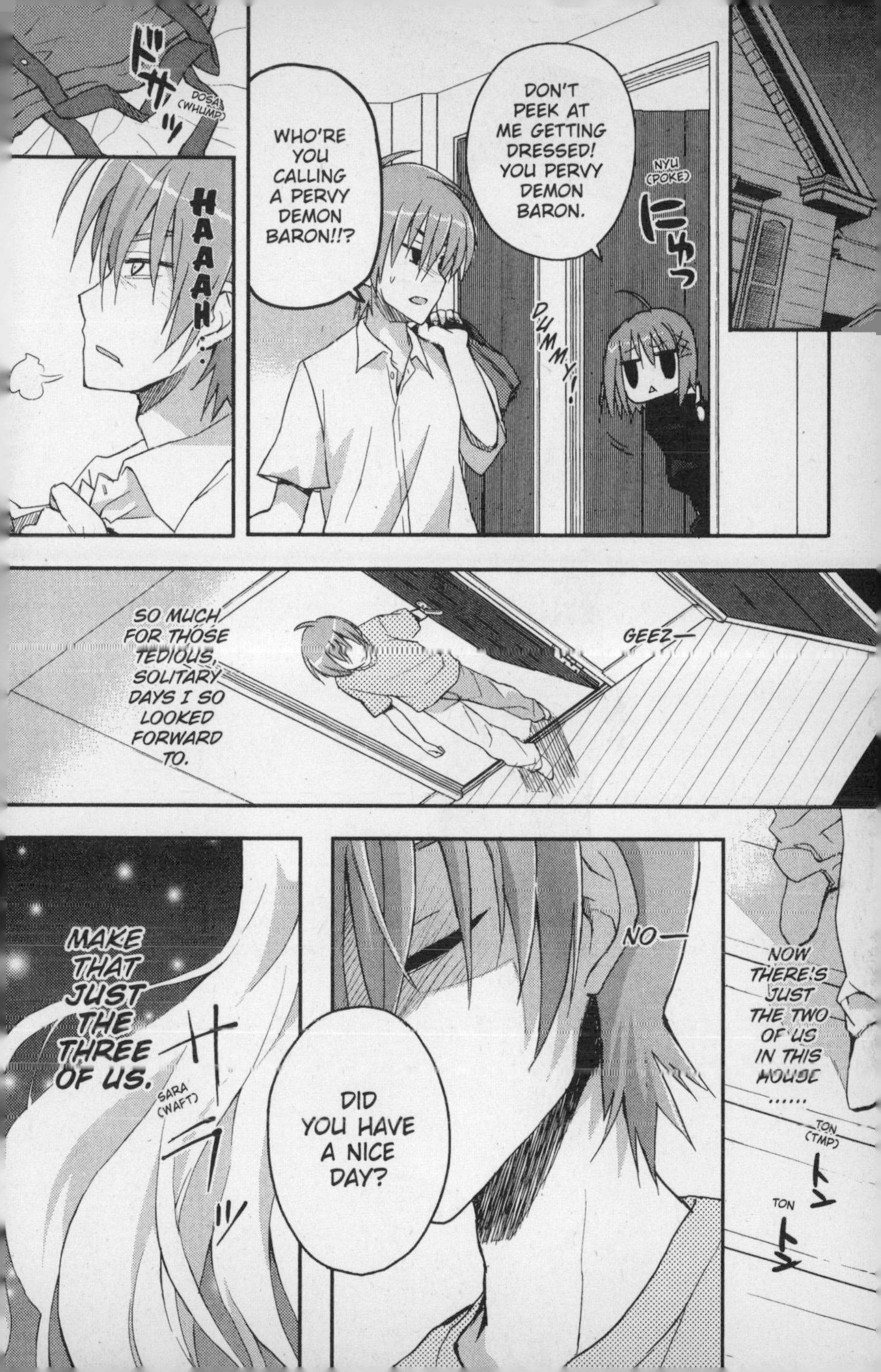
DON'T PEEK AT ME GETTING DRESSED! YOU PERVY DEMON BARON.
NYU (POKE)
にゅっ
WHO'RE YOU CALLING A PERVY DEMON BARON!!?
DUMMY!
DOSA (WHUMP)
ドサッ
HAAAH...
GEEZ—
SO MUCH FOR THOSE TEDIOUS, SOLITARY DAYS I SO LOOKED FORWARD TO.
NOW THERE'S JUST THE TWO OF US IN THIS HOUSE......
TON (TMP)
トン
TON
トン
NO—
DID YOU HAVE A NICE DAY?
MAKE THAT JUST THE THREE OF US.
SARA (WAFT)
サラッ

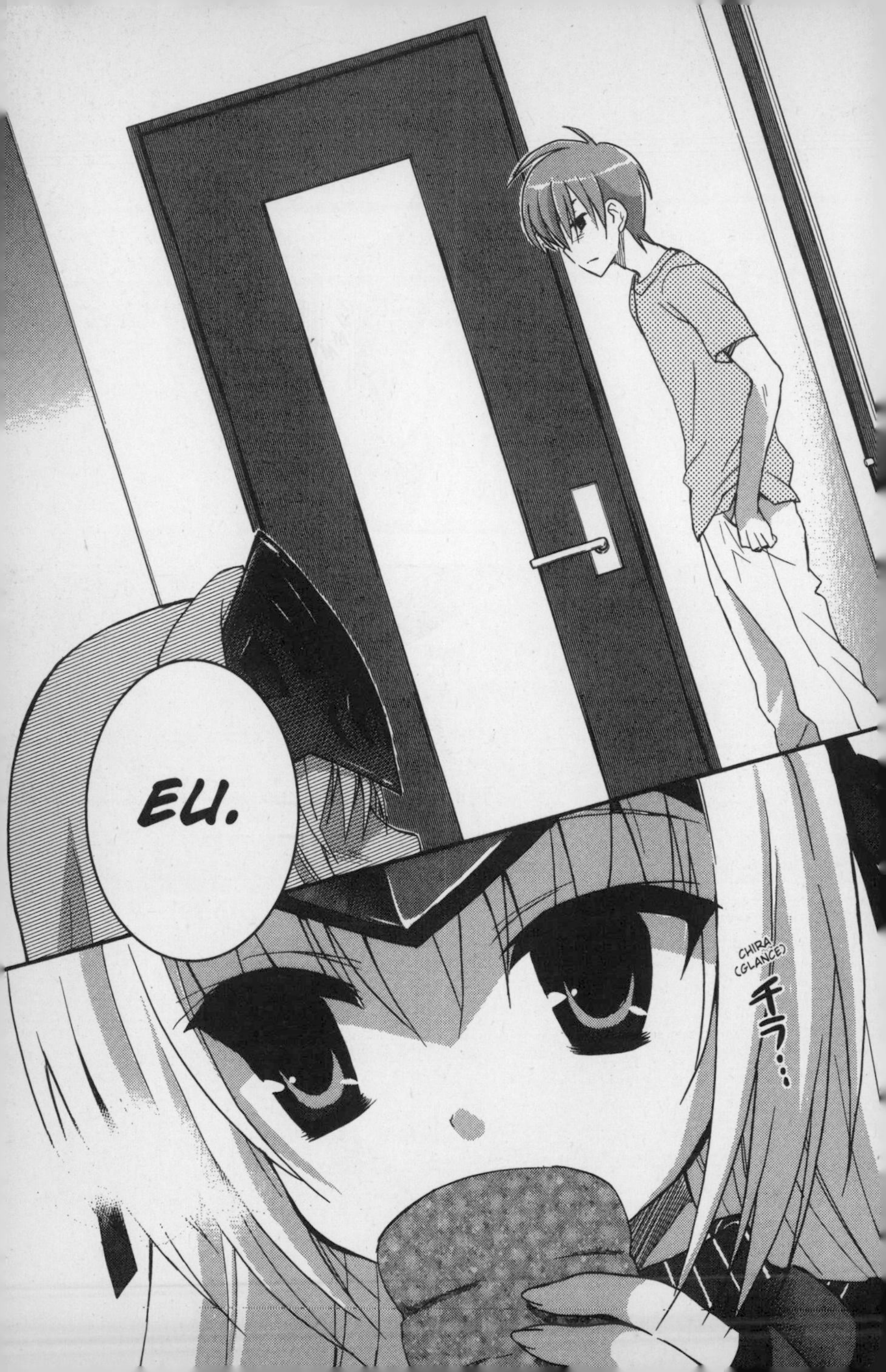
EU.
CHIRA (GLANCE)
チラ…

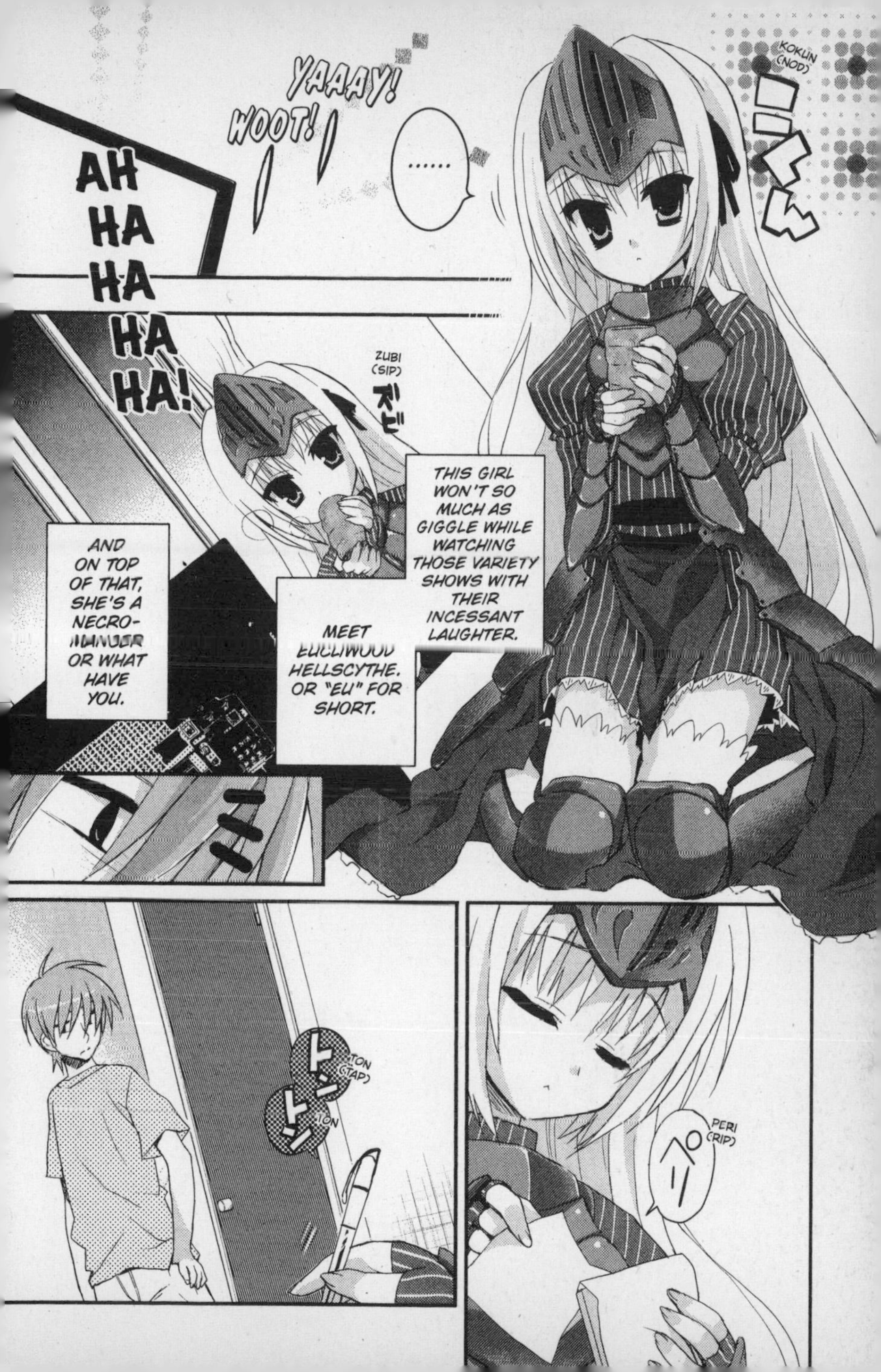
KOKUN (NOD)
THIS GIRL WON'T SO MUCH AS GIGGLE WHILE WATCHING THOSE VARIETY SHOWS WITH THEIR INCESSANT LAUGHTER.
YAAAY! WOOT!
......
AH HA HA HA HA HA!
ZUBI (SIP)
MEET EUCLIWOOD HELLSCYTHE. OR "EU" FOR SHORT.
AND ON TOP OF THAT, SHE'S A NECRO-MANCER OR WHAT HAVE YOU.
PERI (RIP)
TON (TAP)
TON

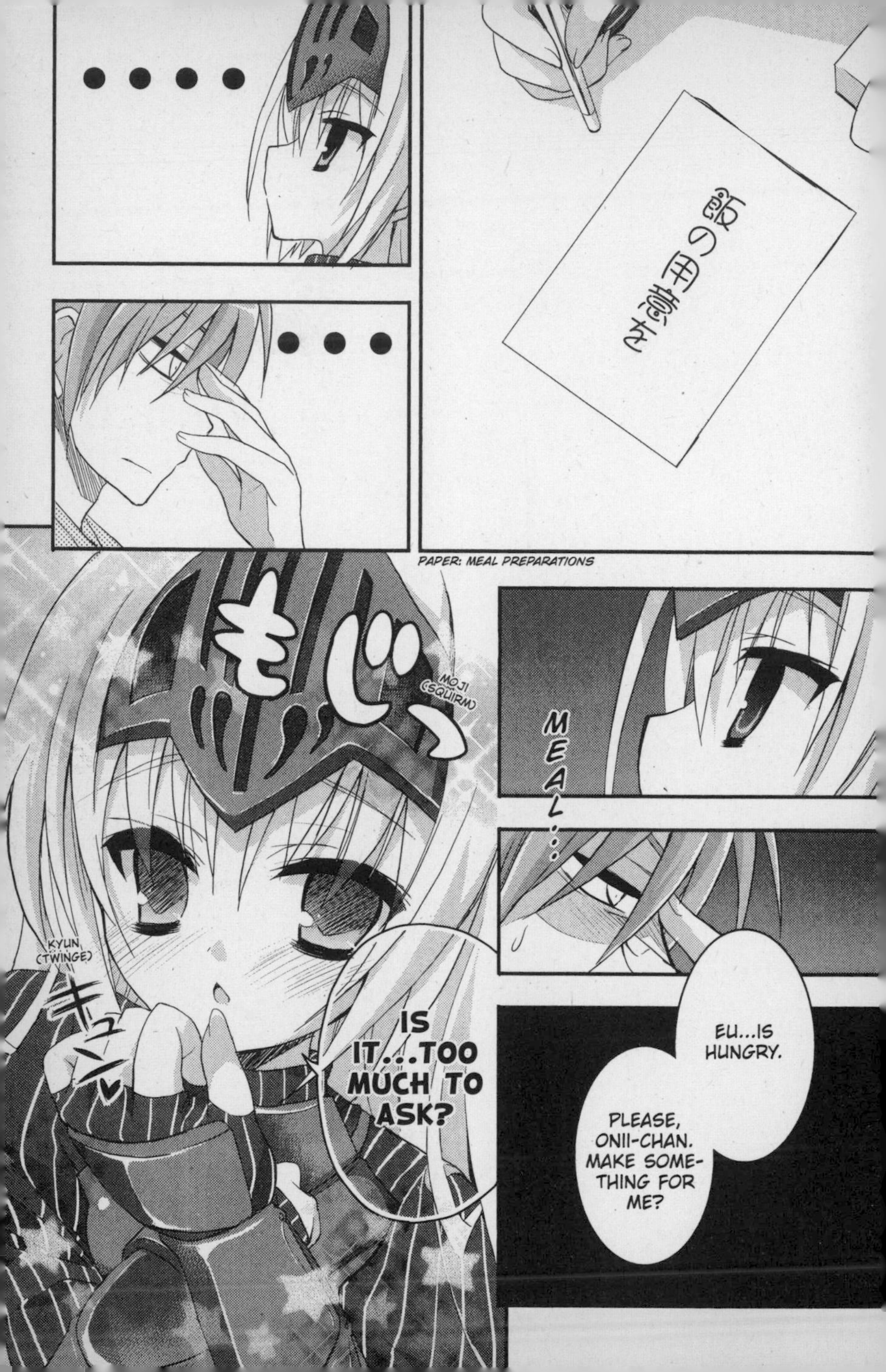
飯の用意を
PAPER: MEAL PREPARATIONS
• • • •
• • •
MEAL...
EU...IS HUNGRY.
PLEASE, ONII-CHAN. MAKE SOMETHING FOR ME?
もじ
MOJI (SQUIRM)
IS IT...TOO MUCH TO ASK?
キュン
KYUN (TWINGE)

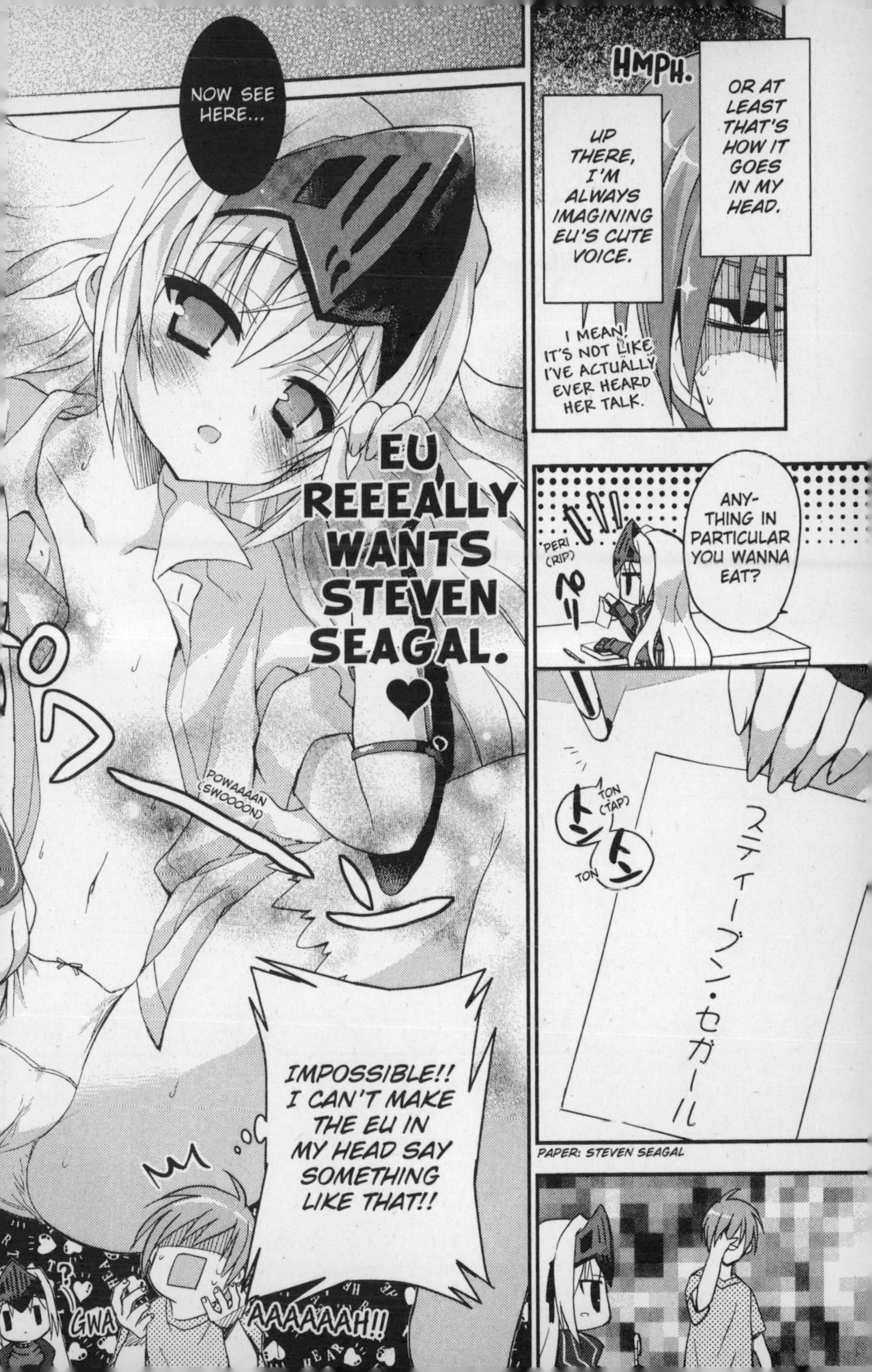

HMPH.
OR AT LEAST THAT'S HOW IT GOES IN MY HEAD.
UP THERE, I'M ALWAYS IMAGINING EU'S CUTE VOICE.
I MEAN, IT'S NOT LIKE I'VE ACTUALLY EVER HEARD HER TALK.
ANY-THING IN PARTICULAR YOU WANNA EAT?
PERI (RIP)
TON (TAP)
TON
ステーブン・セガール
PAPER: STEVEN SEAGAL
NOW SEE HERE...
EU REEEALLY WANTS STEVEN SEAGAL. ♥
POWAAAAN (SWOOOON)
IMPOSSIBLE!! I CAN'T MAKE THE EU IN MY HEAD SAY SOMETHING LIKE THAT!!
GWA
AAAAAAH!!

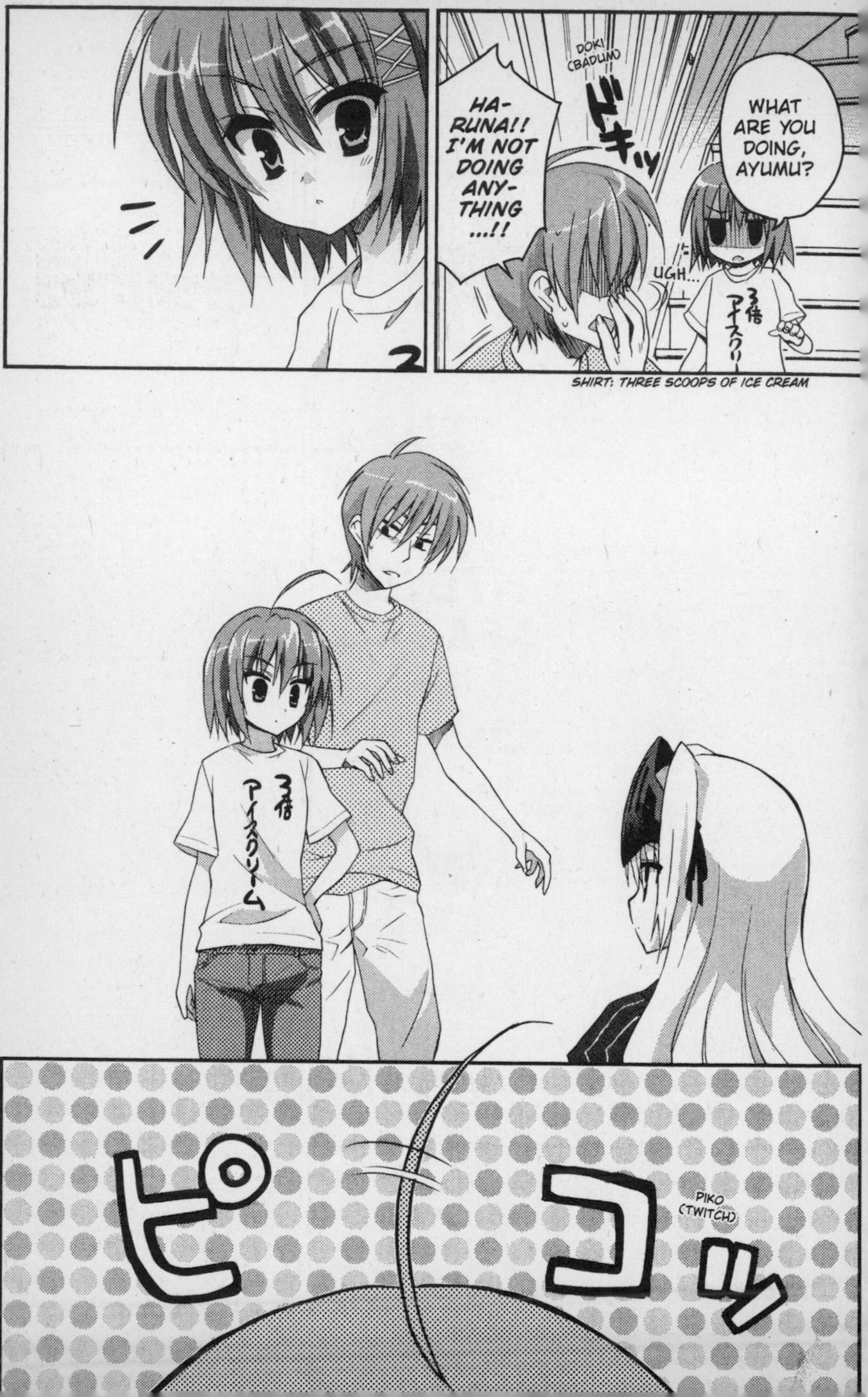
WHAT ARE YOU DOING, AYUMU?
DOKI (BADUM)
ドキッ
HA-RUNA!! I'M NOT DOING ANY-THING ...!!
UGH...
SHIRT: THREE SCOOPS OF ICE CREAM
ピコッ
PIKO (TWITCH)

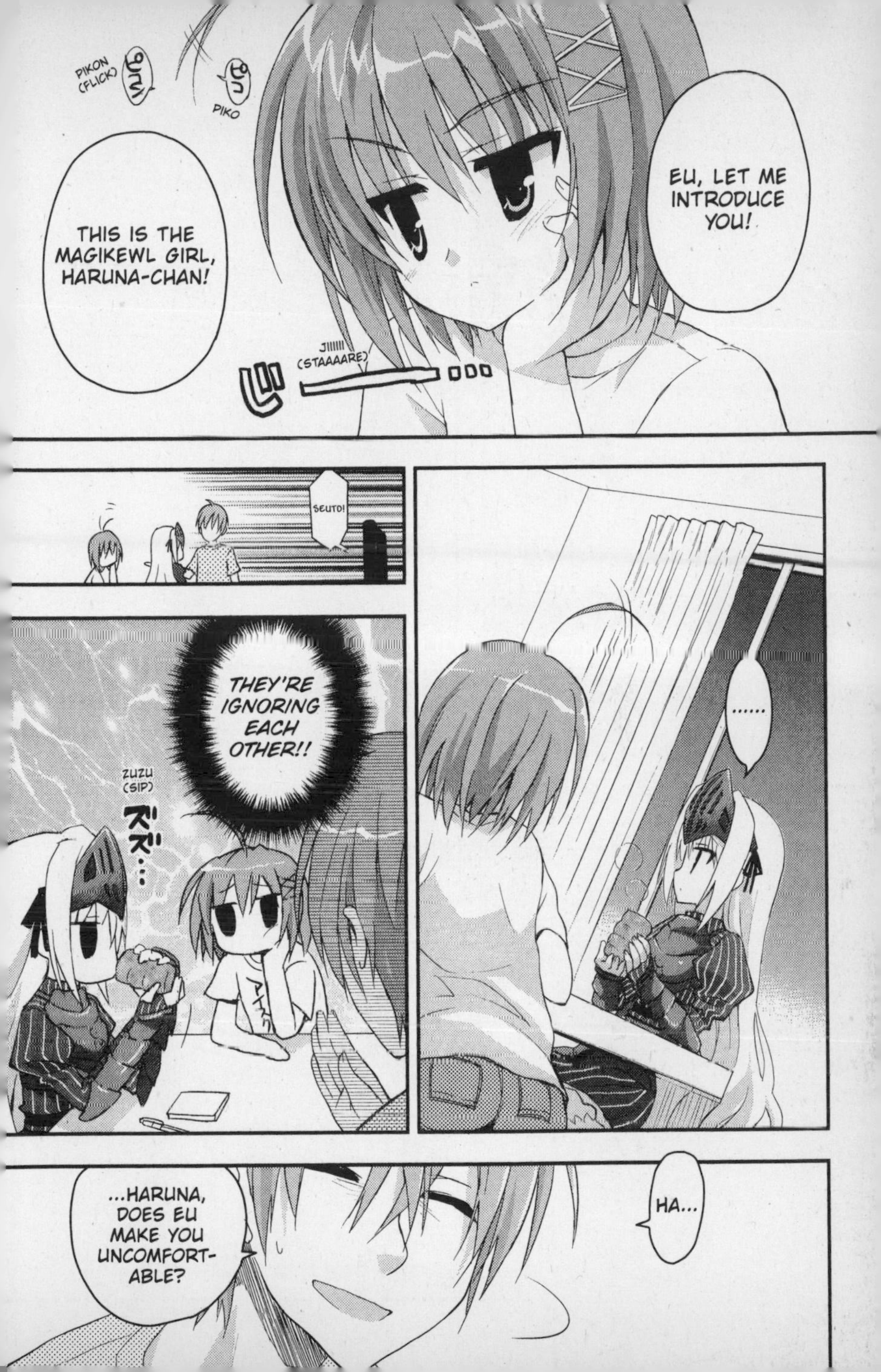
EU, LET ME INTRODUCE YOU!
PIKO
PIKON (FLICK)
THIS IS THE MAGIKEWL GIRL, HARUNA-CHAN!
JIIIII (STAAAARE)
......
SEUTO!
THEY'RE IGNORING EACH OTHER!!
ZUZU (SIP)
HA...
...HARUNA, DOES EU MAKE YOU UNCOMFORT-ABLE?

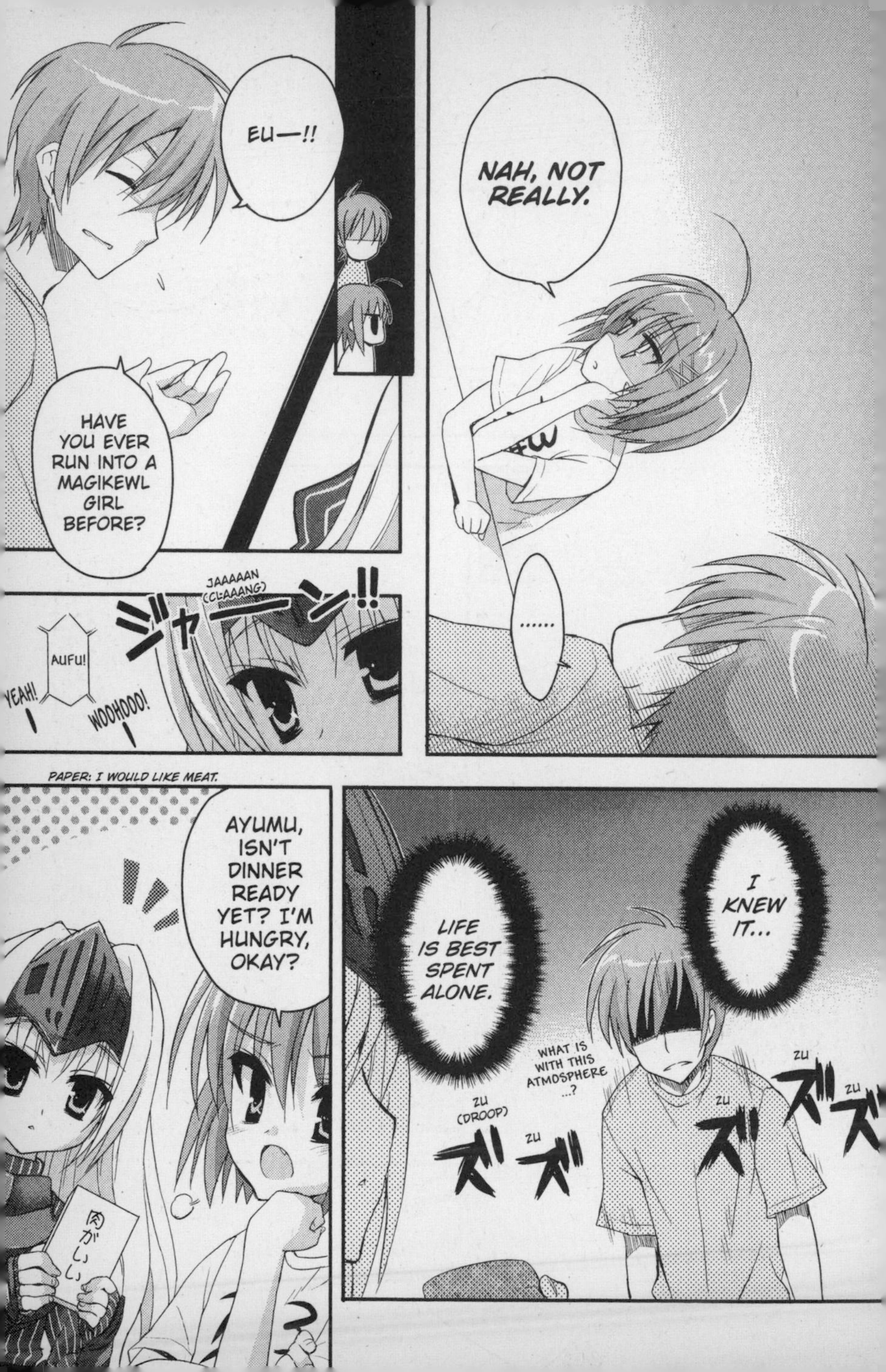
NAH, NOT REALLY.
......
EU—!!
HAVE YOU EVER RUN INTO A MAGIKEWL GIRL BEFORE?
JAAAAAN (CL-AAANG)
AUFU!
YEAH!
WOOHOOO!
PAPER: I WOULD LIKE MEAT.
I KNEW IT...
LIFE IS BEST SPENT ALONE.
WHAT IS WITH THIS ATMOSPHERE ...?
ZU
ZU
ZU
ZU (DROOP)
AYUMU, ISN'T DINNER READY YET? I'M HUNGRY, OKAY?
肉がしい

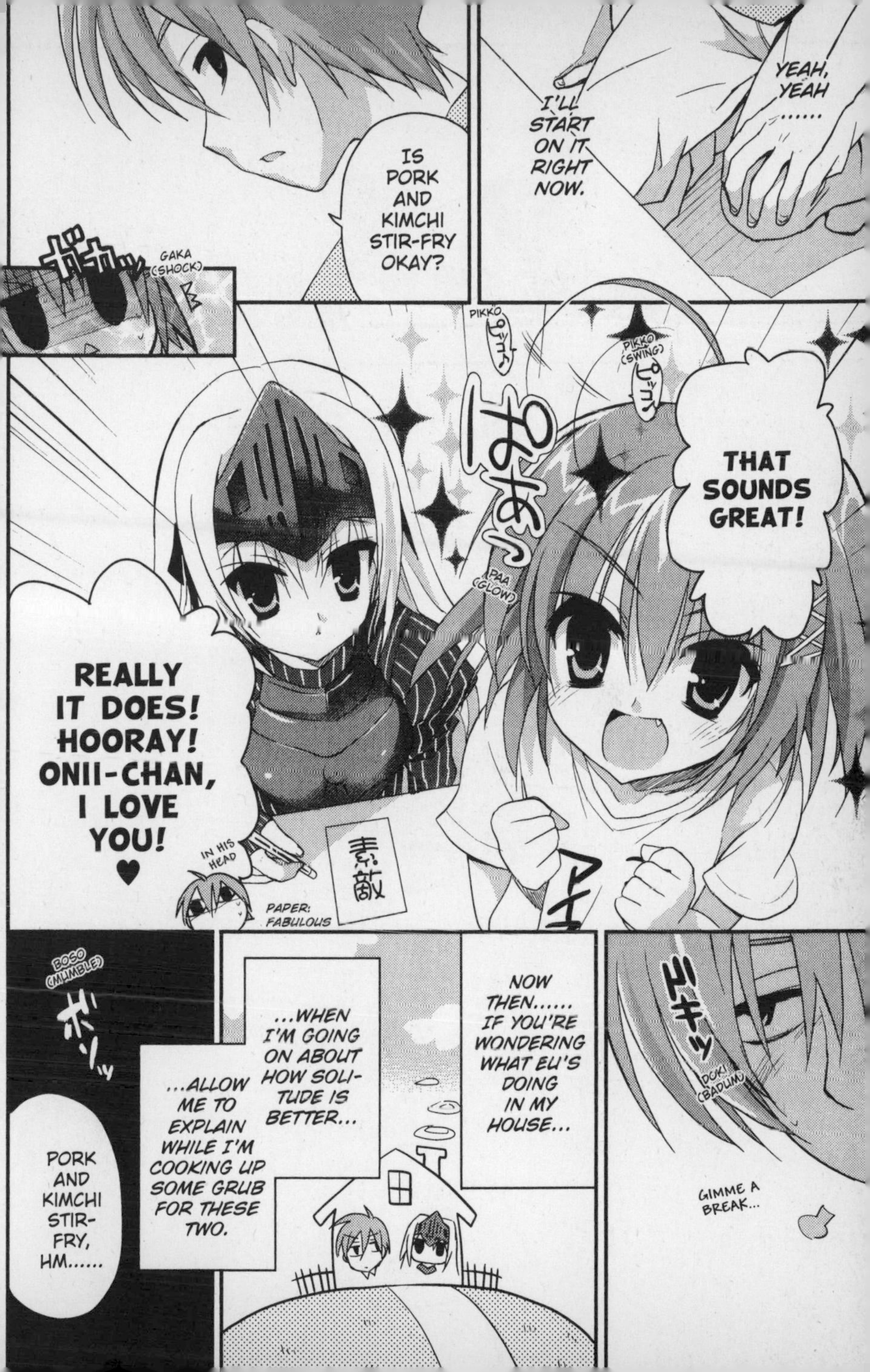
YEAH, YEAH......
I'LL START ON IT RIGHT NOW.
IS PORK AND KIMCHI STIR-FRY OKAY?
GAKA (SHOCK)
PIKKO (SWING)
PIKKO
THAT SOUNDS GREAT!
PAA (GLOW)
REALLY IT DOES! HOORAY! ONII-CHAN, I LOVE YOU! ♥
IN HIS HEAD
素敵
PAPER: FABULOUS
DOKI (BADUM)
GIMME A BREAK...
NOW THEN...... IF YOU'RE WONDERING WHAT EU'S DOING IN MY HOUSE...
...WHEN I'M GOING ON ABOUT HOW SOLI-TUDE IS BETTER...
...ALLOW ME TO EXPLAIN WHILE I'M COOKING UP SOME GRUB FOR THESE TWO.
BOSO (MUMBLE)
PORK AND KIMCHI STIR-FRY, HM......

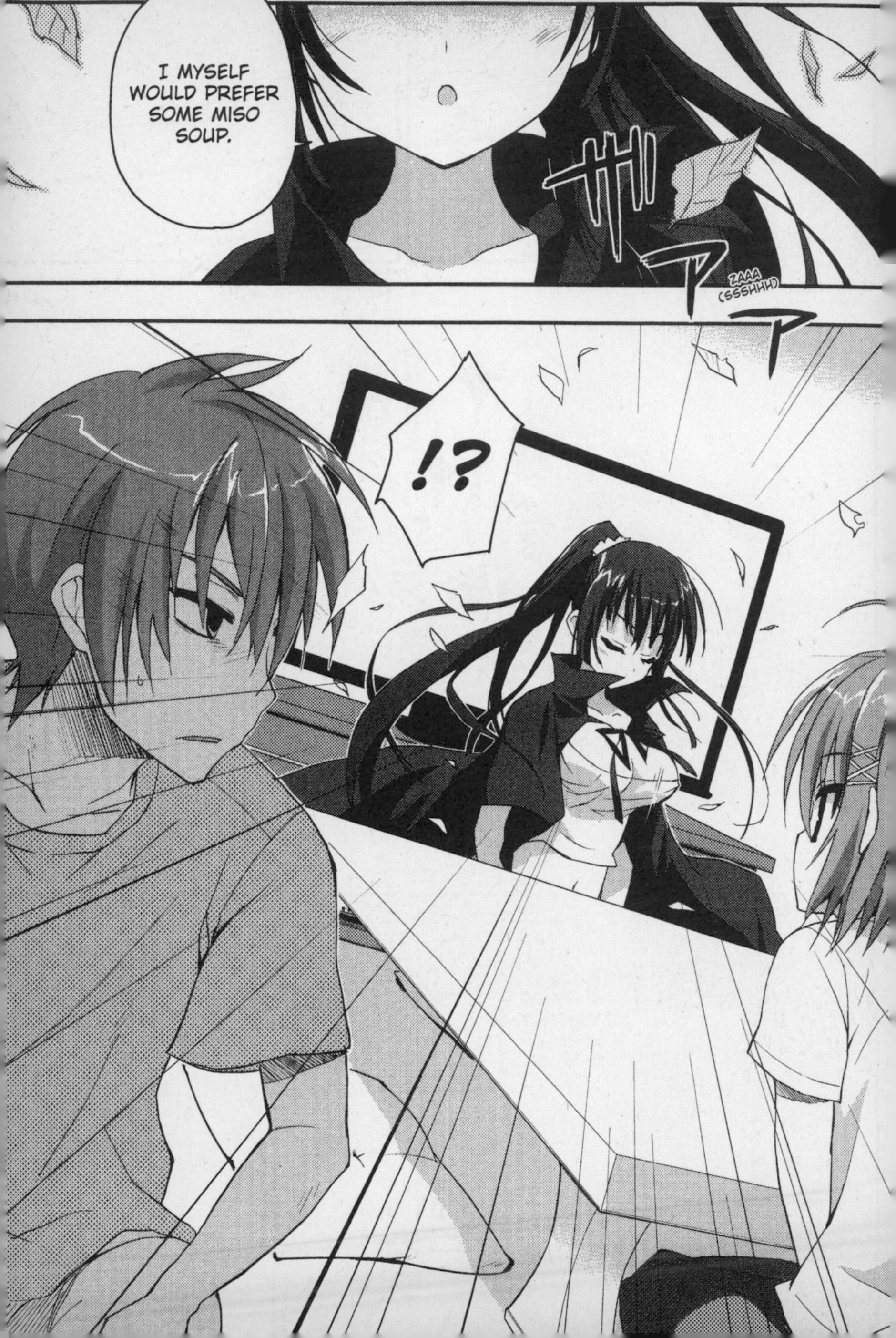
I MYSELF WOULD PREFER SOME MISO SOUP.
ZAAA (SSSHHH)
!?

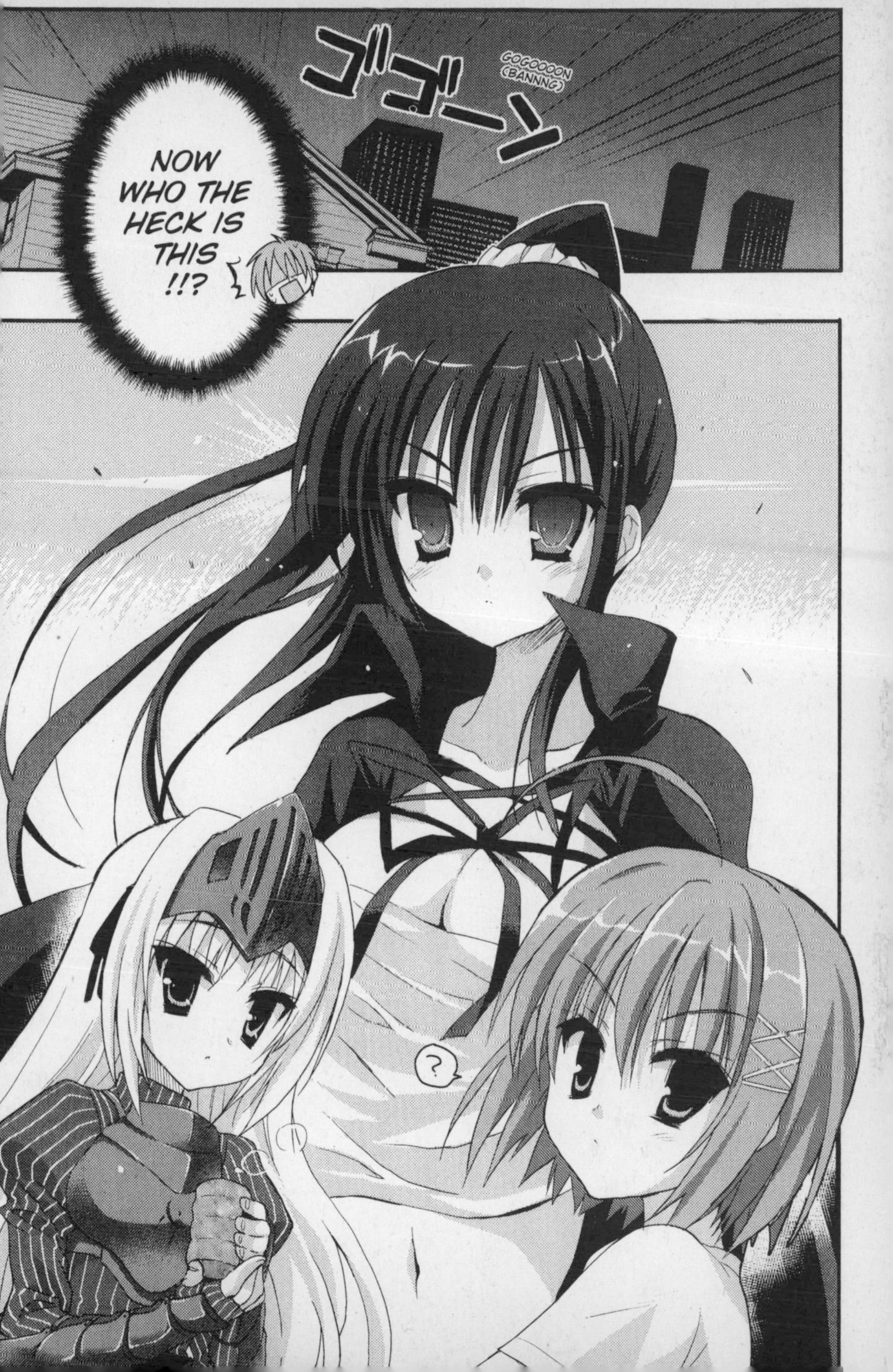
ゴゴーン
GOGOOOON (BANNNG)
NOW WHO THE HECK IS THIS !!?
?

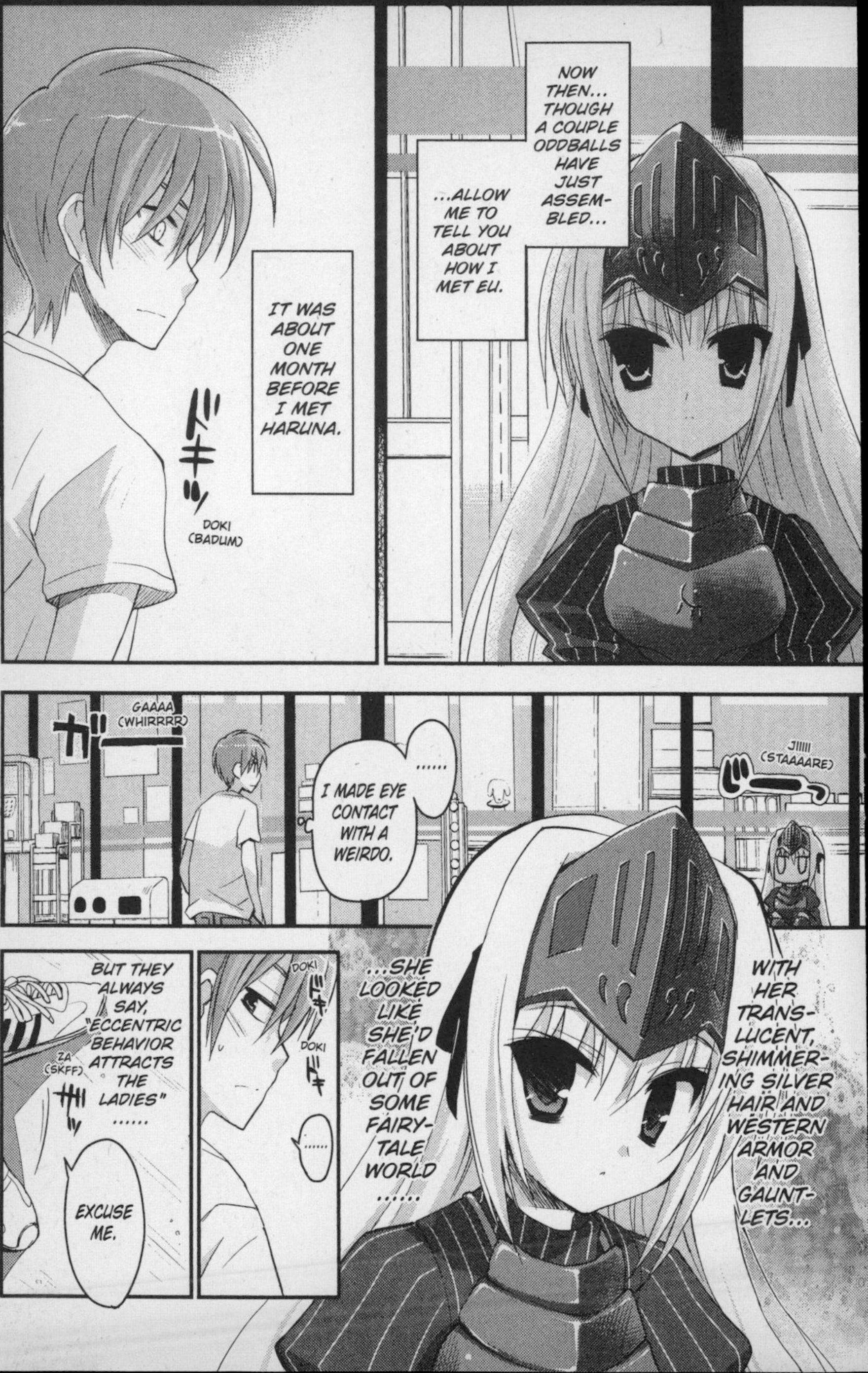
NOW THEN... THOUGH A COUPLE ODDBALLS HAVE JUST ASSEM-BLED...
...ALLOW ME TO TELL YOU ABOUT HOW I MET EU.
IT WAS ABOUT ONE MONTH BEFORE I MET HARUNA.
DOKI (BADUM)
JIIIII (STAAAARE)
......
I MADE EYE CONTACT WITH A WEIRDO.
GAAAA (WHIRRRR)
WITH HER TRANS-LUCENT, SHIMMER-ING SILVER HAIR AND WESTERN ARMOR AND GAUNT-LETS...
...SHE LOOKED LIKE SHE'D FALLEN OUT OF SOME FAIRY-TALE WORLD ......
DOKI
DOKI
......
BUT THEY ALWAYS SAY, "ECCENTRIC BEHAVIOR ATTRACTS THE LADIES" ......
ZA (SKFF)
EXCUSE ME.

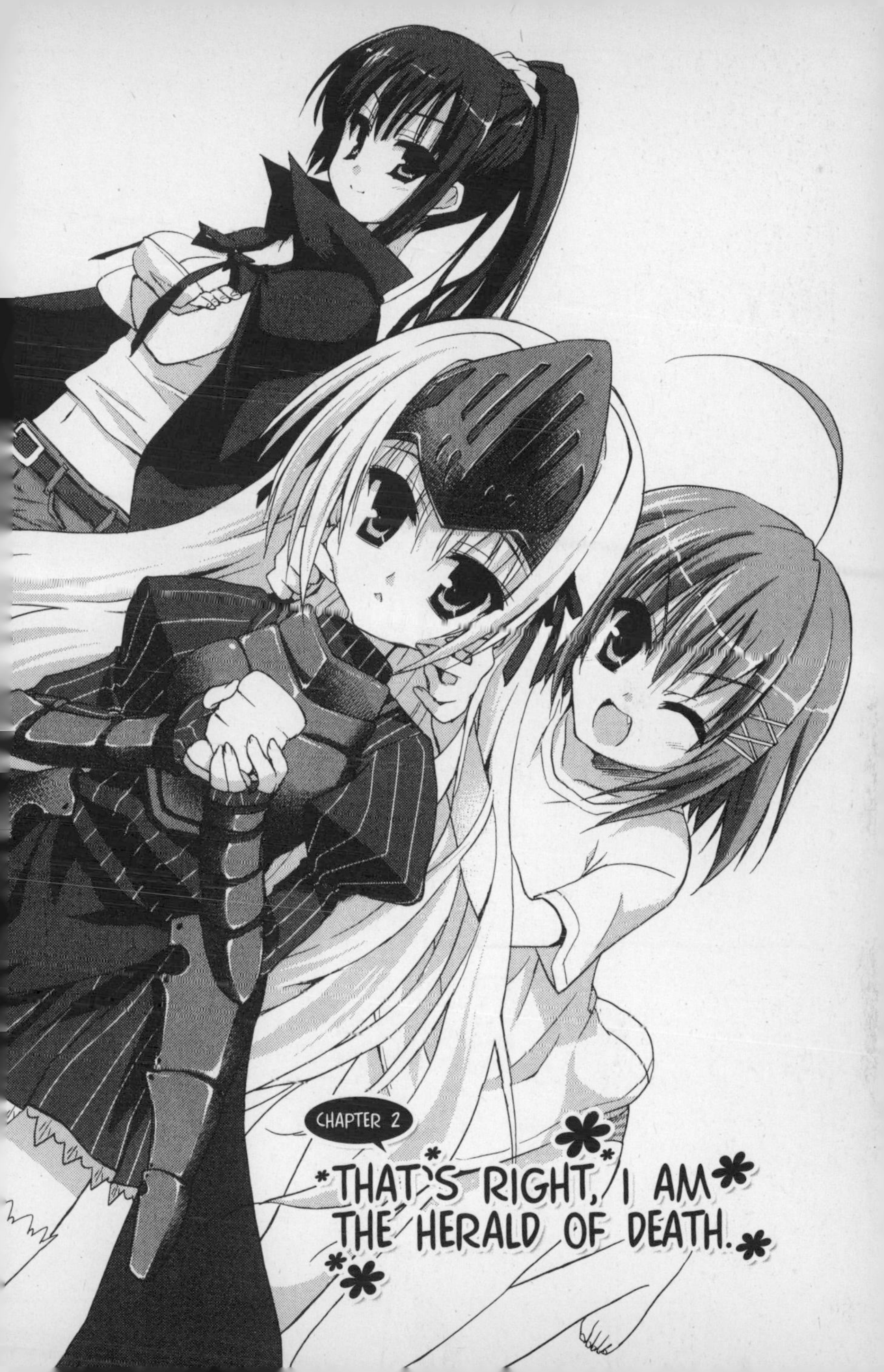
CHAPTER 2
THAT'S RIGHT, I AM
THE HERALD OF DEATH.

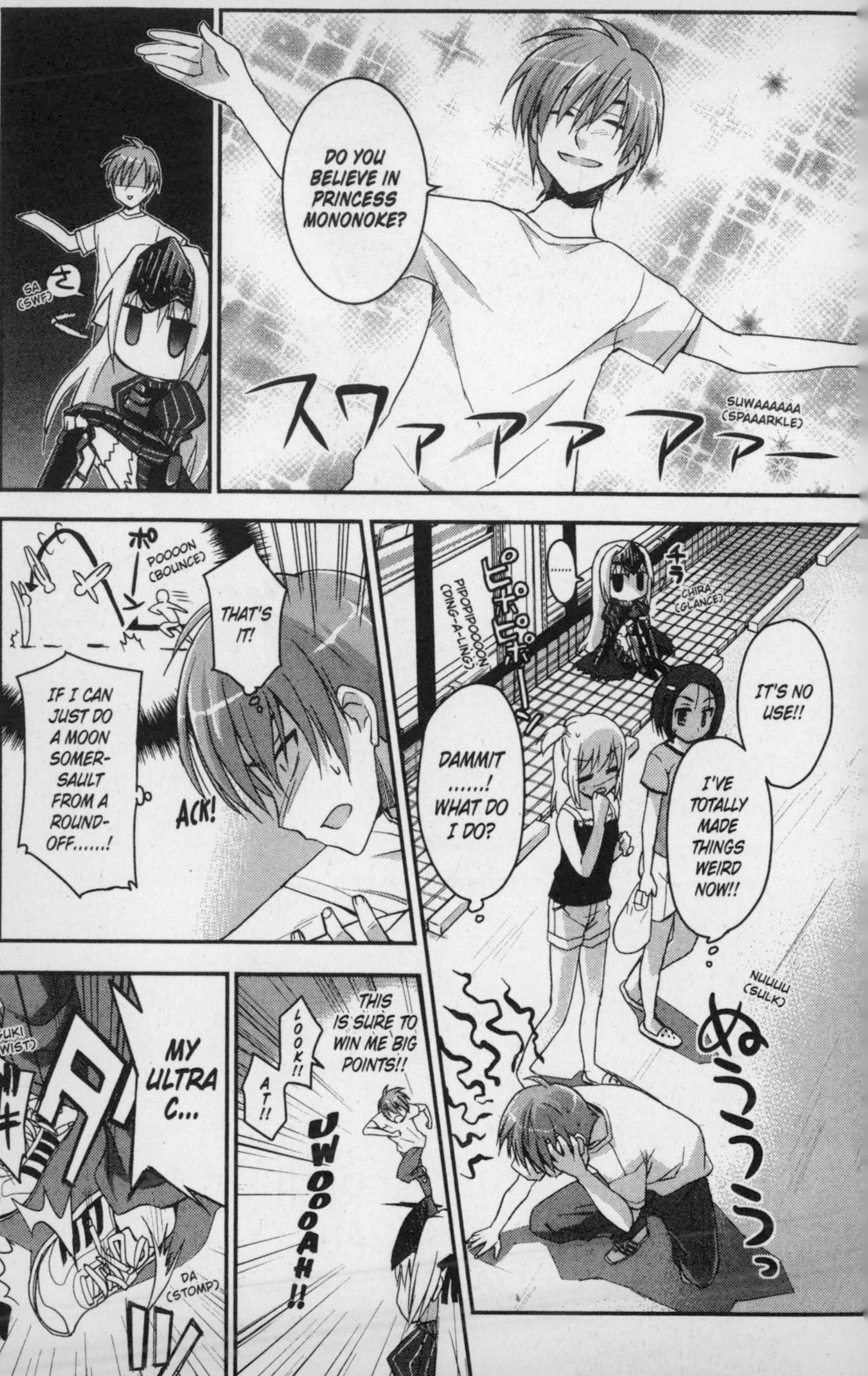
DO YOU BELIEVE IN PRINCESS MONONOKE?
スワァァァ アァー
SUWAAAAAA (SPAAARKLE)
さ
SA (SWF)
......
チラ
CHIRA (GLANCE)
ピポピポ
PIPOPIPOOOON (DING-A-LING)
IT'S NO USE!!
I'VE TOTALLY MADE THINGS WEIRD NOW!!
DAMMIT ......! WHAT DO I DO?
ぬううう
NUUUU (SULK)
THAT'S IT!
ポ
POOOON (BOUNCE)
IF I CAN JUST DO A MOON SOMER-SAULT FROM A ROUND-OFF......!
ACK!
THIS IS SURE TO WIN ME BIG POINTS!!
LOOK!!
AT!!
UWOOOOAH!!
MY ULTRA C...
グキ
GUKI (TWIST)
ダ
DA (STOMP)

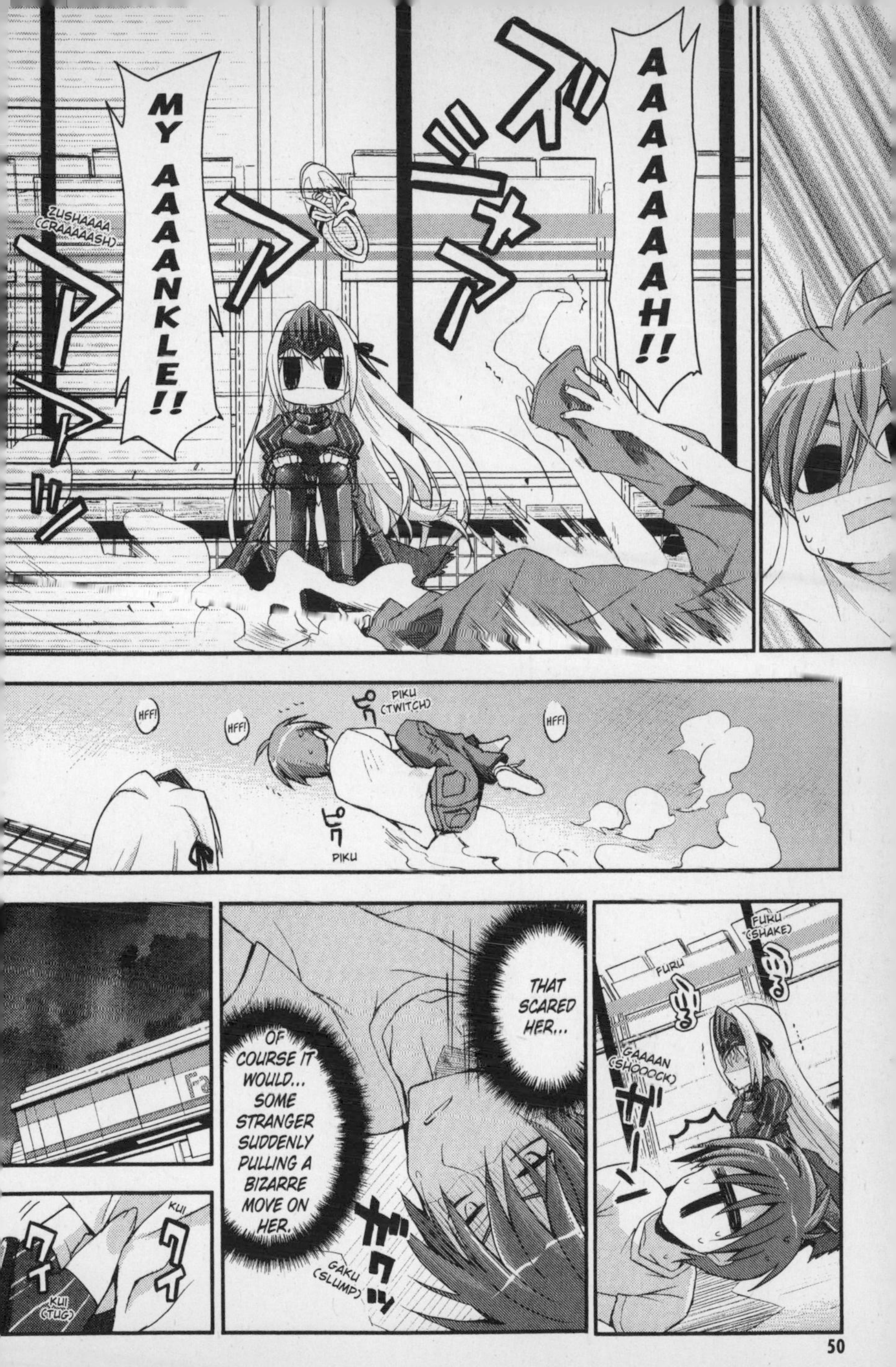
AAAAAAAAAH!!
MY AAAAANKLE!!
ZUSHAAAA (CRAAAAASH)
HFF!
PIKU (TWITCH)
HFF!
HFF!
PIKU
FURU (SHAKE)
FURU
GAAAAN (SHOOOCK)
THAT SCARED HER...
OF COURSE IT WOULD... SOME STRANGER SUDDENLY PULLING A BIZARRE MOVE ON HER.
GAKU (SLUMP)
KUI
KUI (TUG)

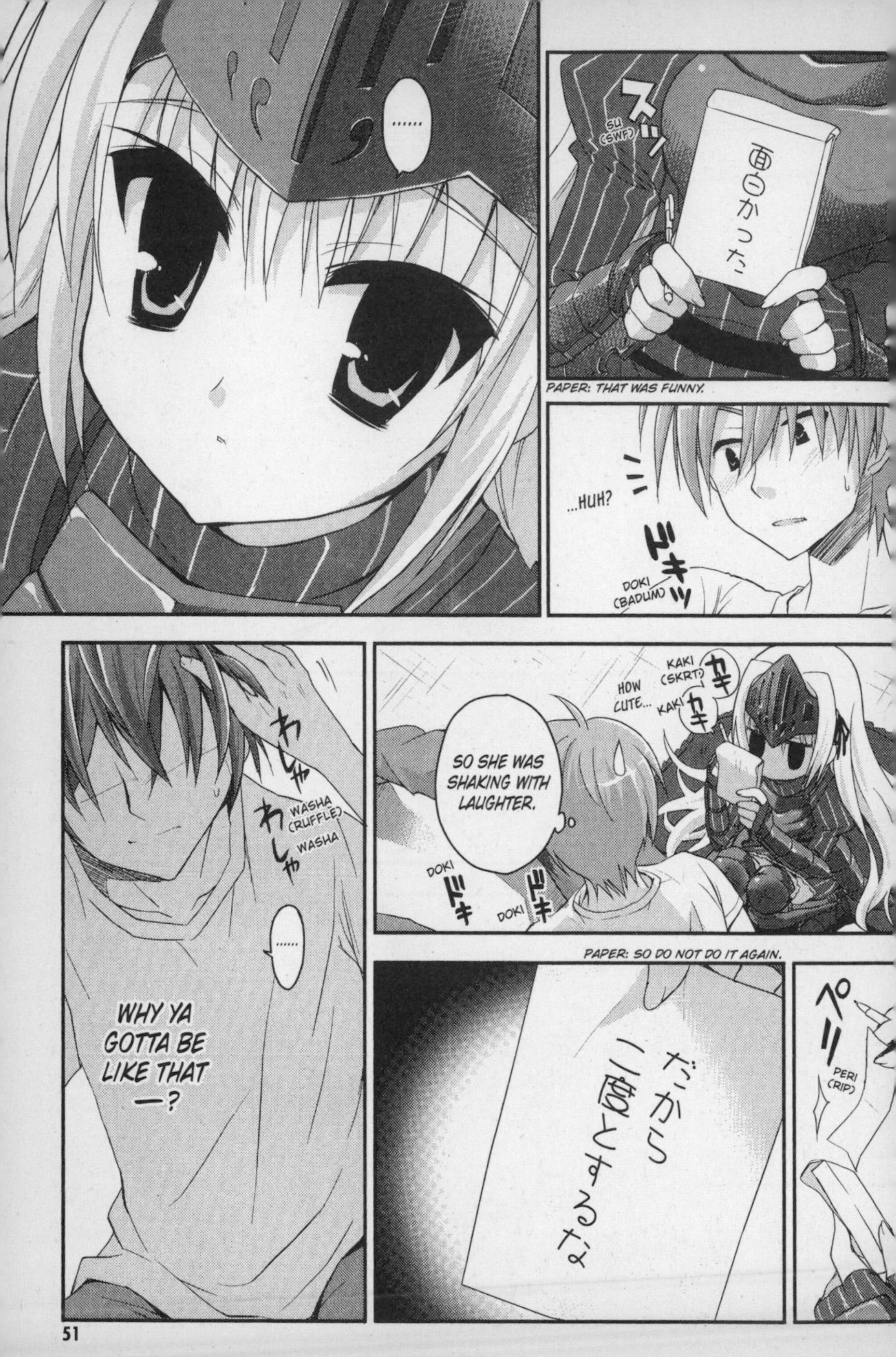
スッ
SU (SWF)
面白かった
PAPER: THAT WAS FUNNY.
…HUH?
ドキッ
DOKI (BADUM)
……
カキ
KAKI (SKRT)
カキ
KAKI
HOW CUTE…
SO SHE WAS SHAKING WITH LAUGHTER.
ドキ
DOKI
ドキ
DOKI
PAPER: SO DO NOT DO IT AGAIN.
ペリ
PERI (RIP)
だから二度とするな
わしゃわしゃ
WASHA (RUFFLE) WASHA
……
WHY YA GOTTA BE LIKE THAT—?

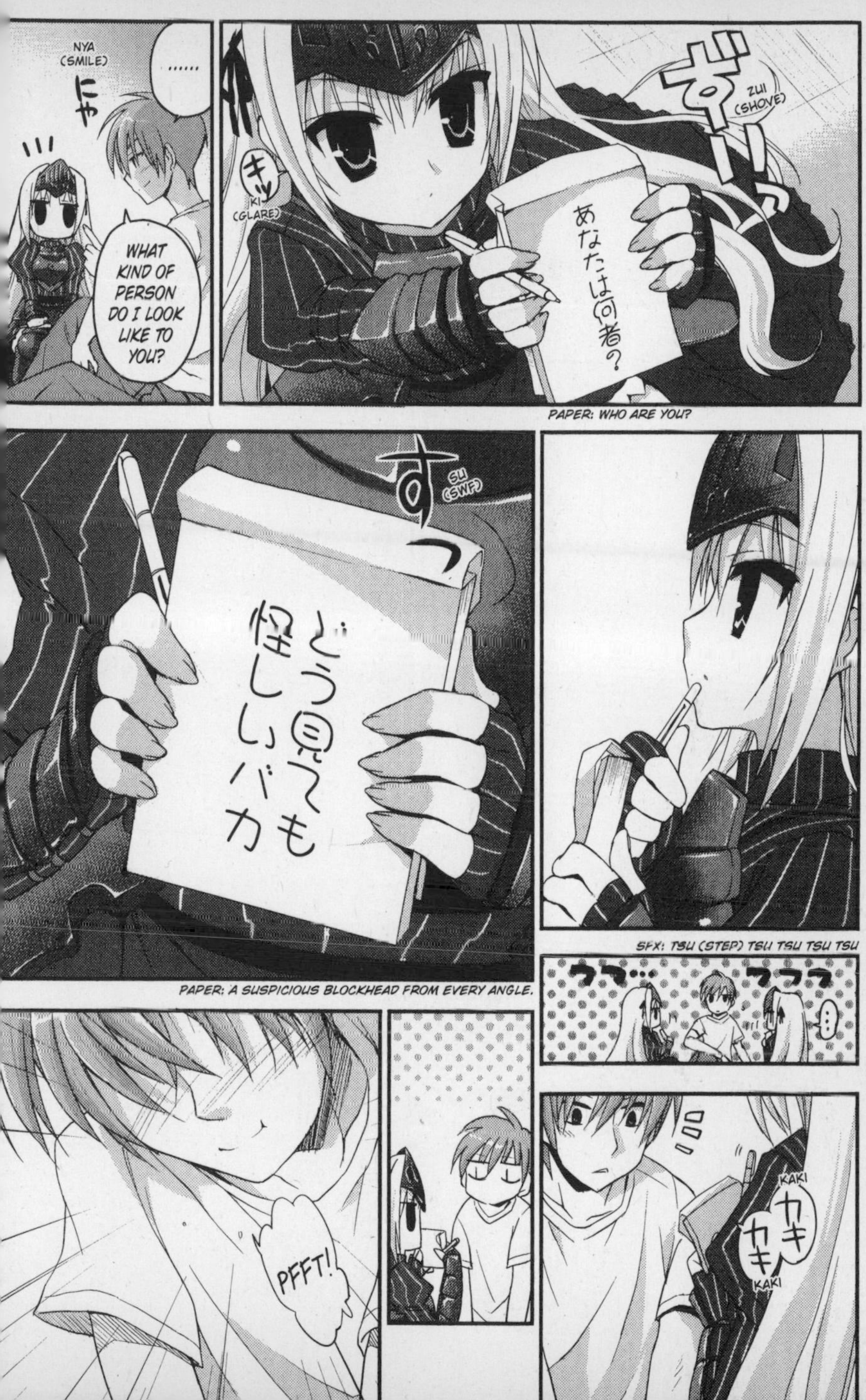
ずいっ
ZUI (SHOVE)
キッ
KI (GLARE)
あなたは何者?
PAPER: WHO ARE YOU?
......
NYA (SMILE)
にゃ
WHAT KIND OF PERSON DO I LOOK LIKE TO YOU?
SFX: TSU (STEP) TSU TSU TSU TSU
ツツ…
ツツツ
…
すっ
SU (SWF)
どう見ても怪しいバカ
PAPER: A SUSPICIOUS BLOCKHEAD FROM EVERY ANGLE.
KAKI
カキ
カキ
KAKI
PFFT!

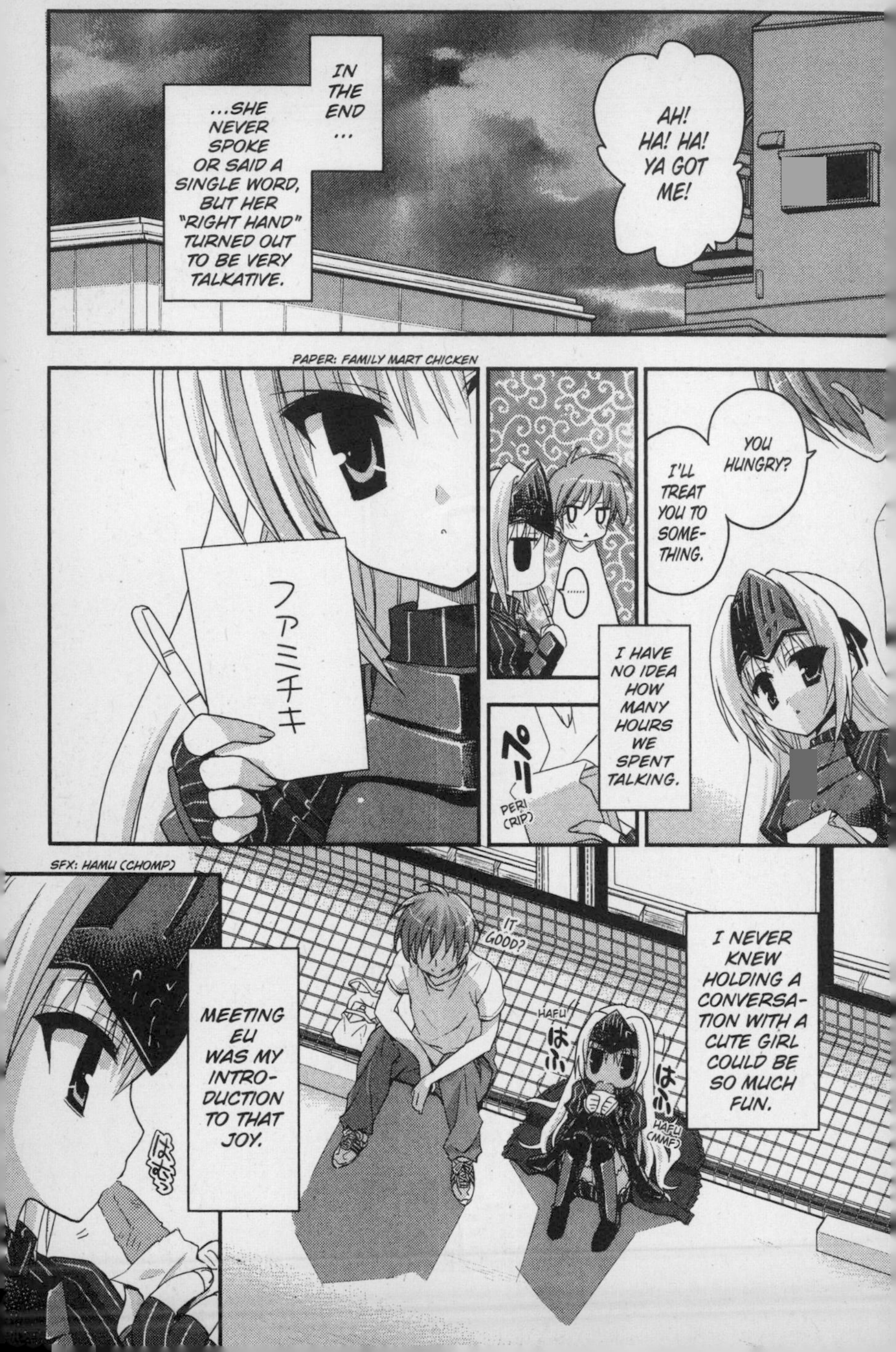
AH! HA! HA! YA GOT ME!
IN THE END...
...SHE NEVER SPOKE OR SAID A SINGLE WORD, BUT HER "RIGHT HAND" TURNED OUT TO BE VERY TALKATIVE.
PAPER: FAMILY MART CHICKEN
YOU HUNGRY?
I'LL TREAT YOU TO SOME-THING.
I HAVE NO IDEA HOW MANY HOURS WE SPENT TALKING.
......
ペリ
PERI (RIP)
ファミチキ
SFX: HAMU (CHOMP)
I NEVER KNEW HOLDING A CONVERSA-TION WITH A CUTE GIRL COULD BE SO MUCH FUN.
IT GOOD?
はふ
HAFU
はふ
HAFU (MMF)
MEETING EU WAS MY INTRO-DUCTION TO THAT JOY.

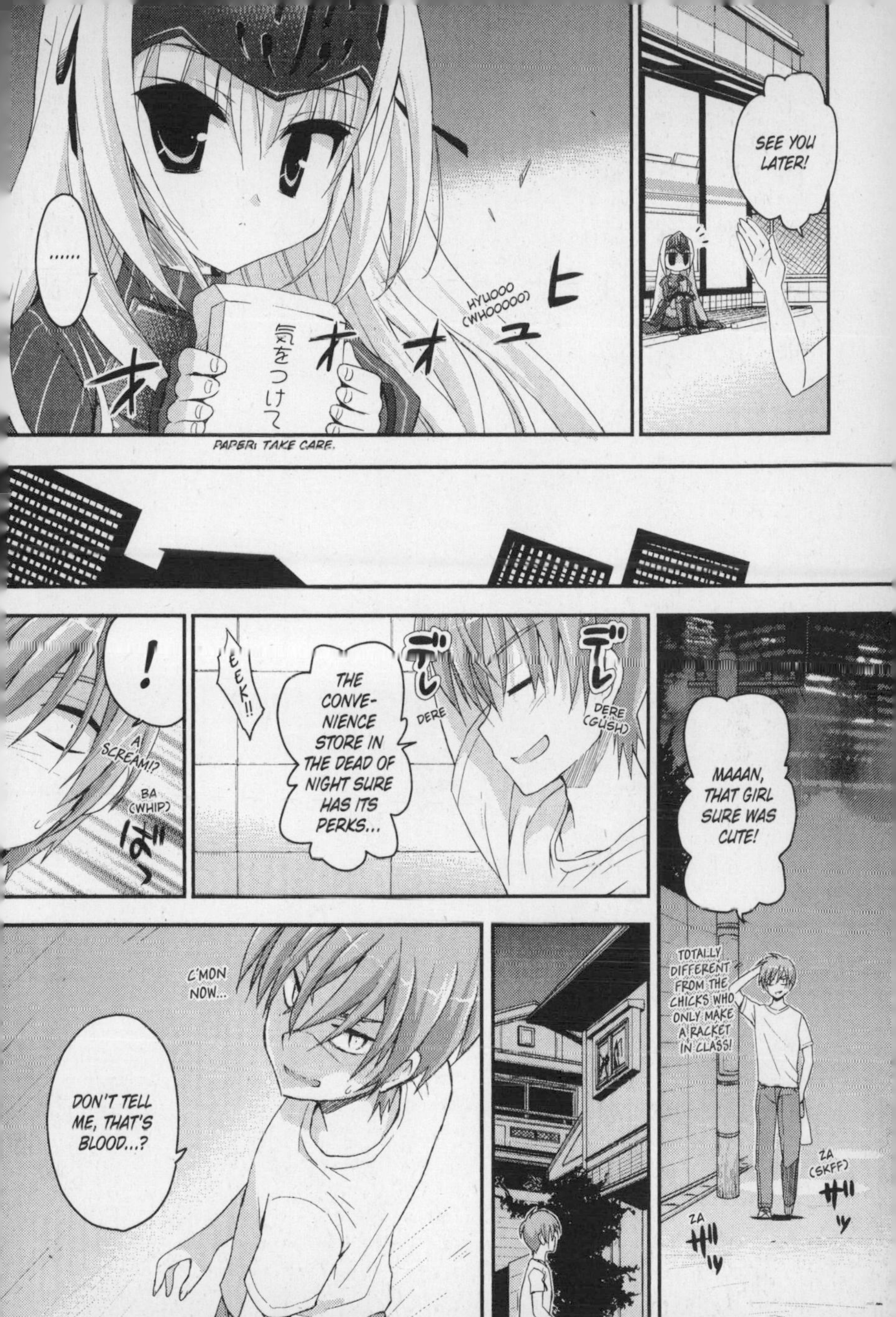
SEE YOU LATER!
......
HYUOOO (WHOOOOO)
ヒュオオオ
気をつけて
PAPER: TAKE CARE.
MAAAN, THAT GIRL SURE WAS CUTE!
TOTALLY DIFFERENT FROM THE CHICKS WHO ONLY MAKE A RACKET IN CLASS!
ZA (SKFF)
ZA
THE CONVENIENCE STORE IN THE DEAD OF NIGHT SURE HAS ITS PERKS...
DERE
DERE (GUSH)
EEK!!
!
A SCREAM!?
BA (WHIP)
C'MON NOW...
DON'T TELL ME, THAT'S BLOOD...?

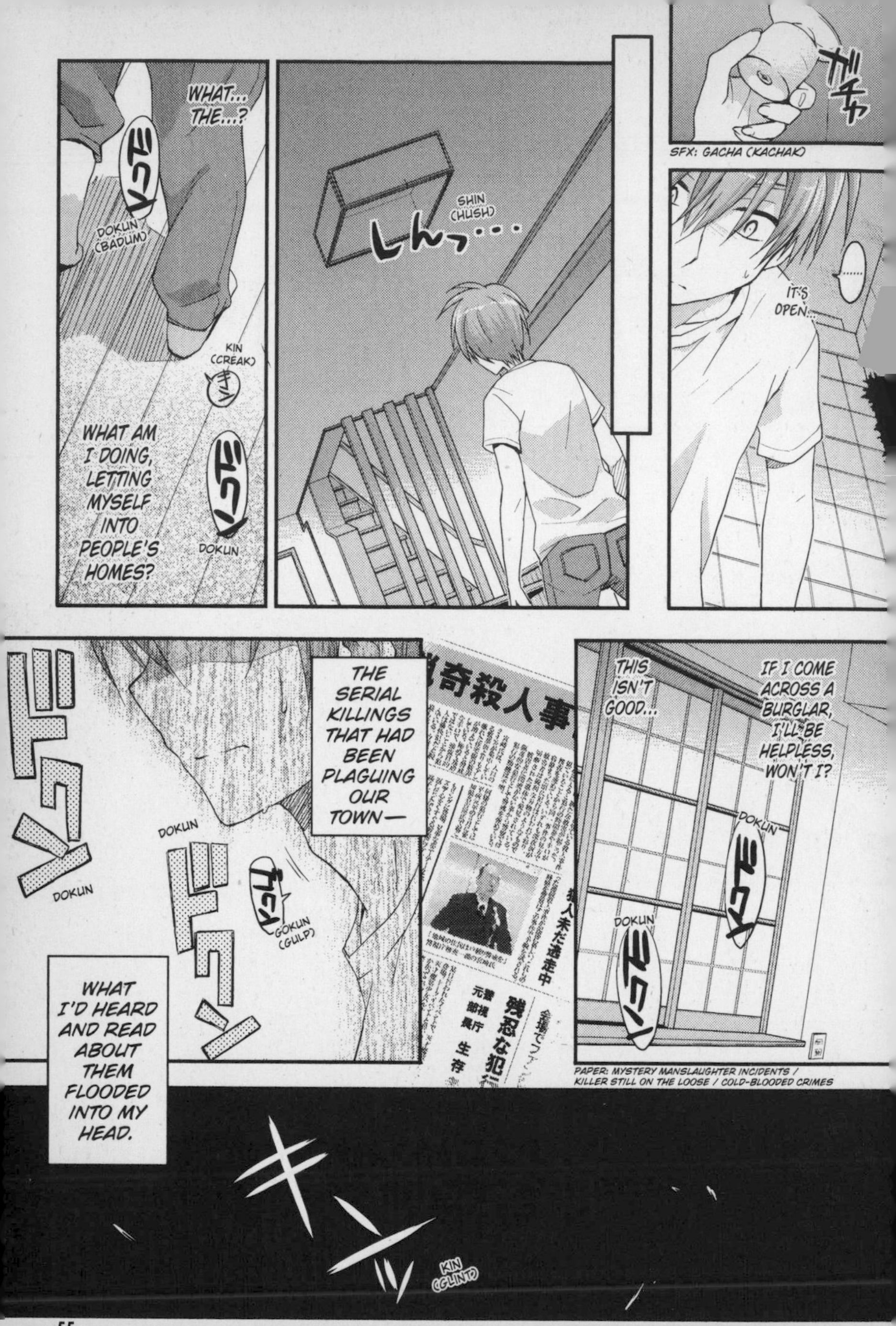

SFX: GACHA (KACHAK)
......
IT'S OPEN...
SHIN (HUSH)
WHAT... THE...?
DOKUN (BADUM)
KIN (CREAK)
WHAT AM I DOING, LETTING MYSELF INTO PEOPLE'S HOMES?
DOKUN
IF I COME ACROSS A BURGLAR, I'LL BE HELPLESS, WON'T I?
THIS ISN'T GOOD...
DOKUN
DOKUN
PAPER: MYSTERY MANSLAUGHTER INCIDENTS / KILLER STILL ON THE LOOSE / COLD-BLOODED CRIMES
THE SERIAL KILLINGS THAT HAD BEEN PLAGUING OUR TOWN—
奇殺人事
犯人未だ逃走中
残忍な犯行
GOKUN (GULP)
DOKUN
DOKUN
WHAT I'D HEARD AND READ ABOUT THEM FLOODED INTO MY HEAD.
KIN (GLINT)

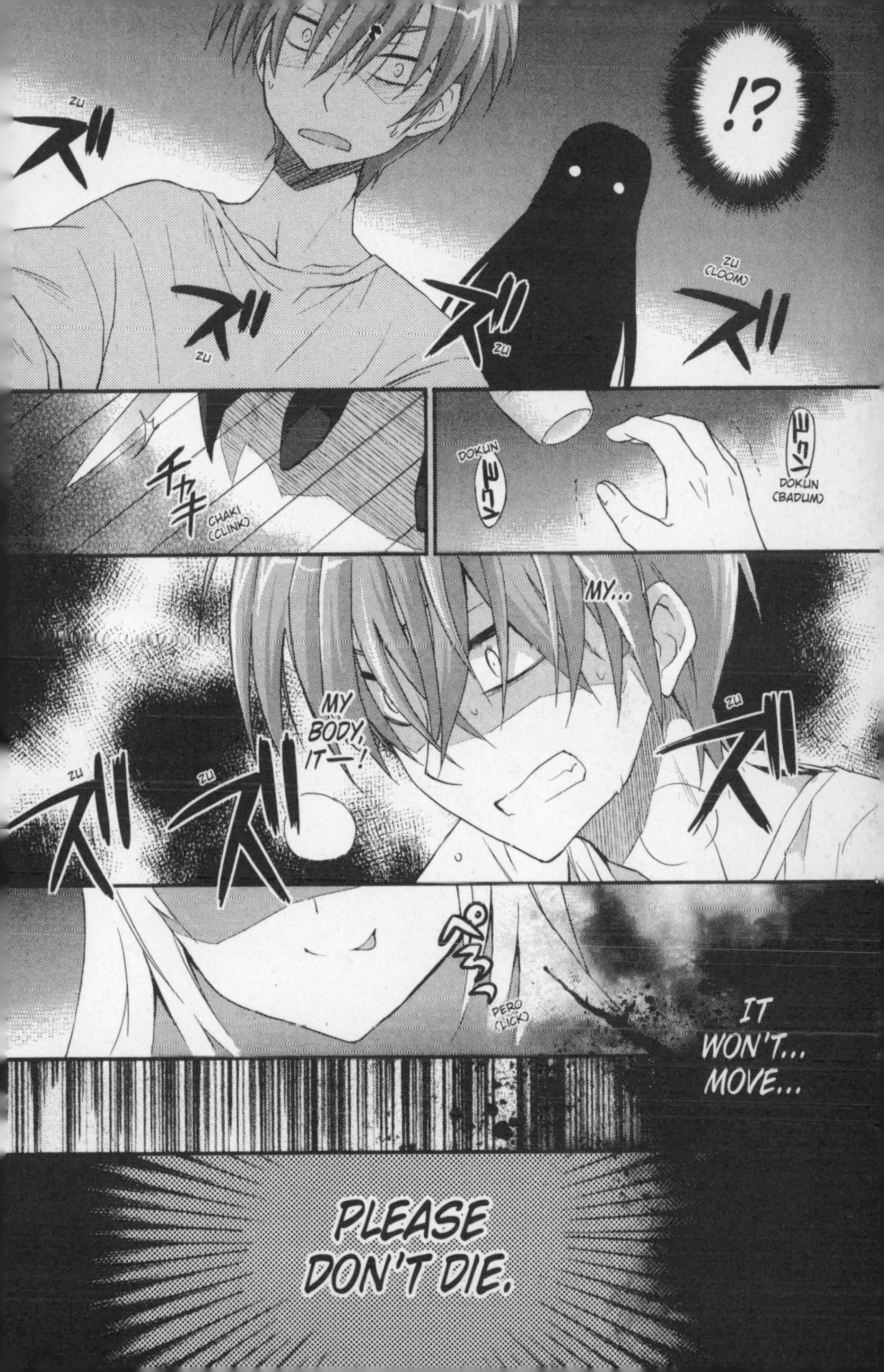
!?
ZU (LOOM)
ZU
ZU
ZU
DOKUN (BADUM)
DOKUN
CHAKI (CLINK)
MY...
ZU
MY BODY, IT—!
ZU
ZU
IT WON'T... MOVE...
PERO (LICK)
PLEASE DON'T DIE.

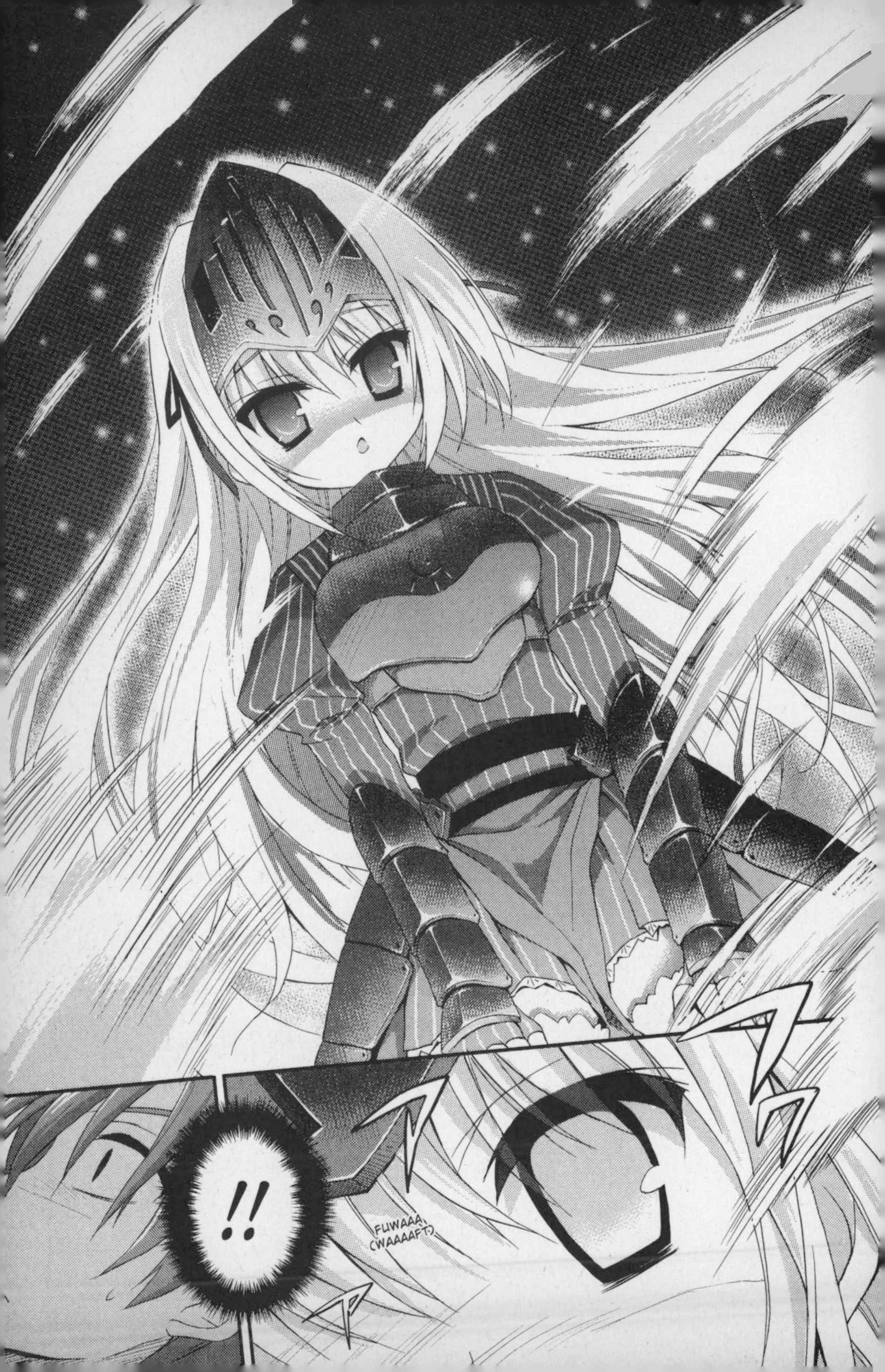
FUWAAA
(WAAAAFT)
!!

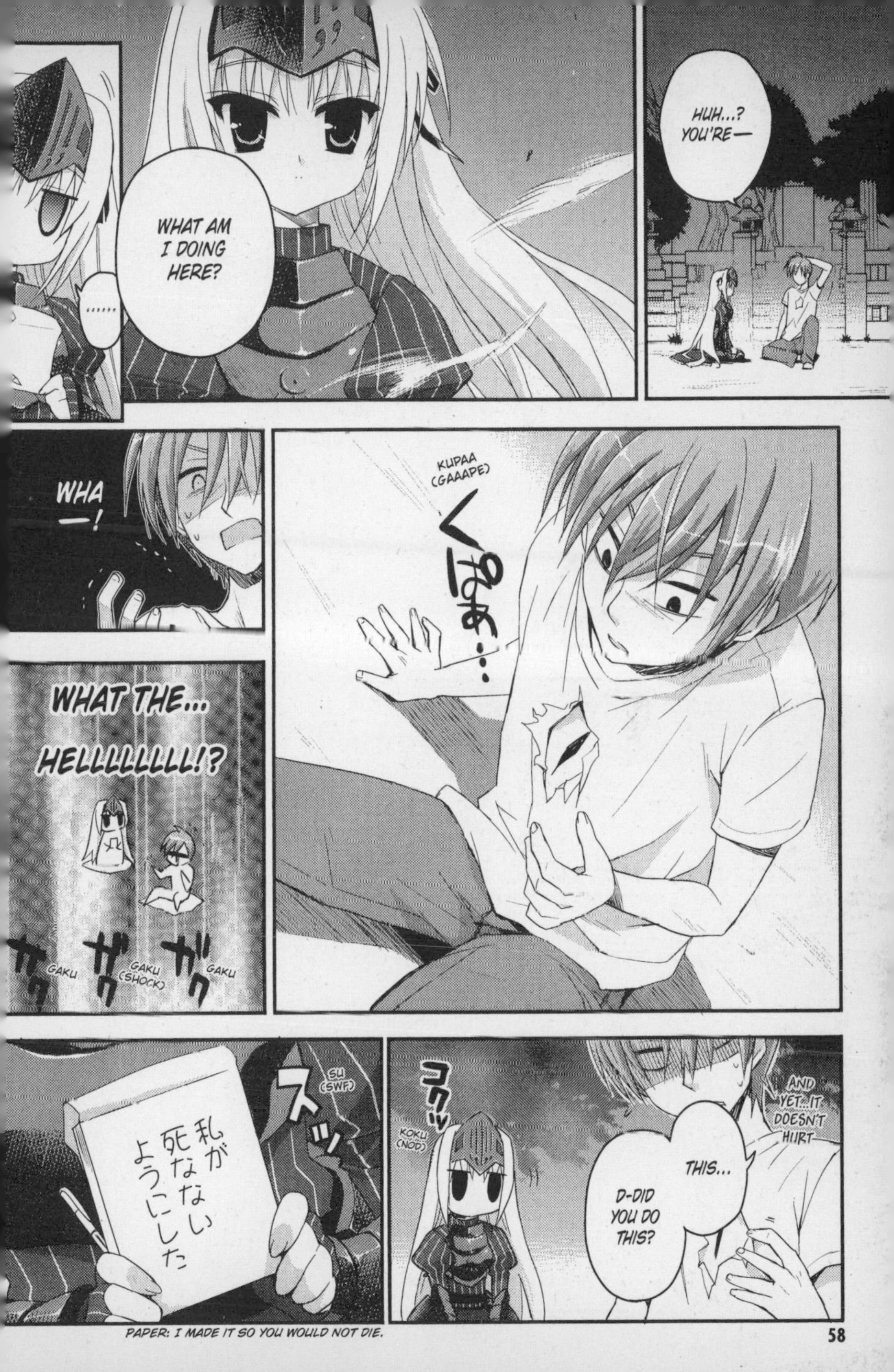
HUH...? YOU'RE—
WHAT AM I DOING HERE?
......
KUPAA (GAAAPE)
くぱあ…
WHA—!
WHAT THE... HELLLLLLLLL!?
ガク GAKU
ガク GAKU (SHOCK)
ガク GAKU
AND YET... IT DOESN'T HURT
THIS...
D-DID YOU DO THIS?
コクッ KOKU (NOD)
スッ SU (SWF)
私が死なないようにした

PAPER: I MADE IT SO YOU WOULD NOT DIE.

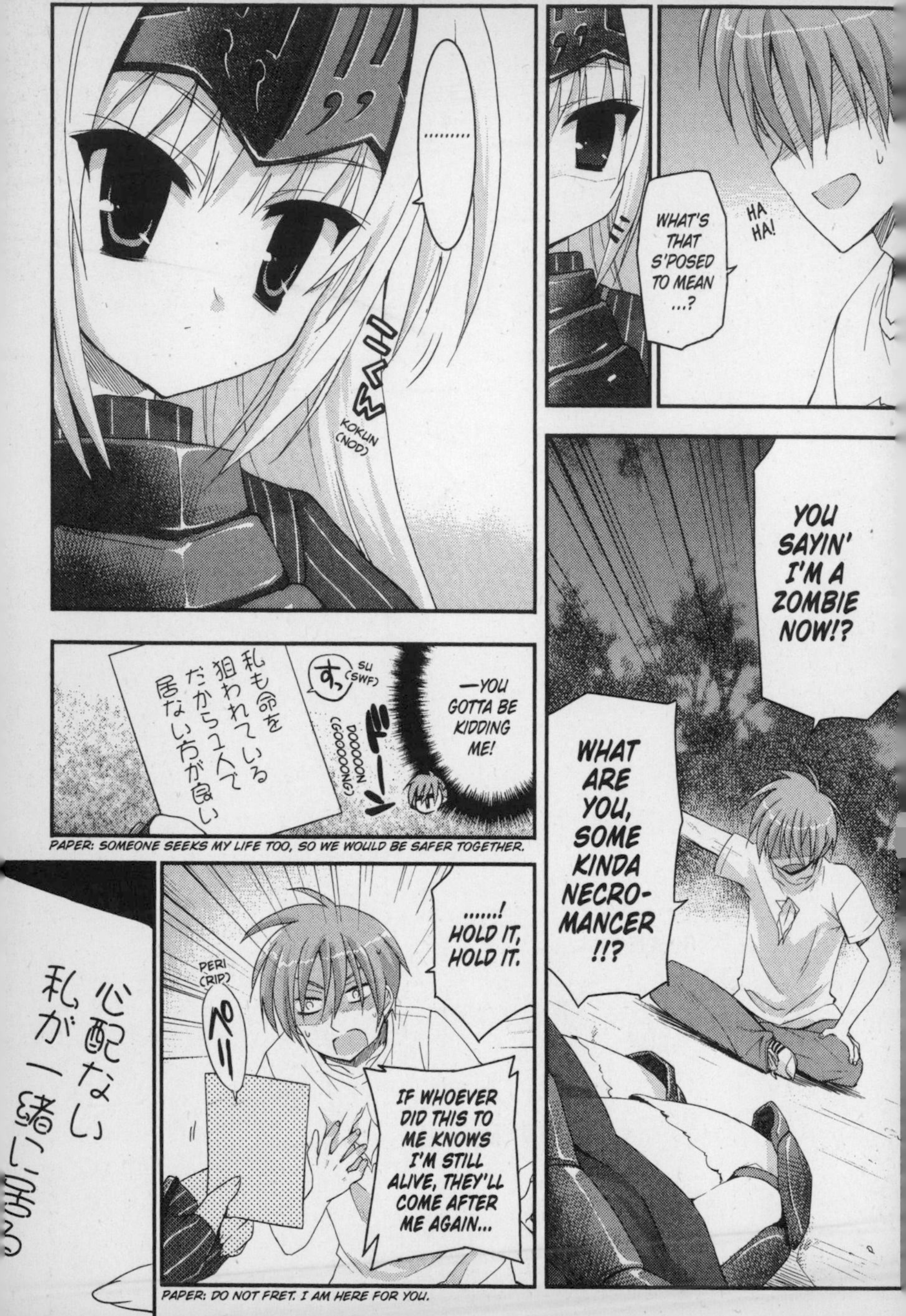

HA HA!
WHAT'S THAT S'POSED TO MEAN ...?
....
コクン
KOKUN (NOD)
YOU SAYIN' I'M A ZOMBIE NOW!?
WHAT ARE YOU, SOME KINDA NECRO-MANCER !!?
一YOU GOTTA BE KIDDING ME!
ドーン
DOOOOON (GOOOOONG)
すっ
SU (SWF)
私も命を狙われている だからユ人で居ない方が良い
PAPER: SOMEONE SEEKS MY LIFE TOO, SO WE WOULD BE SAFER TOGETHER.
......! HOLD IT, HOLD IT.
IF WHOEVER DID THIS TO ME KNOWS I'M STILL ALIVE, THEY'LL COME AFTER ME AGAIN...
ペリ
PERI (RIP)
心配ない 私が一緒に居る
PAPER: DO NOT FRET. I AM HERE FOR YOU.

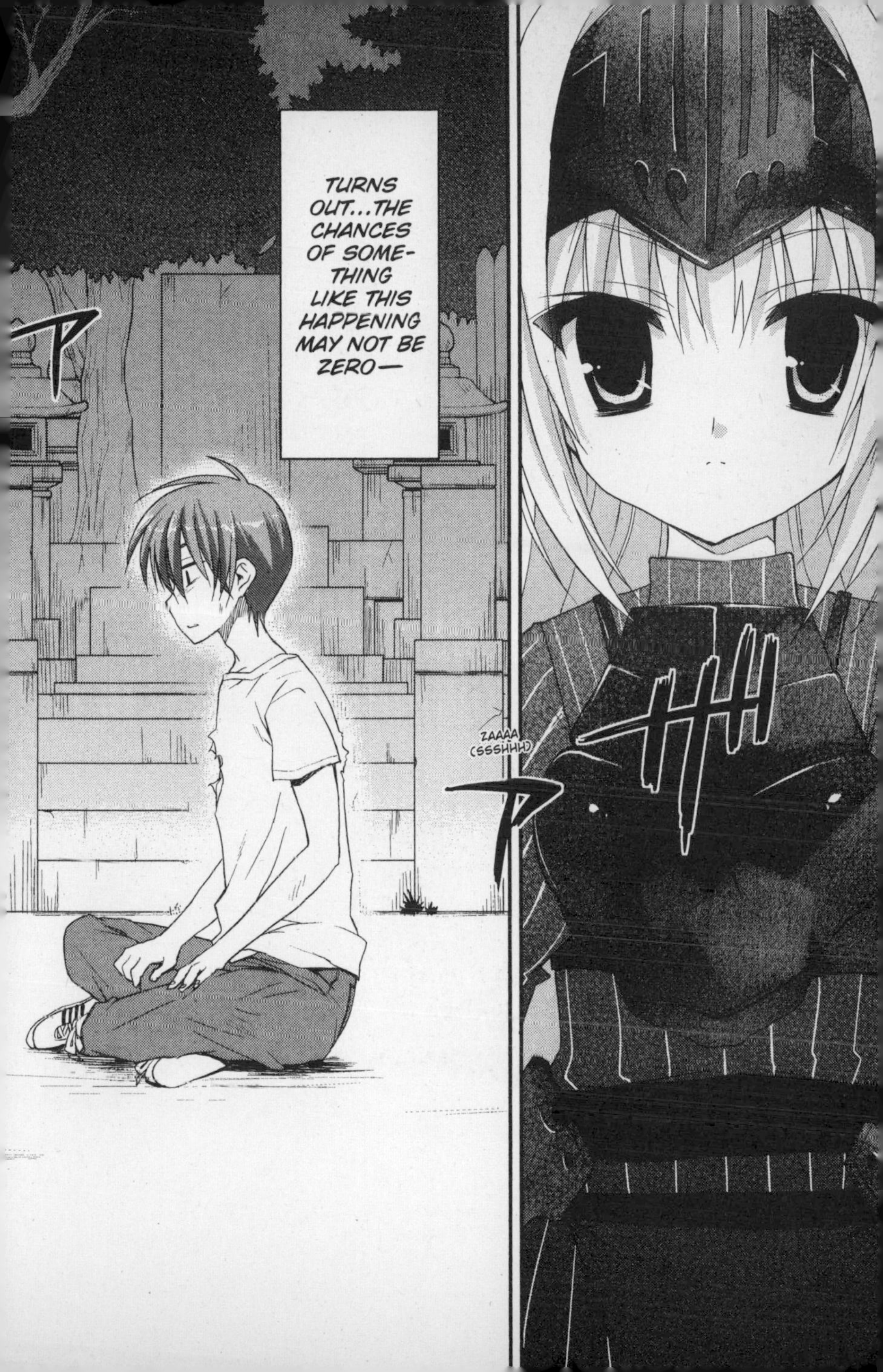
TURNS OUT...THE CHANCES OF SOME-THING LIKE THIS HAPPENING MAY NOT BE ZERO—
ZAAAA (SSSHHH)

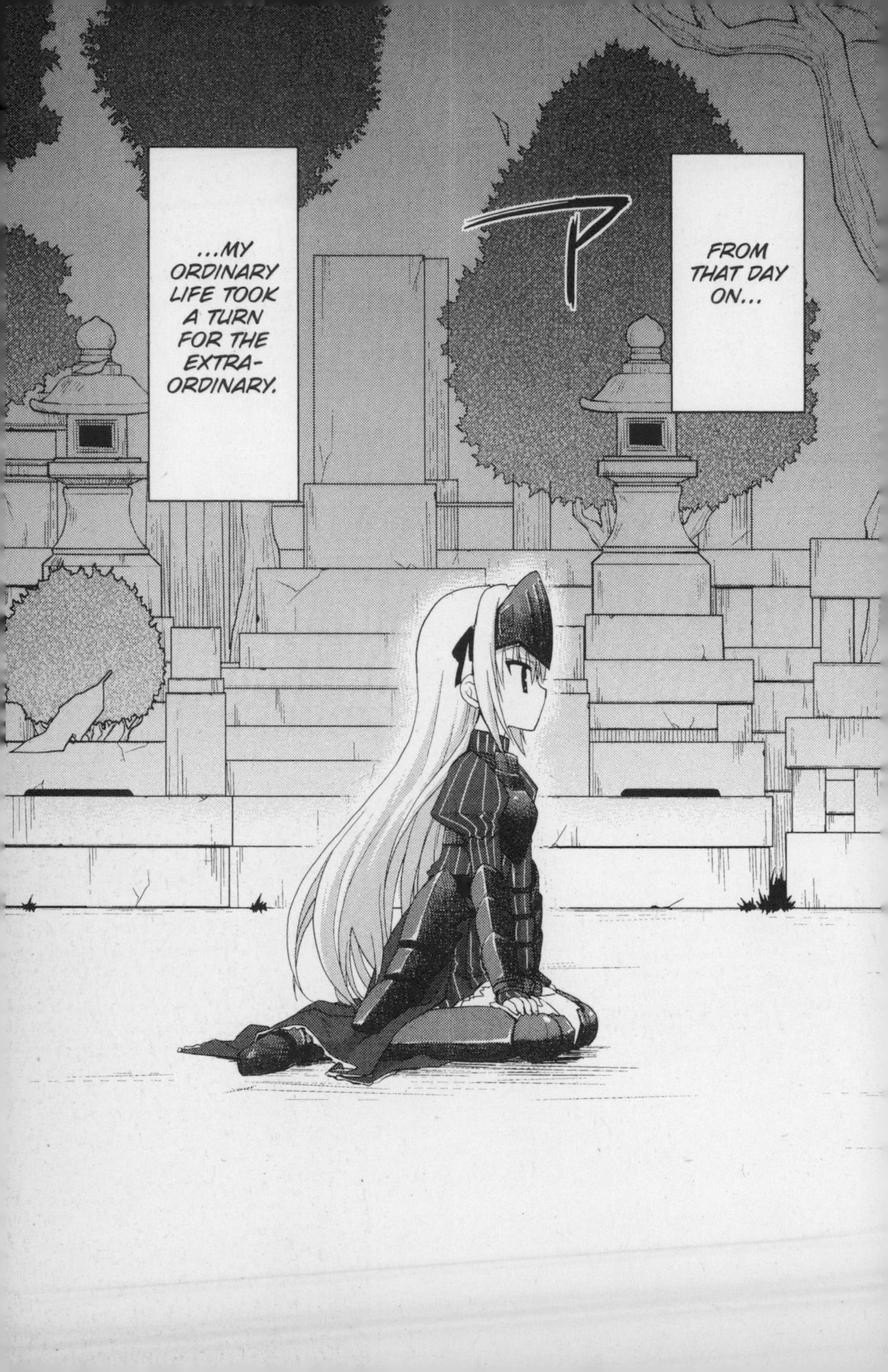
FROM THAT DAY ON...
...MY ORDINARY LIFE TOOK A TURN FOR THE EXTRA-ORDINARY.

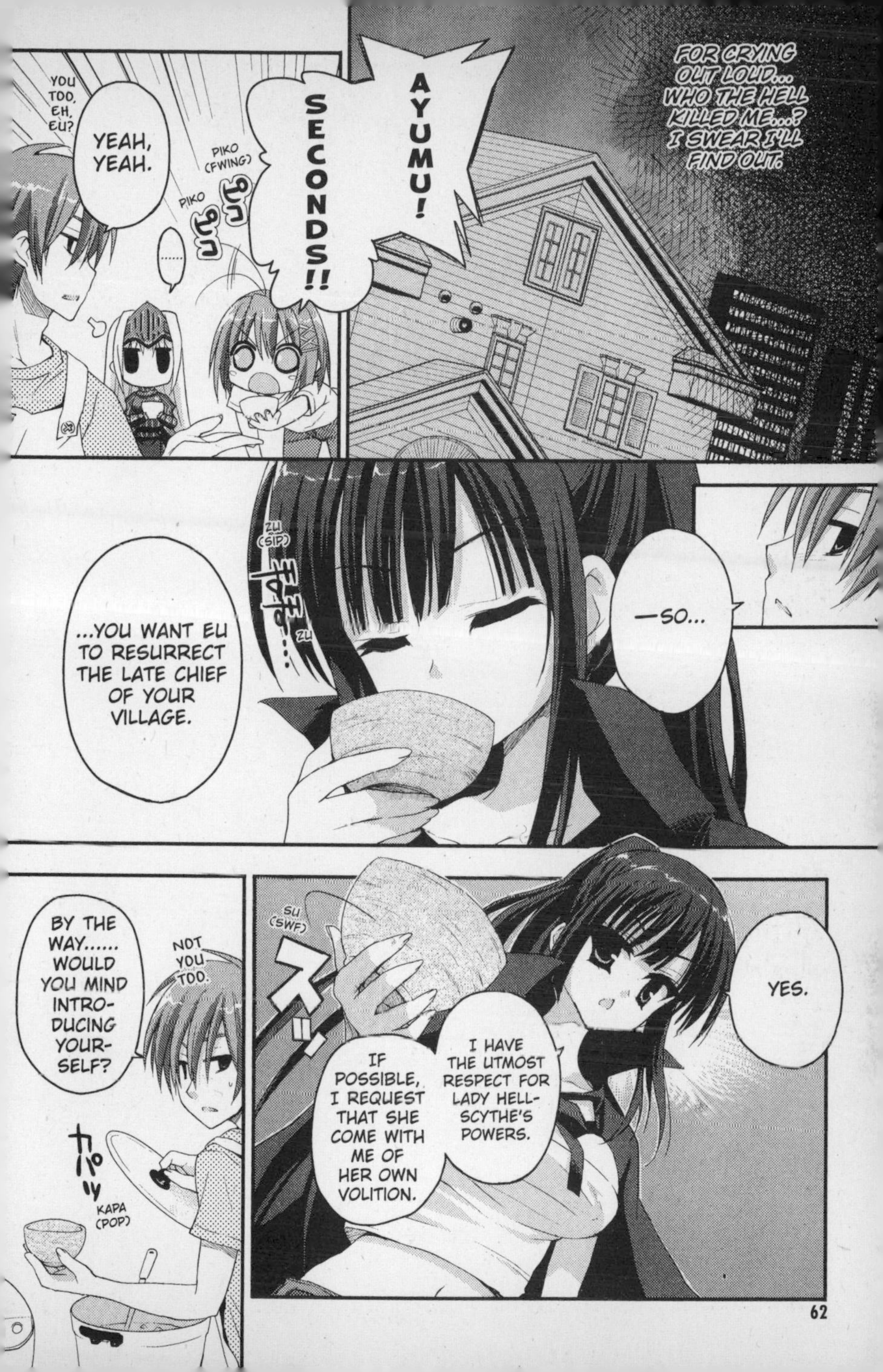
FOR CRYING OUT LOUD... WHO THE HELL KILLED ME...? I SWEAR I'LL FIND OUT.
AYUMU! SECONDS!!
PIKO (FWING)
PIKO
YEAH, YEAH.
YOU TOO, EH, EU?
......
—SO...
ZU (SIP)
ZU
...YOU WANT EU TO RESURRECT THE LATE CHIEF OF YOUR VILLAGE.
YES.
SU (SWF)
I HAVE THE UTMOST RESPECT FOR LADY HELL-SCYTHE'S POWERS.
IF POSSIBLE, I REQUEST THAT SHE COME WITH ME OF HER OWN VOLITION.
NOT YOU TOO.
BY THE WAY...... WOULD YOU MIND INTRO-DUCING YOUR-SELF?
KAPA (POP)

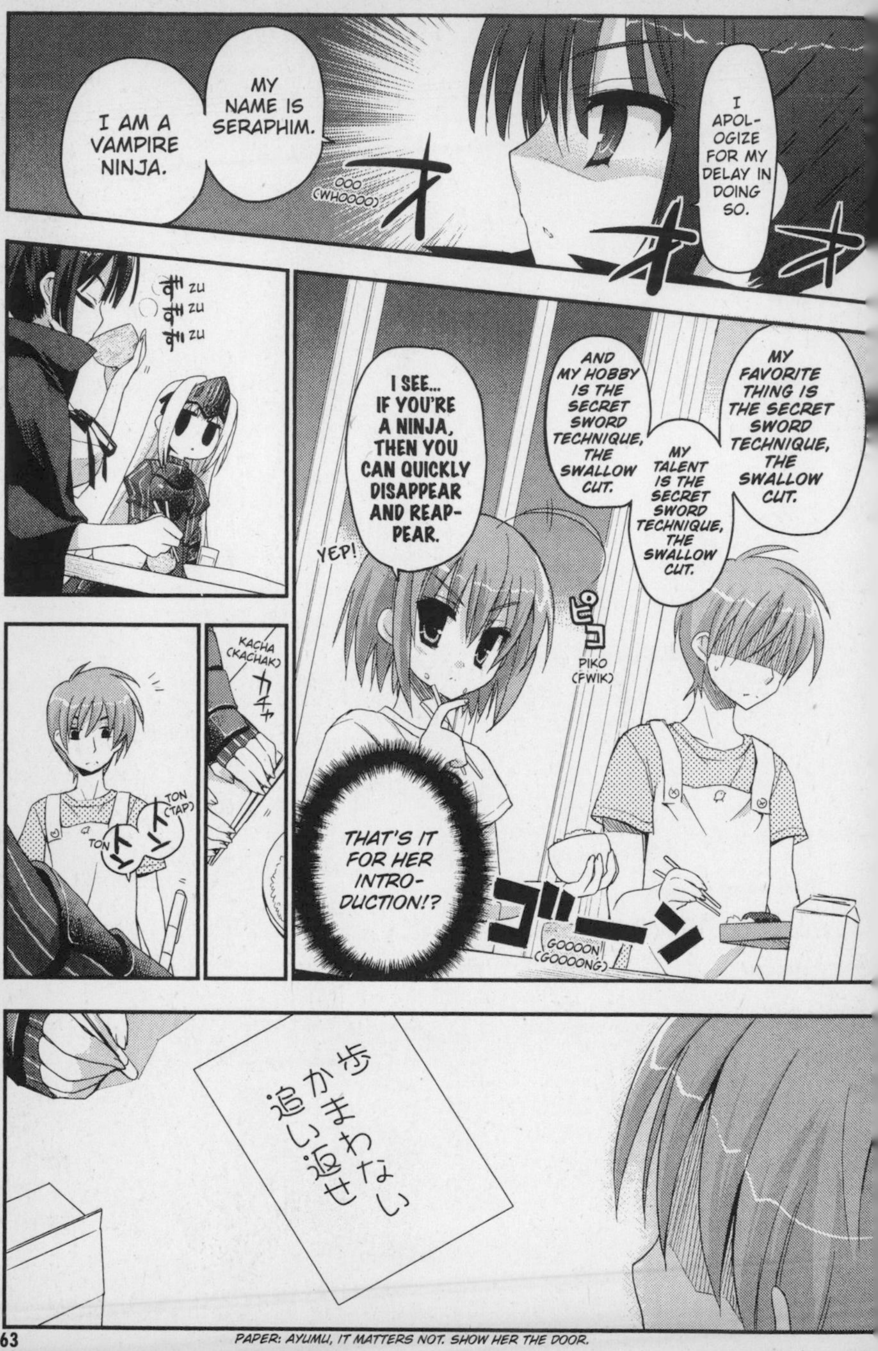
I APOLOGIZE FOR MY DELAY IN DOING SO.
OOO (WHOOOO)
MY NAME IS SERAPHIM.
I AM A VAMPIRE NINJA.
MY FAVORITE THING IS THE SECRET SWORD TECHNIQUE, THE SWALLOW CUT.
MY TALENT IS THE SECRET SWORD TECHNIQUE, THE SWALLOW CUT.
AND MY HOBBY IS THE SECRET SWORD TECHNIQUE, THE SWALLOW CUT.
I SEE... IF YOU'RE A NINJA, THEN YOU CAN QUICKLY DISAPPEAR AND REAPPEAR.
YEP!
PIKO (FWIK)
THAT'S IT FOR HER INTRODUCTION!?
GOOOON (GOOOONG)
ZU ZU ZU
KACHA (KACHAK)
TON TON (TAP)
歩
かまわない
追い返せ

PAPER: AYUMU, IT MATTERS NOT. SHOW HER THE DOOR.

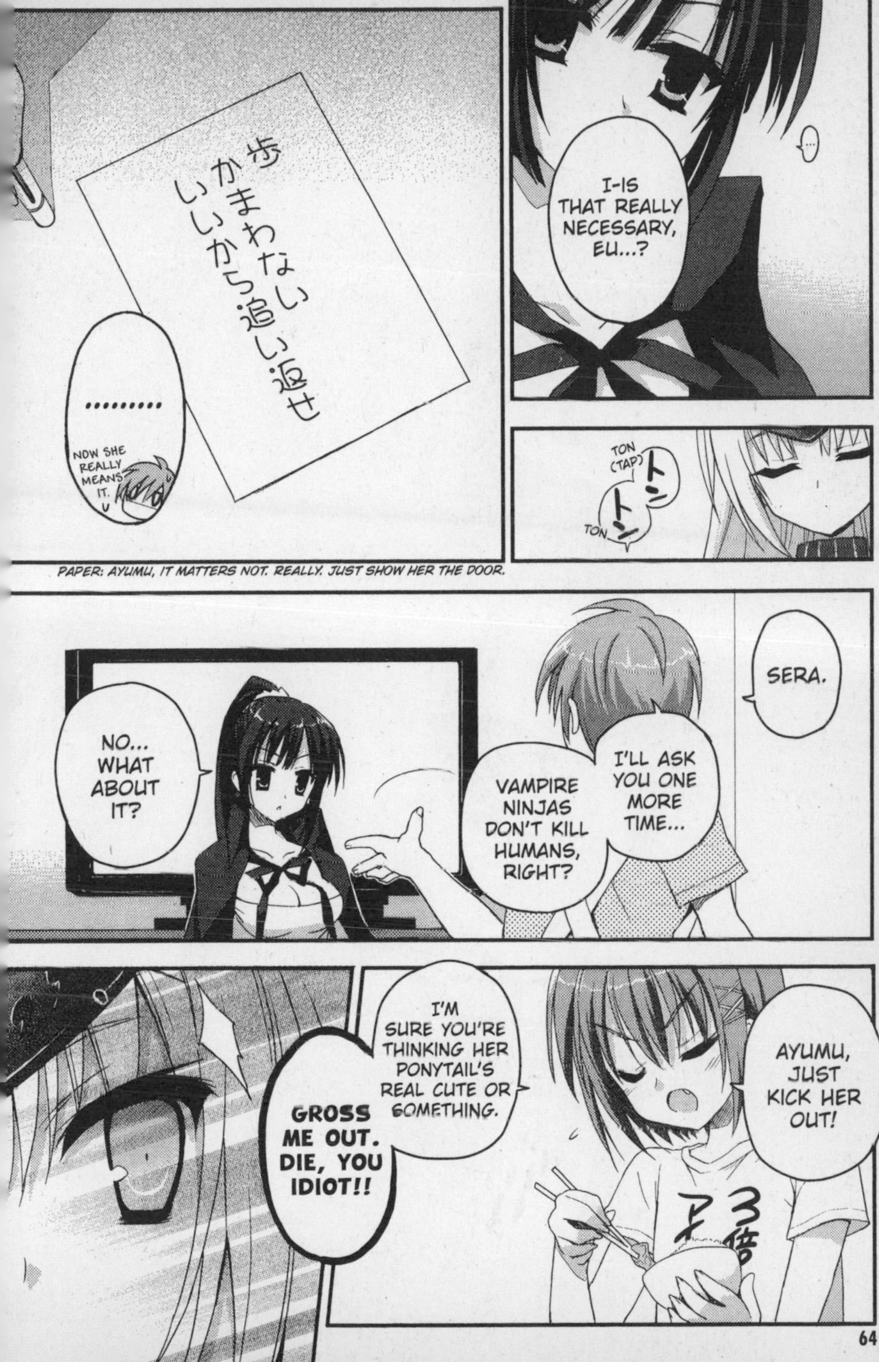
...
I-IS THAT REALLY NECESSARY, EU...?
TON (TAP) TON
歩
かまわない
いいから追い返せ
....
NOW SHE REALLY MEANS IT.
PAPER: AYUMU, IT MATTERS NOT. REALLY. JUST SHOW HER THE DOOR.
SERA.
I'LL ASK YOU ONE MORE TIME...
VAMPIRE NINJAS DON'T KILL HUMANS, RIGHT?
NO... WHAT ABOUT IT?
AYUMU, JUST KICK HER OUT!
I'M SURE YOU'RE THINKING HER PONYTAIL'S REAL CUTE OR SOMETHING.
GROSS ME OUT. DIE, YOU IDIOT!!

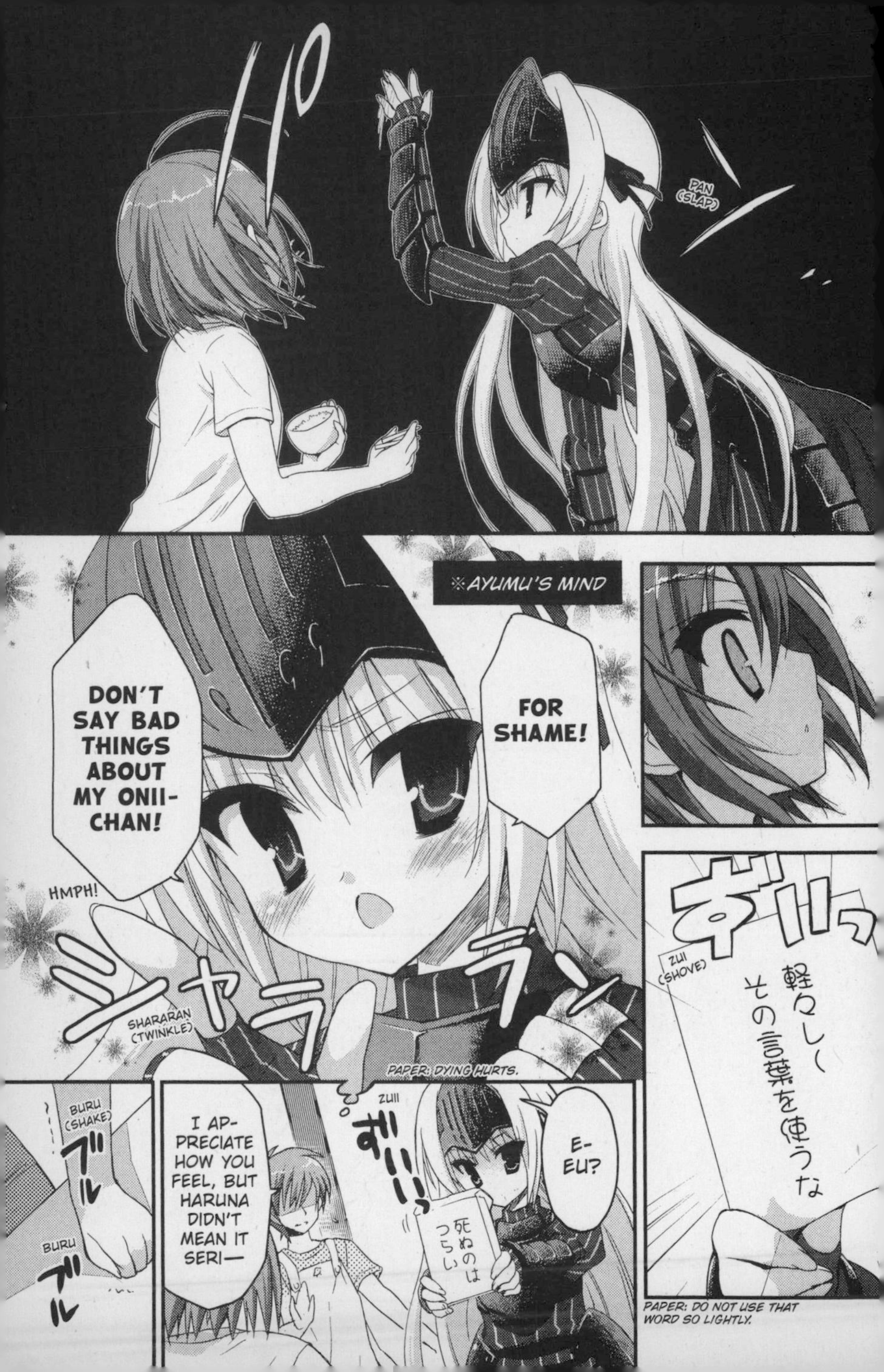
パ
PAN (SLAP)
※AYUMU'S MIND
FOR SHAME!
DON'T SAY BAD THINGS ABOUT MY ONII-CHAN!
HMPH!
シャララン
SHARARAN (TWINKLE)
PAPER: DYING HURTS.
ずいっ
ZUI (SHOVE)
軽々しくその言葉を使うな
PAPER: DO NOT USE THAT WORD SO LIGHTLY.
E-EU?
死ぬのはつらい
ずいいっ
ZUII
I AP-PRECIATE HOW YOU FEEL, BUT HARUNA DIDN'T MEAN IT SERI—
ブル
BURU (SHAKE)
ブル
BURU

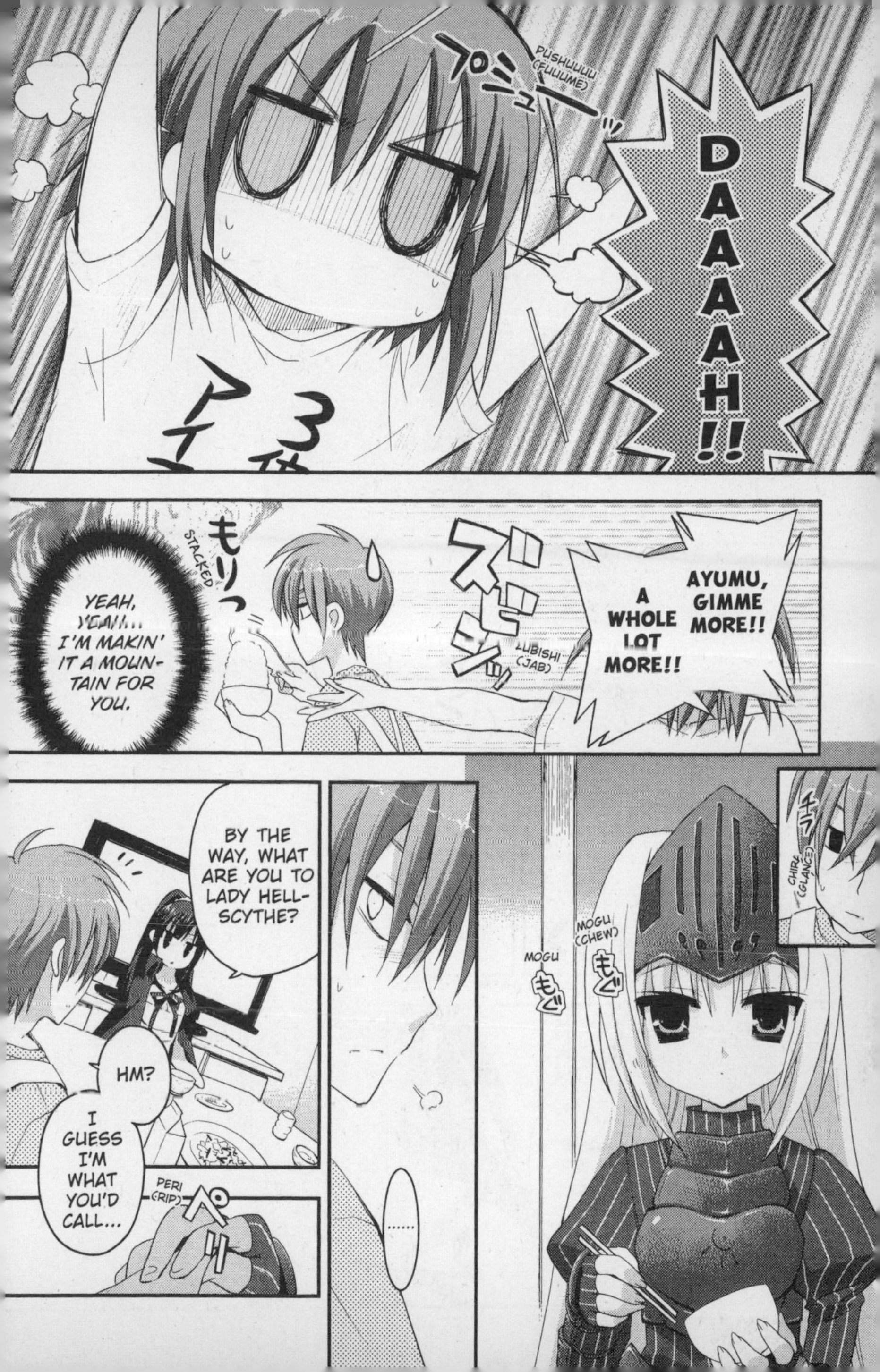
PUSHUUUU (FUUUME)
DAAAAH!!
AYUMU, GIMME MORE!! A WHOLE LOT MORE!!
ZUBISHI (JAB)
STACKED
YEAH, YEAH... I'M MAKIN' IT A MOUNTAIN FOR YOU.
CHIRA (GLANCE)
MOGU (CHEW)
MOGU
BY THE WAY, WHAT ARE YOU TO LADY HELL-SCYTHE?
......
HM?
I GUESS I'M WHAT YOU'D CALL...
PERI (RIP)

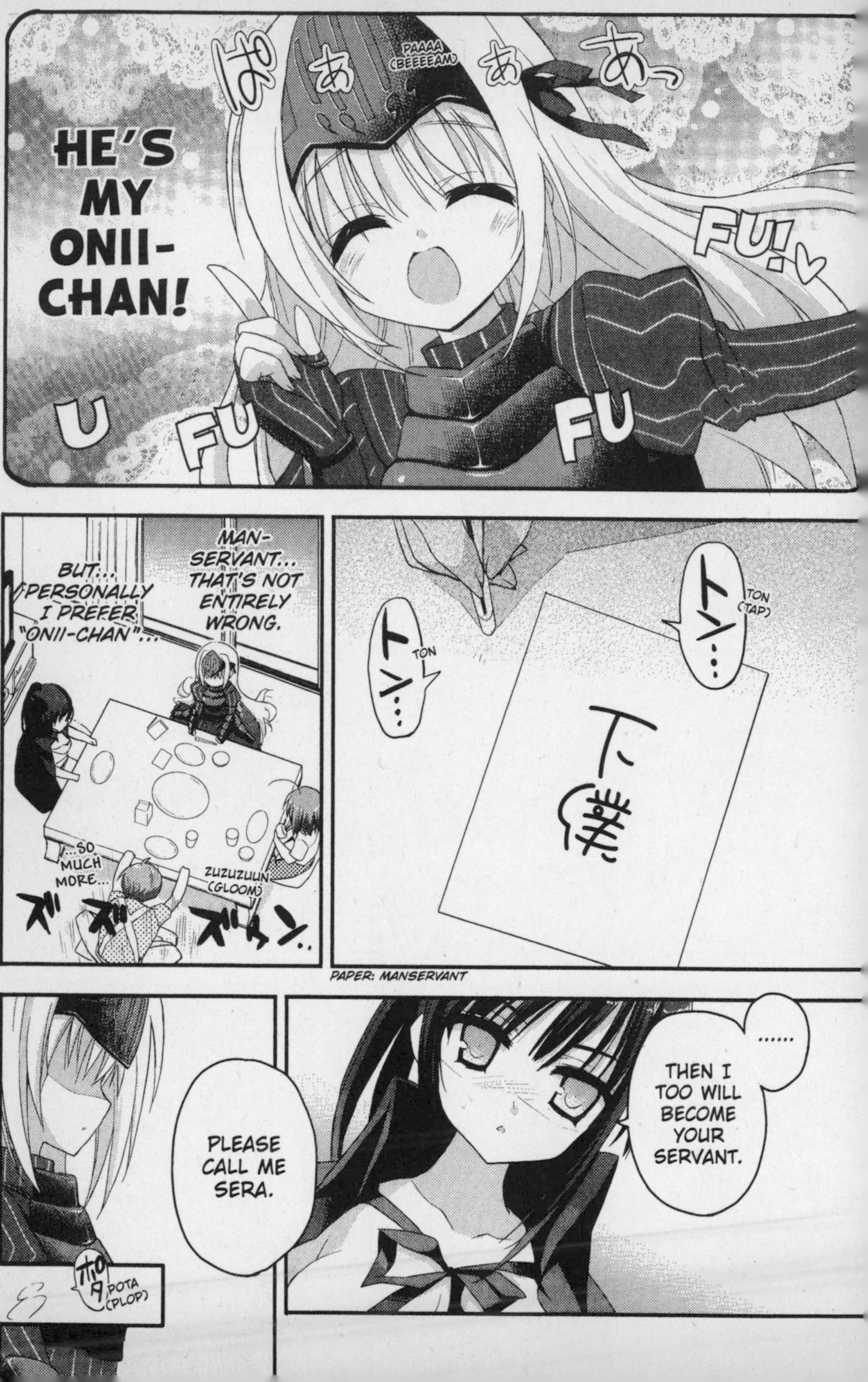
ぱあああっ
PAAAA (BEEEEAM)
FU!♥
HE'S MY ONII-CHAN!
U FU FU
トン…
TON (TAP)
トン…
TON
下僕
PAPER: MANSERVANT
MAN-SERVANT... THAT'S NOT ENTIRELY WRONG.
BUT... PERSONALLY I PREFER "ONII-CHAN"...
...SO MUCH MORE...
ズズズゥン..
ZUZUZUUN (GLOOM)
......
THEN I TOO WILL BECOME YOUR SERVANT.
PLEASE CALL ME SERA.
ポタ
POTA (PLOP)

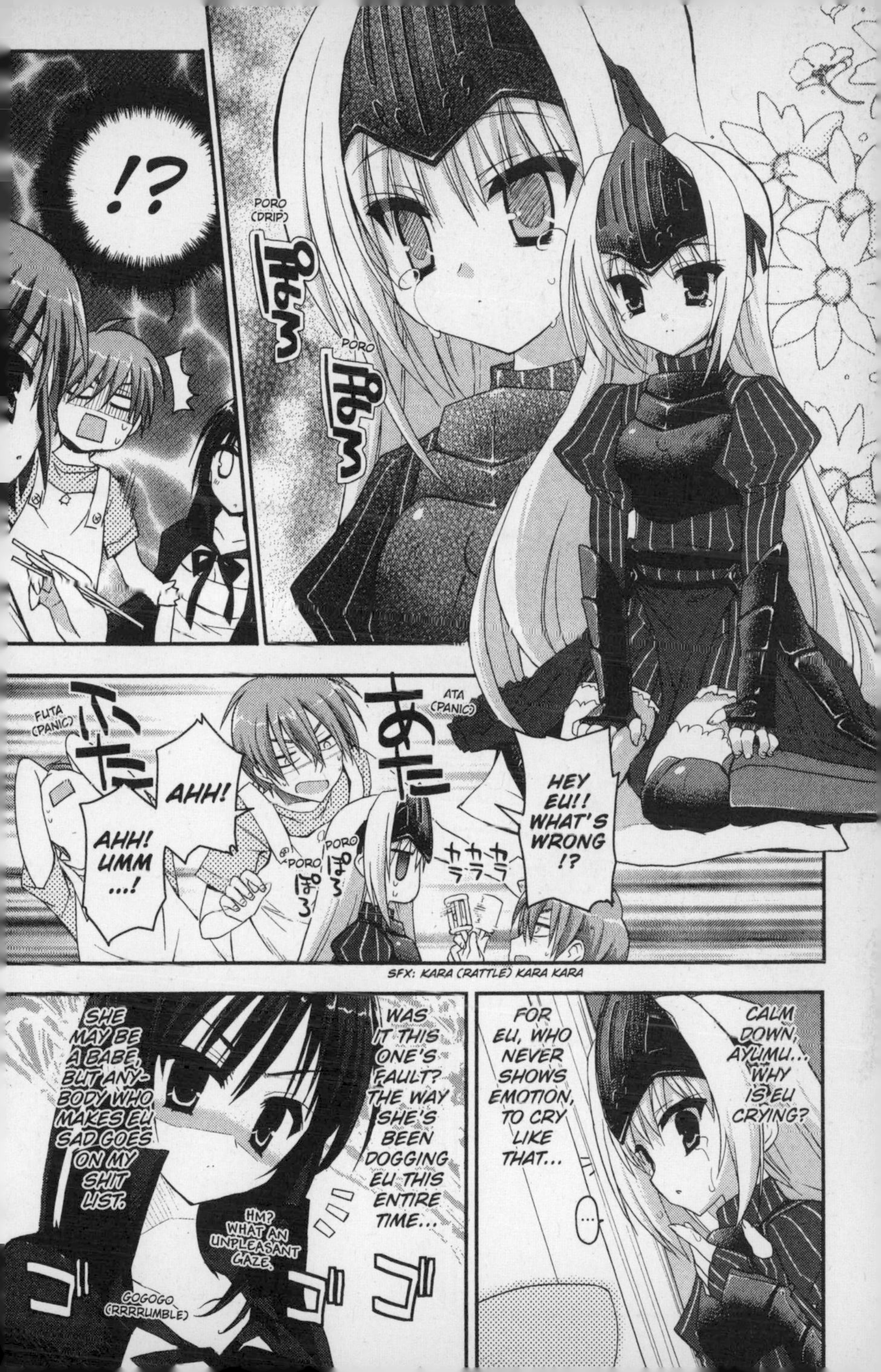
PORO (DRIP)
ぽろ
PORO
ぽろ
!?
HEY EU!! WHAT'S WRONG !?
ATA (PANIC)
あた
AHH!
AHH! UMM ...!
FUTA (PANIC)
ふた
PORO
ぽろ
PORO
ぽろ
カラ カラ カラ
SFX: KARA (RATTLE) KARA KARA
CALM DOWN, AYUMU... WHY IS EU CRYING?
FOR EU, WHO NEVER SHOWS EMOTION, TO CRY LIKE THAT...
...
WAS IT THIS ONE'S FAULT? THE WAY SHE'S BEEN DOGGING EU THIS ENTIRE TIME...
SHE MAY BE A BABE, BUT ANY-BODY WHO MAKES EU SAD GOES ON MY SHIT LIST.
HM? WHAT AN UNPLEASANT GAZE.
GOGOGO (RRRRUMBLE)
ゴゴゴ

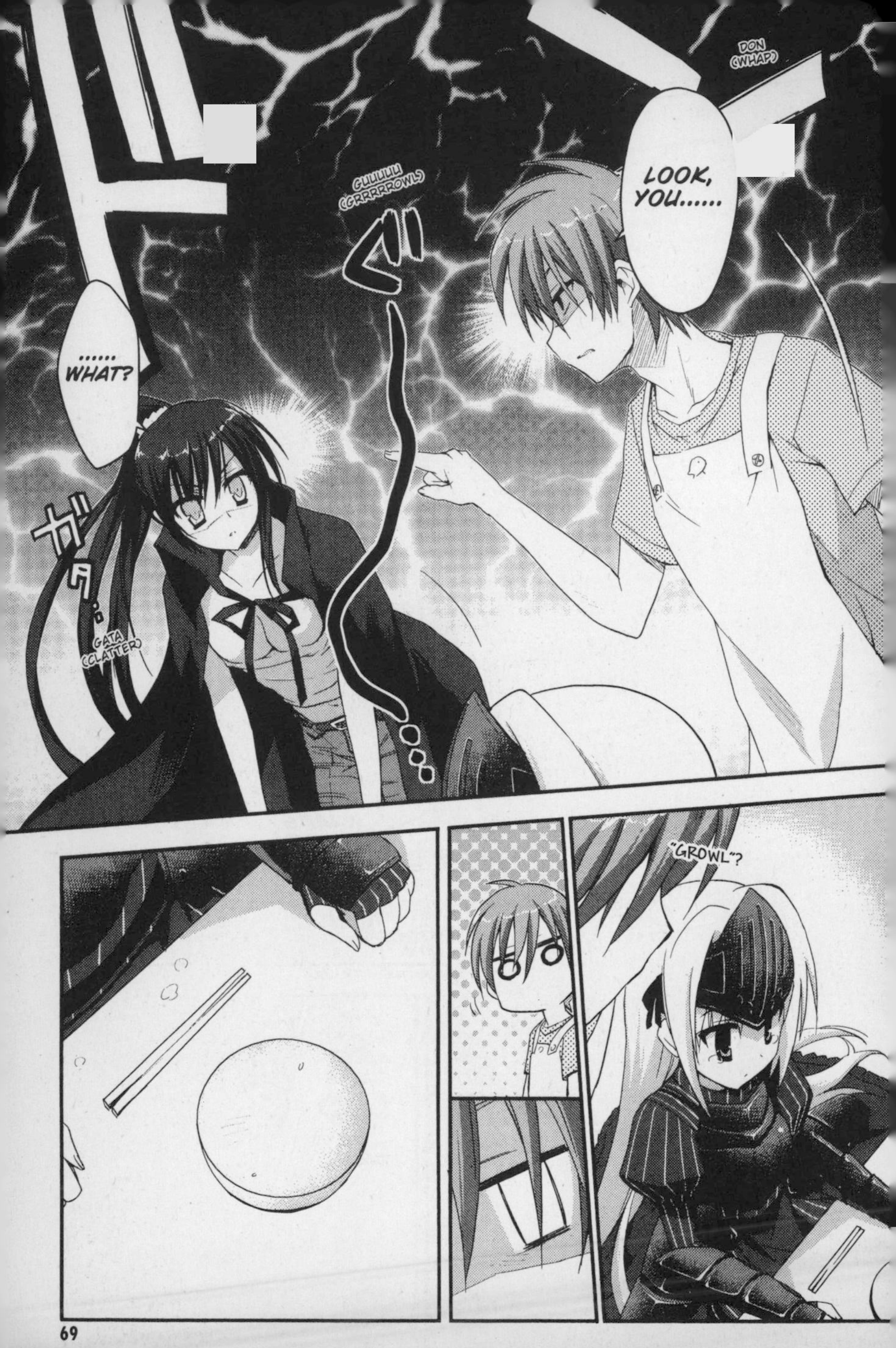
DON (WHAP)
LOOK, YOU......
GUUUUU (GRRRRRROWL)
......WHAT?
GATA (CLATTER)
"GROWL"?

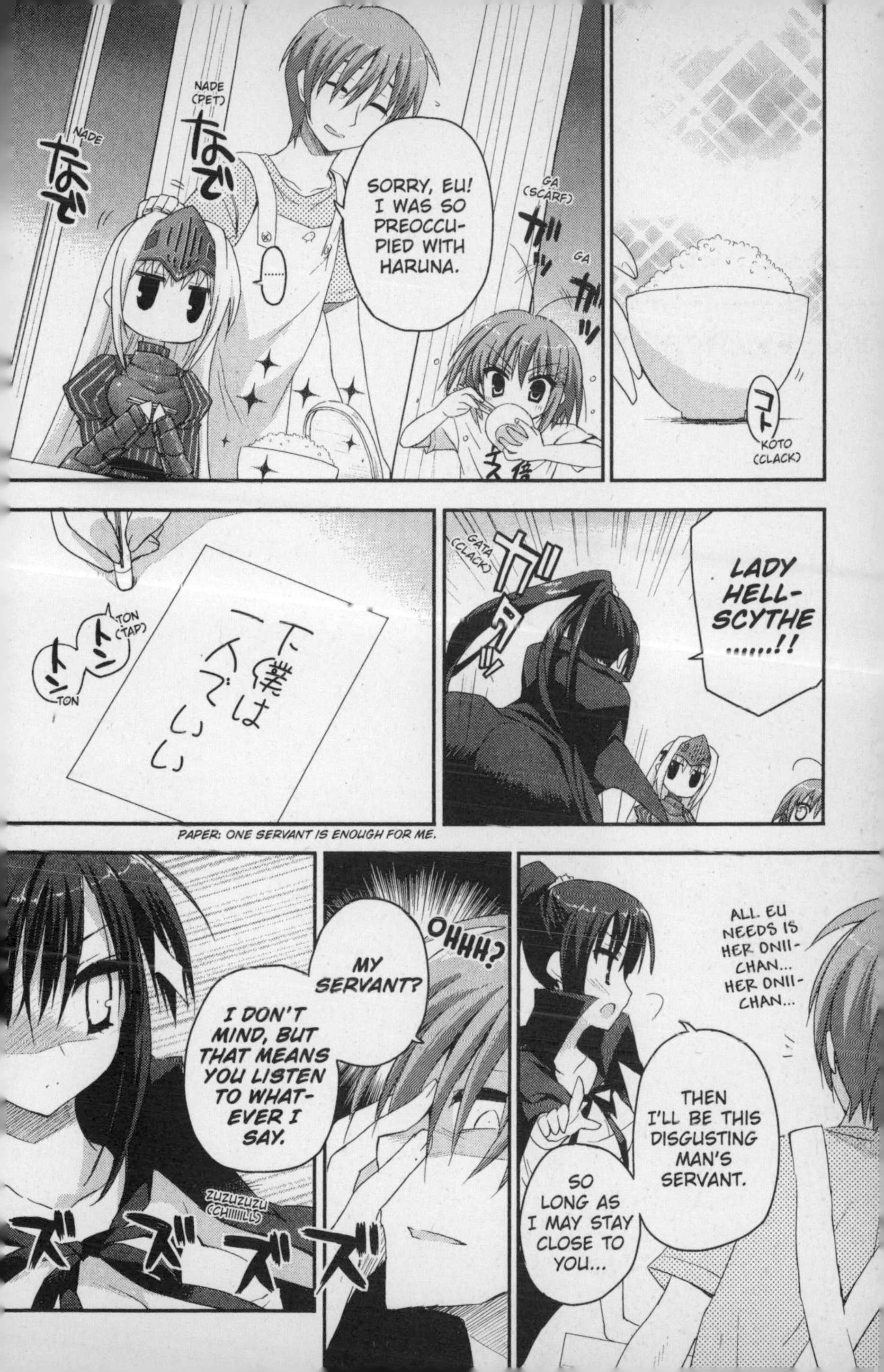
コト
KOTO (CLACK)
GA (SCARF)
ガッ
GA
ガッ
SORRY, EU! I WAS SO PREOCCUPIED WITH HARUNA.
......
NADE (PET)
なで
NADE
なで
LADY HELL-SCYTHE ......!!
GATA (CLACK)
ガタッ
下僕は一人でいい
TON (TAP)
トン
トン
TON
PAPER: ONE SERVANT IS ENOUGH FOR ME.
ALL. EU NEEDS IS HER ONII-CHAN... HER ONII-CHAN...
THEN I'LL BE THIS DISGUSTING MAN'S SERVANT.
SO LONG AS I MAY STAY CLOSE TO YOU...
OHHH?
MY SERVANT?
I DON'T MIND, BUT THAT MEANS YOU LISTEN TO WHATEVER I SAY.
ZUZUZUZU (CHIIIILL)
ズズズズ

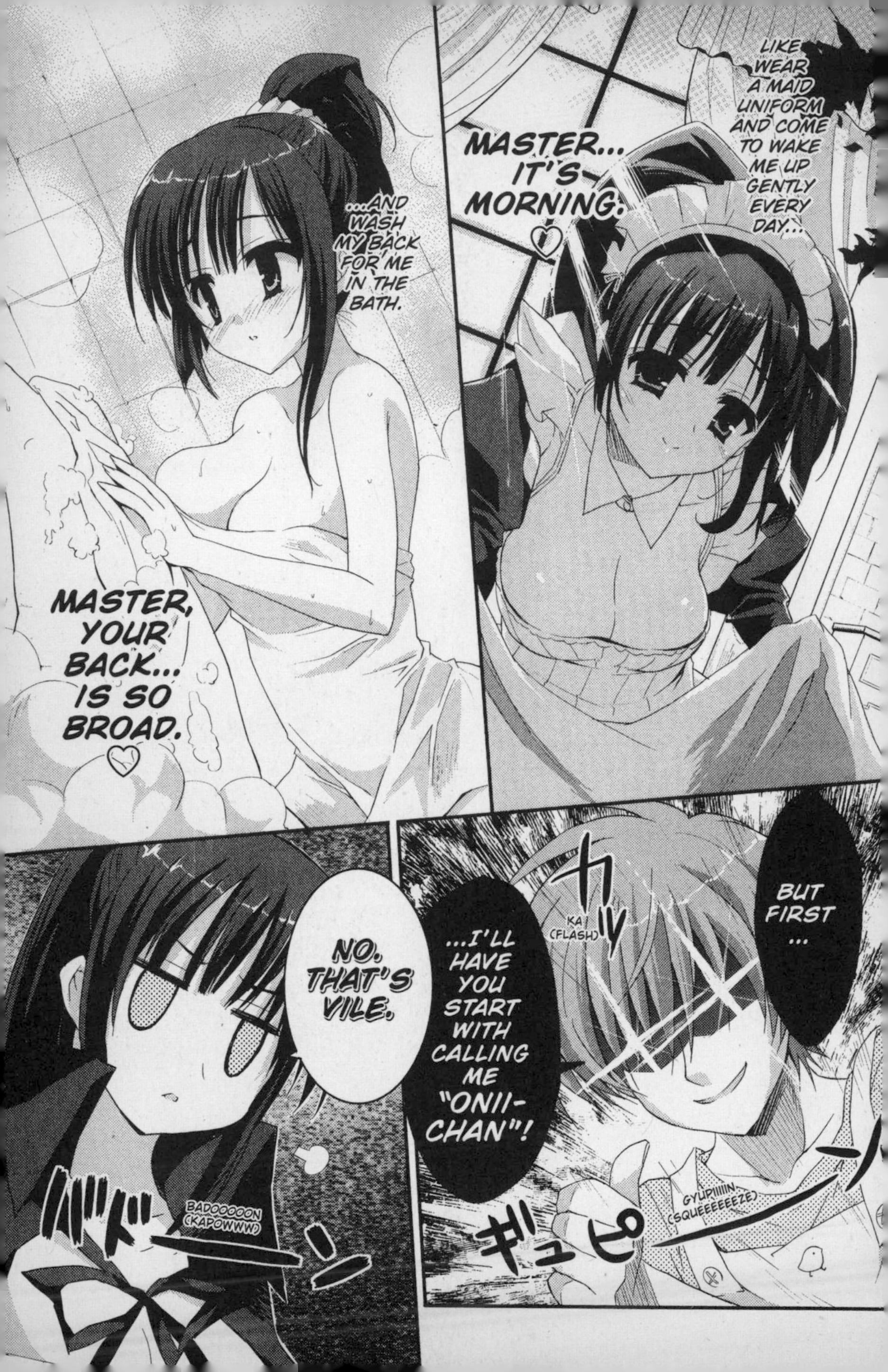

LIKE WEAR A MAID UNIFORM AND COME TO WAKE ME UP GENTLY EVERY DAY...
MASTER... IT'S MORNING. ♡
...AND WASH MY BACK FOR ME IN THE BATH.
MASTER, YOUR BACK... IS SO BROAD. ♡
BUT FIRST ...
KA (FLASH)
...I'LL HAVE YOU START WITH CALLING ME "ONII-CHAN"!
GYUPIIIIIN (SQUEEEEEEEZE)
NO. THAT'S VILE.
BADOOOOOON (KAPOWWW)

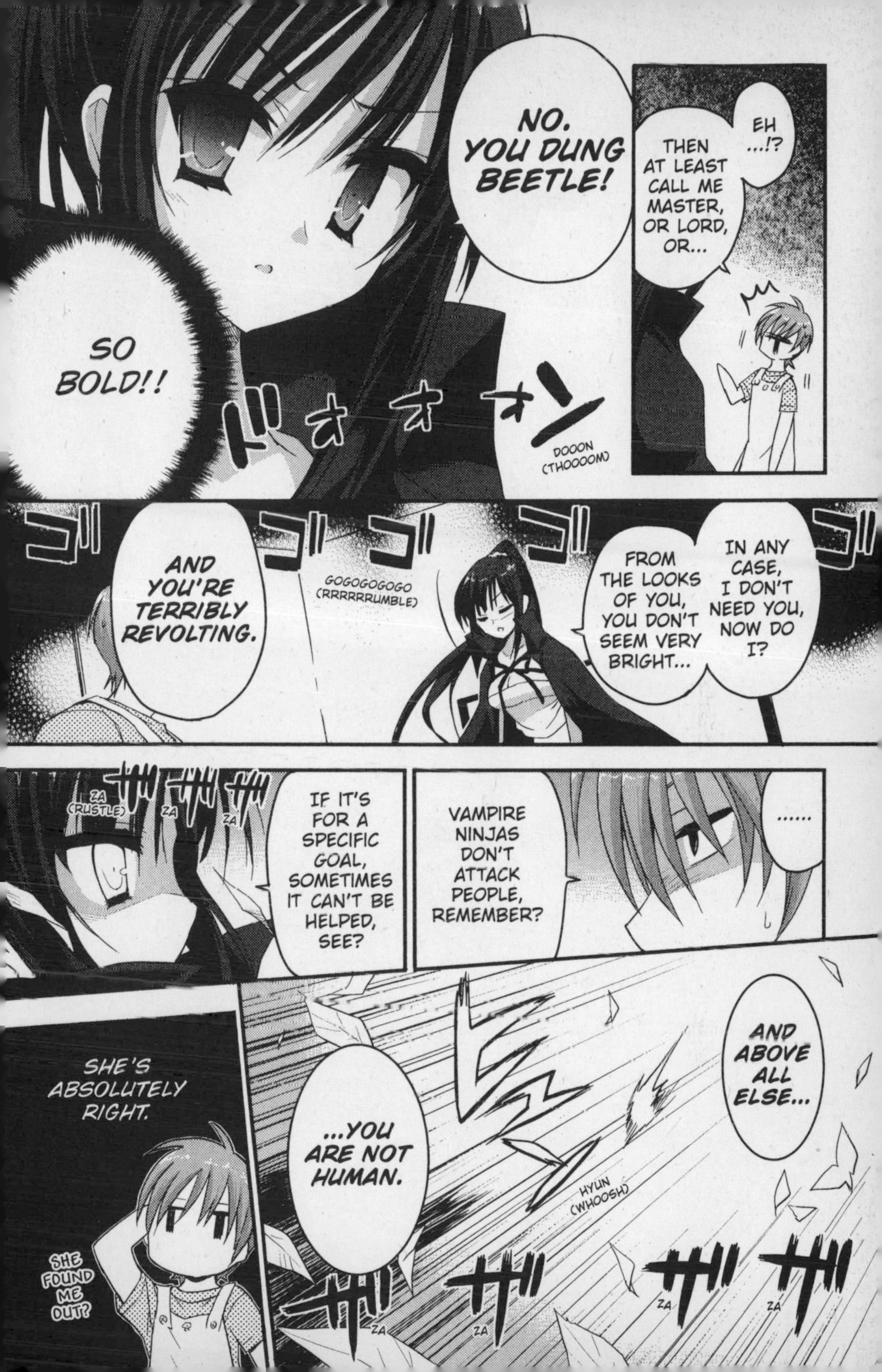
EH ...!?
THEN AT LEAST CALL ME MASTER, OR LORD, OR...
NO. YOU DUNG BEETLE!
SO BOLD!!
DOOON (THOOOOM)
IN ANY CASE, I DON'T NEED YOU, NOW DO I?
FROM THE LOOKS OF YOU, YOU DON'T SEEM VERY BRIGHT...
GOGOGOGOGO (RRRRRRUMBLE)
AND YOU'RE TERRIBLY REVOLTING.
......
VAMPIRE NINJAS DON'T ATTACK PEOPLE, REMEMBER?
IF IT'S FOR A SPECIFIC GOAL, SOMETIMES IT CAN'T BE HELPED, SEE?
ZA (RUSTLE) ZA ZA
AND ABOVE ALL ELSE...
HYUN (WHOOSH)
...YOU ARE NOT HUMAN.
ZA ZA ZA ZA
SHE'S ABSOLUTELY RIGHT.
SHE FOUND ME OUT?

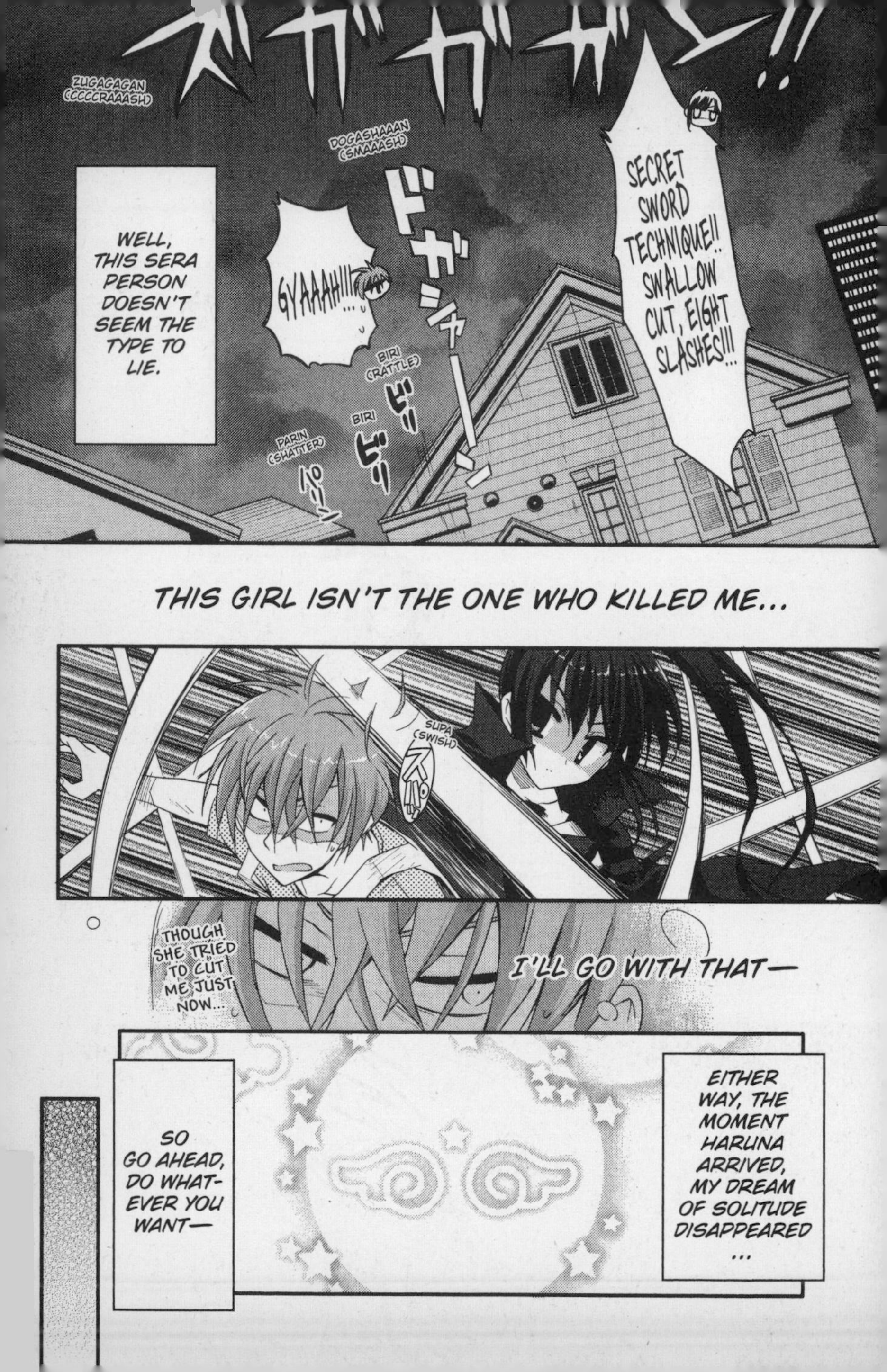
ZUGAGAGAN (CCCCRAAAASH)
SECRET SWORD TECHNIQUE!! SWALLOW CUT, EIGHT SLASHES!!!
DOGASHAAAN (SMAAAASH)
GYAAAH!!!
BIRI (RATTLE)
BIRI
PARIN (SHATTER)
WELL, THIS SERA PERSON DOESN'T SEEM THE TYPE TO LIE.
THIS GIRL ISN'T THE ONE WHO KILLED ME...
SUPA (SWISH)
I'LL GO WITH THAT—
THOUGH SHE TRIED TO CUT ME JUST NOW...
EITHER WAY, THE MOMENT HARUNA ARRIVED, MY DREAM OF SOLITUDE DISAPPEARED ...
SO GO AHEAD, DO WHAT-EVER YOU WANT—

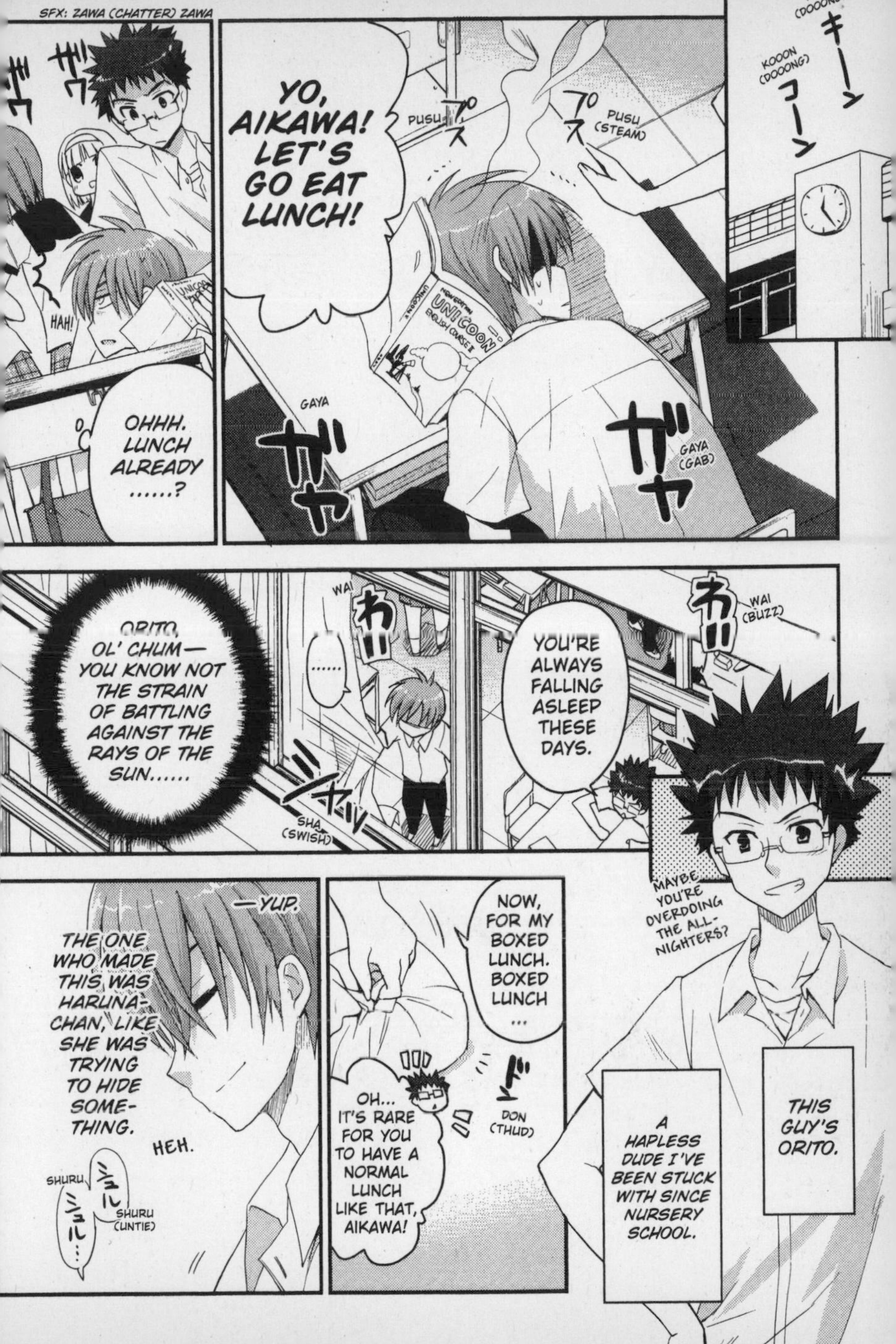
KIIN (DOOONG)
KOOON (DOOONG)
YO, AIKAWA! LET'S GO EAT LUNCH!
PUSU (STEAM)
PUSU
GAYA (GAB)
GAYA
SFX: ZAWA (CHATTER) ZAWA
HAH!
OHHH. LUNCH ALREADY ......?
WAI (BUZZ)
YOU'RE ALWAYS FALLING ASLEEP THESE DAYS.
WAI
......
SHA (SWISH)
ORITO, OL' CHUM— YOU KNOW NOT THE STRAIN OF BATTLING AGAINST THE RAYS OF THE SUN......
MAYBE YOU'RE OVERDOING THE ALL-NIGHTERS?
THIS GUY'S ORITO.
A HAPLESS DUDE I'VE BEEN STUCK WITH SINCE NURSERY SCHOOL.
NOW, FOR MY BOXED LUNCH. BOXED LUNCH ...
DON (THUD)
OH... IT'S RARE FOR YOU TO HAVE A NORMAL LUNCH LIKE THAT, AIKAWA!
—YUP.
THE ONE WHO MADE THIS WAS HARUNA-CHAN, LIKE SHE WAS TRYING TO HIDE SOME-THING.
HEH.
SHURU
SHURU (UNTIE)

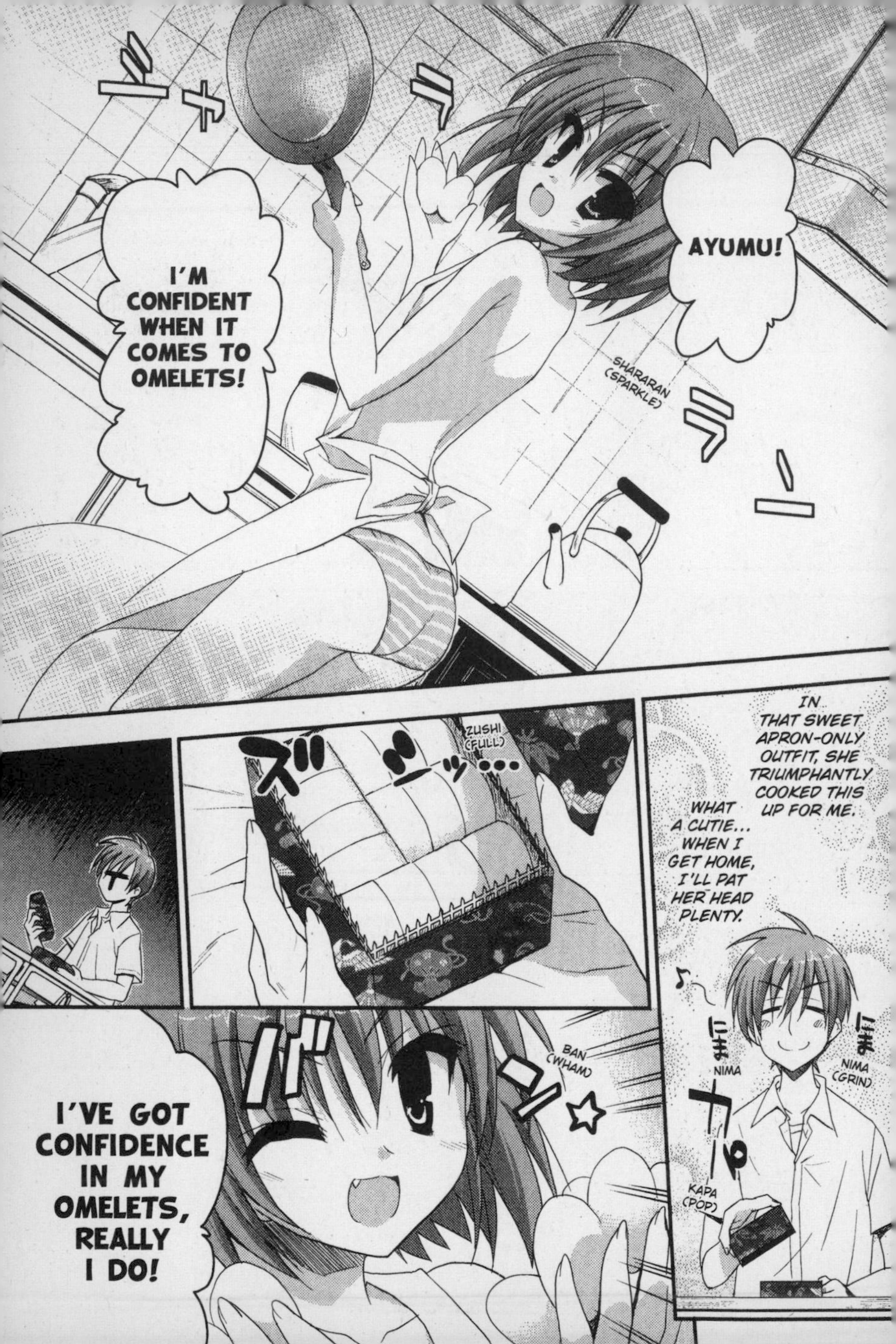

AYUMU!
SHARARAN (SPARKLE)
I'M CONFIDENT WHEN IT COMES TO OMELETS!
IN THAT SWEET APRON-ONLY OUTFIT, SHE TRIUMPHANTLY COOKED THIS UP FOR ME.
WHAT A CUTIE... WHEN I GET HOME, I'LL PAT HER HEAD PLENTY.
NIMA (GRIN)
NIMA
KAPA (POP)
ZUSHI (FULL)
BAN (WHAM)
I'VE GOT CONFIDENCE IN MY OMELETS, REALLY I DO!

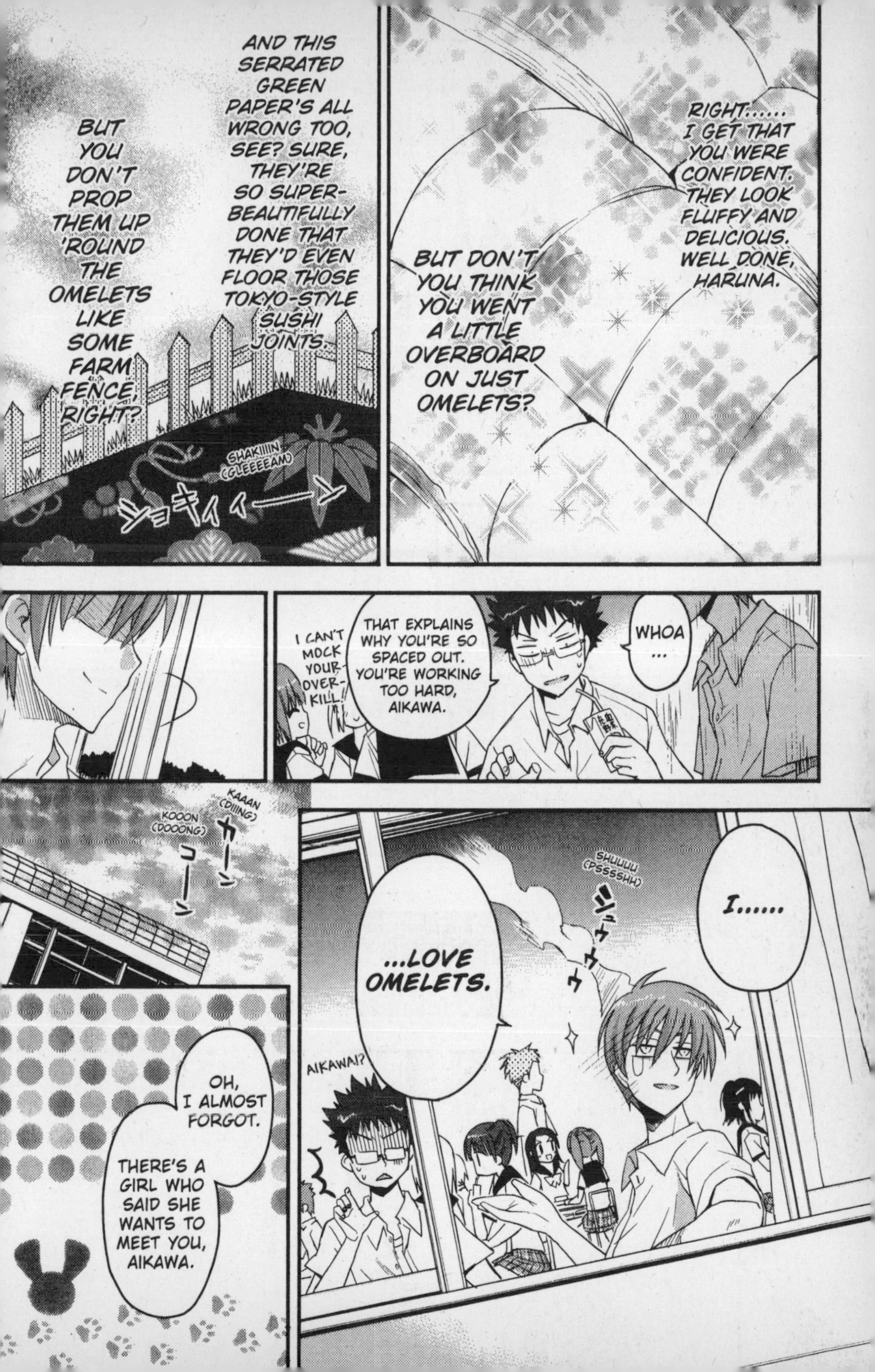
RIGHT...... I GET THAT YOU WERE CONFIDENT. THEY LOOK FLUFFY AND DELICIOUS. WELL DONE, HARUNA.
BUT DON'T YOU THINK YOU WENT A LITTLE OVERBOARD ON JUST OMELETS?
AND THIS SERRATED GREEN PAPER'S ALL WRONG TOO, SEE? SURE, THEY'RE SO SUPER-BEAUTIFULLY DONE THAT THEY'D EVEN FLOOR THOSE TOKYO-STYLE SUSHI JOINTS.
BUT YOU DON'T PROP THEM UP 'ROUND THE OMELETS LIKE SOME FARM FENCE, RIGHT?
SHAKIIIIN (GLEEEEAM)
ショキィーン
WHOA ...
THAT EXPLAINS WHY YOU'RE SO SPACED OUT. YOU'RE WORKING TOO HARD, AIKAWA.
I CAN'T MOCK YOUR OVER-KILL!
I......
...LOVE OMELETS.
SHUUUU (PSSSSHH)
シュゥゥゥ
AIKAWA!?
KAAAN (DIIING)
カーン
KOOON (DOOONG)
コーン
OH, I ALMOST FORGOT.
THERE'S A GIRL WHO SAID SHE WANTS TO MEET YOU, AIKAWA.

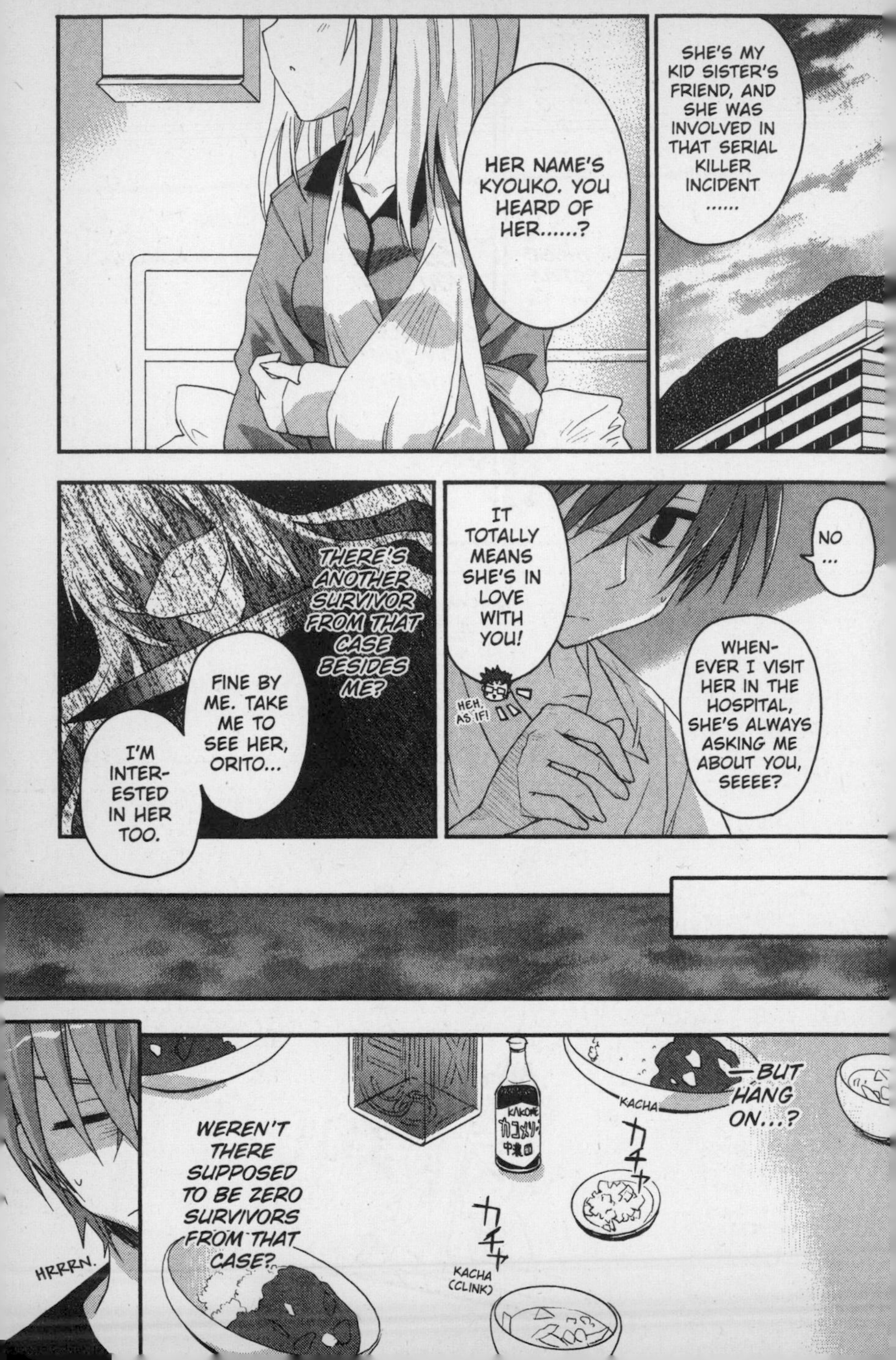
SHE'S MY KID SISTER'S FRIEND, AND SHE WAS INVOLVED IN THAT SERIAL KILLER INCIDENT ......
HER NAME'S KYOUKO. YOU HEARD OF HER......?
NO ...
WHEN-EVER I VISIT HER IN THE HOSPITAL, SHE'S ALWAYS ASKING ME ABOUT YOU, SEEEE?
IT TOTALLY MEANS SHE'S IN LOVE WITH YOU!
HEH, AS IF!
THERE'S ANOTHER SURVIVOR FROM THAT CASE BESIDES ME?
FINE BY ME. TAKE ME TO SEE HER, ORITO...
I'M INTERESTED IN HER TOO.
—BUT HANG ON...?
KACHA
WEREN'T THERE SUPPOSED TO BE ZERO SURVIVORS FROM THAT CASE?
KACHA (CLINK)
HRRRN.

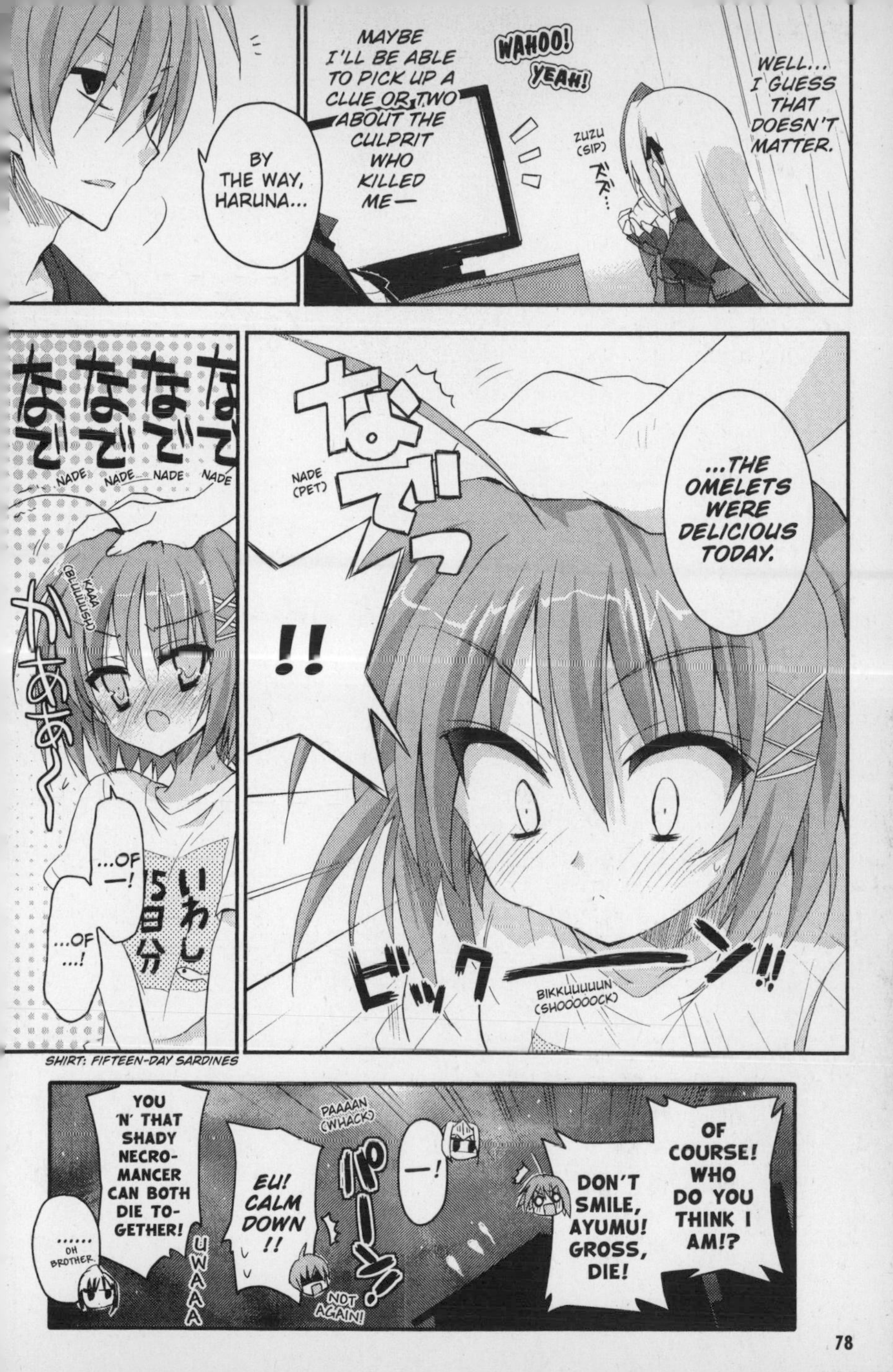
WELL... I GUESS THAT DOESN'T MATTER.
ZUZU (SIP)
ズズ...
WAHOO! YEAH!
MAYBE I'LL BE ABLE TO PICK UP A CLUE OR TWO ABOUT THE CULPRIT WHO KILLED ME—
BY THE WAY, HARUNA...
NADE (PET)
なでっ
...THE OMELETS WERE DELICIOUS TODAY.
!!
ビックーーン!!
BIKKUUUUUN (SHOOOOCK)
なでなでなでなで
NADE NADE NADE NADE
KAAA (BLUUUUSH)
かぁぁ~
...OF—!
...OF...!
いわし15日分
SHIRT: FIFTEEN-DAY SARDINES
OF COURSE! WHO DO YOU THINK I AM!?
DON'T SMILE, AYUMU! GROSS, DIE!
PAAAAN (WHACK)
パーン!
—!
NOT AGAIN!
EU! CALM DOWN!!
UWAAA
YOU 'N' THAT SHADY NECROMANCER CAN BOTH DIE TOGETHER!
......OH BROTHER.

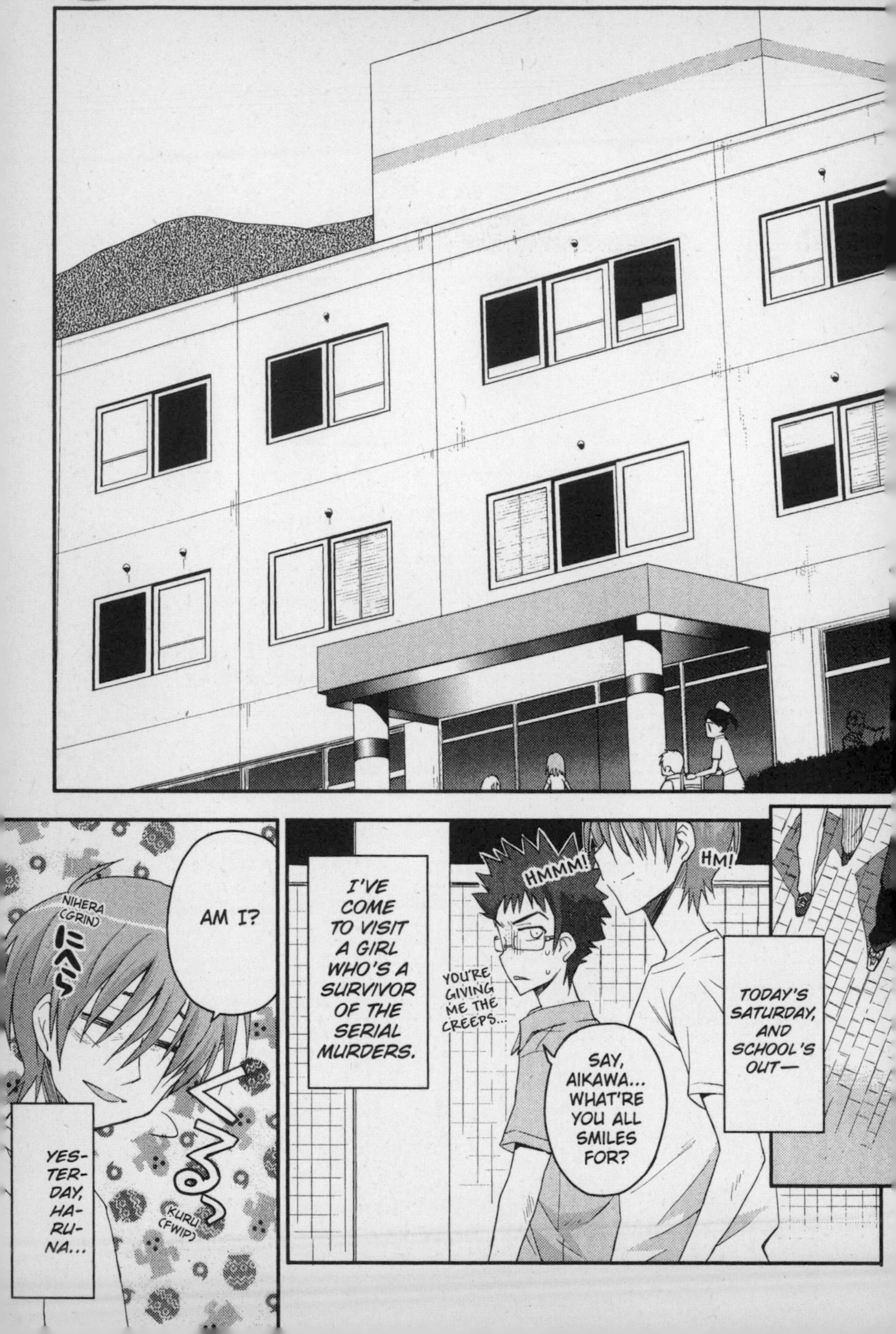
TODAY'S SATURDAY, AND SCHOOL'S OUT—
HM!
HMMM!
SAY, AIKAWA... WHAT'RE YOU ALL SMILES FOR?
YOU'RE GIVING ME THE CREEPS...
I'VE COME TO VISIT A GIRL WHO'S A SURVIVOR OF THE SERIAL MURDERS.
AM I?
NIHERA (GRIN)
KURU (FWIP)
YES-TER-DAY, HA-RU-NA...

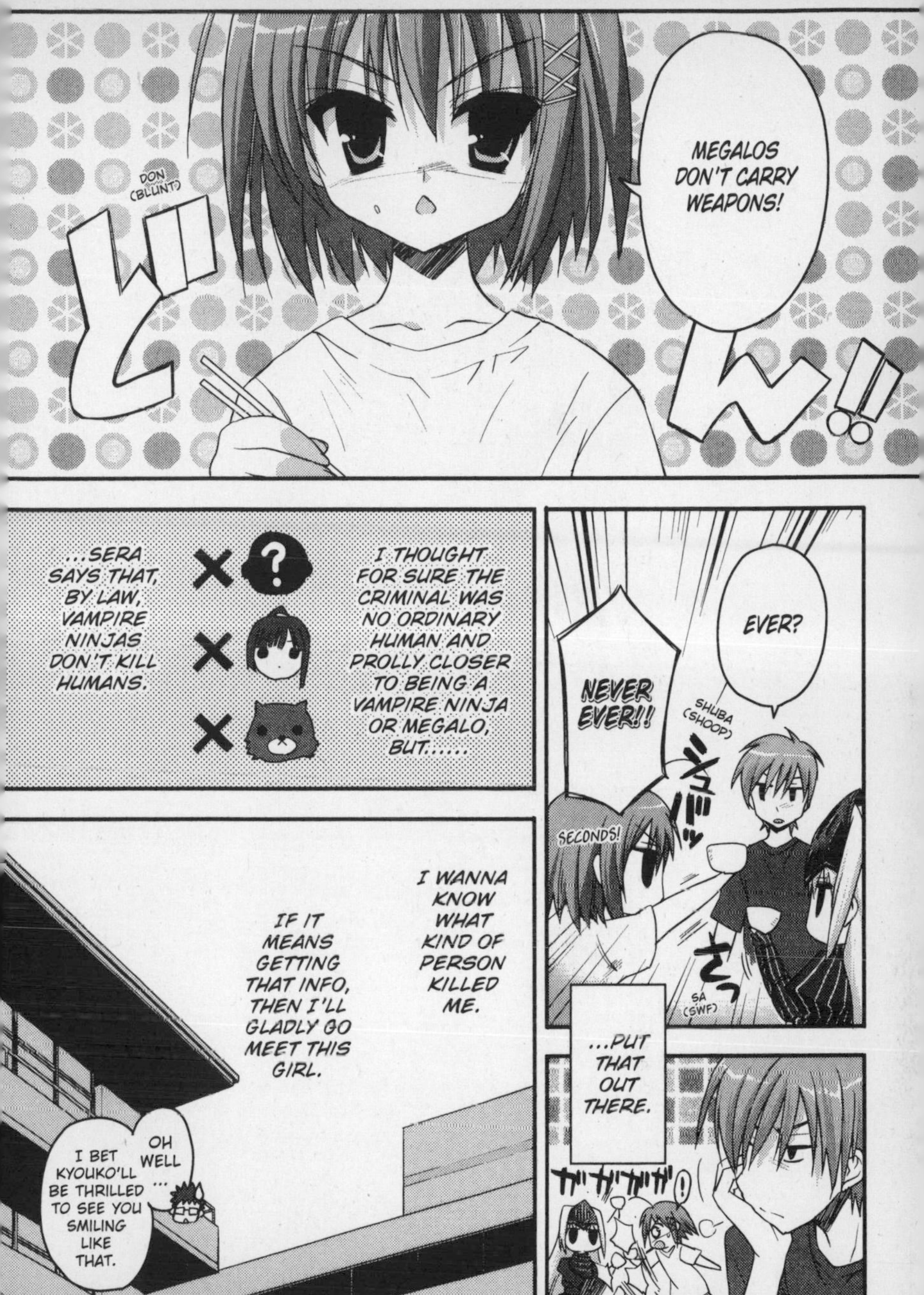
MEGALOS DON'T CARRY WEAPONS!
DON (BLUNT)
EVER?
NEVER EVER!!
SHUBA (SHOOP)
SECONDS!
SA (SWF)
I THOUGHT FOR SURE THE CRIMINAL WAS NO ORDINARY HUMAN AND PROLLY CLOSER TO BEING A VAMPIRE NINJA OR MEGALO, BUT......
...SERA SAYS THAT, BY LAW, VAMPIRE NINJAS DON'T KILL HUMANS.
...PUT THAT OUT THERE.
I WANNA KNOW WHAT KIND OF PERSON KILLED ME.
IF IT MEANS GETTING THAT INFO, THEN I'LL GLADLY GO MEET THIS GIRL.
OH WELL...
I BET KYOUKO'LL BE THRILLED TO SEE YOU SMILING LIKE THAT.

SFX: GA (CLACK) GA GA GA

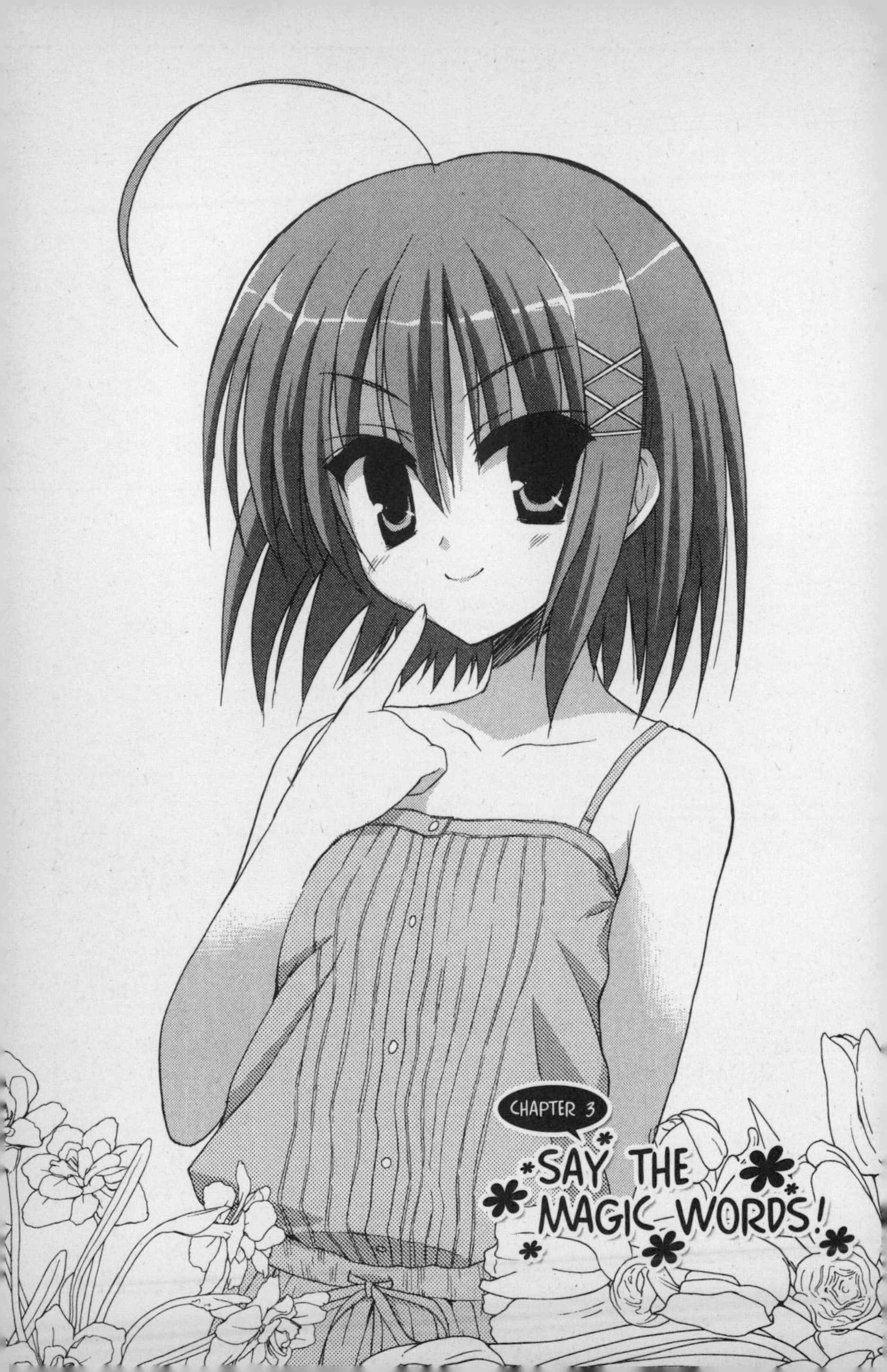
CHAPTER 3
SAY THE MAGIC WORDS!

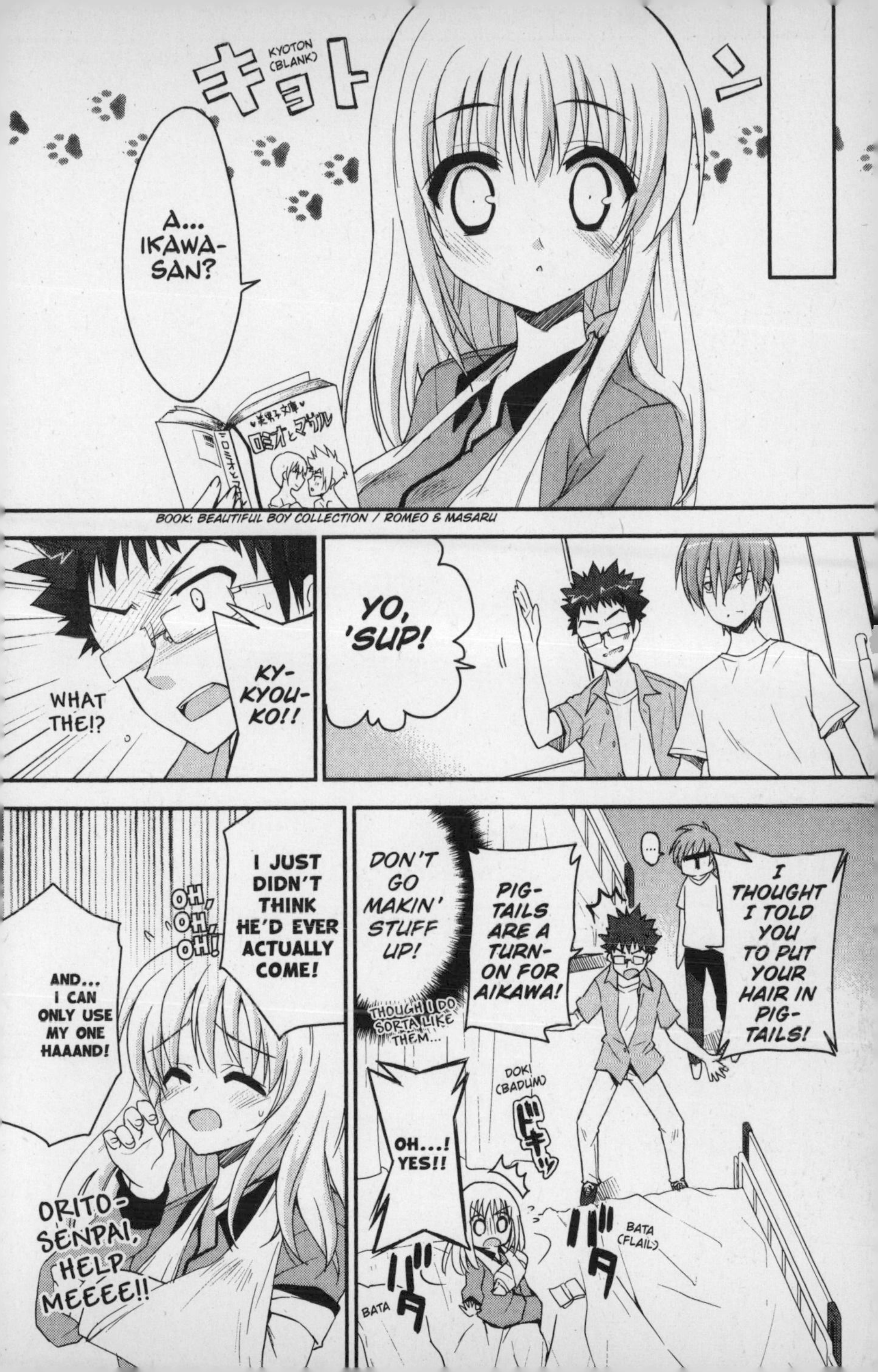
KYOTON (BLANK)
キョトン
A... IKAWA-SAN?
BOOK: BEAUTIFUL BOY COLLECTION / ROMEO & MASARU
YO, 'SUP!
KY-KYOUKO!!
WHAT THE!?
I THOUGHT I TOLD YOU TO PUT YOUR HAIR IN PIG-TAILS!
...
PIG-TAILS ARE A TURN-ON FOR AIKAWA!
DON'T GO MAKIN' STUFF UP!
THOUGH I DO SORTA LIKE THEM...
DOKI (BADUM)
OH...! YES!!
BATA (FLAIL)
BATA
I JUST DIDN'T THINK HE'D EVER ACTUALLY COME!
OH, OH, OH!
AND... I CAN ONLY USE MY ONE HAAAND!
ORITO-SENPAI, HELP MEEEE!!

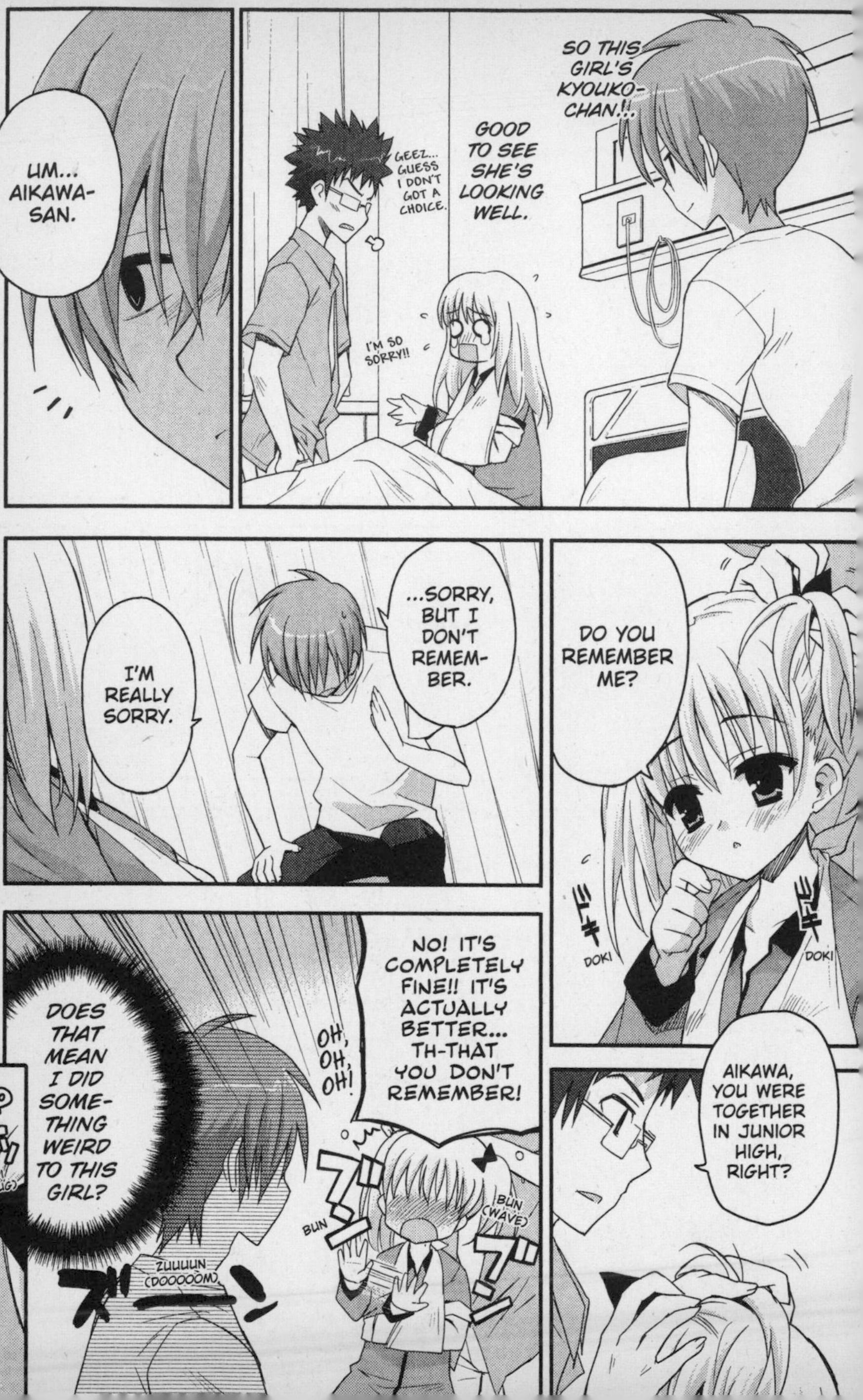
SO THIS GIRL'S KYOUKO-CHAN...!
GOOD TO SEE SHE'S LOOKING WELL.
GEEZ... GUESS I DON'T GOT A CHOICE.
I'M SO SORRY!!
UM... AIKAWA-SAN.
DO YOU REMEMBER ME?
DOKI
DOKI
...SORRY, BUT I DON'T REMEMBER.
I'M REALLY SORRY.
AIKAWA, YOU WERE TOGETHER IN JUNIOR HIGH, RIGHT?
NO! IT'S COMPLETELY FINE!! IT'S ACTUALLY BETTER... TH-THAT YOU DON'T REMEMBER!
OH, OH, OH!
BUN (WAVE)
BUN
ZUUUUN (DOOOOOM)
DOES THAT MEAN I DID SOMETHING WEIRD TO THIS GIRL?
PI (TUG)

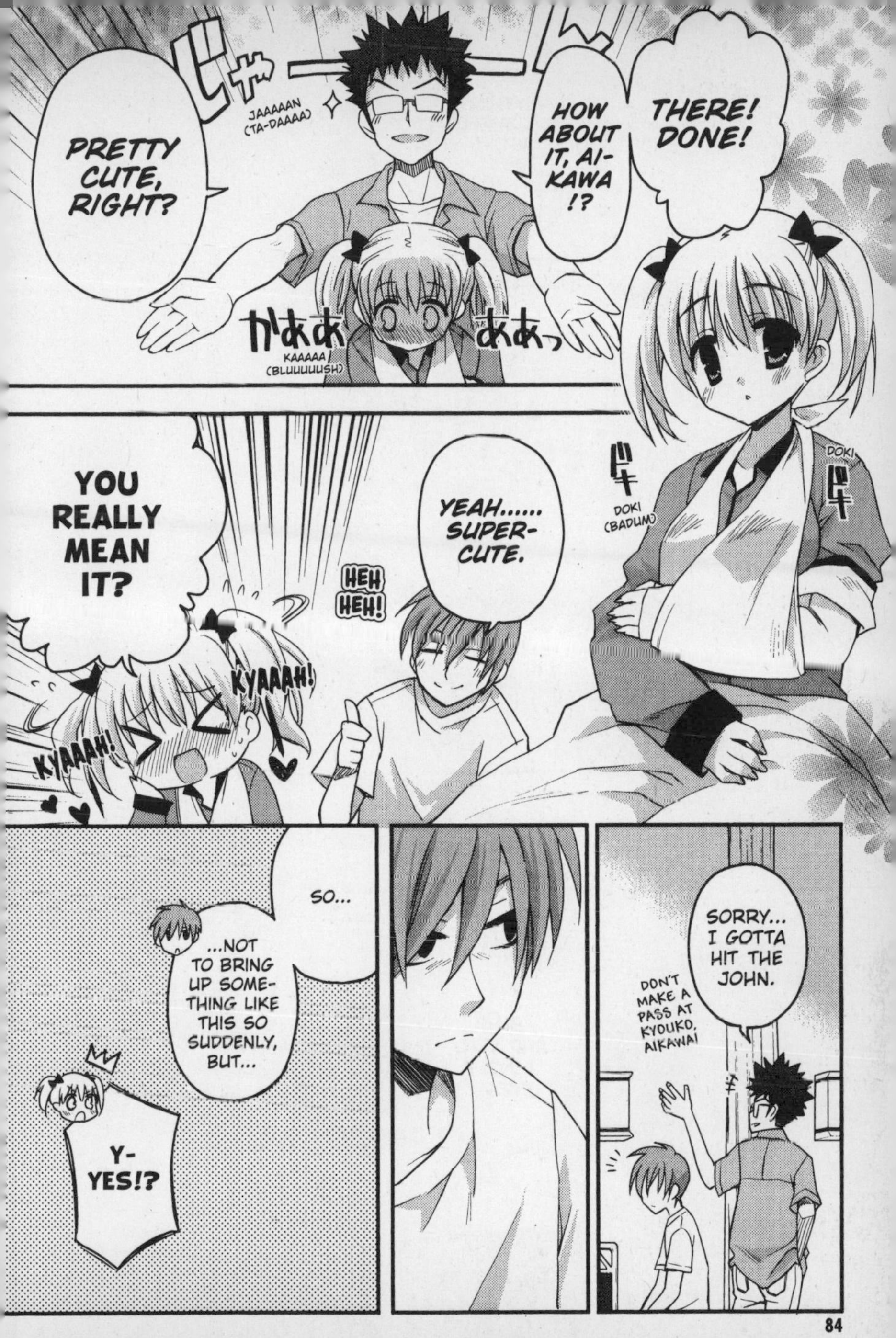
THERE! DONE!
HOW ABOUT IT, AI-KAWA!?
じゃーん
JAAAAAN (TA-DAAAA)
PRETTY CUTE, RIGHT?
かあああああっ
KAAAAA (BLUUUUUSH)
ドキ
DOKI
ドキ
DOKI (BADUM)
YEAH...... SUPER-CUTE.
HEH HEH!
YOU REALLY MEAN IT?
KYAAAH!
KYAAAH!
SORRY... I GOTTA HIT THE JOHN.
DON'T MAKE A PASS AT KYOUKO, AIKAWA!
SO...
...NOT TO BRING UP SOME-THING LIKE THIS SO SUDDENLY, BUT...
Y-YES!?

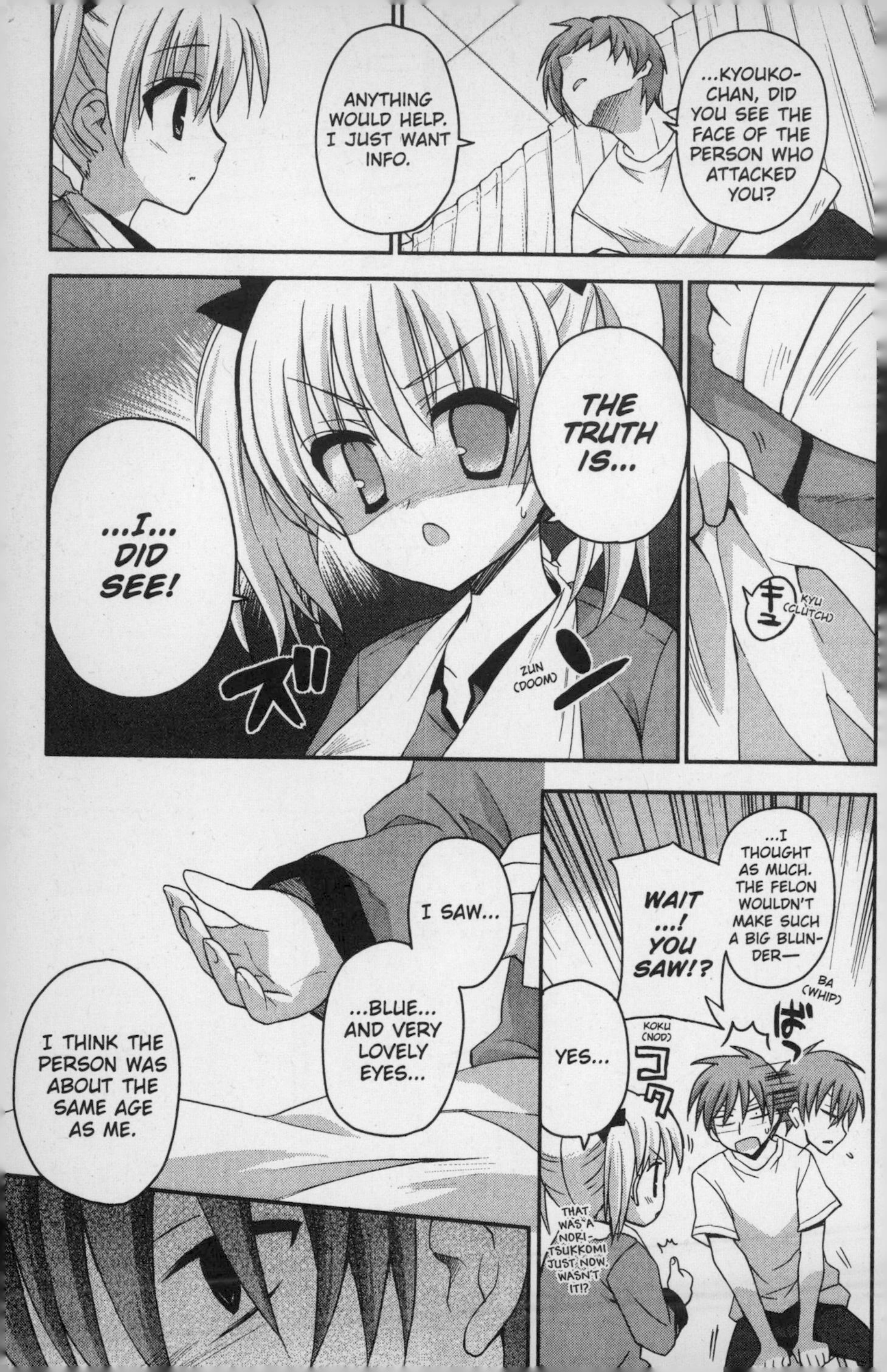
...KYOUKO-CHAN, DID YOU SEE THE FACE OF THE PERSON WHO ATTACKED YOU?
ANYTHING WOULD HELP. I JUST WANT INFO.
KYU (CLUTCH)
THE TRUTH IS...
ZUN (DOOM)
...I... DID SEE!
...I THOUGHT AS MUCH. THE FELON WOULDN'T MAKE SUCH A BIG BLUN-DER—
BA (WHIP)
WAIT ...! YOU SAW!?
KOKU (NOD)
YES...
THAT WAS A NORI-TSUKKOMI JUST NOW, WASN'T IT!?
I SAW...
...BLUE... AND VERY LOVELY EYES...
I THINK THE PERSON WAS ABOUT THE SAME AGE AS ME.

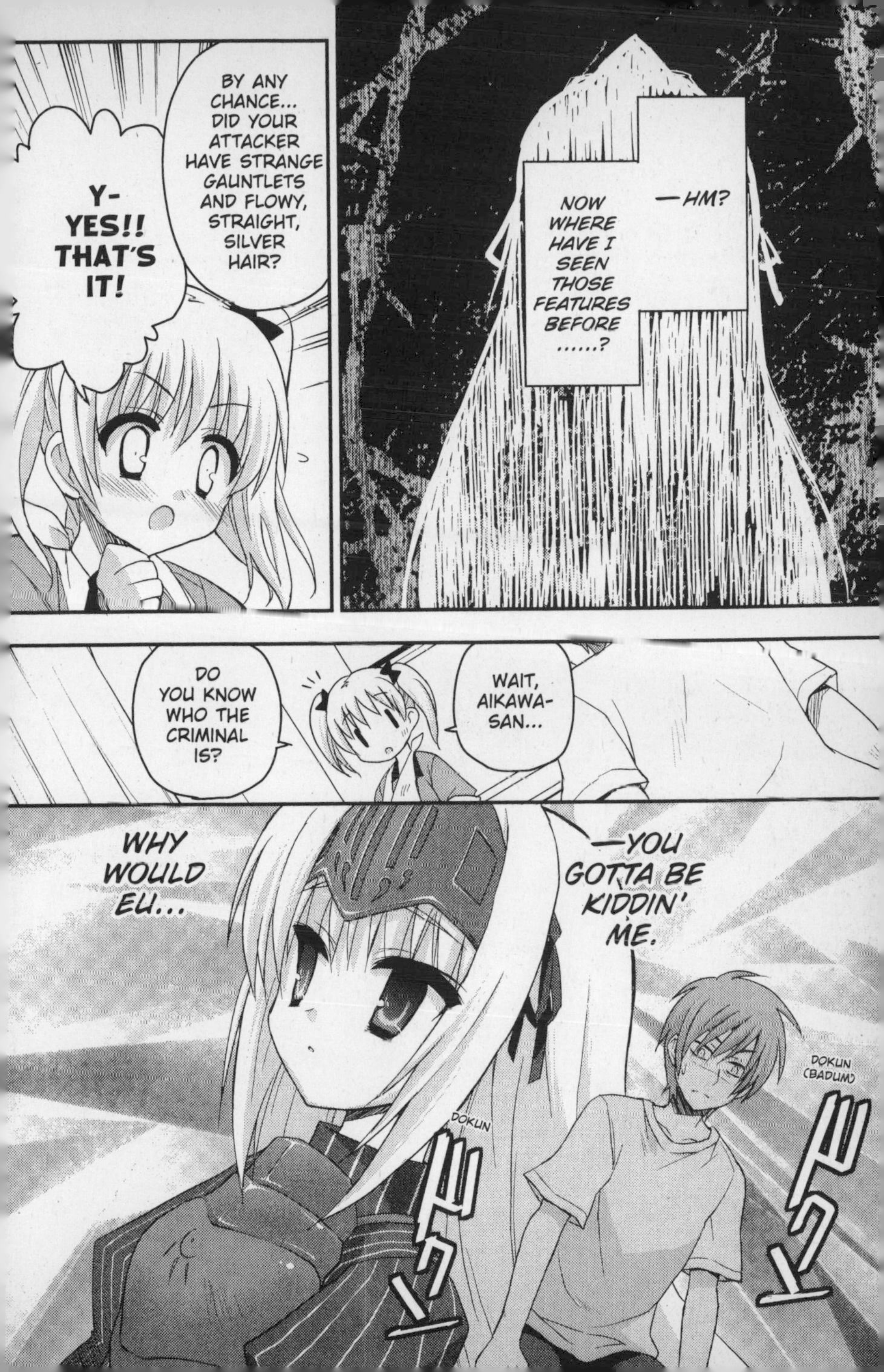
—HM?
NOW WHERE HAVE I SEEN THOSE FEATURES BEFORE ......?
BY ANY CHANCE... DID YOUR ATTACKER HAVE STRANGE GAUNTLETS AND FLOWY, STRAIGHT, SILVER HAIR?
Y-YES!! THAT'S IT!
WAIT, AIKAWA-SAN...
DO YOU KNOW WHO THE CRIMINAL IS?
—YOU GOTTA BE KIDDIN' ME.
WHY WOULD EU...
DOKUN (BADUM)
DOKUN

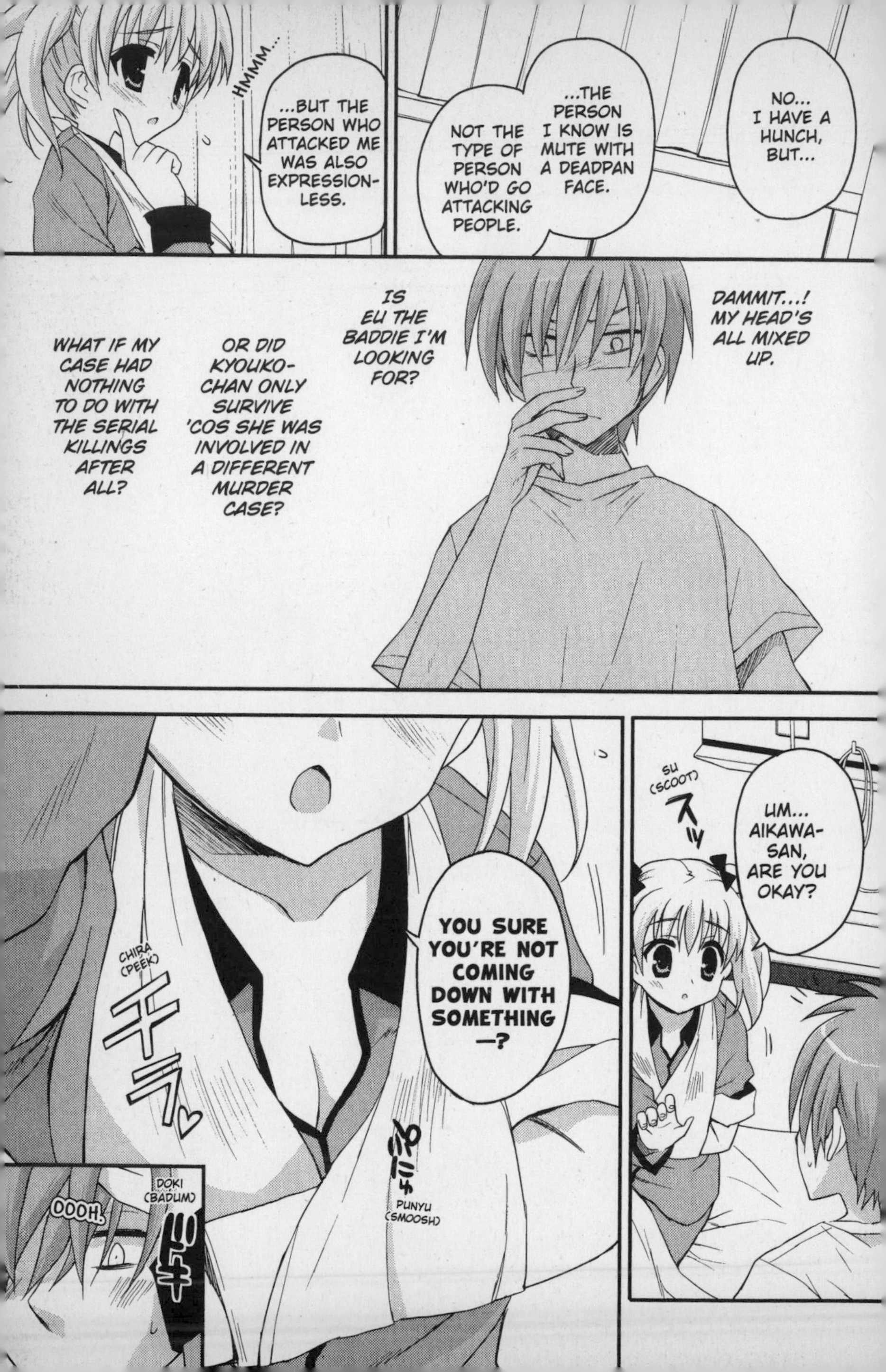
NO... I HAVE A HUNCH, BUT...
...THE PERSON I KNOW IS MUTE WITH A DEADPAN FACE.
NOT THE TYPE OF PERSON WHO'D GO ATTACKING PEOPLE.
HMMM...
...BUT THE PERSON WHO ATTACKED ME WAS ALSO EXPRESSIONLESS.
DAMMIT...! MY HEAD'S ALL MIXED UP.
IS EU THE BADDIE I'M LOOKING FOR?
OR DID KYOUKO-CHAN ONLY SURVIVE 'COS SHE WAS INVOLVED IN A DIFFERENT MURDER CASE?
WHAT IF MY CASE HAD NOTHING TO DO WITH THE SERIAL KILLINGS AFTER ALL?
SU (SCOOT)
UM... AIKAWA-SAN, ARE YOU OKAY?
YOU SURE YOU'RE NOT COMING DOWN WITH SOMETHING—?
CHIRA (PEEK)
PUNYU (SMOOSH)
DOKI (BADUM)
OOOH.

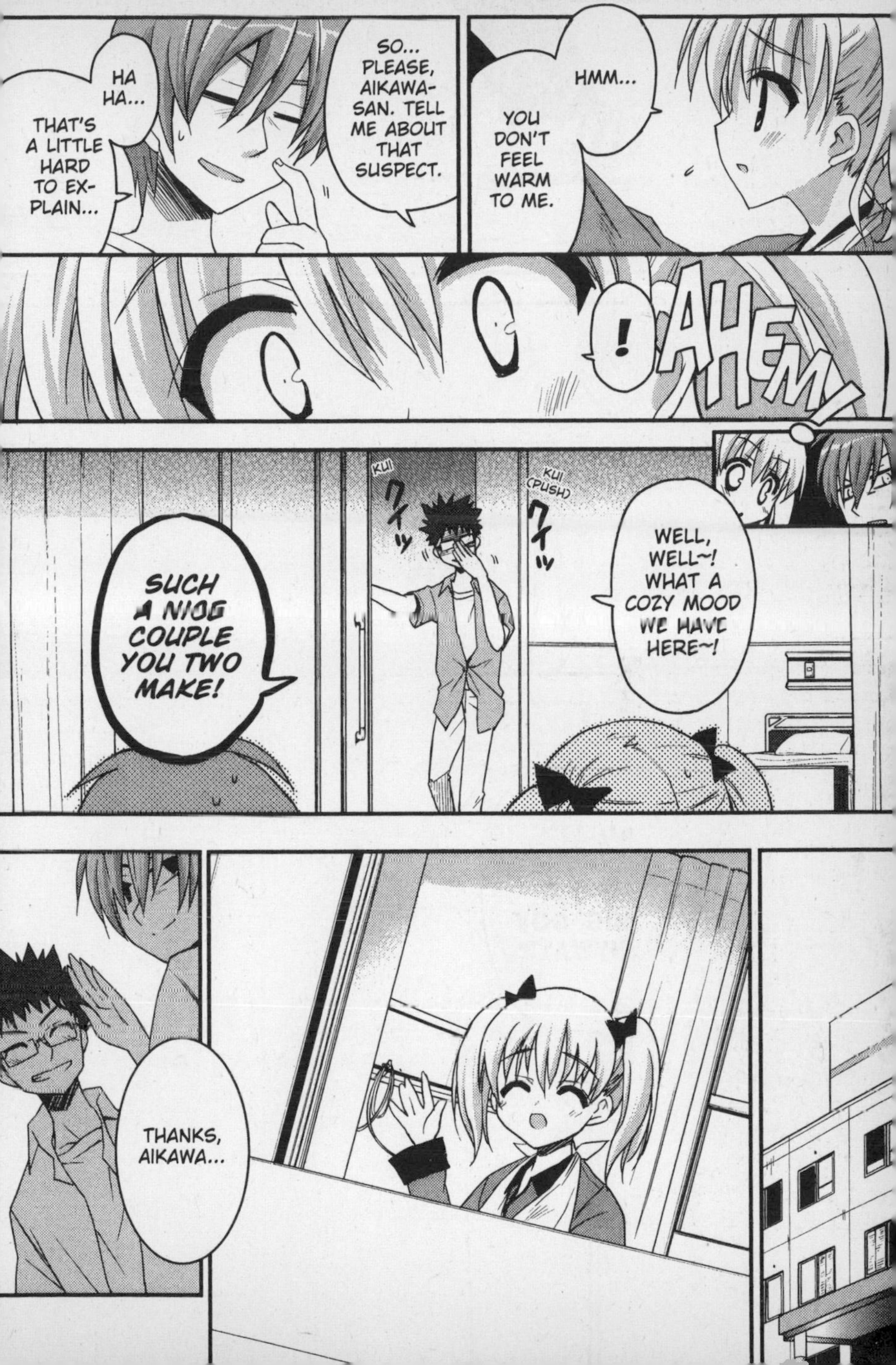
HMM...
YOU DON'T FEEL WARM TO ME.
SO... PLEASE, AIKAWA-SAN. TELL ME ABOUT THAT SUSPECT.
HA HA...
THAT'S A LITTLE HARD TO EX-PLAIN...
!
AHEM!
KUI (PUSH)
クイッ
KUI
クイッ
WELL, WELL~! WHAT A COZY MOOD WE HAVE HERE~!
SUCH A NICE COUPLE YOU TWO MAKE!
THANKS, AIKAWA...

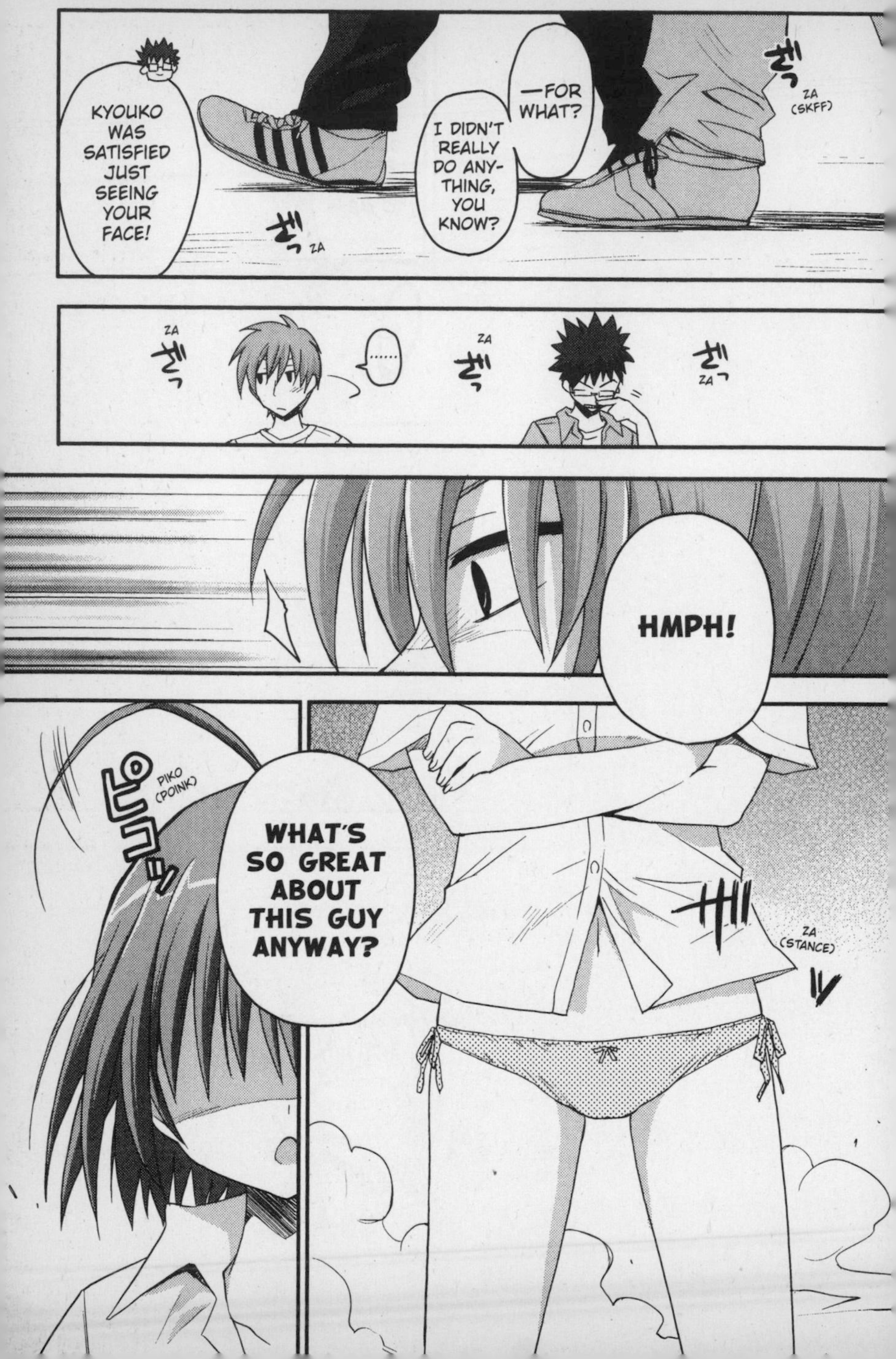
ZA (SKFF)
—FOR WHAT?
I DIDN'T REALLY DO ANY-THING, YOU KNOW?
ZA
KYOUKO WAS SATISFIED JUST SEEING YOUR FACE!
ZA
ZA
......
ZA
HMPH!
ZA (STANCE)
WHAT'S SO GREAT ABOUT THIS GUY ANYWAY?
PIKO (POINK)

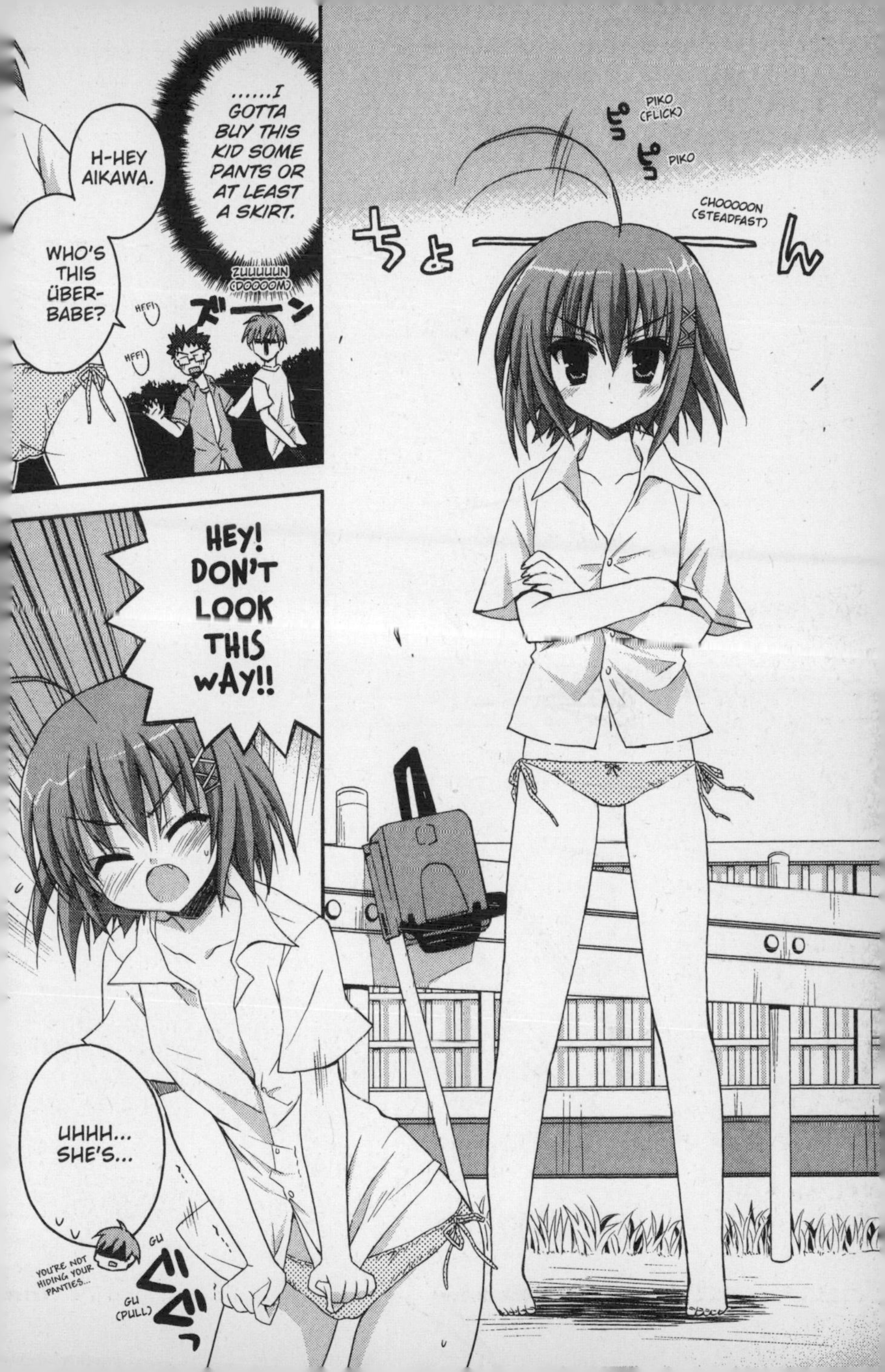
PIKO (FLICK)
PIKO
CHOOOOON (STEADFAST)
......I GOTTA BUY THIS KID SOME PANTS OR AT LEAST A SKIRT.
ZUUUUUN (DOOOOM)
HFF!
HFF!
H-HEY AIKAWA.
WHO'S THIS ÜBER-BABE?
HEY! DON'T LOOK THIS WAY!!
UHHH... SHE'S...
GU
GU (PULL)
YOU'RE NOT HIDING YOUR PANTIES...

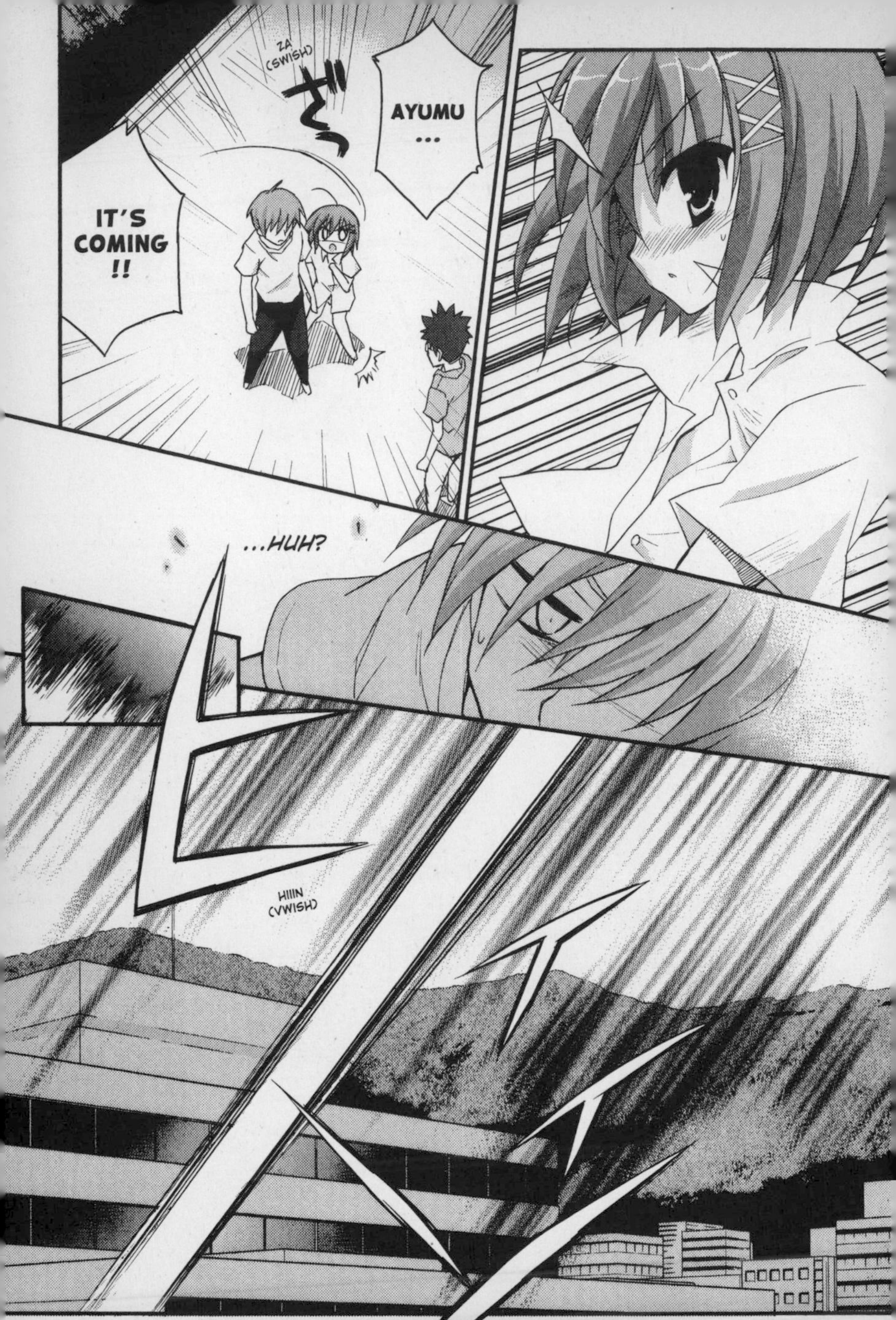
AYUMU...
ZA (SWISH)
IT'S COMING!!
...HUH?
HIIIN (VWISH)

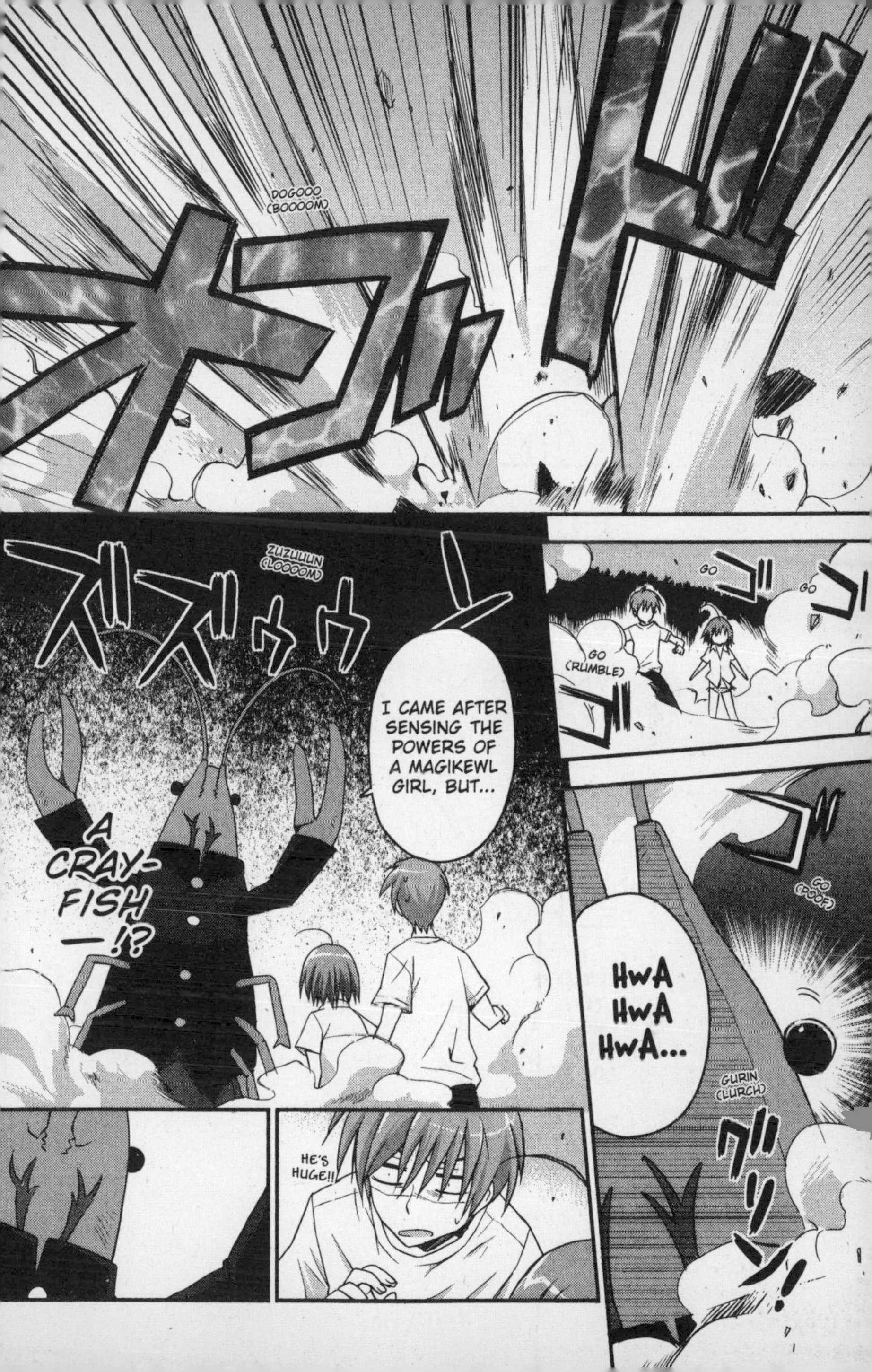
DOGOOO (BOOOOM)
GO
GO
GO (RUMBLE)
GO (POOF)
HWA HWA HWA...
GURIN (LURCH)
ZUZUUUN (LOOOOM)
I CAME AFTER SENSING THE POWERS OF A MAGIKEWL GIRL, BUT...
A CRAY-FISH—!?
HE'S HUGE!!

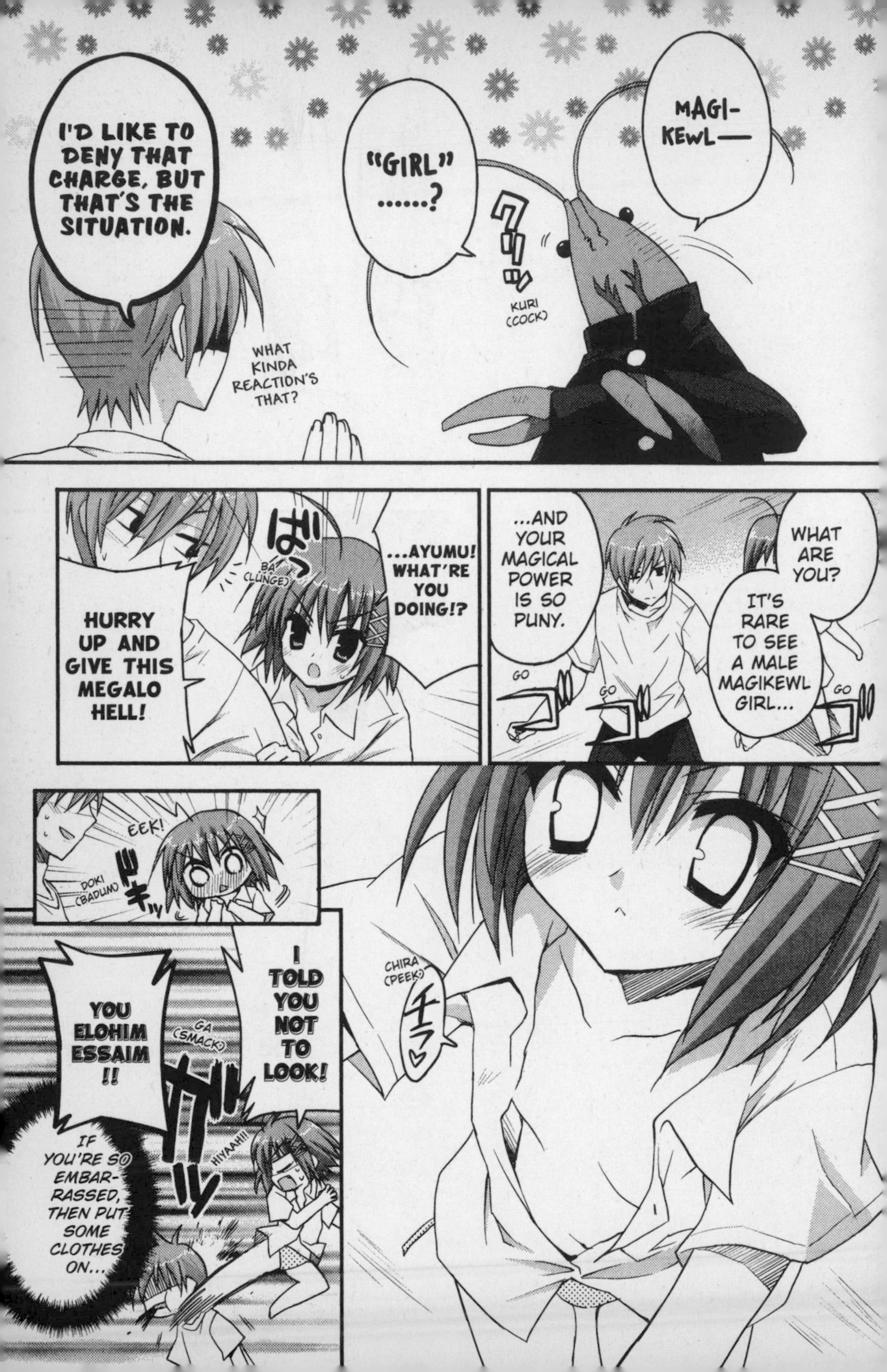
MAGI-KEWL—
KURI (COCK)
"GIRL" ......?
WHAT KINDA REACTION'S THAT?
I'D LIKE TO DENY THAT CHARGE, BUT THAT'S THE SITUATION.
WHAT ARE YOU?
IT'S RARE TO SEE A MALE MAGIKEWL GIRL...
GO
GO
GO
...AND YOUR MAGICAL POWER IS SO PUNY.
...AYUMU! WHAT'RE YOU DOING!?
BA (LUNGE)
HURRY UP AND GIVE THIS MEGALO HELL!
CHIRA (PEEK)
EEK!
DOKI (BADUMP)
I TOLD YOU NOT TO LOOK!
YOU ELOHIM ESSAIM !!
GA (SMACK)
HIYAAH!!!
IF YOU'RE SO EMBARRASSED, THEN PUT SOME CLOTHES ON...

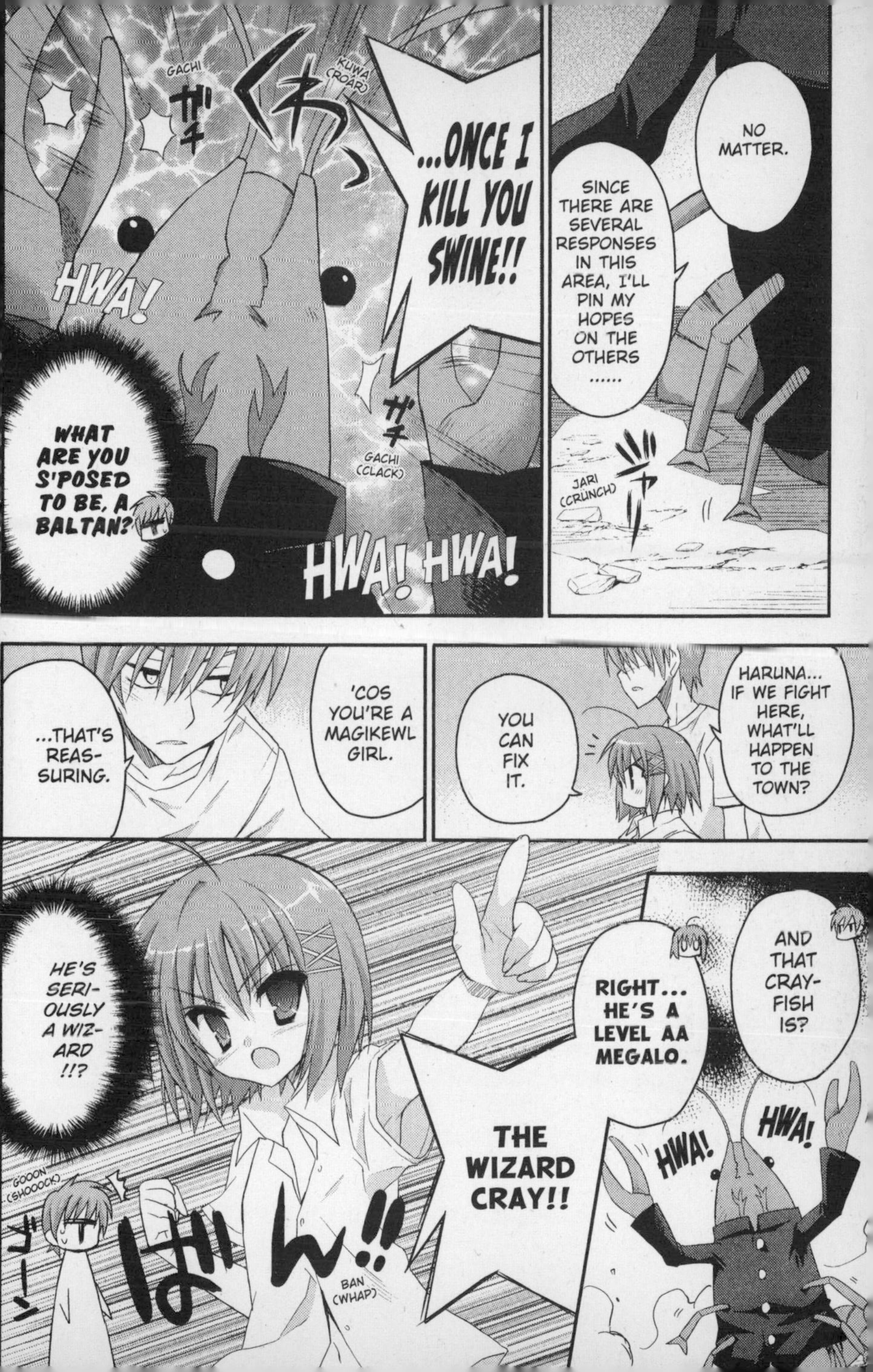
NO MATTER.
SINCE THERE ARE SEVERAL RESPONSES IN THIS AREA, I'LL PIN MY HOPES ON THE OTHERS ......
JARI (CRUNCH)
KUWA (ROAR)
...ONCE I KILL YOU SWINE!!
GACHI
HWA!
GACHI (CLACK)
WHAT ARE YOU S'POSED TO BE, A BALTAN?
HWA! HWA!
HARUNA... IF WE FIGHT HERE, WHAT'LL HAPPEN TO THE TOWN?
YOU CAN FIX IT.
'COS YOU'RE A MAGIKEWL GIRL.
...THAT'S REAS-SURING.
AND THAT CRAY-FISH IS?
RIGHT... HE'S A LEVEL AA MEGALO.
HWA!
HWA!
THE WIZARD CRAY!!
HE'S SERI-OUSLY A WIZ-ARD!!?
BAN (WHAP)
GOOON (SHOOOCK)

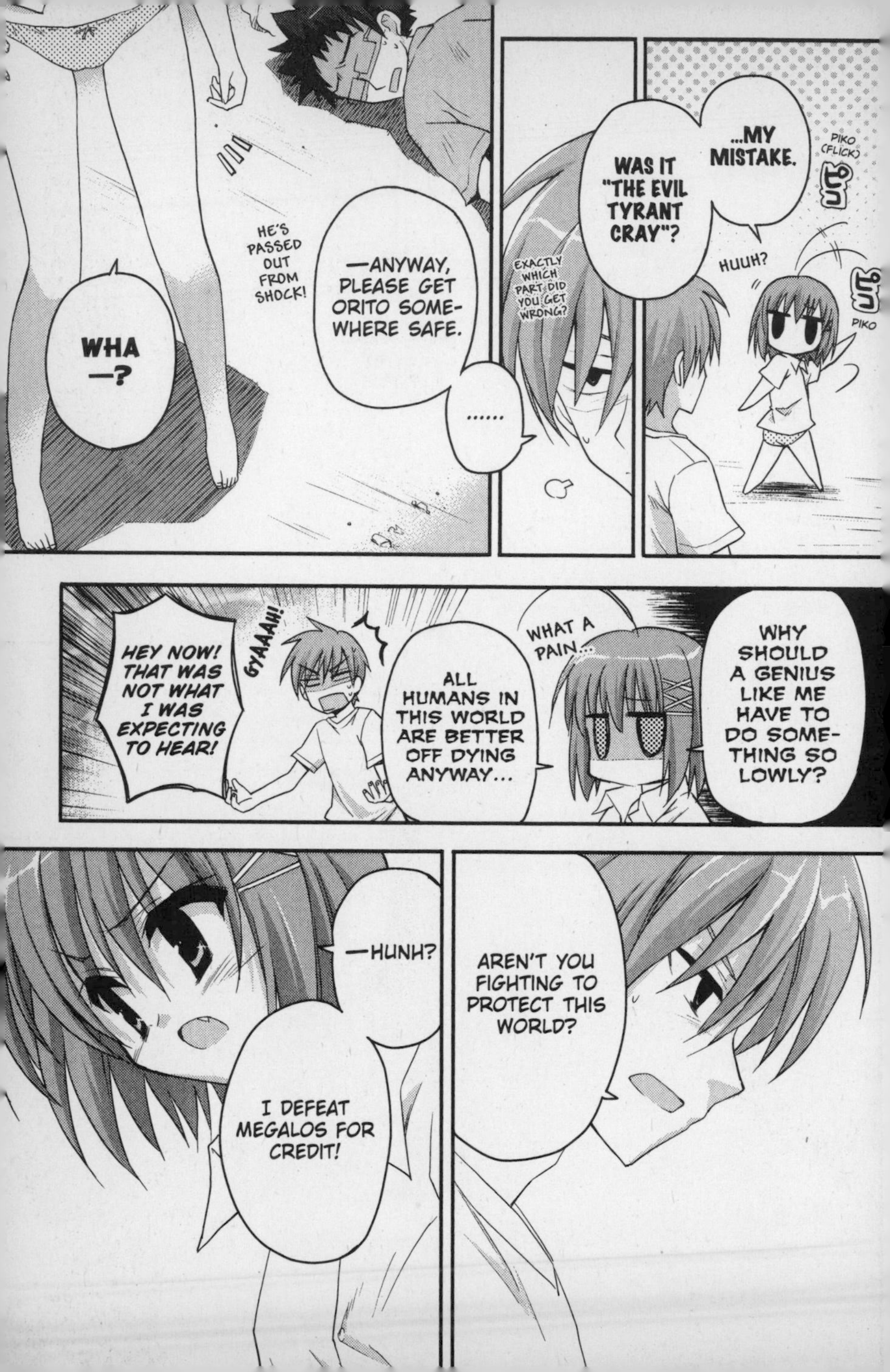
...MY MISTAKE.
PIKO (FLICK)
HUUH?
PIKO
WAS IT "THE EVIL TYRANT CRAY"?
EXACTLY WHICH PART DID YOU GET WRONG?
—ANYWAY, PLEASE GET ORITO SOMEWHERE SAFE.
......
HE'S PASSED OUT FROM SHOCK!
WHA—?
WHY SHOULD A GENIUS LIKE ME HAVE TO DO SOMETHING SO LOWLY?
WHAT A PAIN...
ALL HUMANS IN THIS WORLD ARE BETTER OFF DYING ANYWAY...
GYAAAH!
HEY NOW! THAT WAS NOT WHAT I WAS EXPECTING TO HEAR!
AREN'T YOU FIGHTING TO PROTECT THIS WORLD?
—HUNH?
I DEFEAT MEGALOS FOR CREDIT!

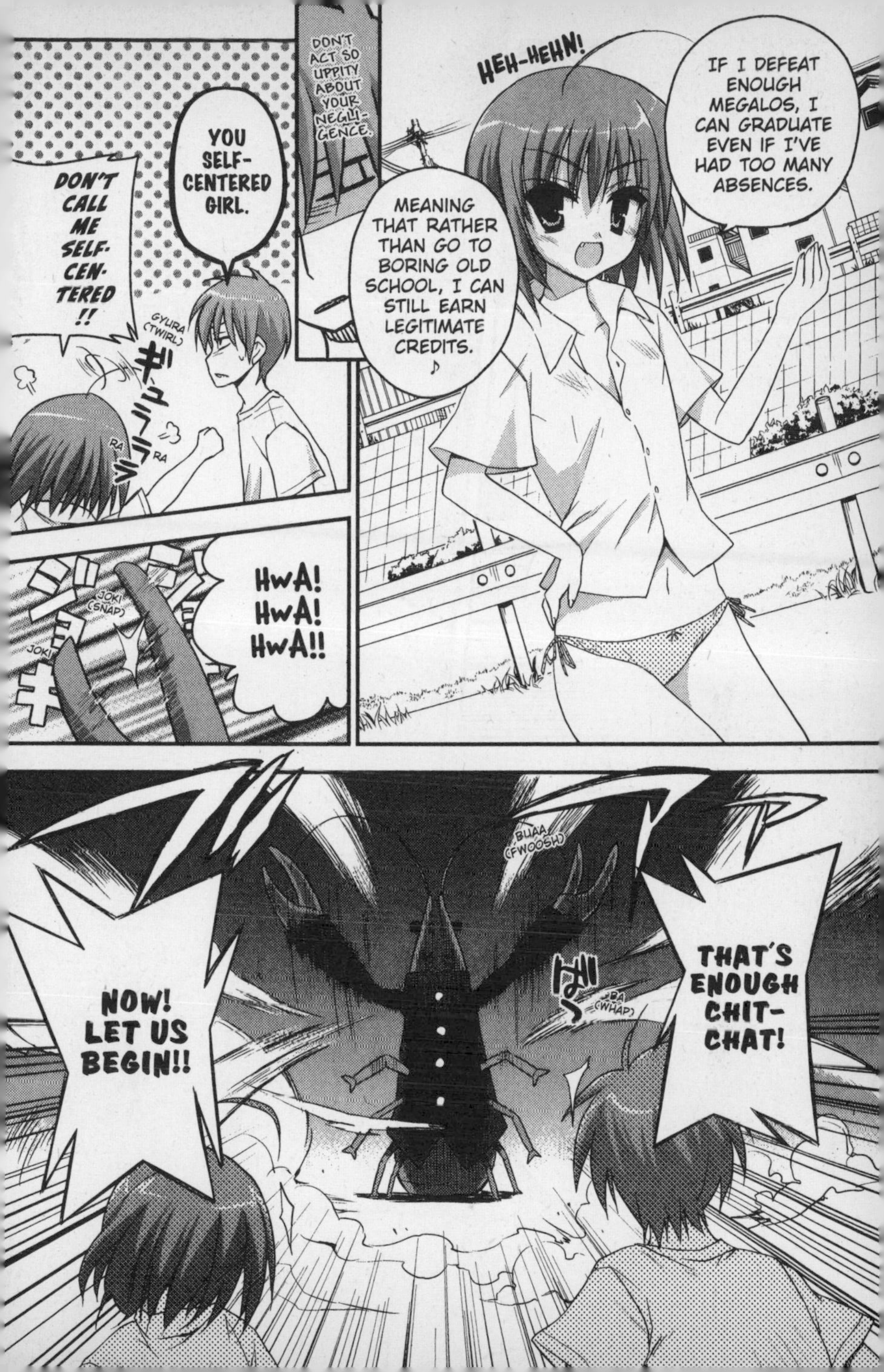
HEH-HEHN!
IF I DEFEAT ENOUGH MEGALOS, I CAN GRADUATE EVEN IF I'VE HAD TOO MANY ABSENCES.
MEANING THAT RATHER THAN GO TO BORING OLD SCHOOL, I CAN STILL EARN LEGITIMATE CREDITS. ♪
DON'T ACT SO UPPITY ABOUT YOUR NEGLI-GENCE.
YOU SELF-CENTERED GIRL.
DON'T CALL ME SELF-CENTERED!!
GYURA (TWIRL)
RA
RA
HWA! HWA! HWA!!
JOKI (SNAP)
JOKI
BUAA (FWOOSH)
THAT'S ENOUGH CHIT-CHAT!
BA (WHAP)
NOW! LET US BEGIN!!

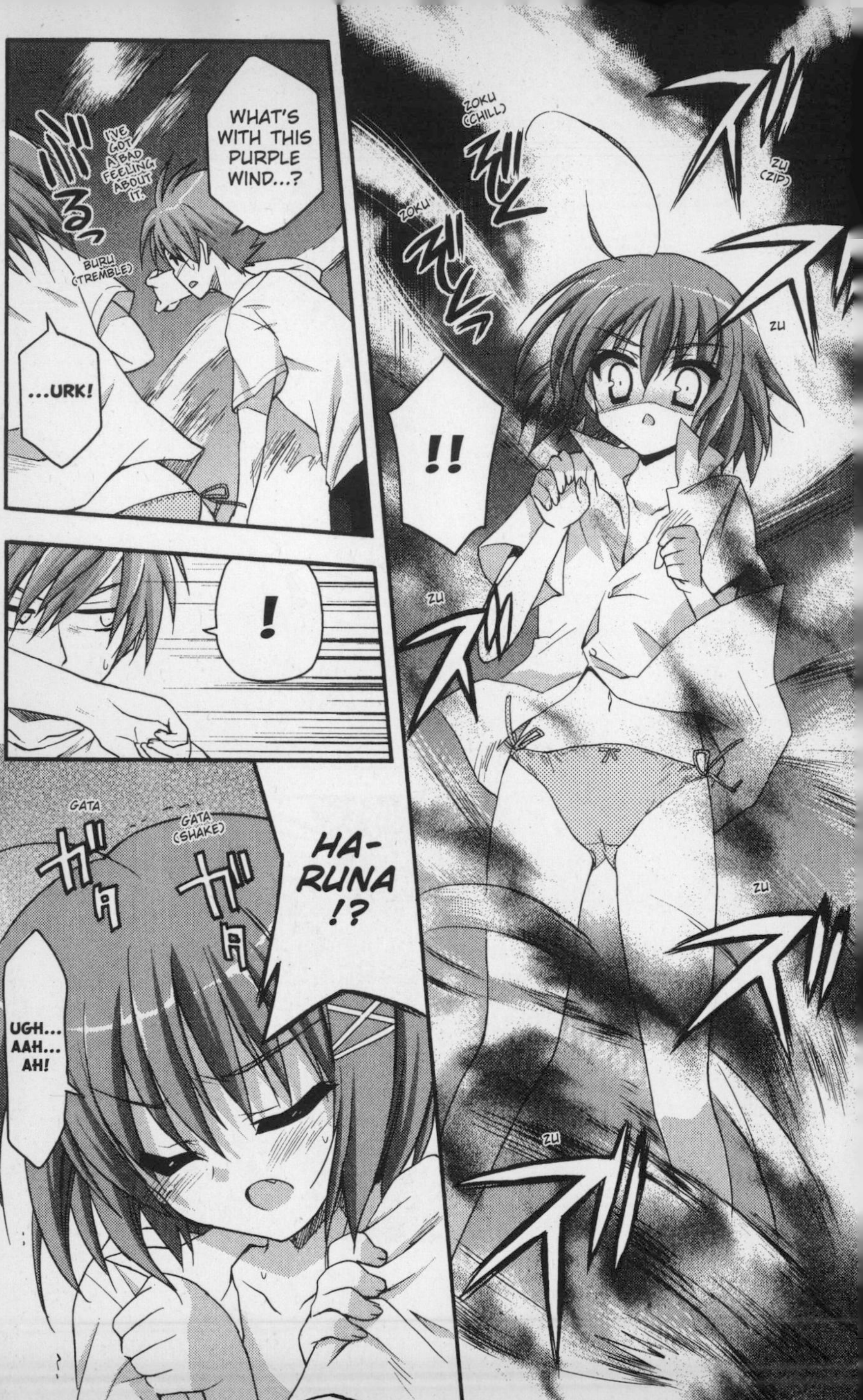
ZU (ZIP)
ZOKU (CHILL)
ZOKU
ZU
!!
ZU
ZU
ZU
WHAT'S WITH THIS PURPLE WIND...?
I'VE GOT A BAD FEELING ABOUT IT.
BURU (TREMBLE)
...URK!
!
HA-RUNA!?
GATA (SHAKE)
GATA
UGH... AAH... AH!

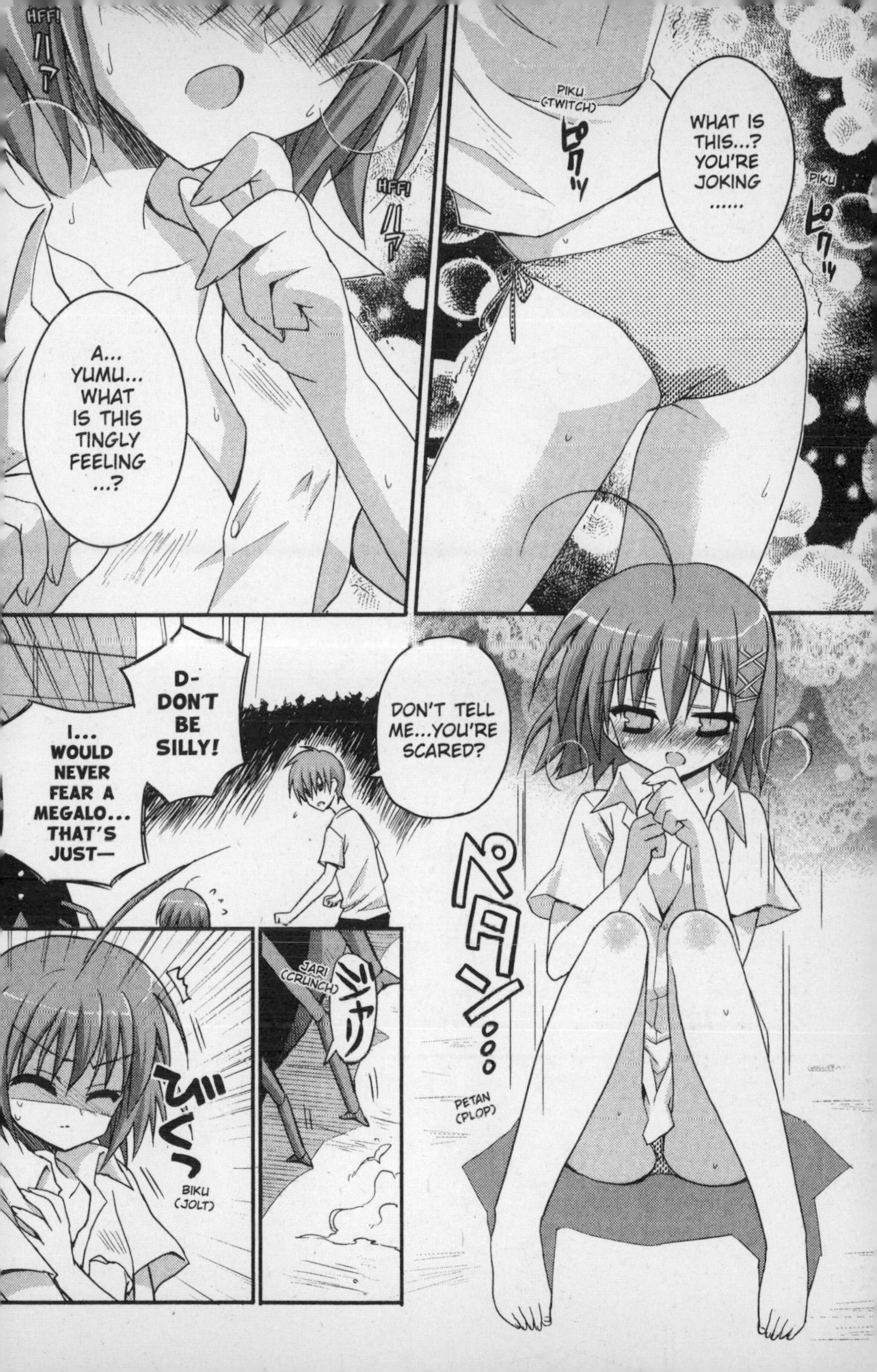
WHAT IS THIS...? YOU'RE JOKING ......
PIKU
PIKU (TWITCH)
HFF!
HFF!
A... YUMU... WHAT IS THIS TINGLY FEELING ...?
DON'T TELL ME...YOU'RE SCARED?
PETAN (PLOP)
D-DON'T BE SILLY!
I... WOULD NEVER FEAR A MEGALO... THAT'S JUST—
JARI (CRUNCH)
BIKU (JOLT)

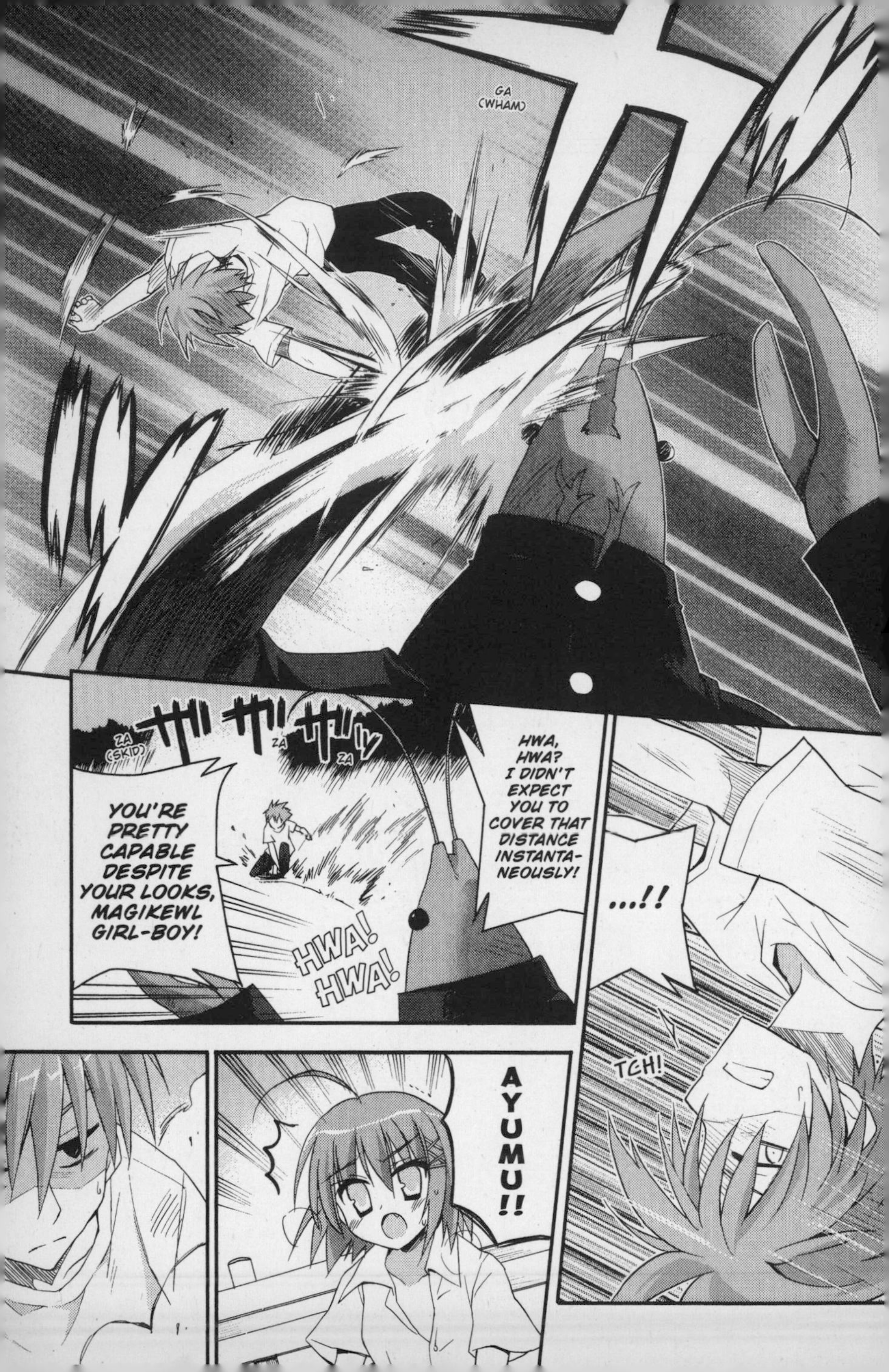
GA (WHAM)
...!!
TCH!
HWA, HWA? I DIDN'T EXPECT YOU TO COVER THAT DISTANCE INSTANTANEOUSLY!
ZA (SKID) ZA ZA
YOU'RE PRETTY CAPABLE DESPITE YOUR LOOKS, MAGIKEWL GIRL-BOY!
HWA! HWA!
AYUMU!!

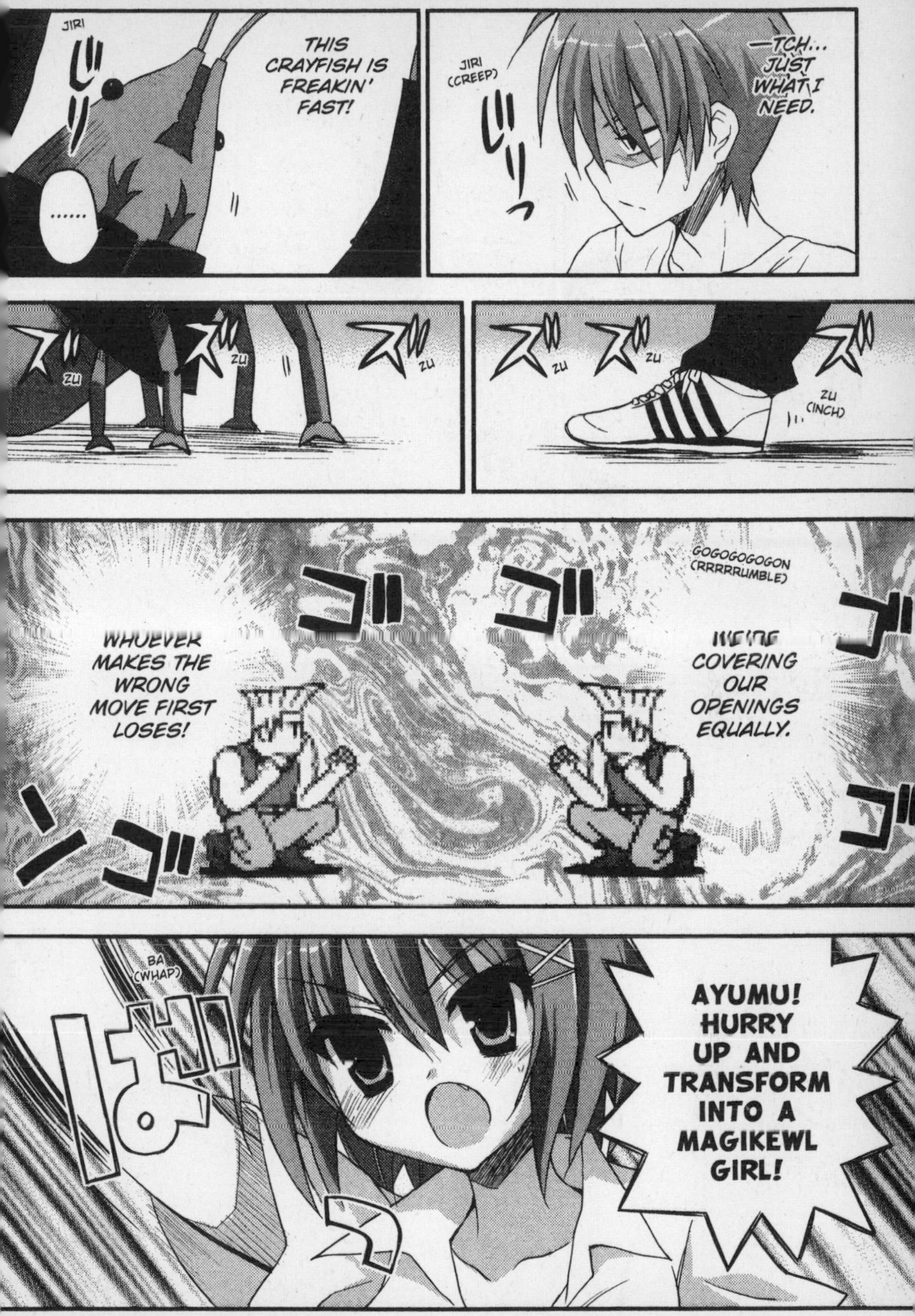
JIRI (CREEP)
—TCH... JUST WHAT I NEED.
JIRI
THIS CRAYFISH IS FREAKIN' FAST!
......
ZU
ZU
ZU (INCH)
ZU
ZU
ZU
GOGOGOGOGON (RRRRRUMBLE)
COVERING OUR OPENINGS EQUALLY.
WHOEVER MAKES THE WRONG MOVE FIRST LOSES!
BA (WHAP)
AYUMU! HURRY UP AND TRANSFORM INTO A MAGIKEWL GIRL!

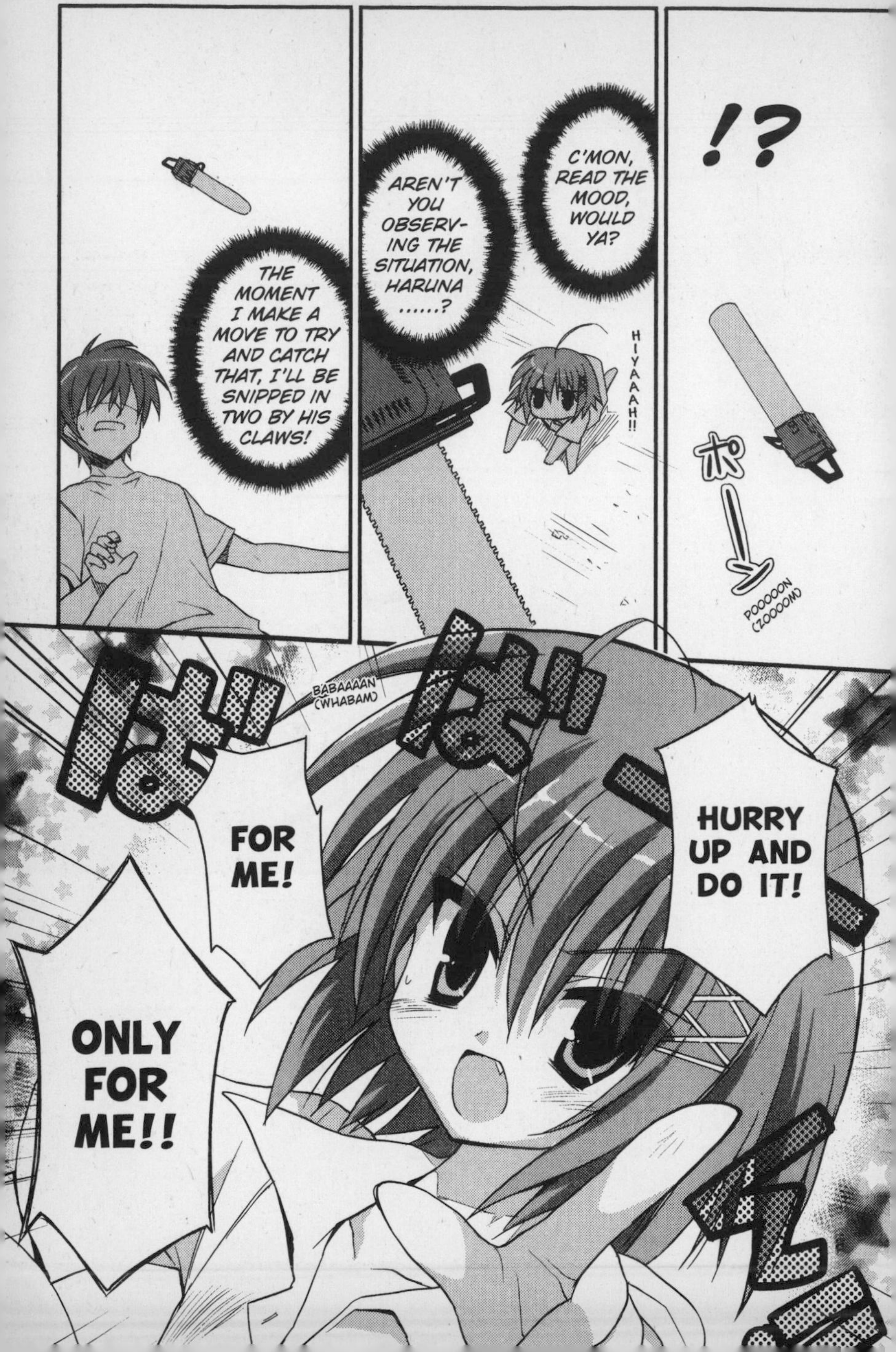

!?
ポーン
POOOOON (ZOOOOOM)
C'MON, READ THE MOOD, WOULD YA?
AREN'T YOU OBSERV-ING THE SITUATION, HARUNA ......?
HIYAAAH!!
THE MOMENT I MAKE A MOVE TO TRY AND CATCH THAT, I'LL BE SNIPPED IN TWO BY HIS CLAWS!
HURRY UP AND DO IT!
BABAAAAN (WHABAM)
FOR ME!
ONLY FOR ME!!

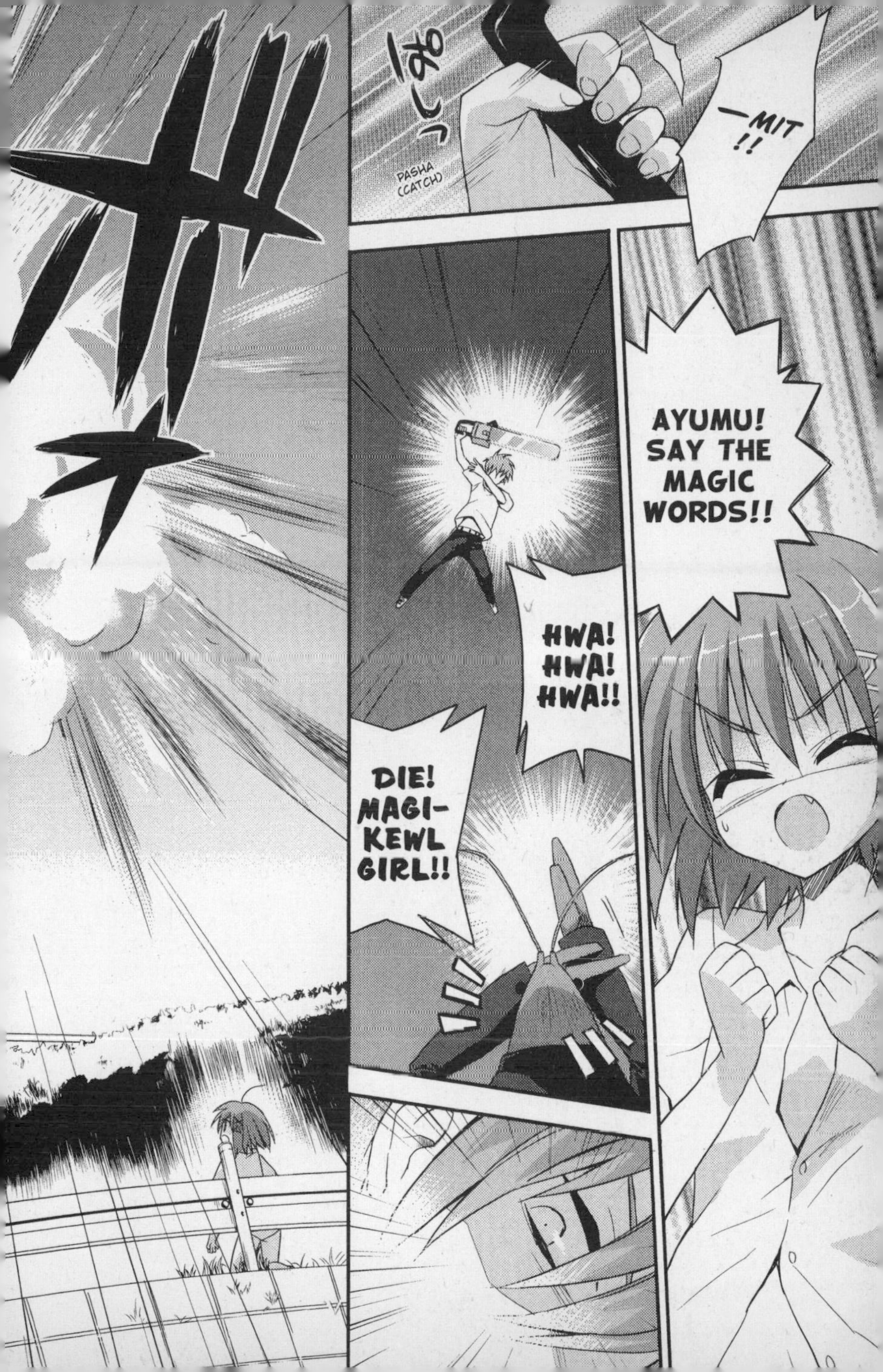

—MIT !!
ぱしっ
PASHA (CATCH)
AYUMU! SAY THE MAGIC WORDS!!
HWA! HWA! HWA!!
DIE! MAGI-KEWL GIRL!!

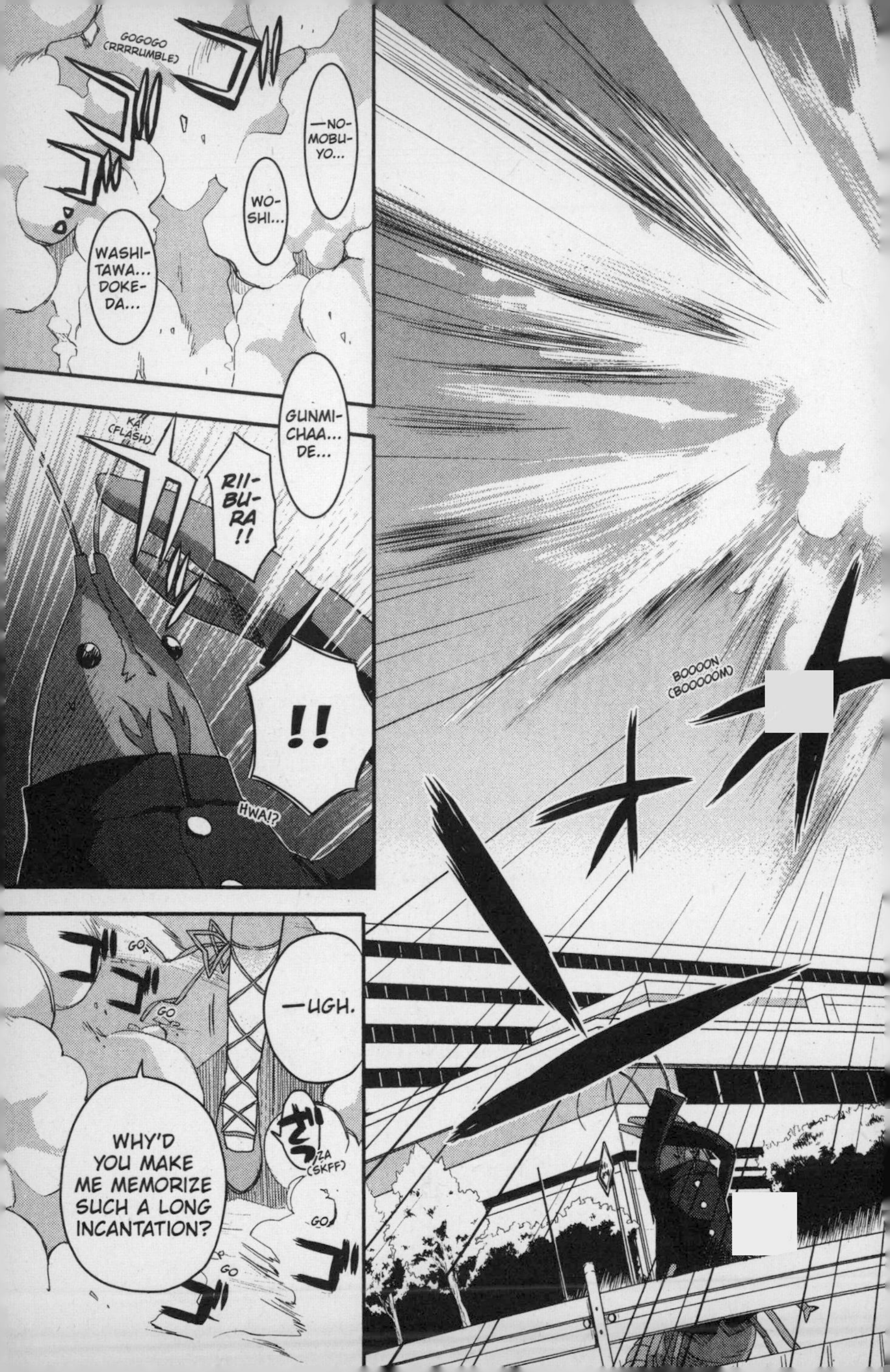
GOGOGO (RRRRUMBLE)
—NO-MOBU-YO...
WO-SHI...
WASHI-TAWA... DOKE-DA...
GUNMI-CHAA... DE...
RII-BU-RA!!
KA (FLASH)
!!
HWA!?
BOOOON (BOOOOOM)
—UGH.
GO
GO
WHY'D YOU MAKE ME MEMORIZE SUCH A LONG INCANTATION?
ZA (SKFF)
GO
GO

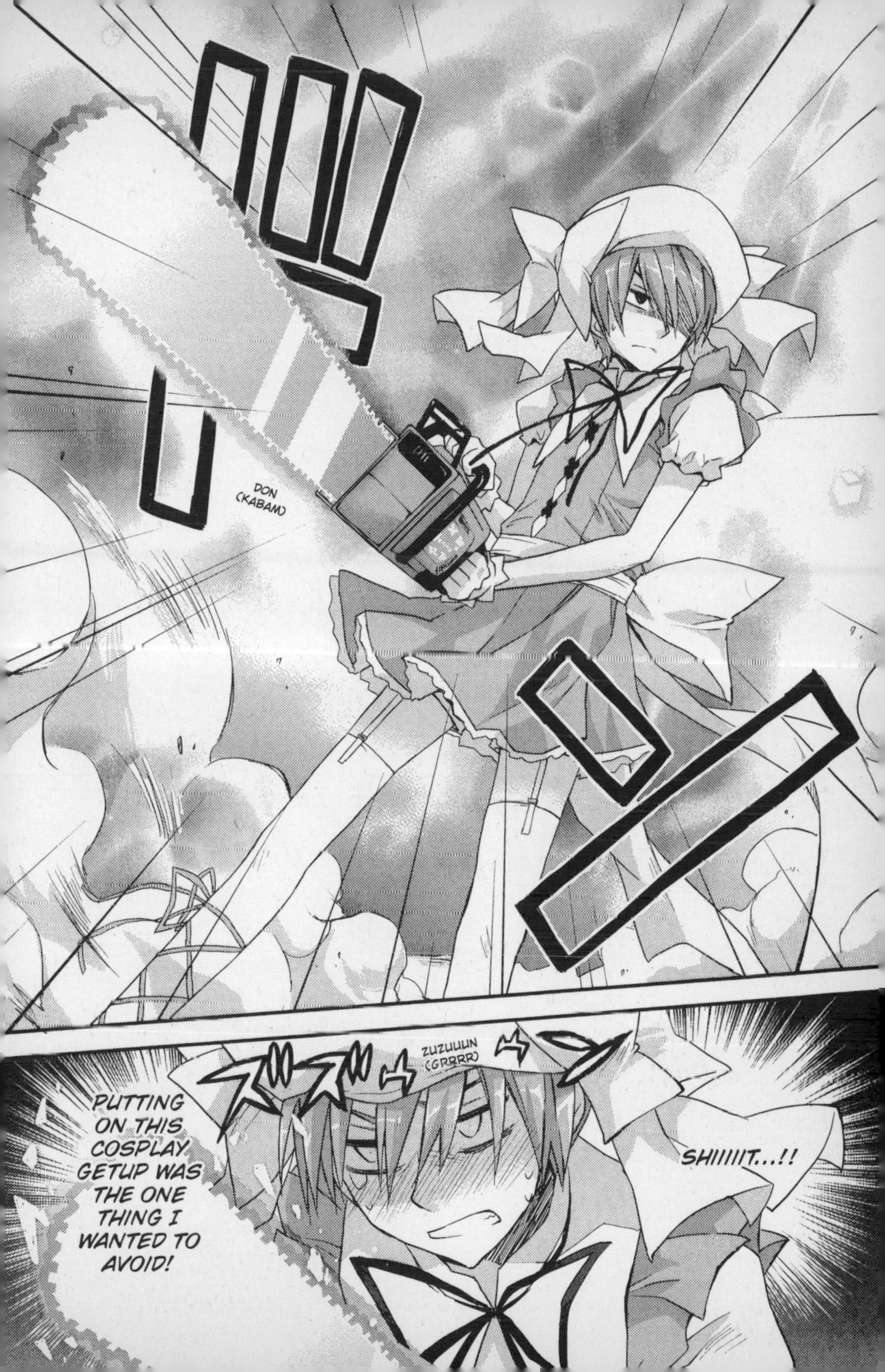
DON
(KABAM)
ZUZUUUN
(GRRRR)
SHIIIIIT...!!
PUTTING ON THIS COSPLAY GETUP WAS THE ONE THING I WANTED TO AVOID!

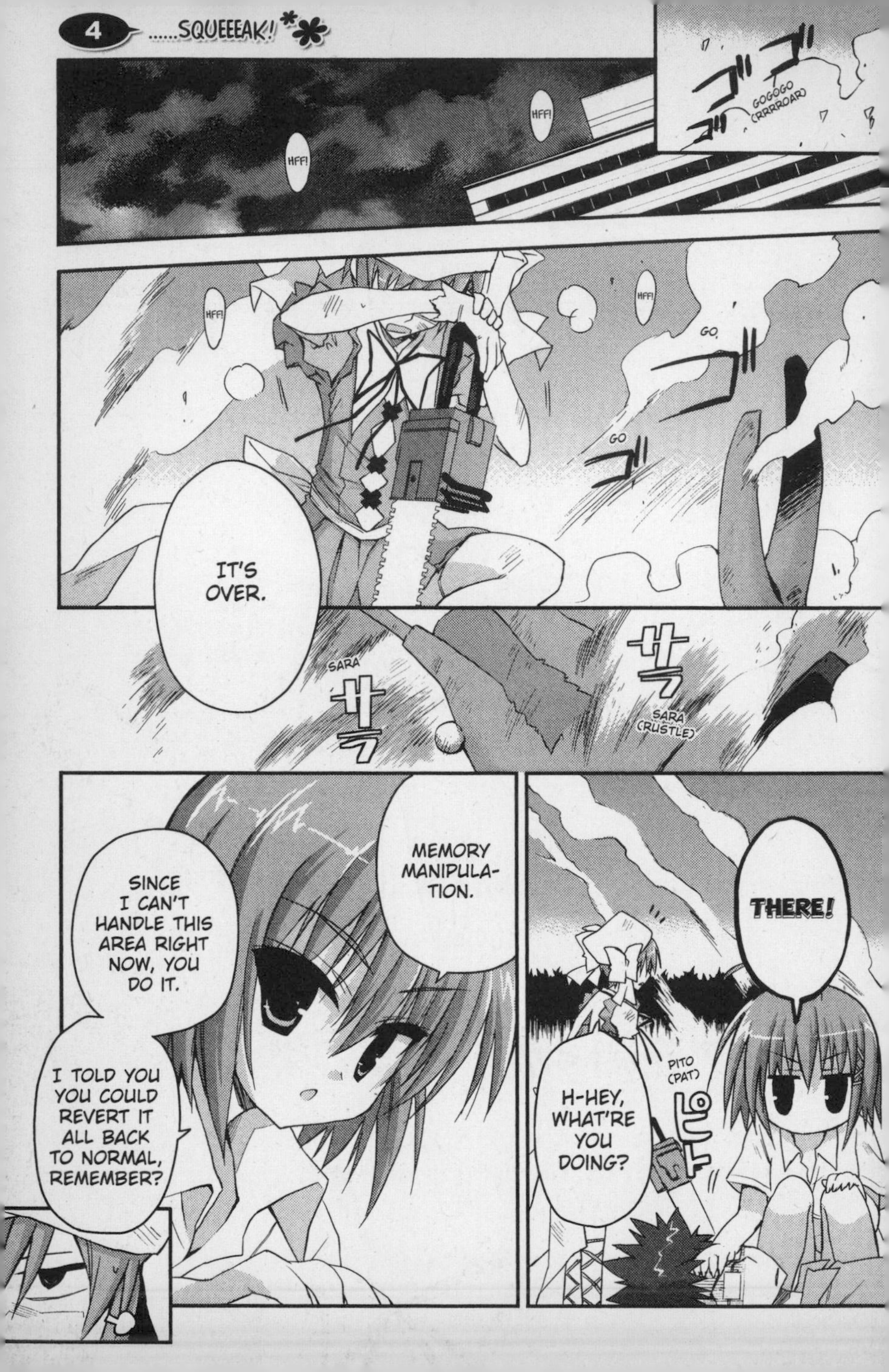
GOGOGO (RRRROAR)
HFF!
HFF!
HFF!
HFF!
GO
GO
IT'S OVER.
SARA (RUSTLE)
SARA
THERE!
PITO (PAT)
H-HEY, WHAT'RE YOU DOING?
MEMORY MANIPULATION.
SINCE I CAN'T HANDLE THIS AREA RIGHT NOW, YOU DO IT.
I TOLD YOU YOU COULD REVERT IT ALL BACK TO NORMAL, REMEMBER?

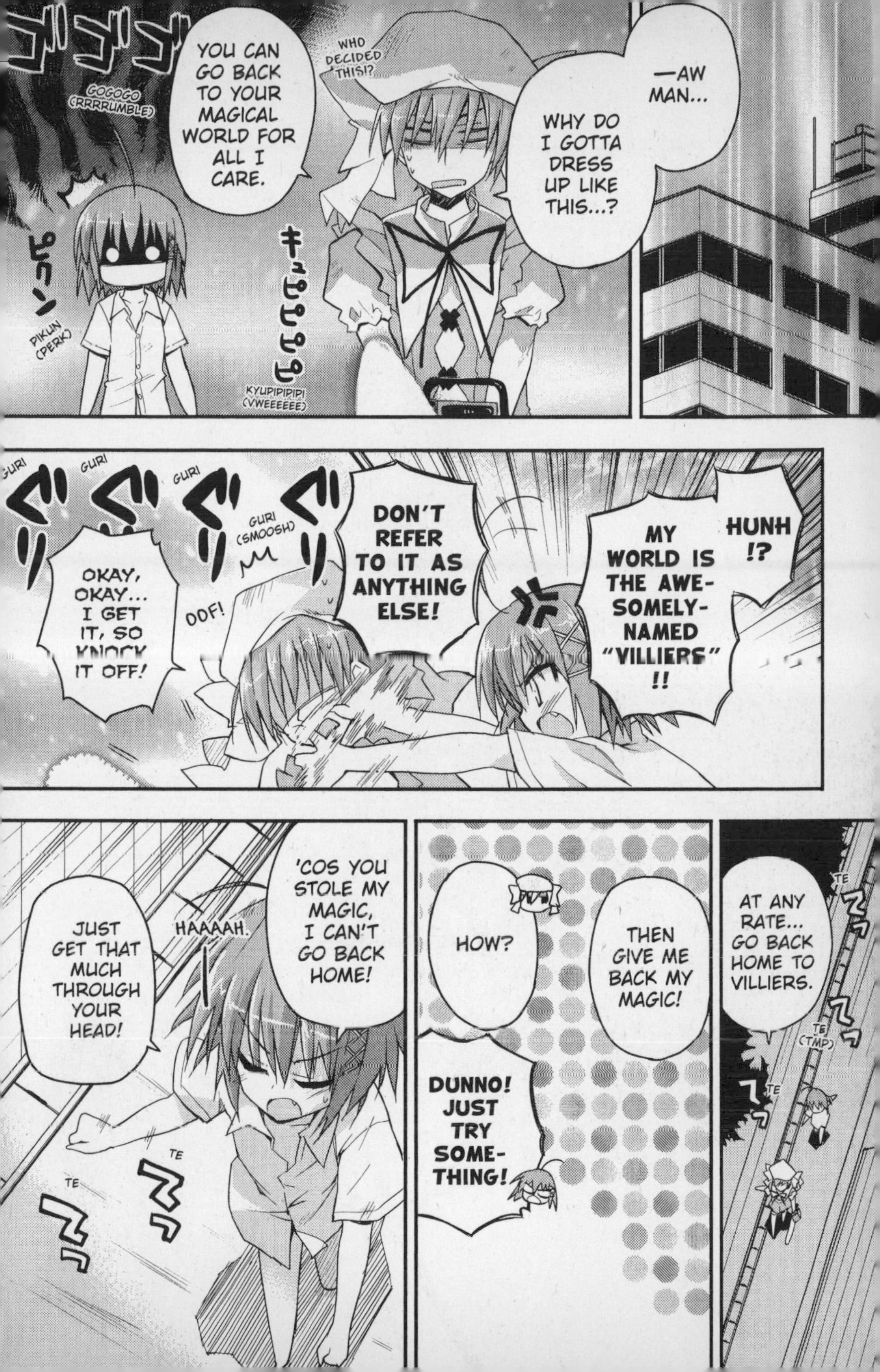
—AW MAN...
WHY DO I GOTTA DRESS UP LIKE THIS...?
WHO DECIDED THIS!?
YOU CAN GO BACK TO YOUR MAGICAL WORLD FOR ALL I CARE.
GOGOGO (RRRRUMBLE)
KYUPIPIPIPI (VWEEEEEE)
PIKUN (PERK)
HUNH !?
MY WORLD IS THE AWE-SOMELY-NAMED "VILLIERS" !!
DON'T REFER TO IT AS ANYTHING ELSE!
GURI
GURI (SMOOSH)
GURI
GURI
OOF!
OKAY, OKAY... I GET IT, SO KNOCK IT OFF!
AT ANY RATE... GO BACK HOME TO VILLIERS.
TE
TE (TMP)
TE
THEN GIVE ME BACK MY MAGIC!
HOW?
DUNNO! JUST TRY SOME-THING!
'COS YOU STOLE MY MAGIC, I CAN'T GO BACK HOME!
HAAAAH.
JUST GET THAT MUCH THROUGH YOUR HEAD!
TE
TE

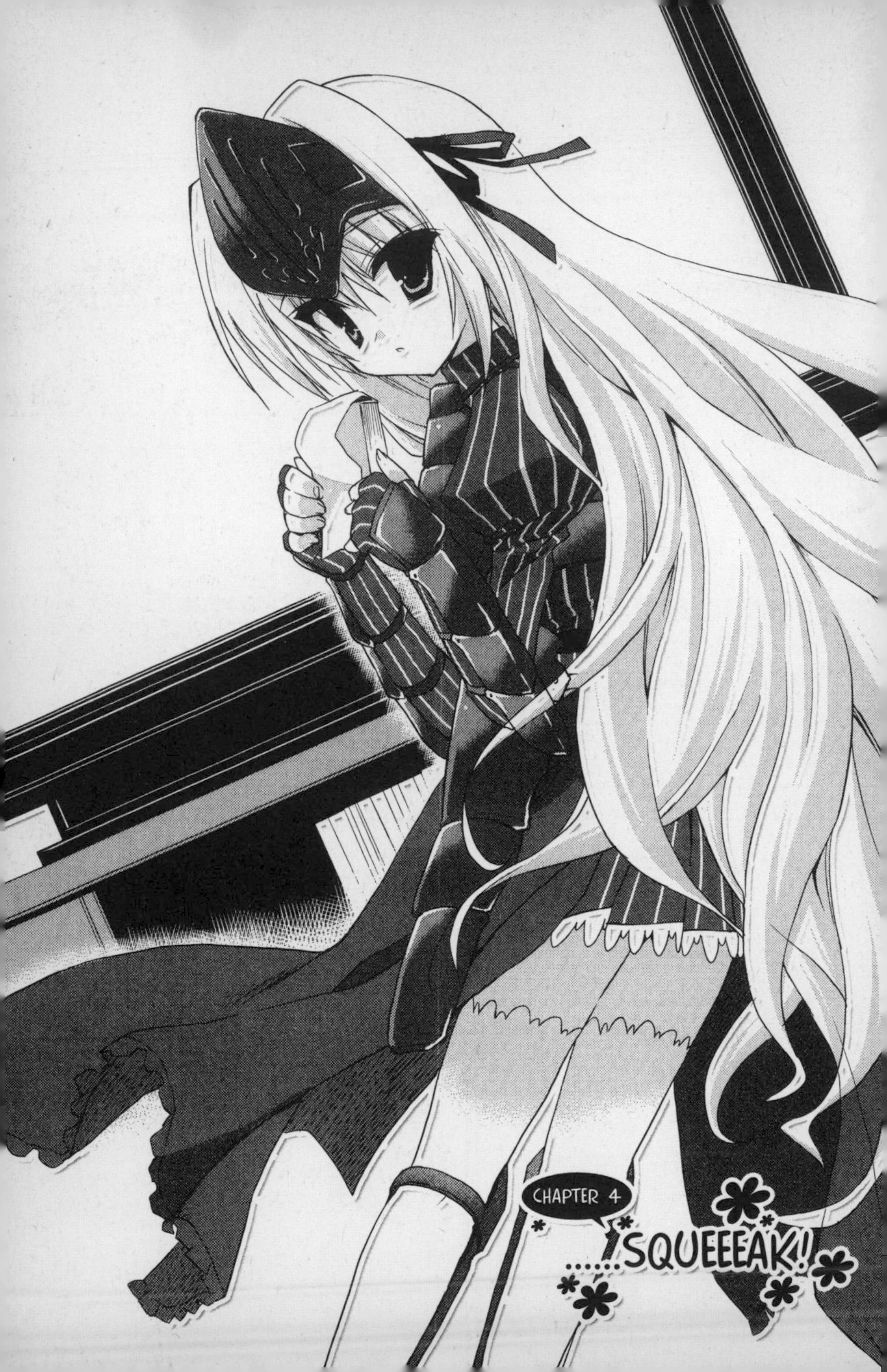
CHAPTER 4
......SQUEEEAK!

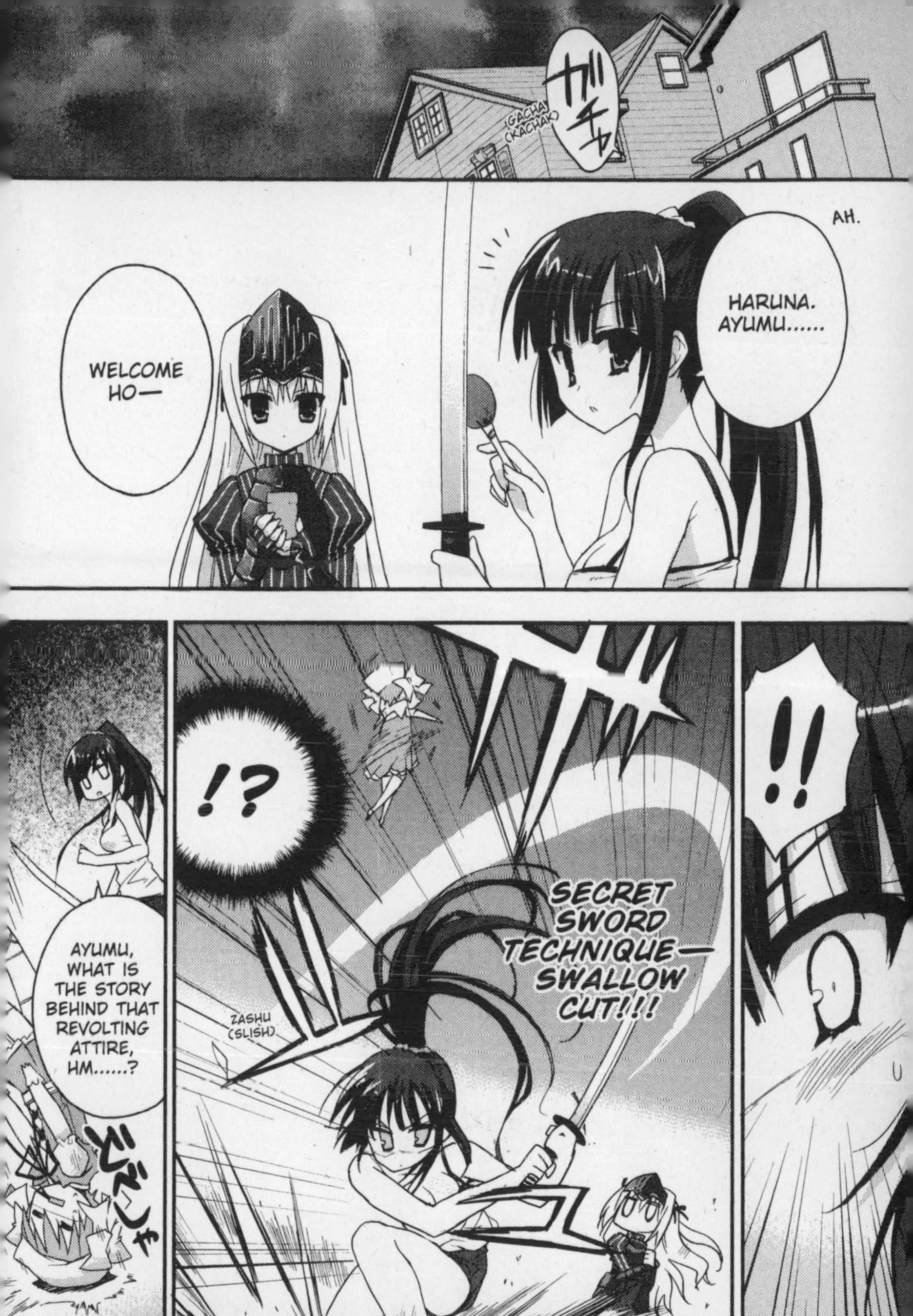
ガチャ
GACHA (KACHAK)
AH.
HARUNA. AYUMU......
WELCOME HO—
!!
SECRET SWORD TECHNIQUE—SWALLOW CUT!!!
!?
ZASHU (SLISH)
AYUMU, WHAT IS THE STORY BEHIND THAT REVOLTING ATTIRE, HM......?
どべしゃ

SFX: DOBESHA (CRUNCH)

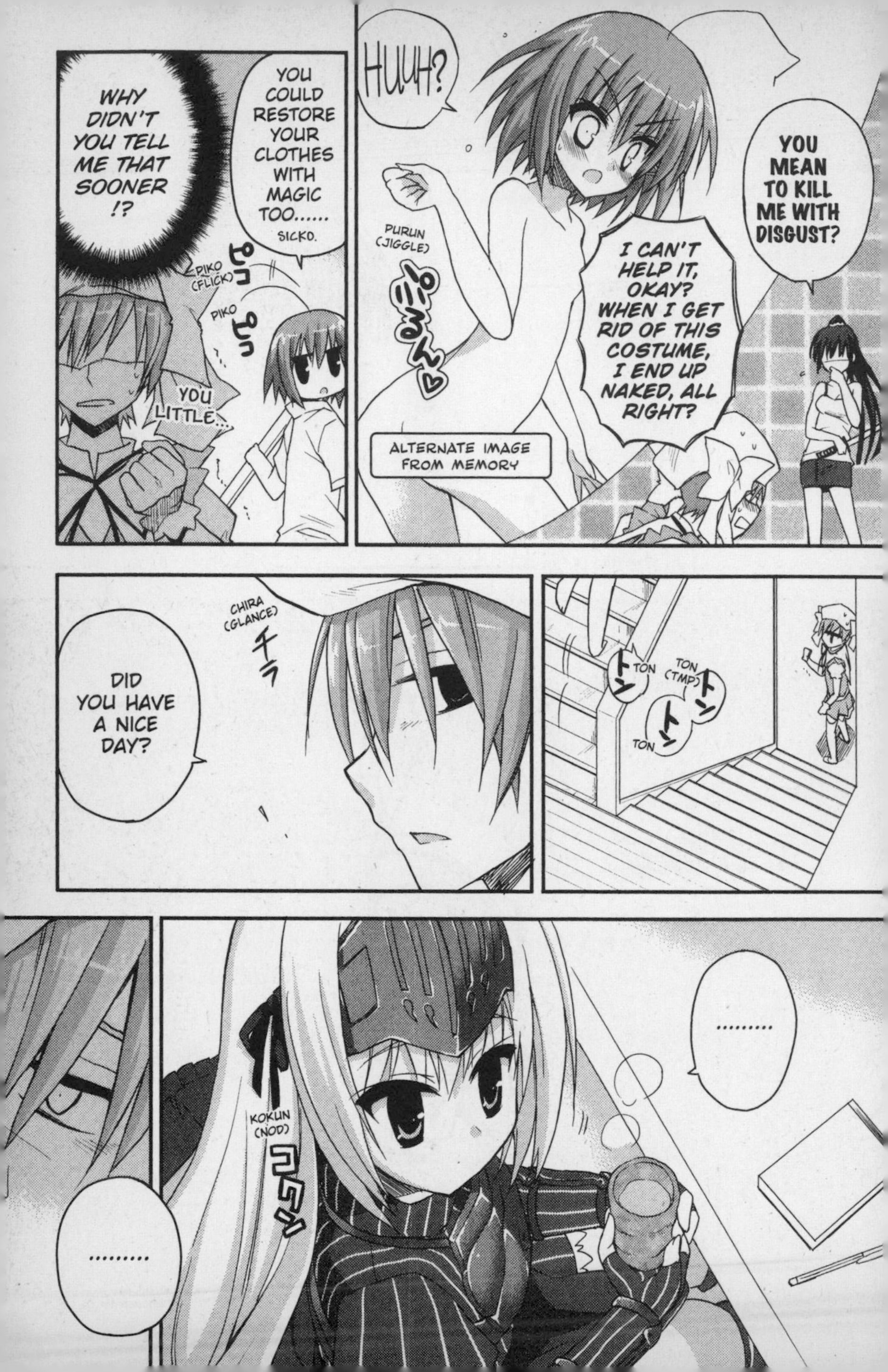

YOU MEAN TO KILL ME WITH DISGUST?
HUUH?
I CAN'T HELP IT, OKAY? WHEN I GET RID OF THIS COSTUME, I END UP NAKED, ALL RIGHT?
PURUN (JIGGLE)
ALTERNATE IMAGE FROM MEMORY
YOU COULD RESTORE YOUR CLOTHES WITH MAGIC TOO......
SICKO.
WHY DIDN'T YOU TELL ME THAT SOONER !?
PIKO (FLICK)
PIKO
YOU LITTLE....
TON
TON (TMP)
TON
CHIRA (GLANCE)
DID YOU HAVE A NICE DAY?
....
KOKUN (NOD)
....

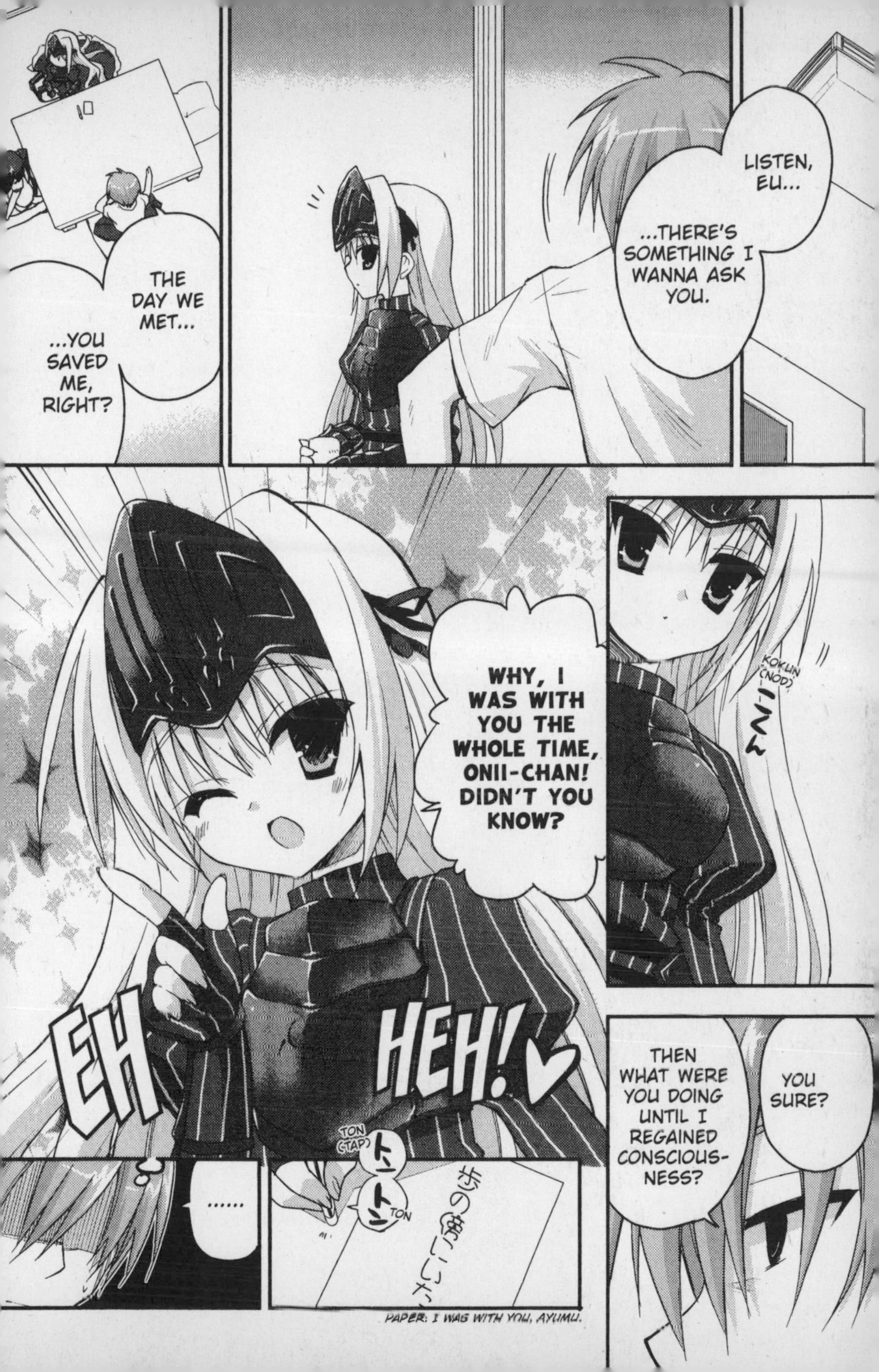
LISTEN, EU...
...THERE'S SOMETHING I WANNA ASK YOU.
THE DAY WE MET...
...YOU SAVED ME, RIGHT?
KOKUN (NOD)
WHY, I WAS WITH YOU THE WHOLE TIME, ONII-CHAN! DIDN'T YOU KNOW?
EH HEH!♥
YOU SURE?
THEN WHAT WERE YOU DOING UNTIL I REGAINED CONSCIOUS-NESS?
TON (TAP)
TON
......
PAPER: I WAS WITH YOU, AYUMU.

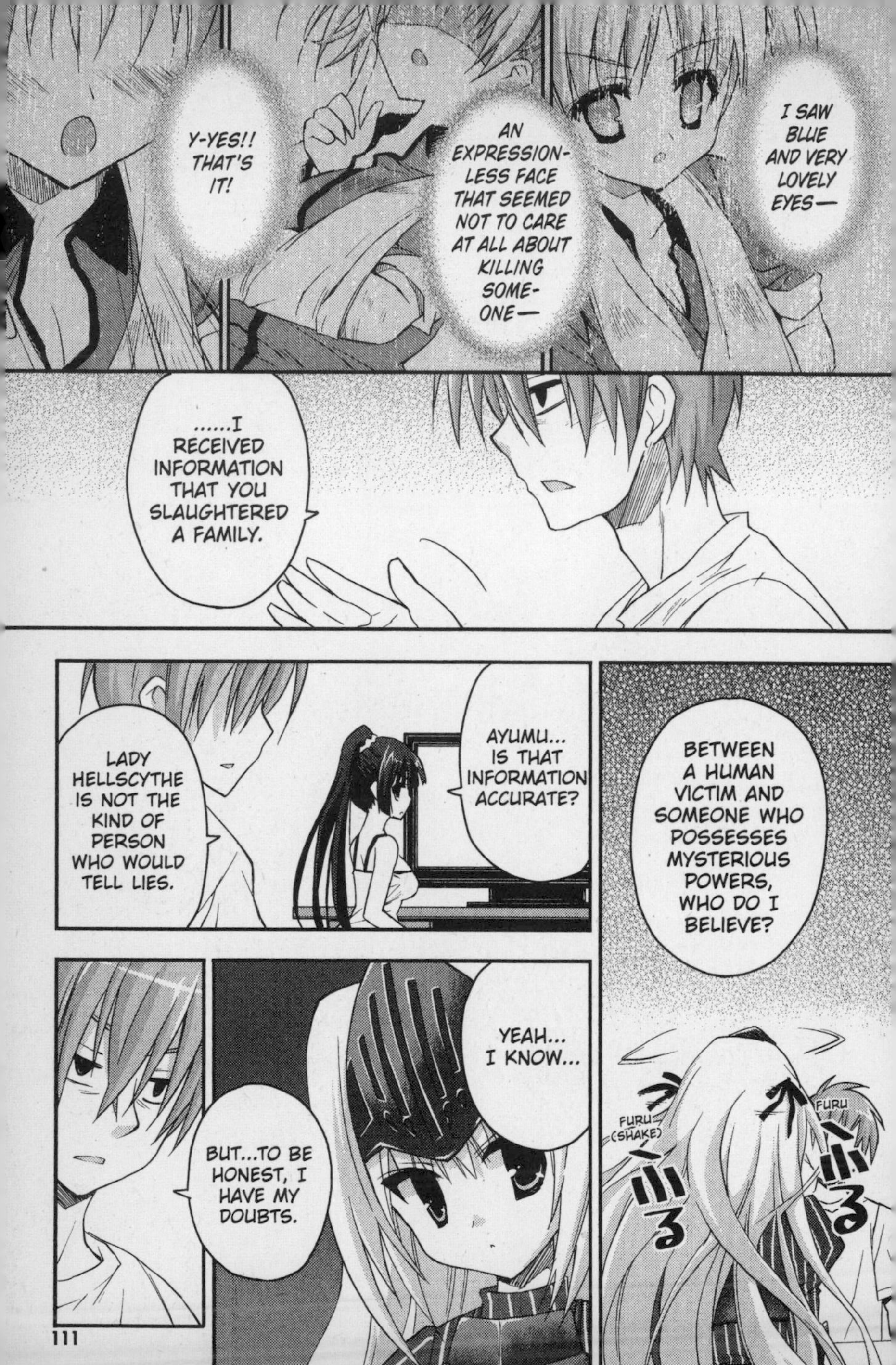
I SAW BLUE AND VERY LOVELY EYES—
AN EXPRESSIONLESS FACE THAT SEEMED NOT TO CARE AT ALL ABOUT KILLING SOMEONE—
Y-YES!! THAT'S IT!
......I RECEIVED INFORMATION THAT YOU SLAUGHTERED A FAMILY.
BETWEEN A HUMAN VICTIM AND SOMEONE WHO POSSESSES MYSTERIOUS POWERS, WHO DO I BELIEVE?
AYUMU... IS THAT INFORMATION ACCURATE?
LADY HELLSCYTHE IS NOT THE KIND OF PERSON WHO WOULD TELL LIES.
ふる
FURU
ふる
FURU (SHAKE)
YEAH... I KNOW...
BUT...TO BE HONEST, I HAVE MY DOUBTS.

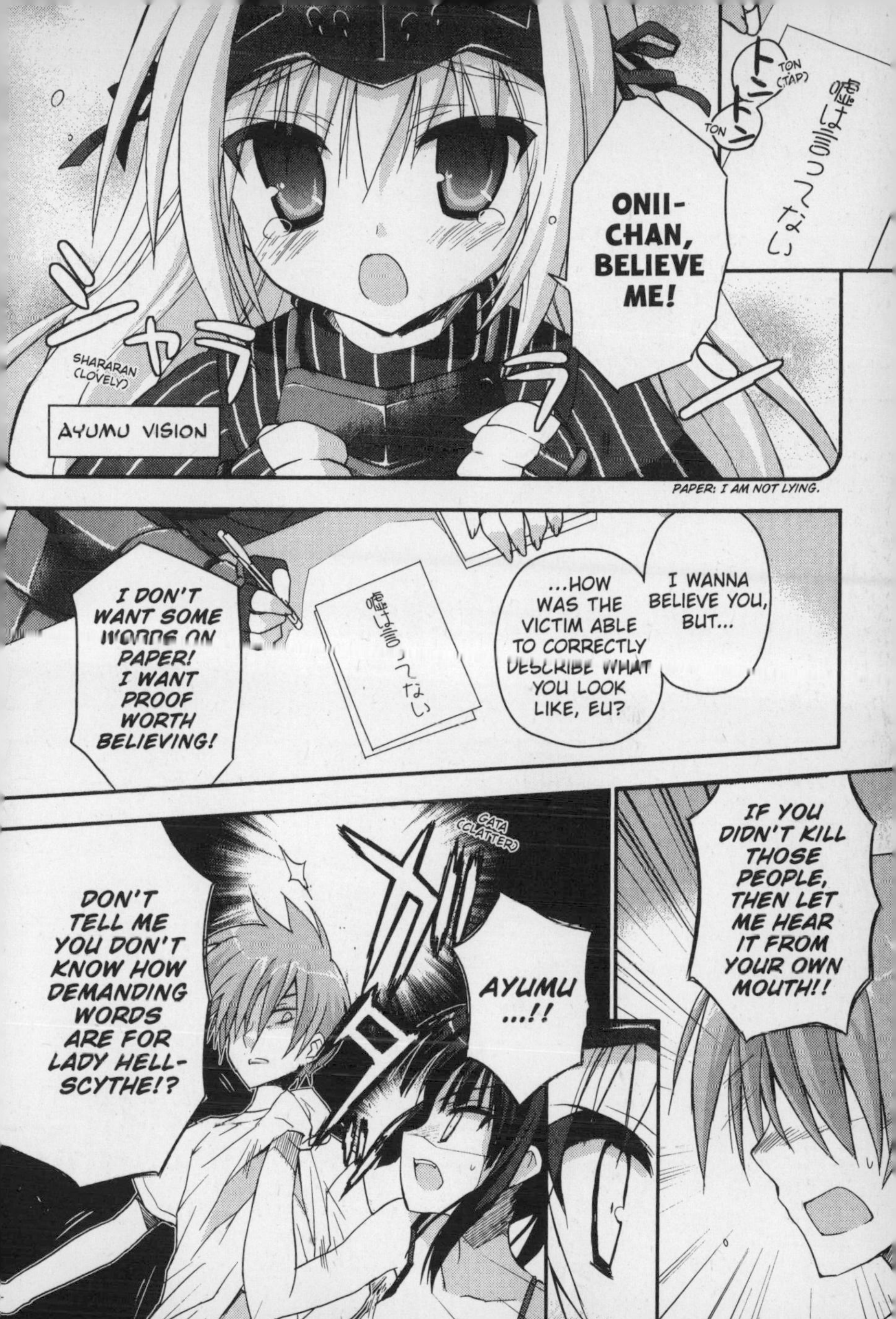
TON (TAP)
TON
嘘は言ってない
ONII-CHAN, BELIEVE ME!
SHARARAN (LOVELY)
AYUMU VISION
PAPER: I AM NOT LYING.
I WANNA BELIEVE YOU, BUT...
...HOW WAS THE VICTIM ABLE TO CORRECTLY DESCRIBE WHAT YOU LOOK LIKE, EU?
嘘は言ってない
I DON'T WANT SOME WORDS ON PAPER! I WANT PROOF WORTH BELIEVING!
IF YOU DIDN'T KILL THOSE PEOPLE, THEN LET ME HEAR IT FROM YOUR OWN MOUTH!!
GATA (CLATTER)
AYUMU ...!!
DON'T TELL ME YOU DON'T KNOW HOW DEMANDING WORDS ARE FOR LADY HELL-SCYTHE!?

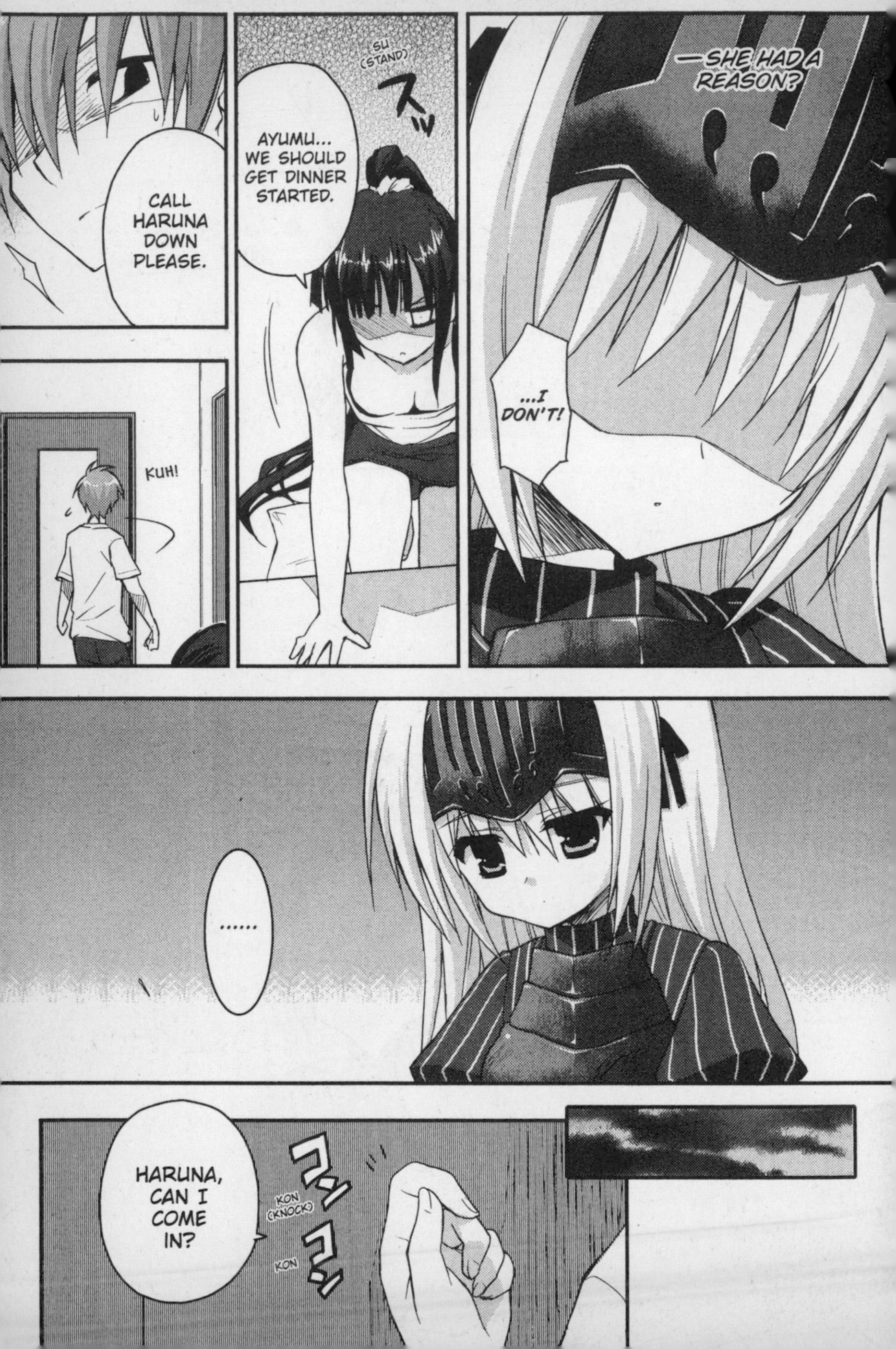
—SHE HAD A REASON?
...I DON'T!
SU (STAND)
AYUMU... WE SHOULD GET DINNER STARTED.
CALL HARUNA DOWN PLEASE.
KUH!
......
HARUNA, CAN I COME IN?
KON (KNOCK)
KON

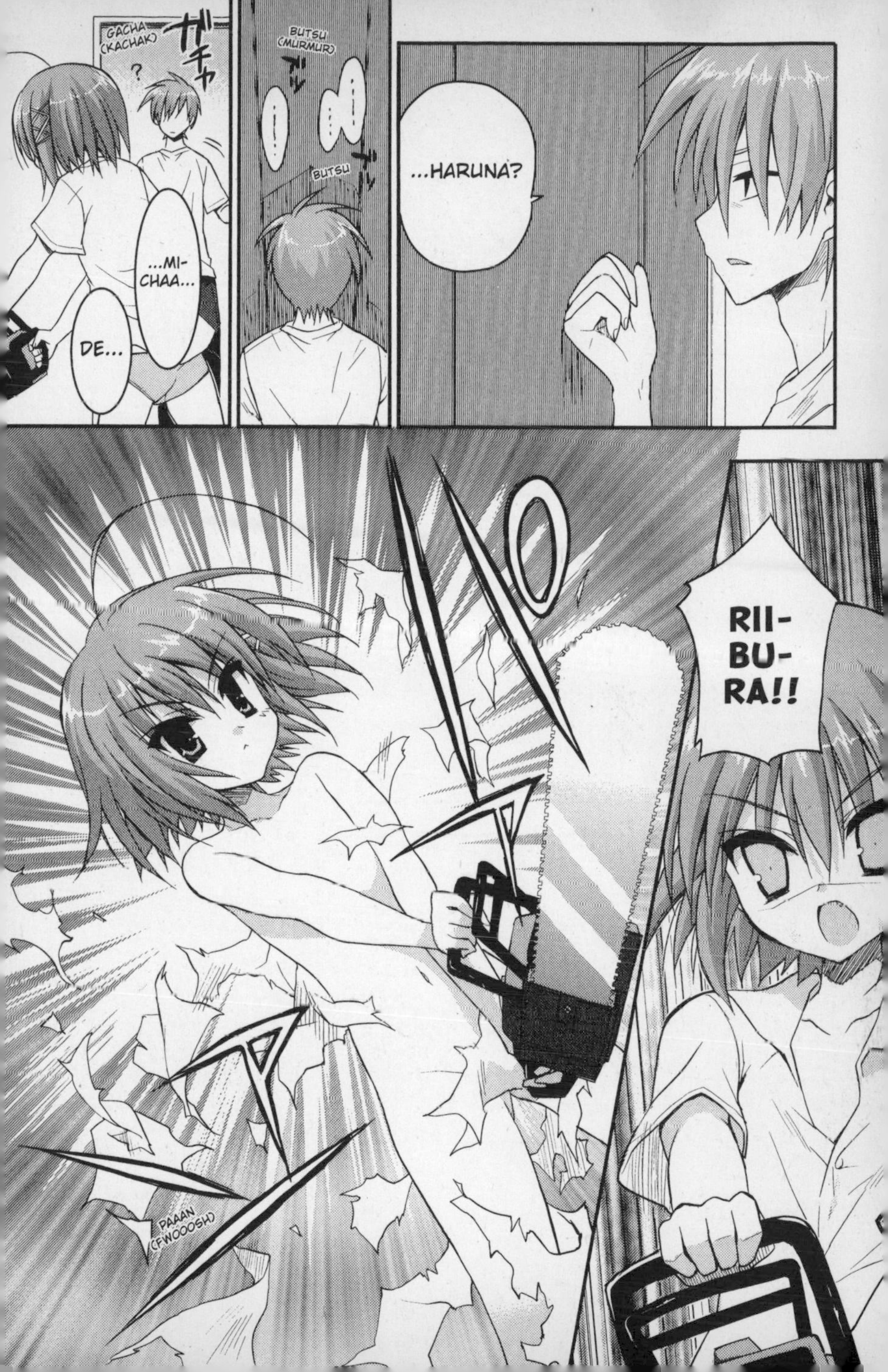
...HARUNA?
BUTSU (MURMUR)
ブツ
...!
...
...!
BUTSU
ブツ
GACHA (KACHAK)
ガチャ
?
...MI-CHAA...
DE...
RII-BU-RA!!
PAAAN (FWOOOSH)

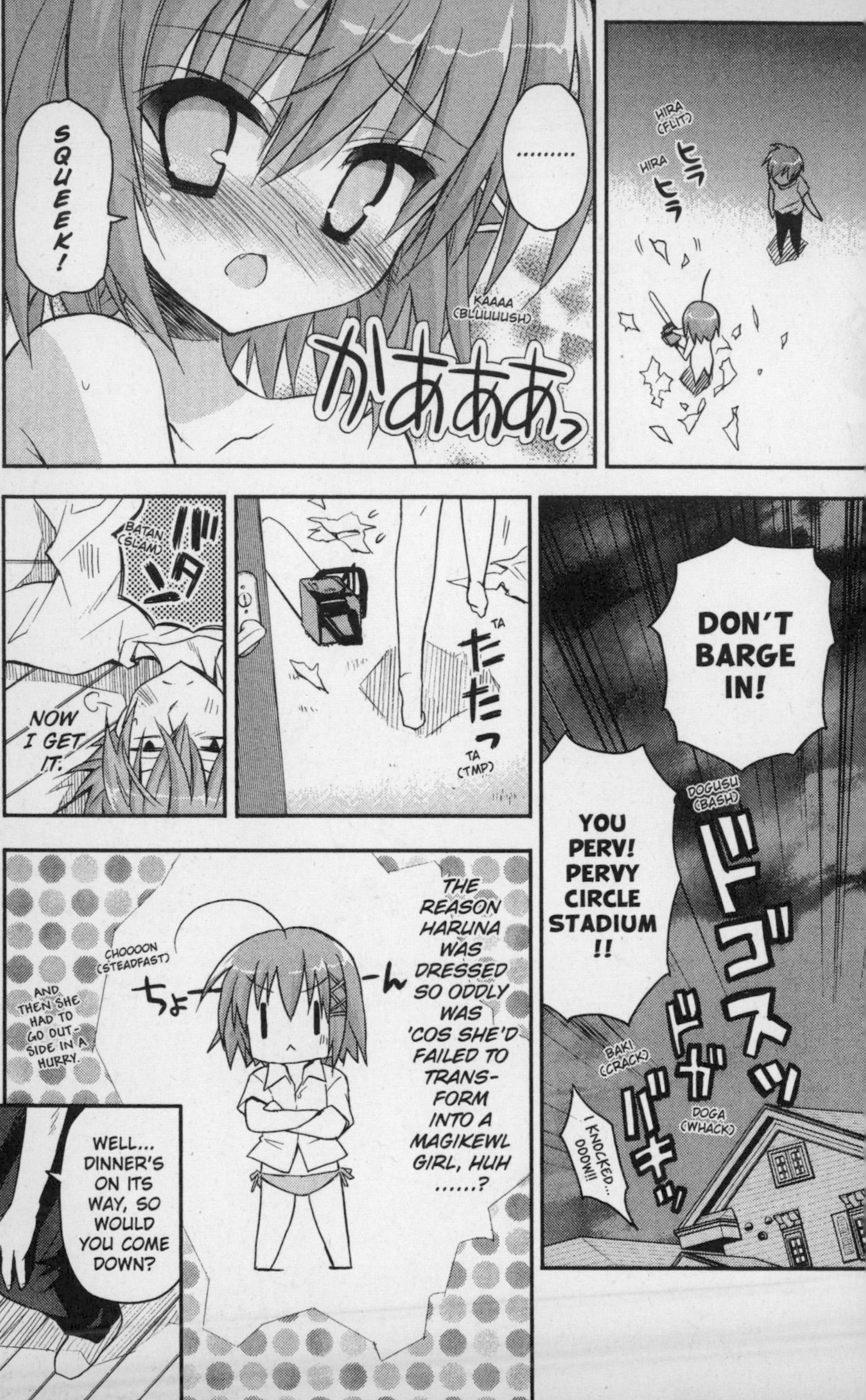
HIRA (FLIT)
ヒラ
HIRA
ヒラ
....
KAAAA (BLUUUUSH)
かあああっ
SQUEEK!
DON'T BARGE IN!
YOU PERV! PERVY CIRCLE STADIUM !!
DOGUSU (BASH)
ドゴスッ
DOGA (WHACK)
ドガ
BAKI (CRACK)
バキッ
I KNOCKED... DOOW!!
TA
たたっ
TA (TMP)
BATAN (SLAM)
バタン
NOW I GET IT.
THE REASON HARUNA WAS DRESSED SO ODDLY WAS 'COS SHE'D FAILED TO TRANS-FORM INTO A MAGIKEWL GIRL, HUH ......?
CHOOOON (STEADFAST)
ちょーん
AND THEN SHE HAD TO GO OUT-SIDE IN A HURRY.
WELL... DINNER'S ON ITS WAY, SO WOULD YOU COME DOWN?

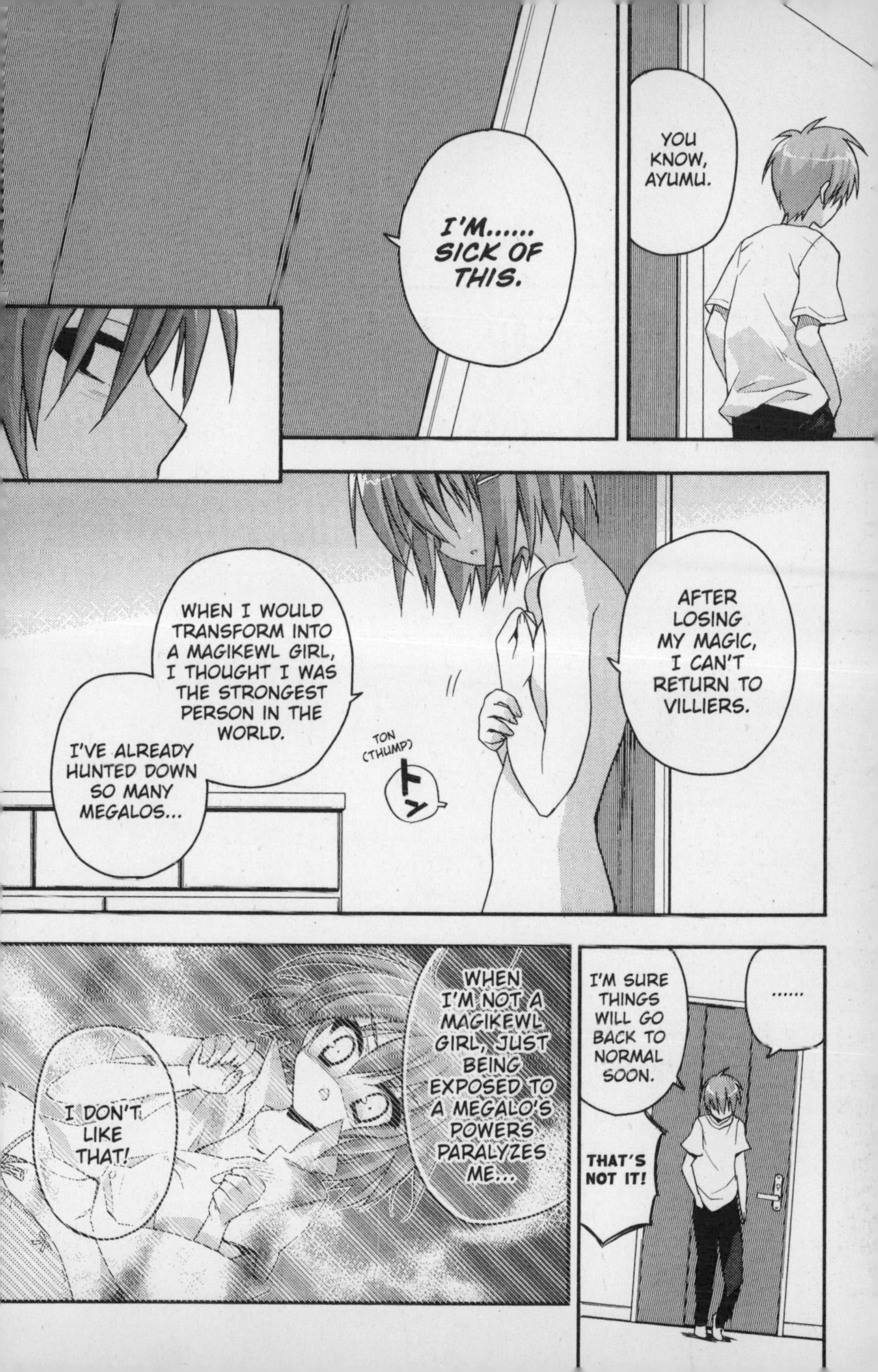

YOU KNOW, AYUMU.
I'M...... SICK OF THIS.
AFTER LOSING MY MAGIC, I CAN'T RETURN TO VILLIERS.
トン
TON (THUMP)
WHEN I WOULD TRANSFORM INTO A MAGIKEWL GIRL, I THOUGHT I WAS THE STRONGEST PERSON IN THE WORLD.
I'VE ALREADY HUNTED DOWN SO MANY MEGALOS...
......
I'M SURE THINGS WILL GO BACK TO NORMAL SOON.
THAT'S NOT IT!
WHEN I'M NOT A MAGIKEWL GIRL, JUST BEING EXPOSED TO A MEGALO'S POWERS PARALYZES ME...
I DON'T LIKE THAT!

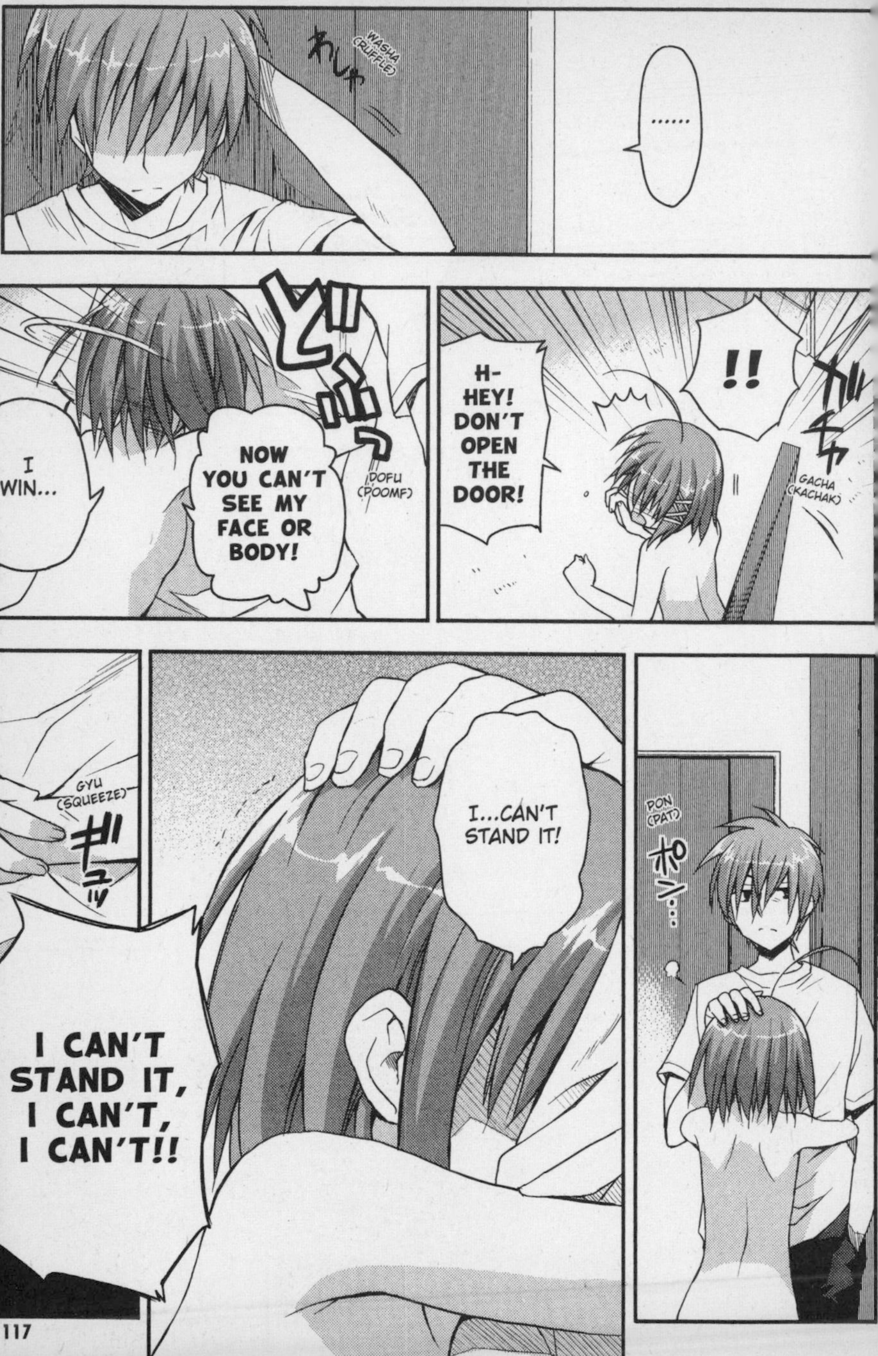
......
わしゃ
WASHA (RUFFLE)
!!
GACHA (KACHAK)
H-HEY! DON'T OPEN THE DOOR!
DOFU (POOMF)
NOW YOU CAN'T SEE MY FACE OR BODY!
I WIN...
PON (PAT)
I...CAN'T STAND IT!
GYU (SQUEEZE)
I CAN'T STAND IT, I CAN'T, I CAN'T!!

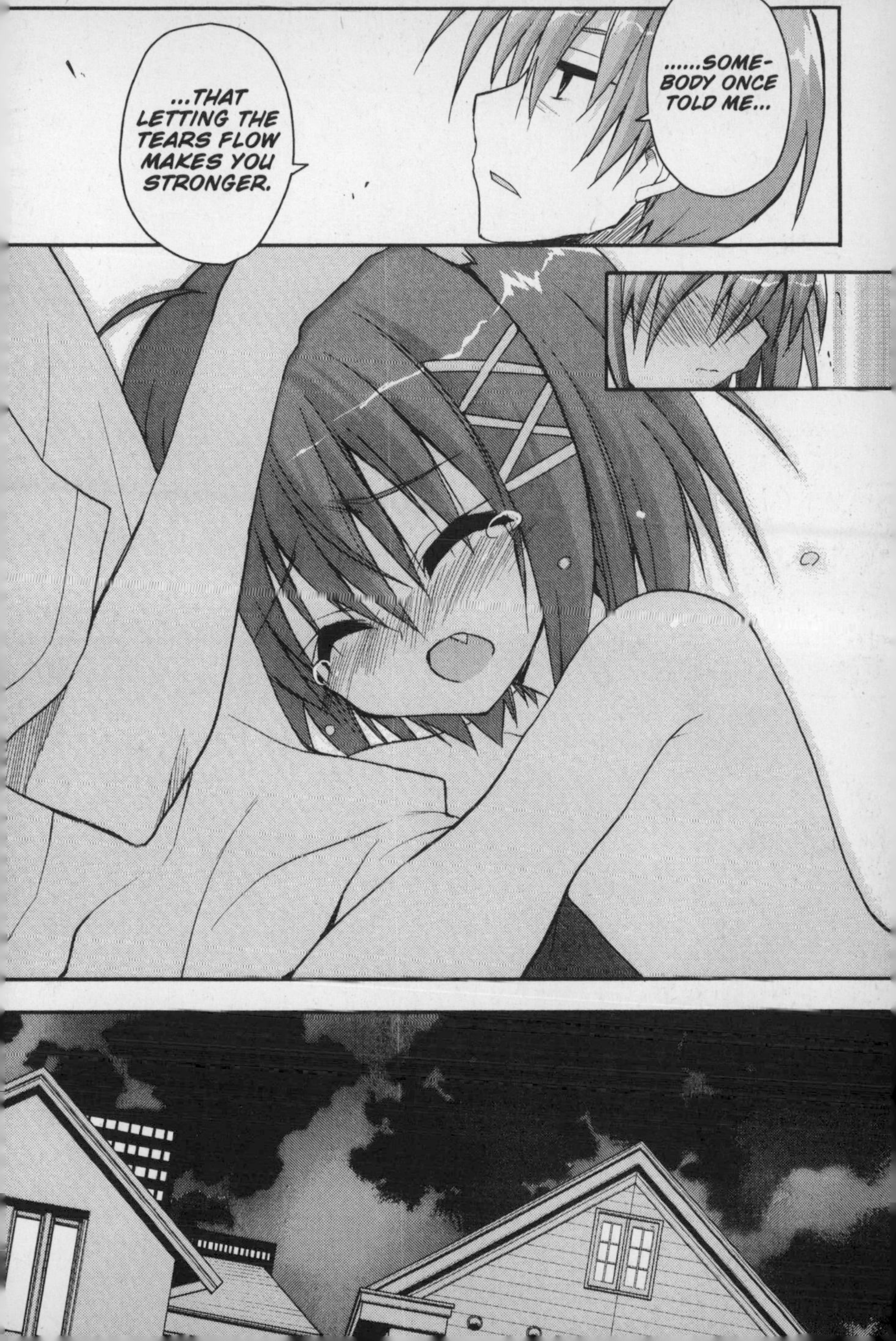
......SOME-BODY ONCE TOLD ME...
...THAT LETTING THE TEARS FLOW MAKES YOU STRONGER.

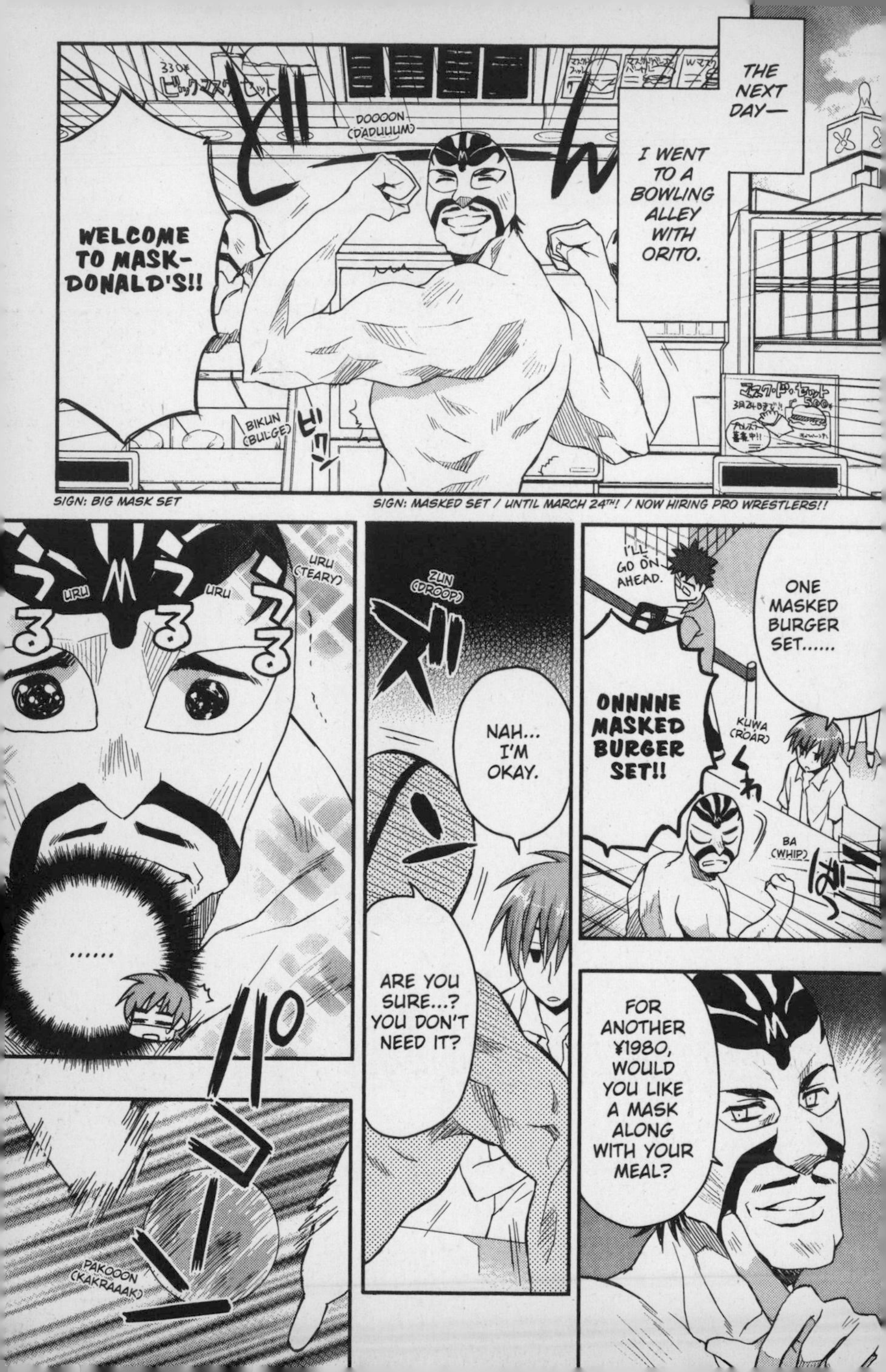
THE NEXT DAY—
I WENT TO A BOWLING ALLEY WITH ORITO.
DOOOON (DADUUUM)
WELCOME TO MASK-DONALD'S!!
BIKUN (BULGE)
SIGN: BIG MASK SET
SIGN: MASKED SET / UNTIL MARCH 24TH! / NOW HIRING PRO WRESTLERS!!
ONE MASKED BURGER SET......
I'LL GO ON AHEAD.
ONNNNE MASKED BURGER SET!!
KUWA (ROAR)
BA (WHIP)
FOR ANOTHER ¥1980, WOULD YOU LIKE A MASK ALONG WITH YOUR MEAL?
ZUN (DROOP)
NAH... I'M OKAY.
ARE YOU SURE...? YOU DON'T NEED IT?
URU (TEARY)
URU
URU
......
PAKOOON (KAKRAAAK)

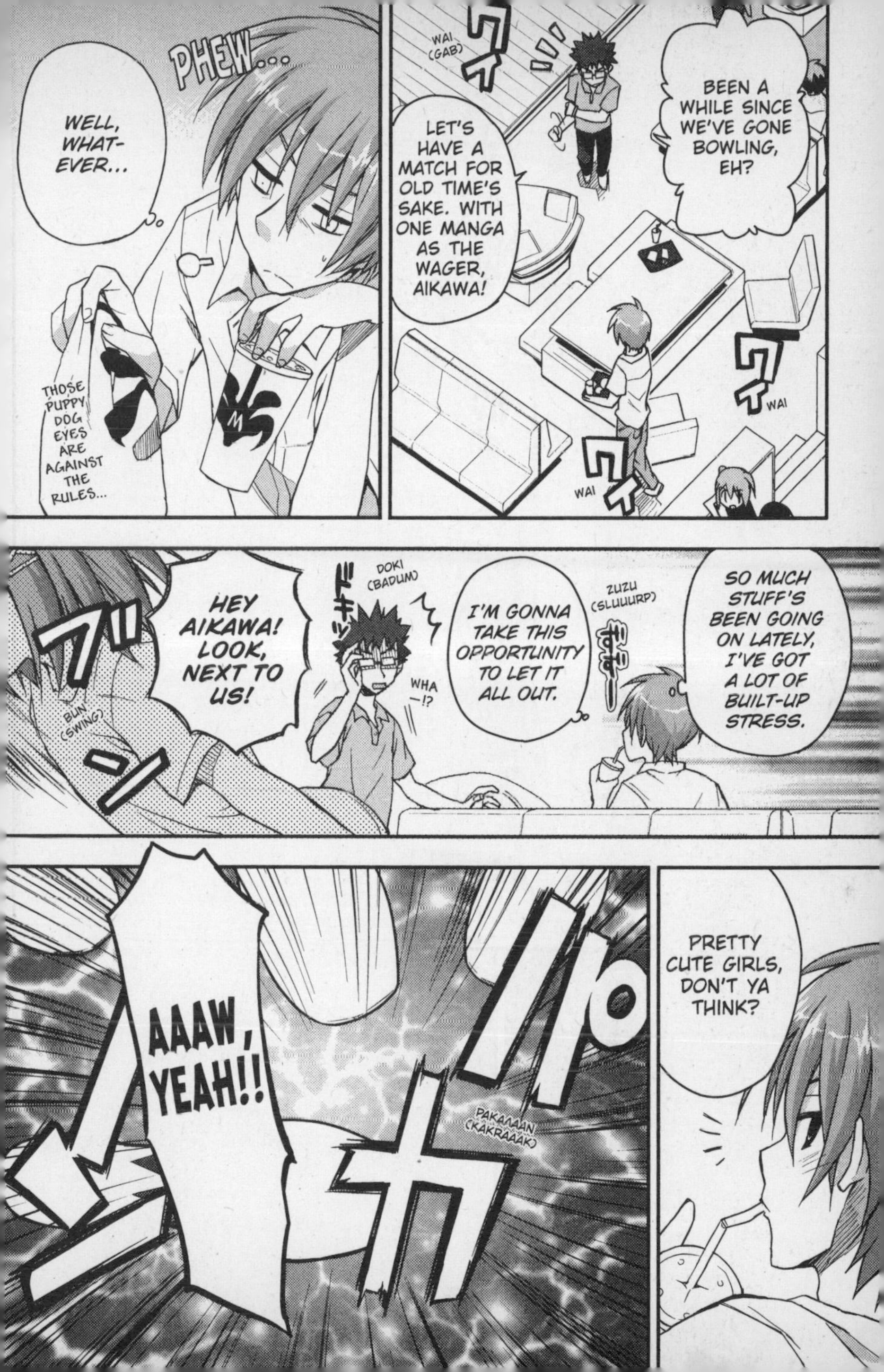
WAI (GAB)
BEEN A WHILE SINCE WE'VE GONE BOWLING, EH?
LET'S HAVE A MATCH FOR OLD TIME'S SAKE. WITH ONE MANGA AS THE WAGER, AIKAWA!
WAI
WAI
PHEW...
WELL, WHATEVER...
THOSE PUPPY DOG EYES ARE AGAINST THE RULES...
SO MUCH STUFF'S BEEN GOING ON LATELY, I'VE GOT A LOT OF BUILT-UP STRESS.
ZUZU (SLUUURP)
I'M GONNA TAKE THIS OPPORTUNITY TO LET IT ALL OUT.
DOKI (BADUM)
WHA—!?
HEY AIKAWA! LOOK, NEXT TO US!
BUN (SWING)
PRETTY CUTE GIRLS, DON'T YA THINK?
PAKAAAAN (KAKRAAAK)
AAAW, YEAH!!

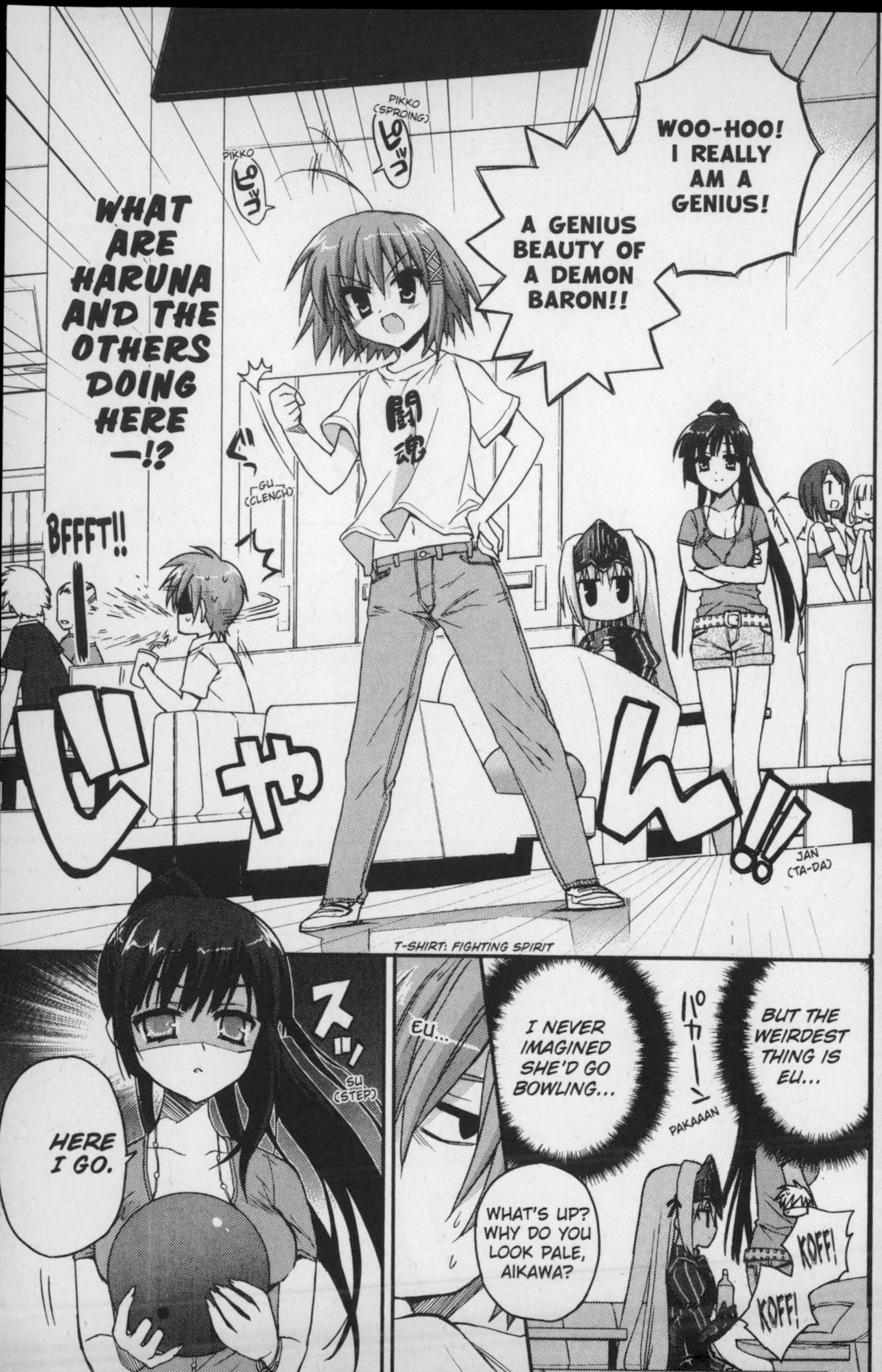
WOO-HOO! I REALLY AM A GENIUS!
A GENIUS BEAUTY OF A DEMON BARON!!
PIKKO (SPROING)
PIKKO
WHAT ARE HARUNA AND THE OTHERS DOING HERE—!?
GU (CLENCH)
BFFFT!!
JAN (TA-DA)
T-SHIRT: FIGHTING SPIRIT
BUT THE WEIRDEST THING IS EU...
I NEVER IMAGINED SHE'D GO BOWLING...
PAKAAAN
EU...
WHAT'S UP? WHY DO YOU LOOK PALE, AIKAWA?
KOFF!
KOFF!
SU (STEP)
HERE I GO.

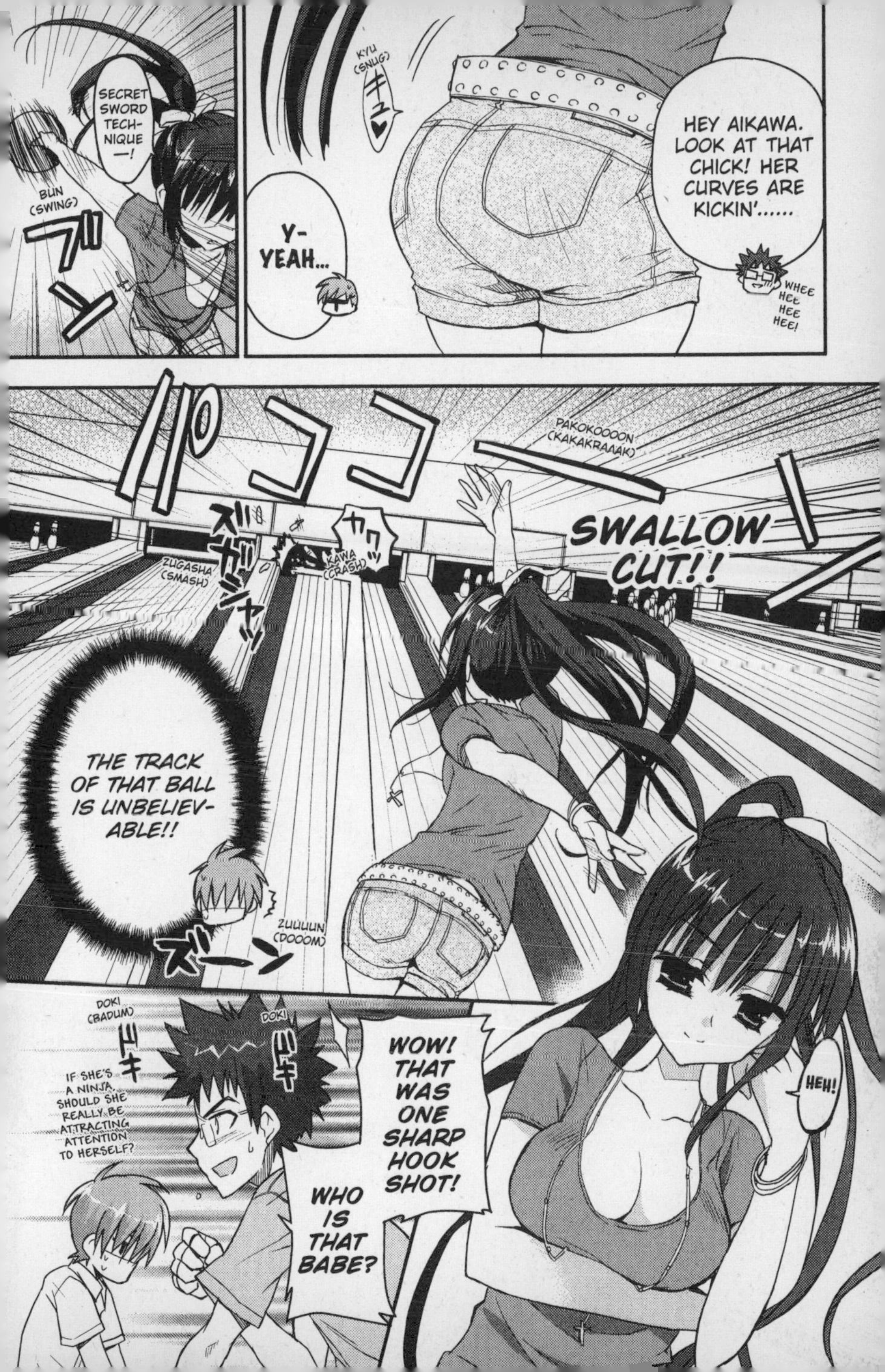
HEY AIKAWA. LOOK AT THAT CHICK! HER CURVES ARE KICKIN'......
WHEE HEE HEE HEE!
KYU (SNUG)
Y-YEAH...
SECRET SWORD TECH-NIQUE—!
BUN (SWING)
PAKOKOOOON (KAKAKRAAAK)
SWALLOW CUT!!
KAWA (CRASH)
ZUGASHA (SMASH)
THE TRACK OF THAT BALL IS UNBELIEV-ABLE!!
ZUUUUN (DOOOM)
HEH!
WOW! THAT WAS ONE SHARP HOOK SHOT!
WHO IS THAT BABE?
DOKI
DOKI (BADUM)
IF SHE'S A NINJA, SHOULD SHE REALLY BE ATTRACTING ATTENTION TO HERSELF?

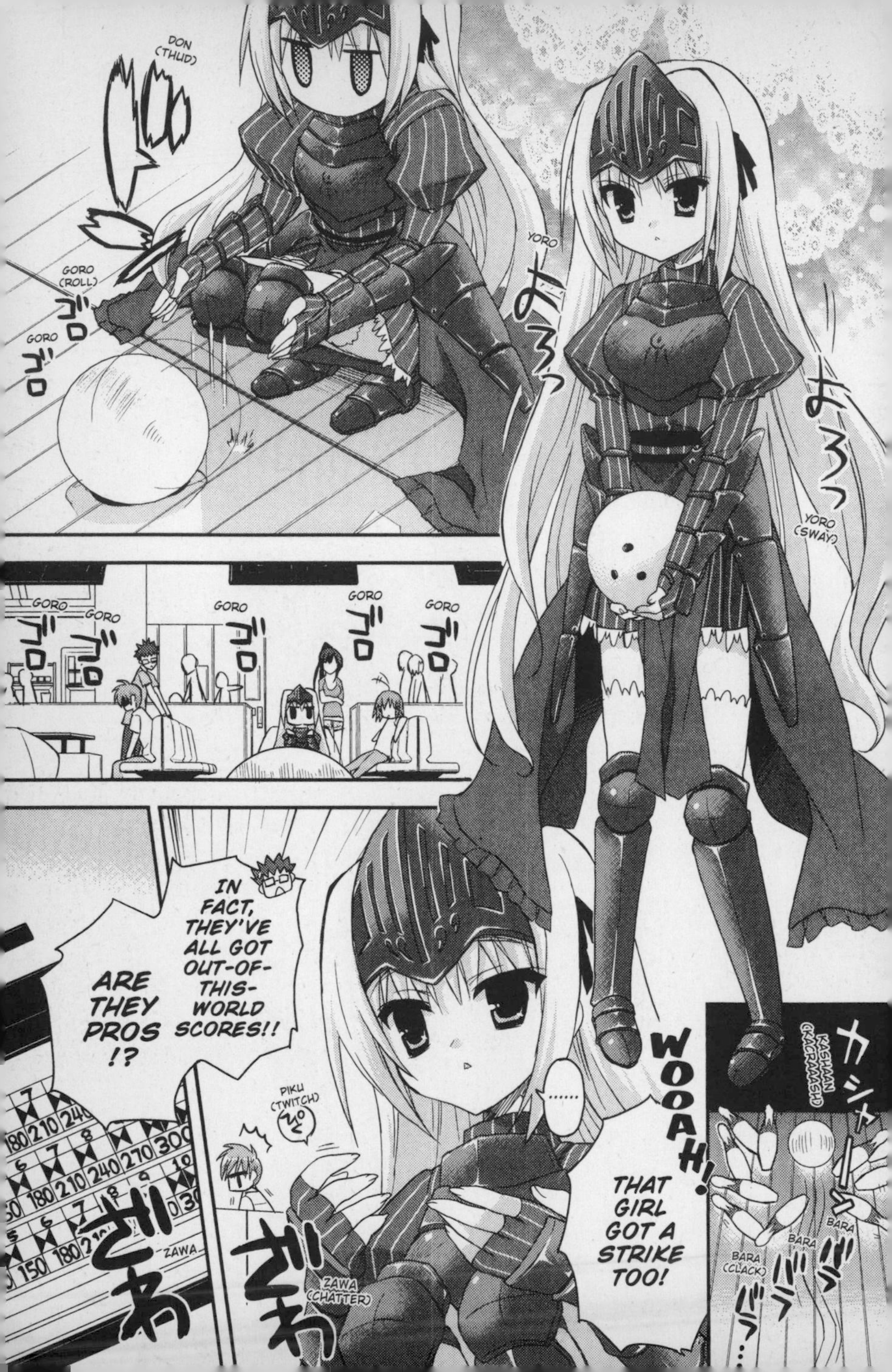

YORO
YORO (SWAY)
DON (THUD)
GORO (ROLL)
GORO
GORO
GORO
GORO
GORO
KASHAN (KACRAAASH)
BARA (CLACK)
BARA
BARA
WOOAH!
THAT GIRL GOT A STRIKE TOO!
......
PIKU (TWITCH)
IN FACT, THEY'VE ALL GOT OUT-OF-THIS-WORLD SCORES!!
ARE THEY PROS!?
ZAWA
ZAWA (CHATTER)

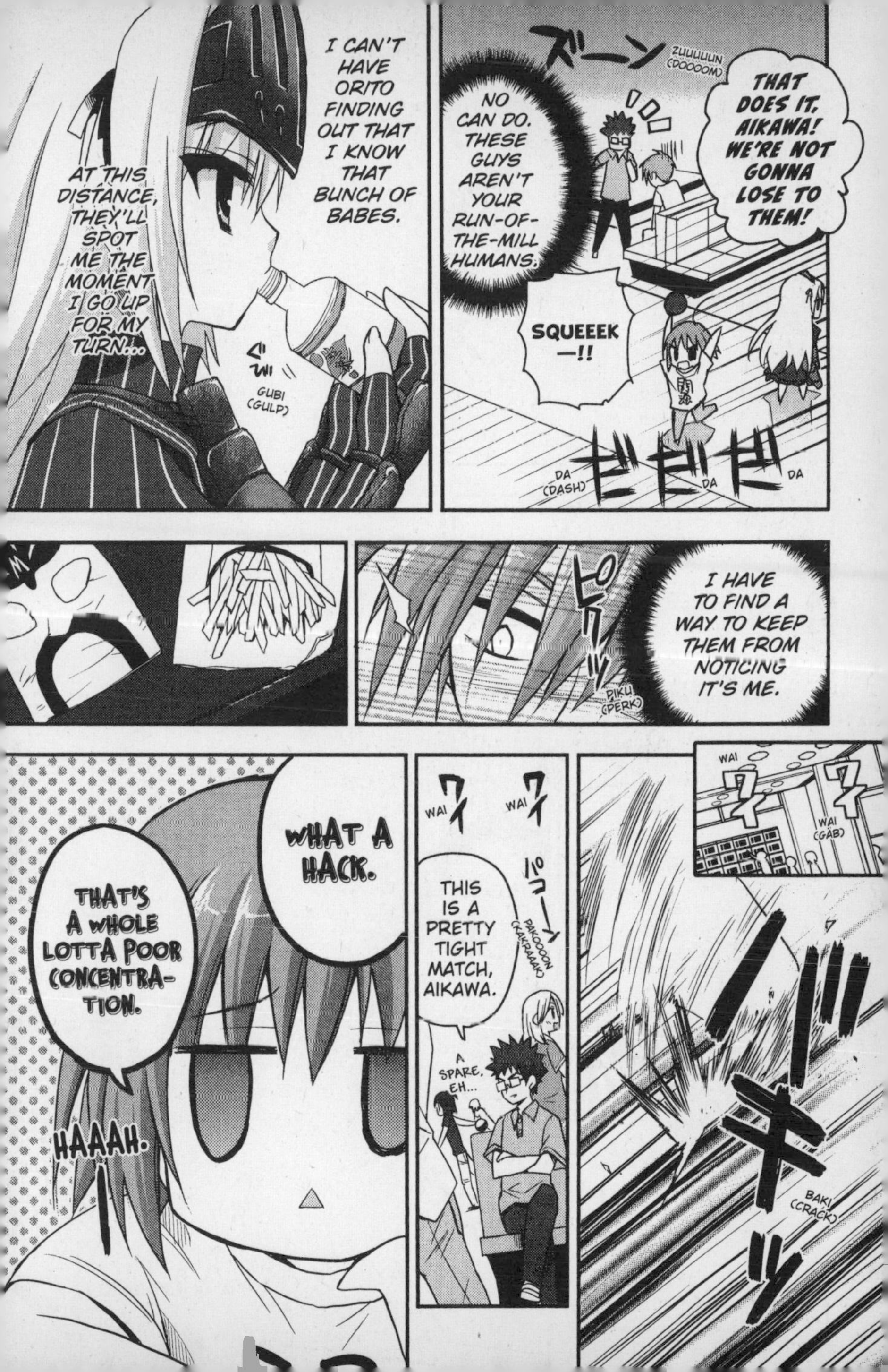
ZUUUUUN (DOOOOM)
THAT DOES IT, AIKAWA! WE'RE NOT GONNA LOSE TO THEM!
NO CAN DO. THESE GUYS AREN'T YOUR RUN-OF-THE-MILL HUMANS.
SQUEEEK—!!
DA (DASH) DA DA
I CAN'T HAVE ORITO FINDING OUT THAT I KNOW THAT BUNCH OF BABES.
AT THIS DISTANCE, THEY'LL SPOT ME THE MOMENT I GO UP FOR MY TURN...
GUBI (GULP)
I HAVE TO FIND A WAY TO KEEP THEM FROM NOTICING IT'S ME.
PIKU (PERK)
WAI WAI WAI (GÄB)
BAKI (CRACK)
WAI WAI
PAKOOOON (KAKRAAAK)
THIS IS A PRETTY TIGHT MATCH, AIKAWA.
A SPARE, EH...
WHAT A HACK.
THAT'S A WHOLE LOTTA POOR CONCENTRATION.
HAAAH.

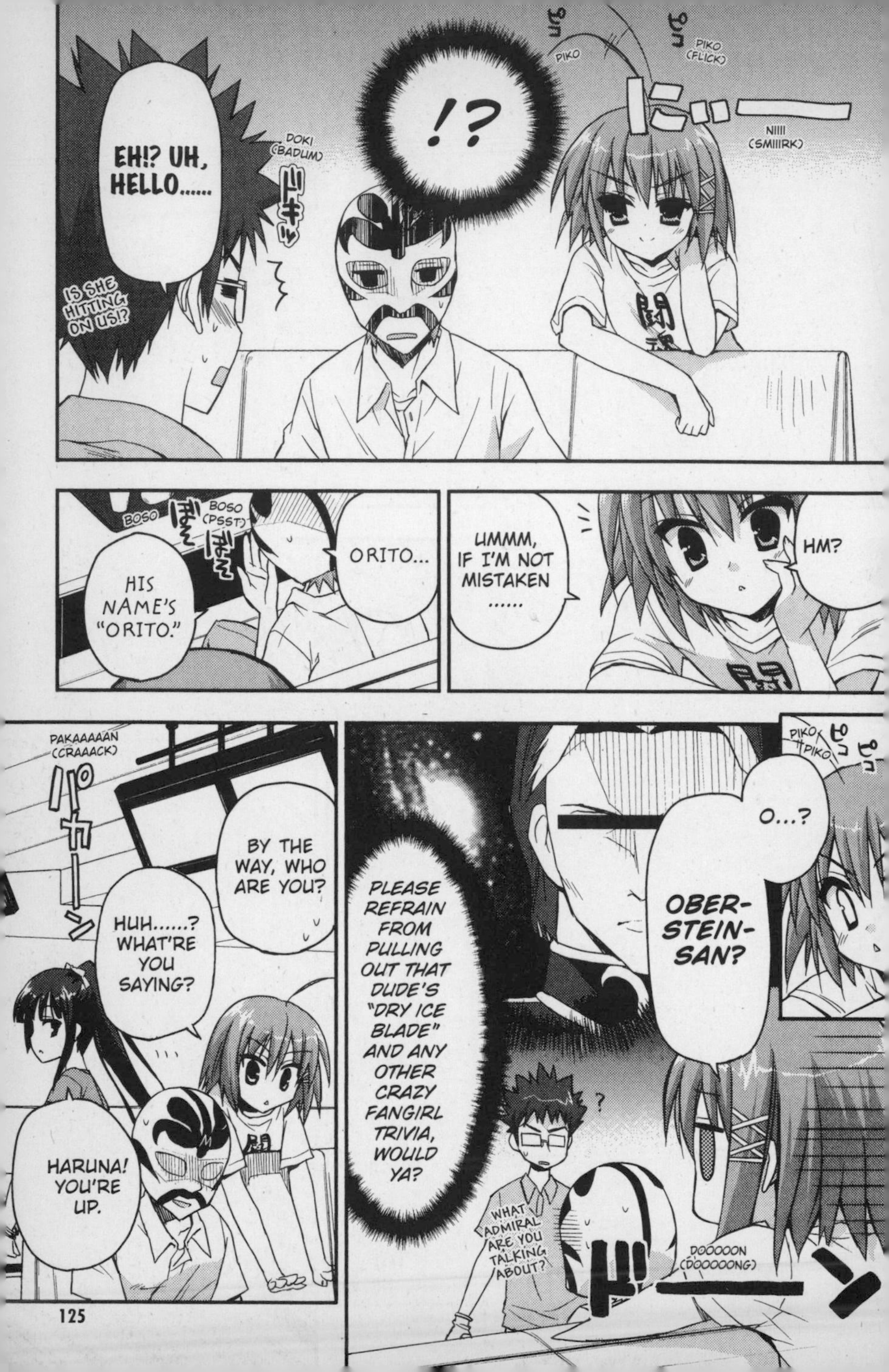
PIKO
PIKO (FLICK)
NIIII (SMIIIRK)
!?
DOKI (BADUM)
EH!? UH, HELLO......
IS SHE HITTING ON US!?
HM?
UMMM, IF I'M NOT MISTAKEN ......
ORITO...
BOSO (PSST)
BOSO
HIS NAME'S "ORITO."
PIKO PIKO
O...?
OBER-STEIN-SAN?
PLEASE REFRAIN FROM PULLING OUT THAT DUDE'S "DRY ICE BLADE" AND ANY OTHER CRAZY FANGIRL TRIVIA, WOULD YA?
WHAT ADMIRAL ARE YOU TALKING ABOUT?
DOOOOON (DOOOOONG)
PAKAAAAAN (CRAAACK)
BY THE WAY, WHO ARE YOU?
HUH......? WHAT'RE YOU SAYING?
HARUNA! YOU'RE UP.

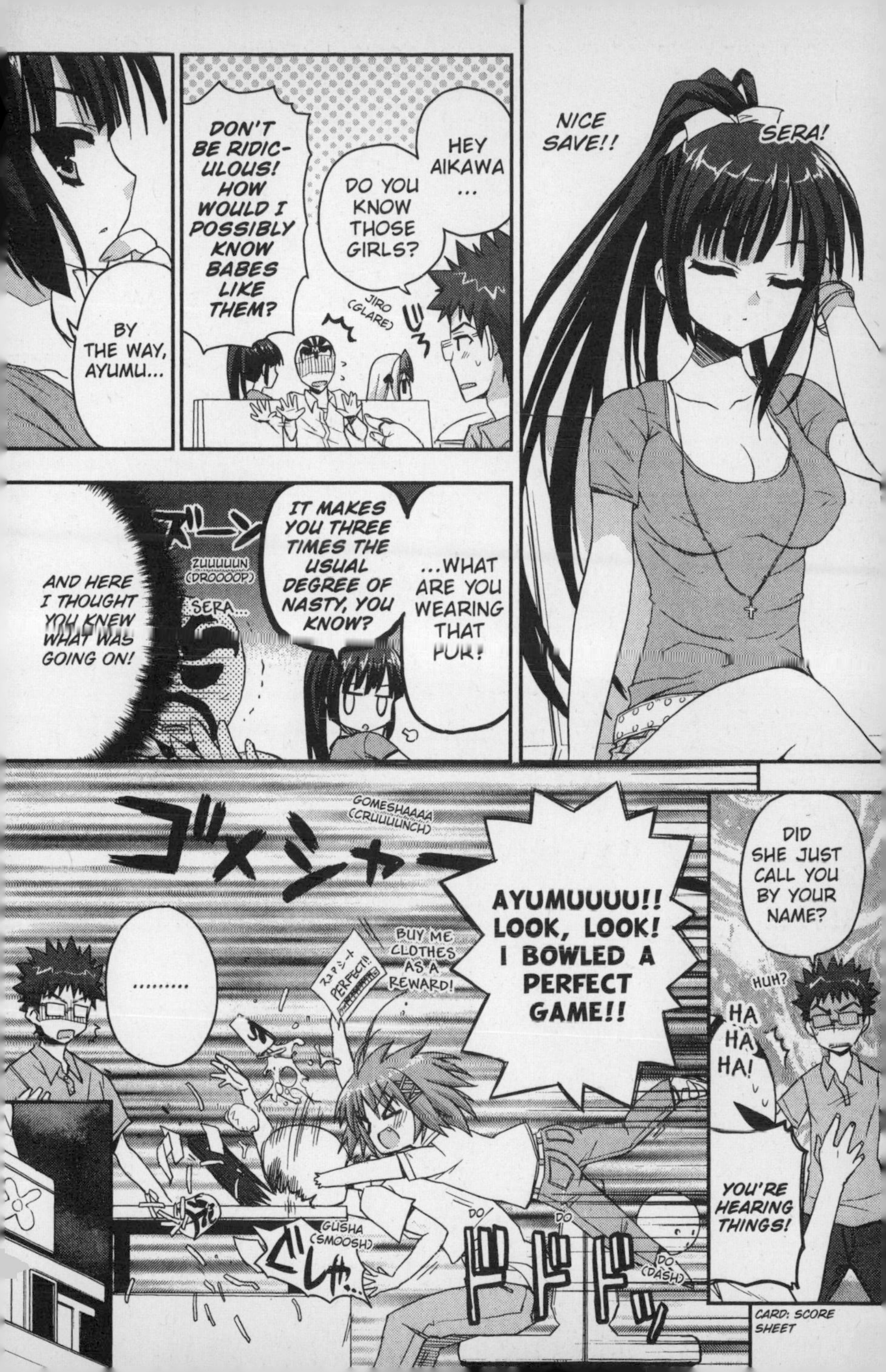
NICE SAVE!!
SERA!
HEY AIKAWA...
DO YOU KNOW THOSE GIRLS?
JIRO (GLARE)
DON'T BE RIDICULOUS! HOW WOULD I POSSIBLY KNOW BABES LIKE THEM?
BY THE WAY, AYUMU...
...WHAT ARE YOU WEARING THAT FOR!
IT MAKES YOU THREE TIMES THE USUAL DEGREE OF NASTY, YOU KNOW?
ZUUUUUN (DROOOOP)
SERA...
AND HERE I THOUGHT YOU KNEW WHAT WAS GOING ON!
DID SHE JUST CALL YOU BY YOUR NAME?
HUH?
HA HA HA!
YOU'RE HEARING THINGS!
GOMESHAAAA (CRUUUUNCH)
AYUMUUUU!! LOOK, LOOK! I BOWLED A PERFECT GAME!!
BUY ME CLOTHES AS A REWARD!
PERFECT!!
....
GUSHA (SMOOSH)
DO DO DO (DASH)
CARD: SCORE SHEET

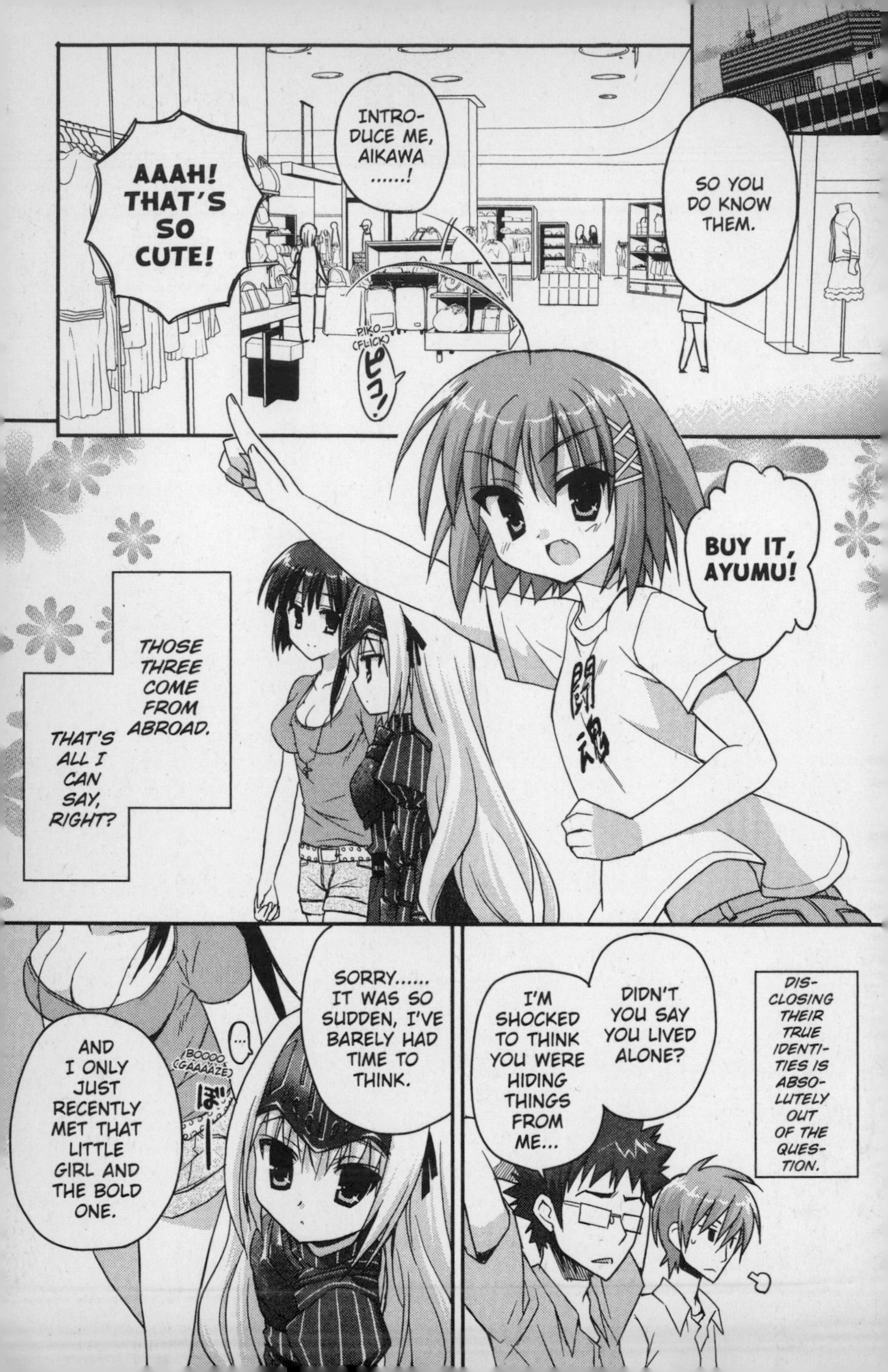

SO YOU DO KNOW THEM.
INTRO-DUCE ME, AIKAWA ......!
AAAH! THAT'S SO CUTE!
PIKO (FLICK)
ピコ!
BUY IT, AYUMU!
THOSE THREE COME FROM ABROAD.
THAT'S ALL I CAN SAY, RIGHT?
DIS-CLOSING THEIR TRUE IDENTI-TIES IS ABSO-LUTELY OUT OF THE QUES-TION.
DIDN'T YOU SAY YOU LIVED ALONE?
I'M SHOCKED TO THINK YOU WERE HIDING THINGS FROM ME...
SORRY...... IT WAS SO SUDDEN, I'VE BARELY HAD TIME TO THINK.
...
BOOOOO (GAAAAZE)
AND I ONLY JUST RECENTLY MET THAT LITTLE GIRL AND THE BOLD ONE.

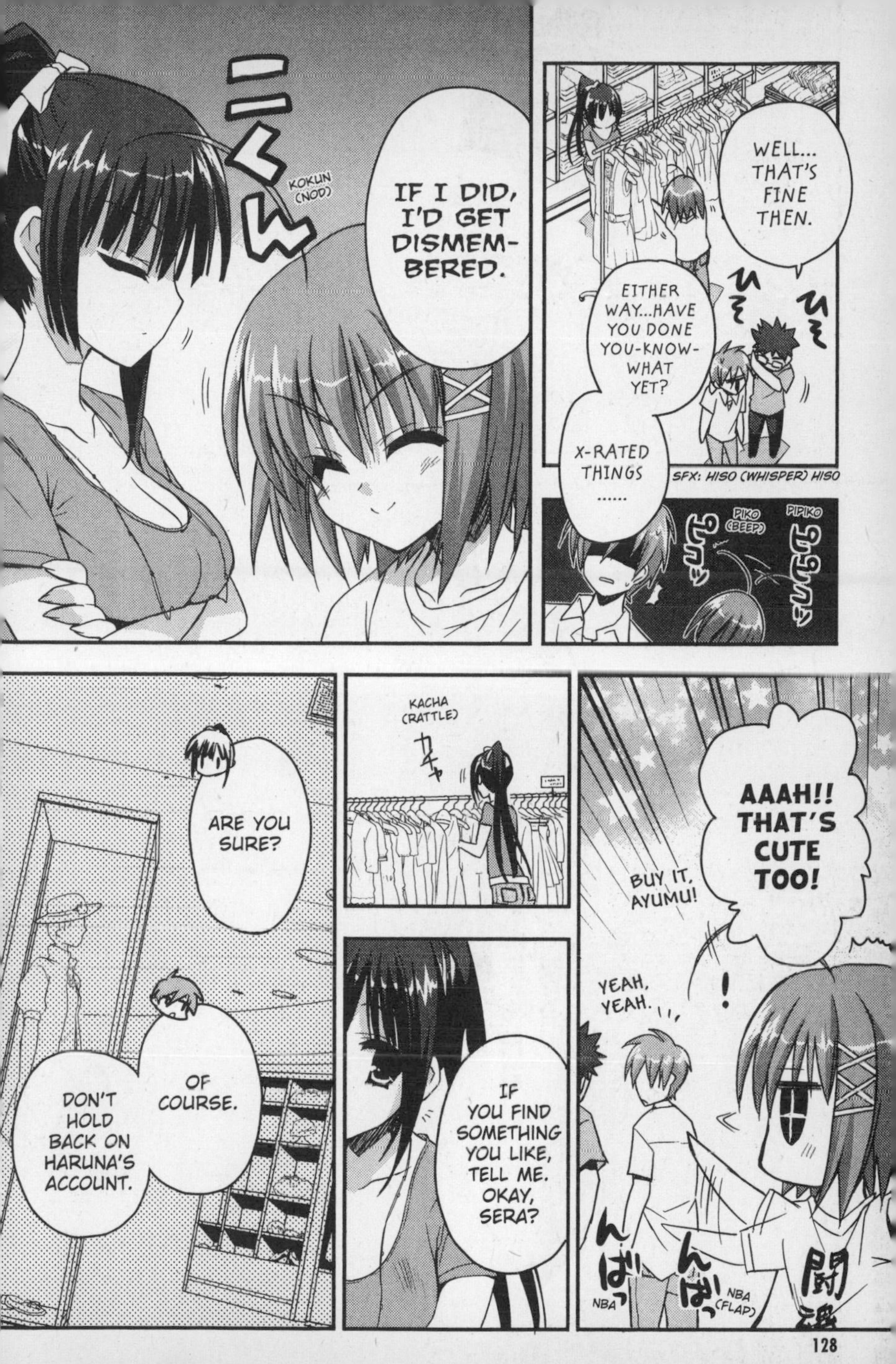
WELL... THAT'S FINE THEN.
EITHER WAY...HAVE YOU DONE YOU-KNOW-WHAT YET?
X-RATED THINGS ......
SFX: HISO (WHISPER) HISO
PIPIKO
PIKO (BEEP)
IF I DID, I'D GET DISMEMBERED.
KOKUN (NOD)
AAAH!! THAT'S CUTE TOO!
BUY IT, AYUMU!
!
YEAH, YEAH.
NBA (FLAP)
NBA
KACHA (RATTLE)
IF YOU FIND SOMETHING YOU LIKE, TELL ME. OKAY, SERA?
ARE YOU SURE?
OF COURSE.
DON'T HOLD BACK ON HARUNA'S ACCOUNT.

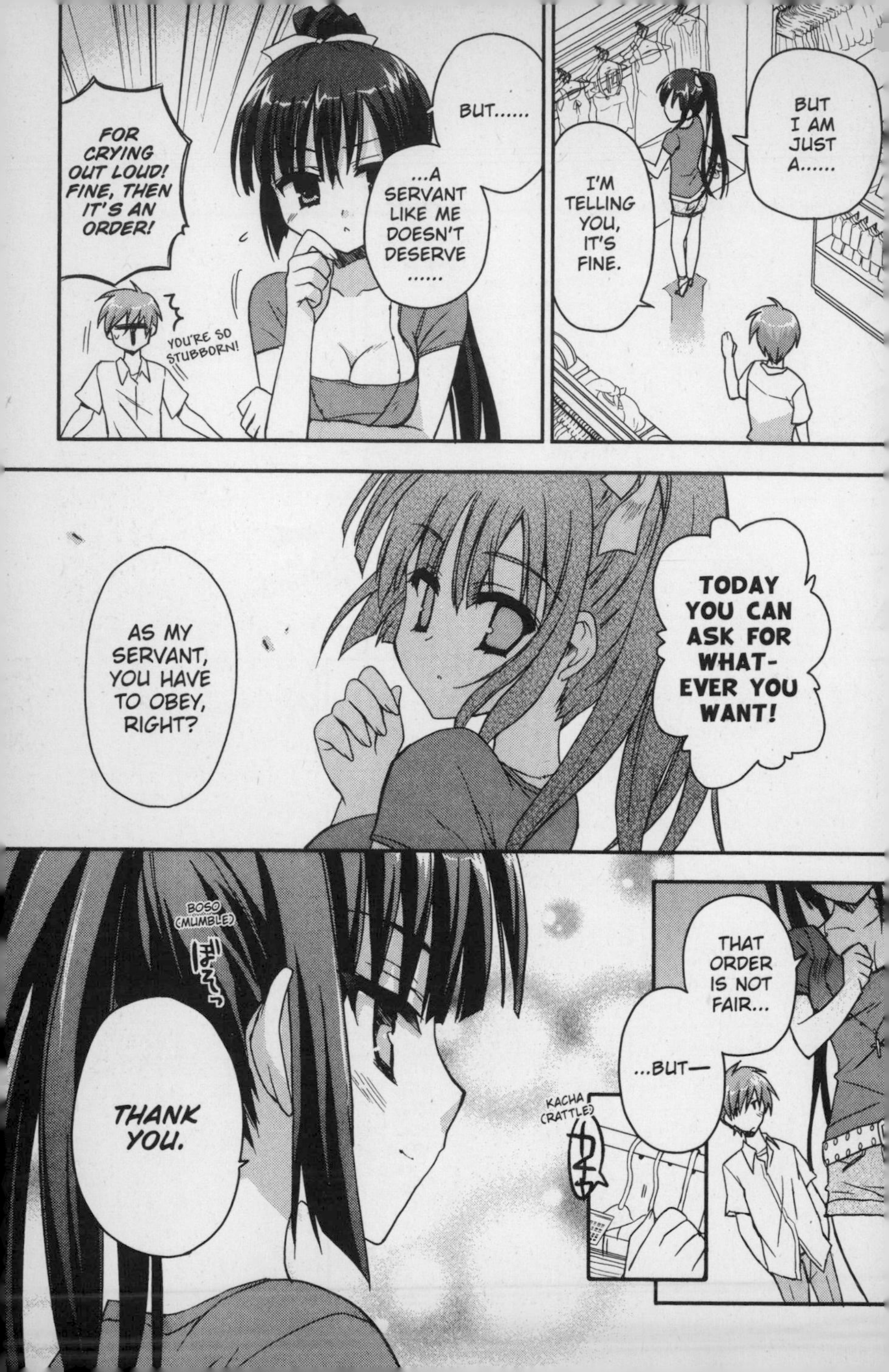
BUT I AM JUST A......
I'M TELLING YOU, IT'S FINE.
BUT......
...A SERVANT LIKE ME DOESN'T DESERVE ......
FOR CRYING OUT LOUD! FINE, THEN IT'S AN ORDER!
YOU'RE SO STUBBORN!
TODAY YOU CAN ASK FOR WHAT-EVER YOU WANT!
AS MY SERVANT, YOU HAVE TO OBEY, RIGHT?
THAT ORDER IS NOT FAIR...
...BUT—
KACHA (RATTLE)
BOSO (MUMBLE)
THANK YOU.

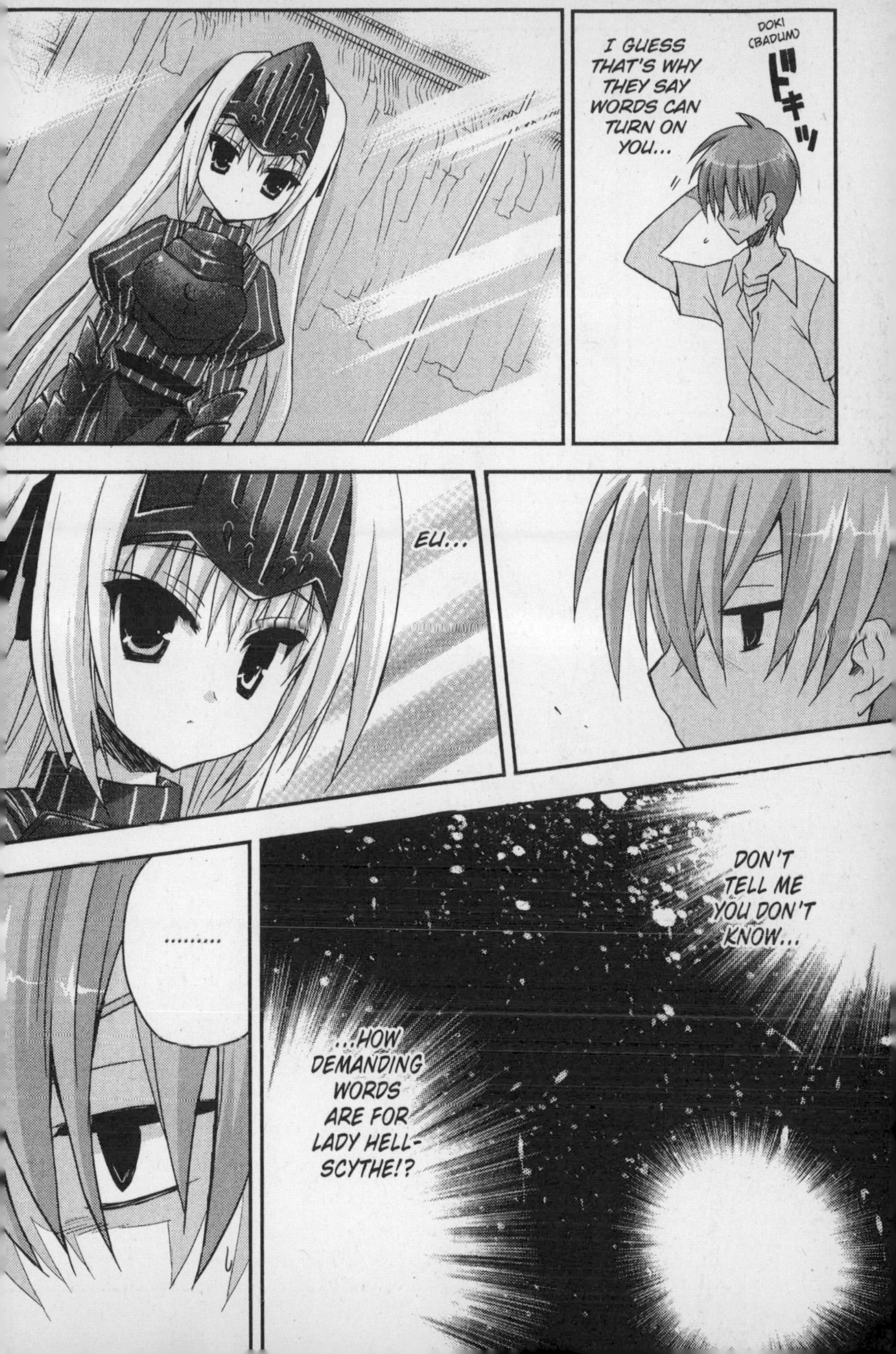
DOKI (BADUM)
ドキッ
I GUESS THAT'S WHY THEY SAY WORDS CAN TURN ON YOU...
EU...
DON'T TELL ME YOU DON'T KNOW...
...HOW DEMANDING WORDS ARE FOR LADY HELL-SCYTHE!?
....

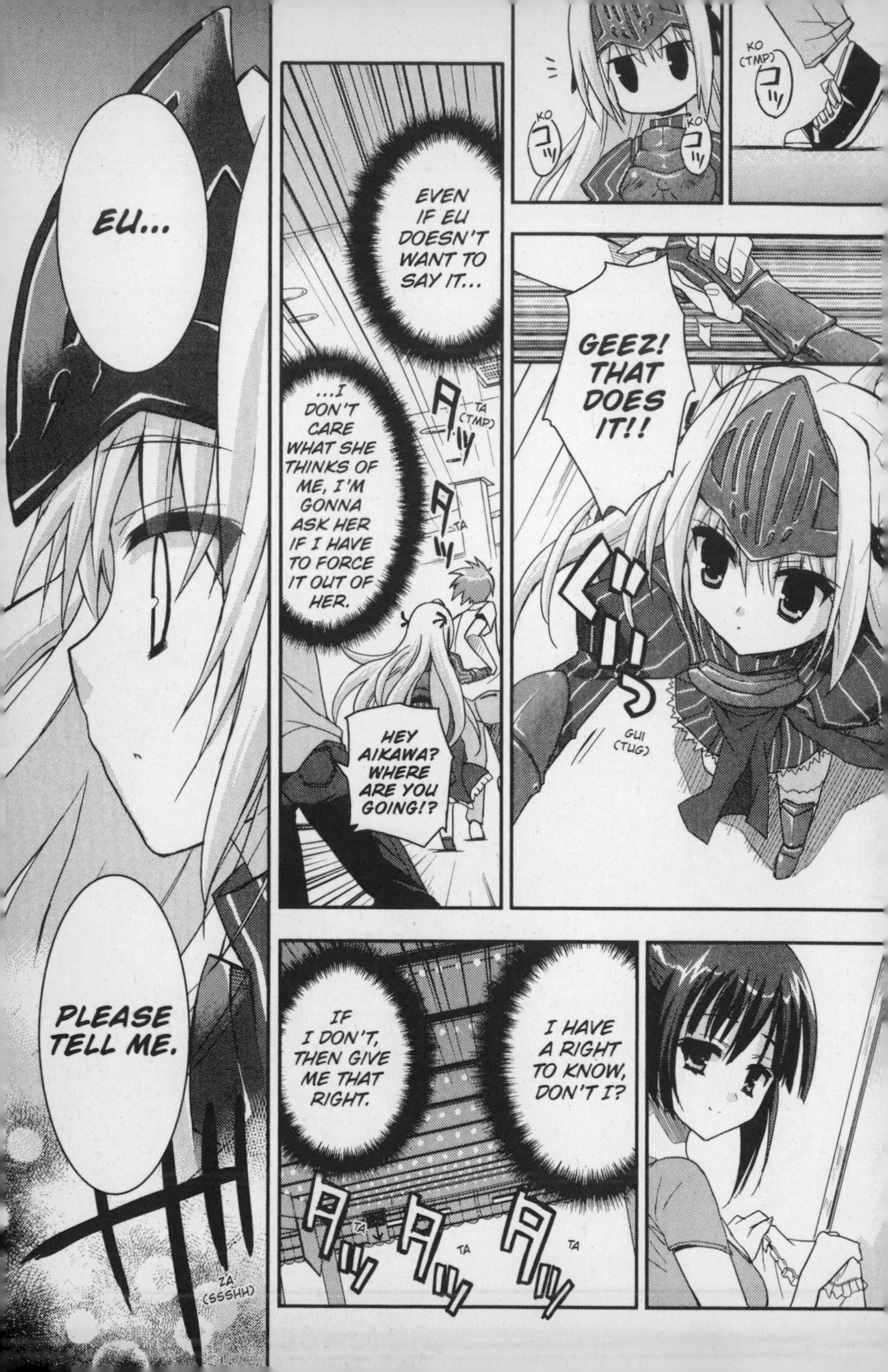
KO (TMP)
KO
KO
GEEZ! THAT DOES IT!!
GUI (TUG)
EVEN IF EU DOESN'T WANT TO SAY IT...
...I DON'T CARE WHAT SHE THINKS OF ME, I'M GONNA ASK HER IF I HAVE TO FORCE IT OUT OF HER.
TA (TMP)
TA
HEY AIKAWA? WHERE ARE YOU GOING!?
I HAVE A RIGHT TO KNOW, DON'T I?
IF I DON'T, THEN GIVE ME THAT RIGHT.
TA
TA
TA
EU...
PLEASE TELL ME.
ZA (SSSHH)

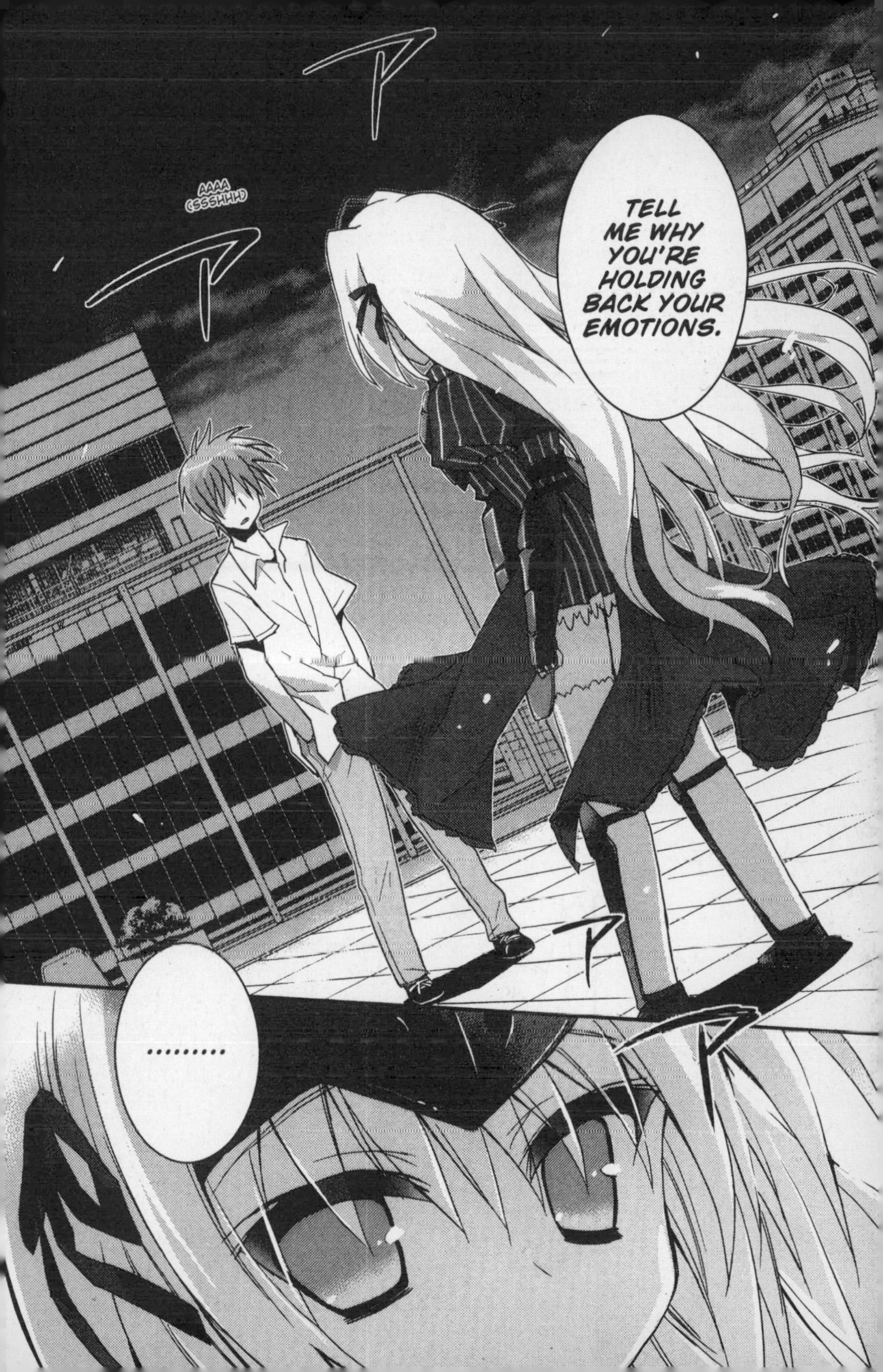
AAAA (SSSHHH)
TELL ME WHY YOU'RE HOLDING BACK YOUR EMOTIONS.
....

5 AYUMU......I'VE NEVER EATEN ANYTHING OTHER THAN JAPANESE COOKING.

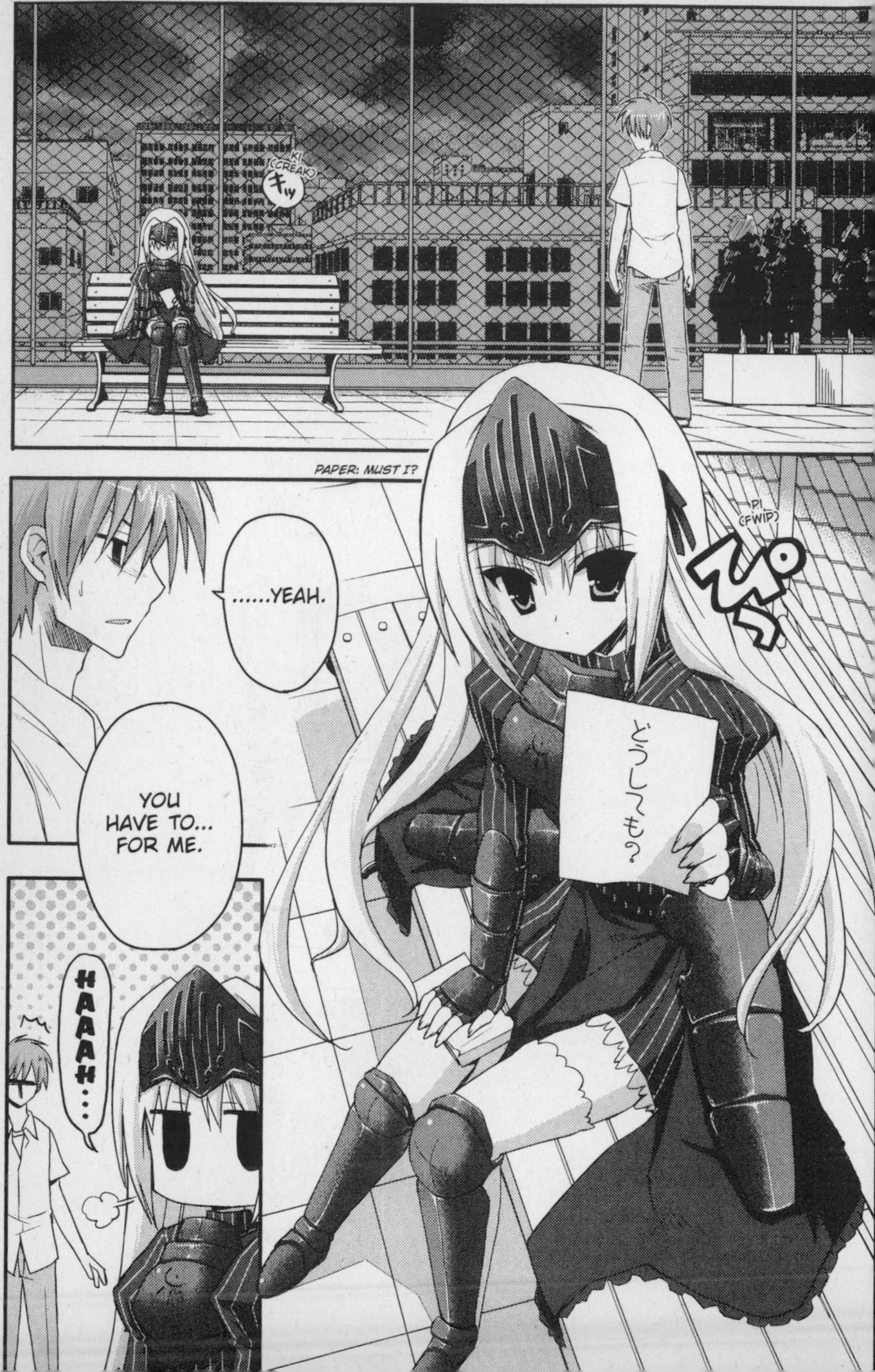
KI (CREAK)
キッ
PI (FWIP)
ぴっ
どうしても？
PAPER: MUST I?
......YEAH.
YOU HAVE TO... FOR ME.
HAAAH...

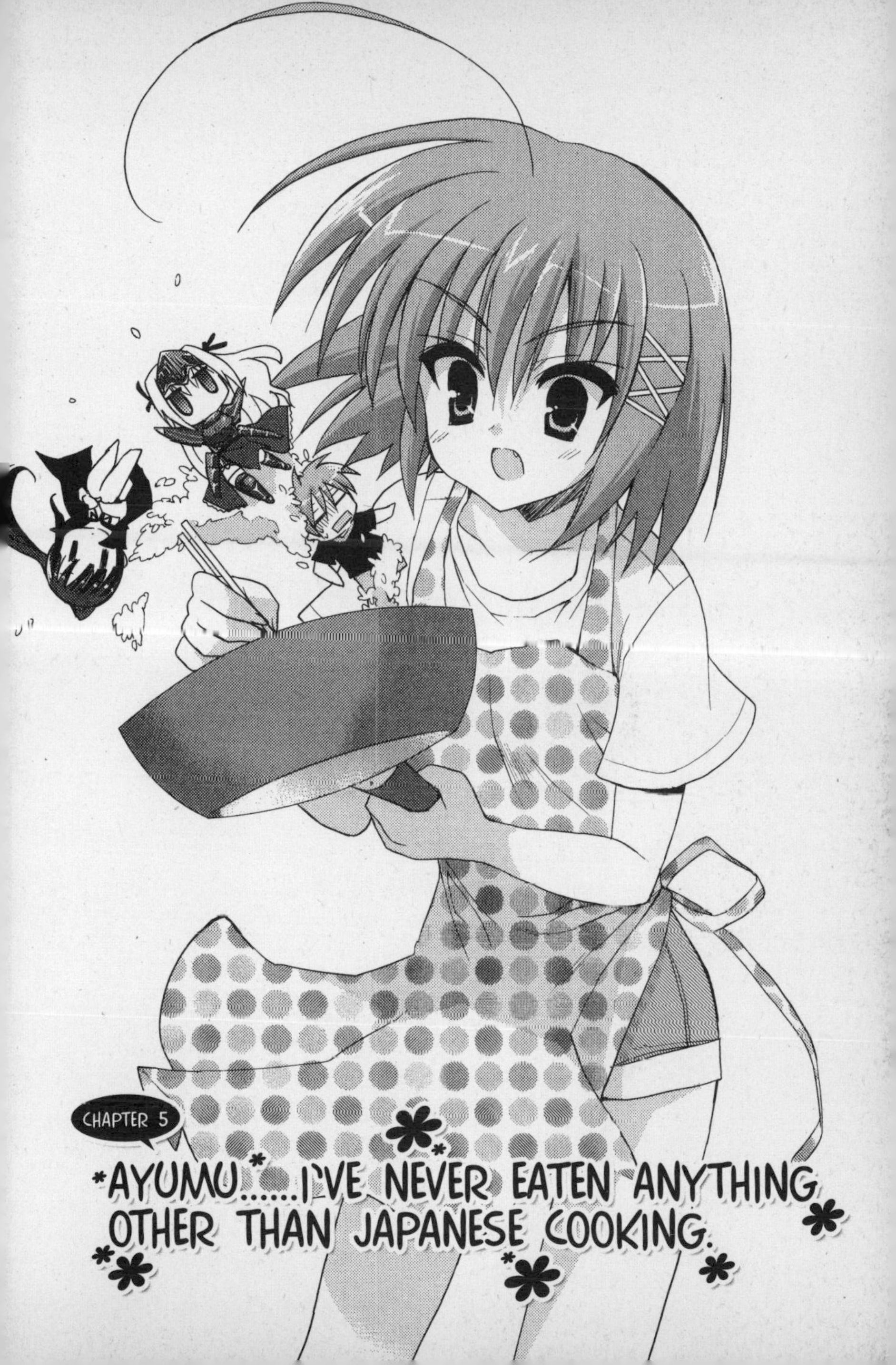
CHAPTER 5
AYUMU......I'VE NEVER EATEN ANYTHING OTHER THAN JAPANESE COOKING.

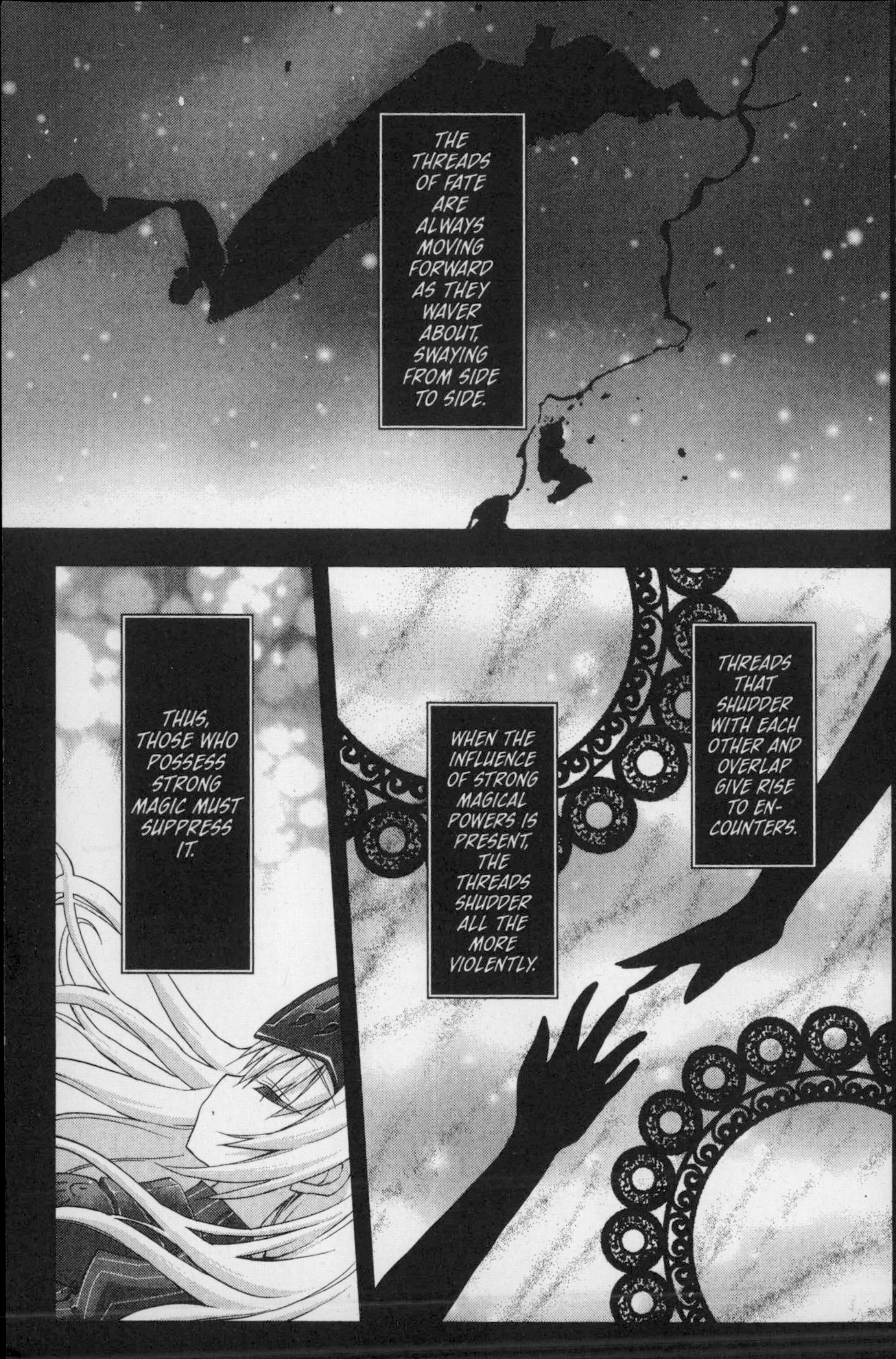
THE THREADS OF FATE ARE ALWAYS MOVING FORWARD AS THEY WAVER ABOUT, SWAYING FROM SIDE TO SIDE.
THREADS THAT SHUDDER WITH EACH OTHER AND OVERLAP GIVE RISE TO EN-COUNTERS.
WHEN THE INFLUENCE OF STRONG MAGICAL POWERS IS PRESENT, THE THREADS SHUDDER ALL THE MORE VIOLENTLY.
THUS, THOSE WHO POSSESS STRONG MAGIC MUST SUPPRESS IT.

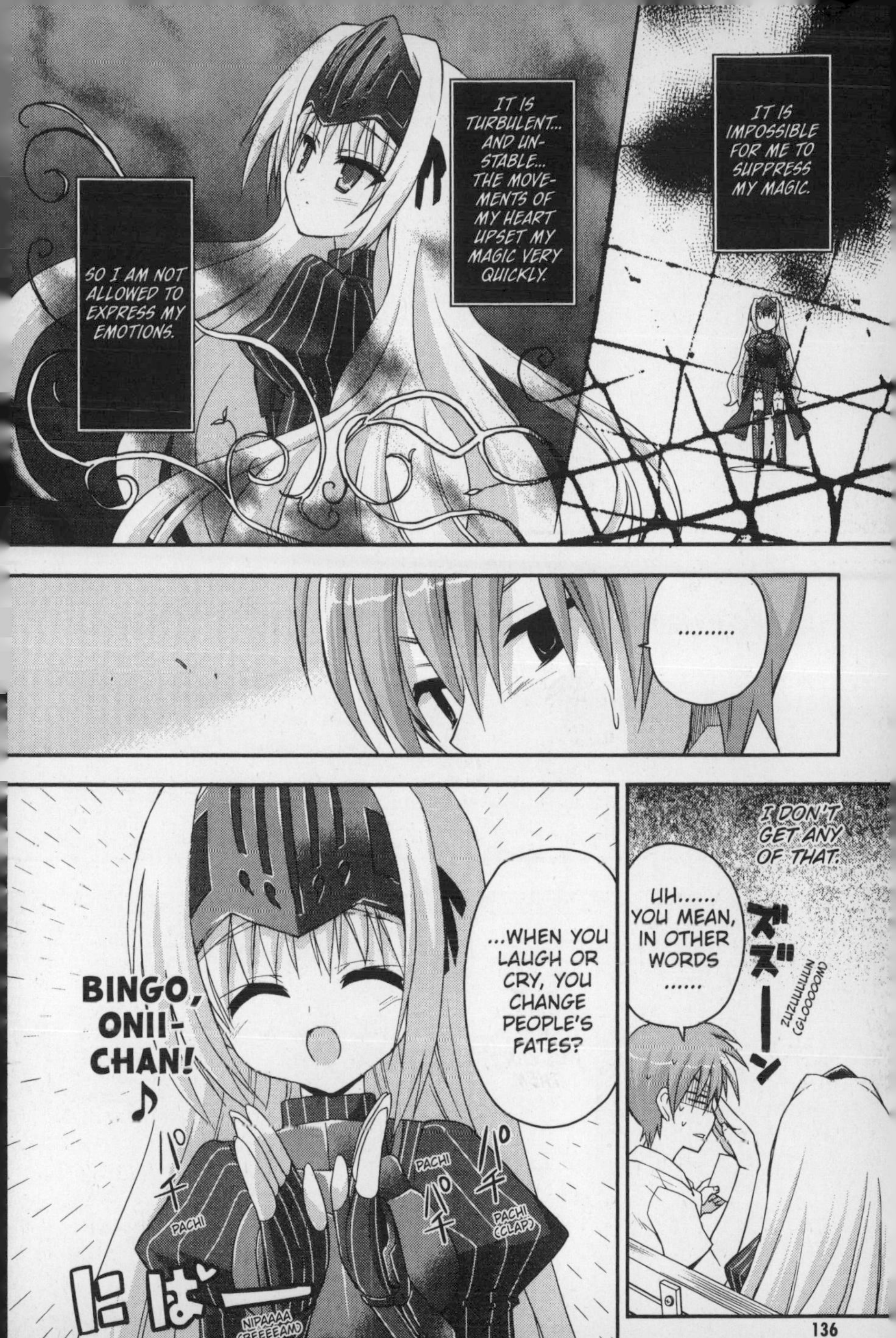
IT IS IMPOSSIBLE FOR ME TO SUPPRESS MY MAGIC.
IT IS TURBULENT... AND UN-STABLE... THE MOVE-MENTS OF MY HEART UPSET MY MAGIC VERY QUICKLY.
SO I AM NOT ALLOWED TO EXPRESS MY EMOTIONS.
....
I DON'T GET ANY OF THAT.
UH...... YOU MEAN, IN OTHER WORDS ......
ズズーン
ZUZUUUUUN (GLOOOOOM)
...WHEN YOU LAUGH OR CRY, YOU CHANGE PEOPLE'S FATES?
BINGO, ONII-CHAN! ♪
パチ
PACHI
パチパチ
PACHI
PACHI (CLAP)
にぱー
NIPAAAA (BEEEEAM)

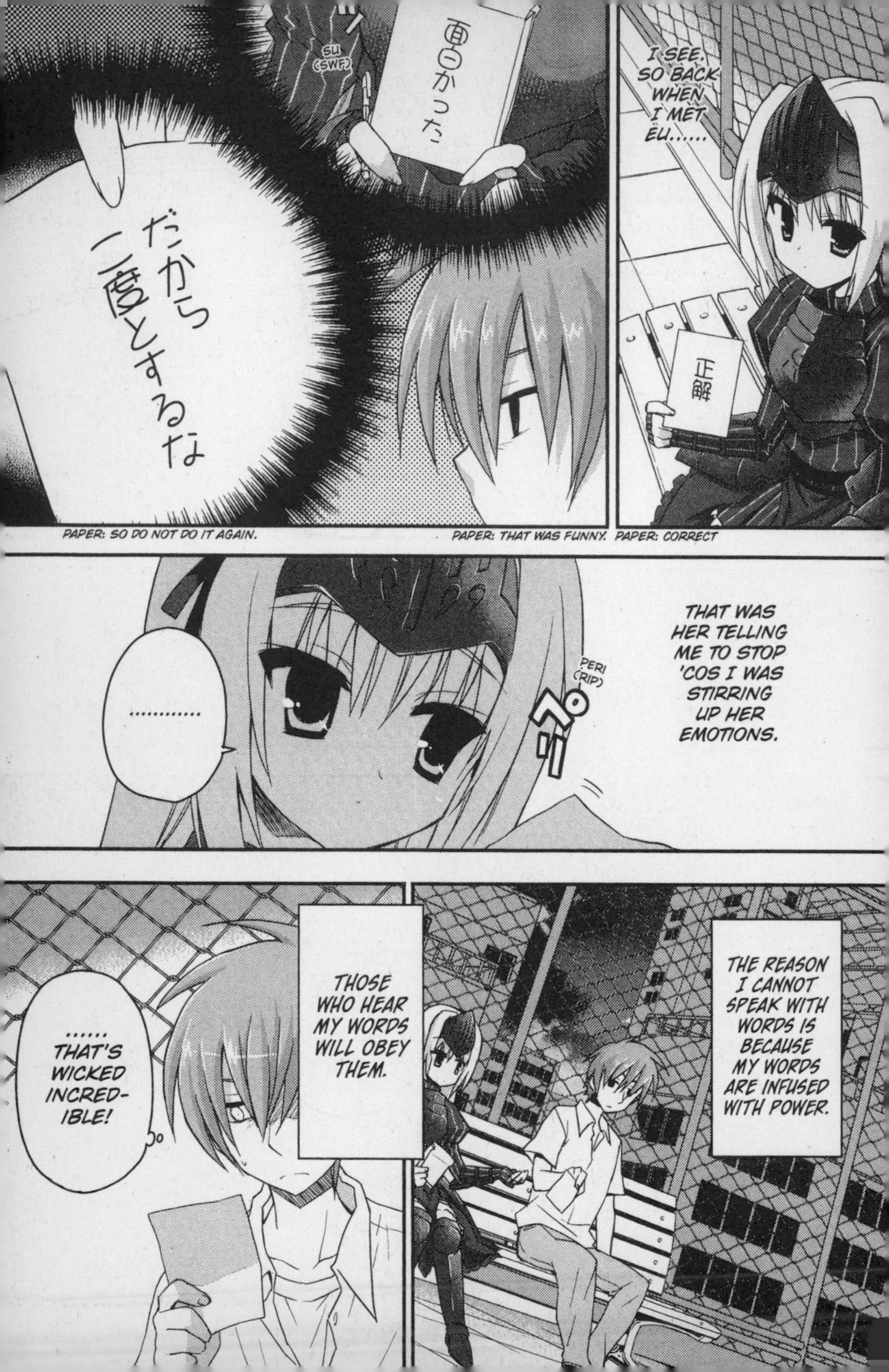

I SEE, SO BACK WHEN I MET EU......
正解
面白かった
SU (SWF)
だから二度とするな
PAPER: SO DO NOT DO IT AGAIN.
PAPER: THAT WAS FUNNY.
PAPER: CORRECT
THAT WAS HER TELLING ME TO STOP 'COS I WAS STIRRING UP HER EMOTIONS.
PERI (RIP)
ペリ
....
THE REASON I CANNOT SPEAK WITH WORDS IS BECAUSE MY WORDS ARE INFUSED WITH POWER.
THOSE WHO HEAR MY WORDS WILL OBEY THEM.
......THAT'S WICKED INCREDIBLE!

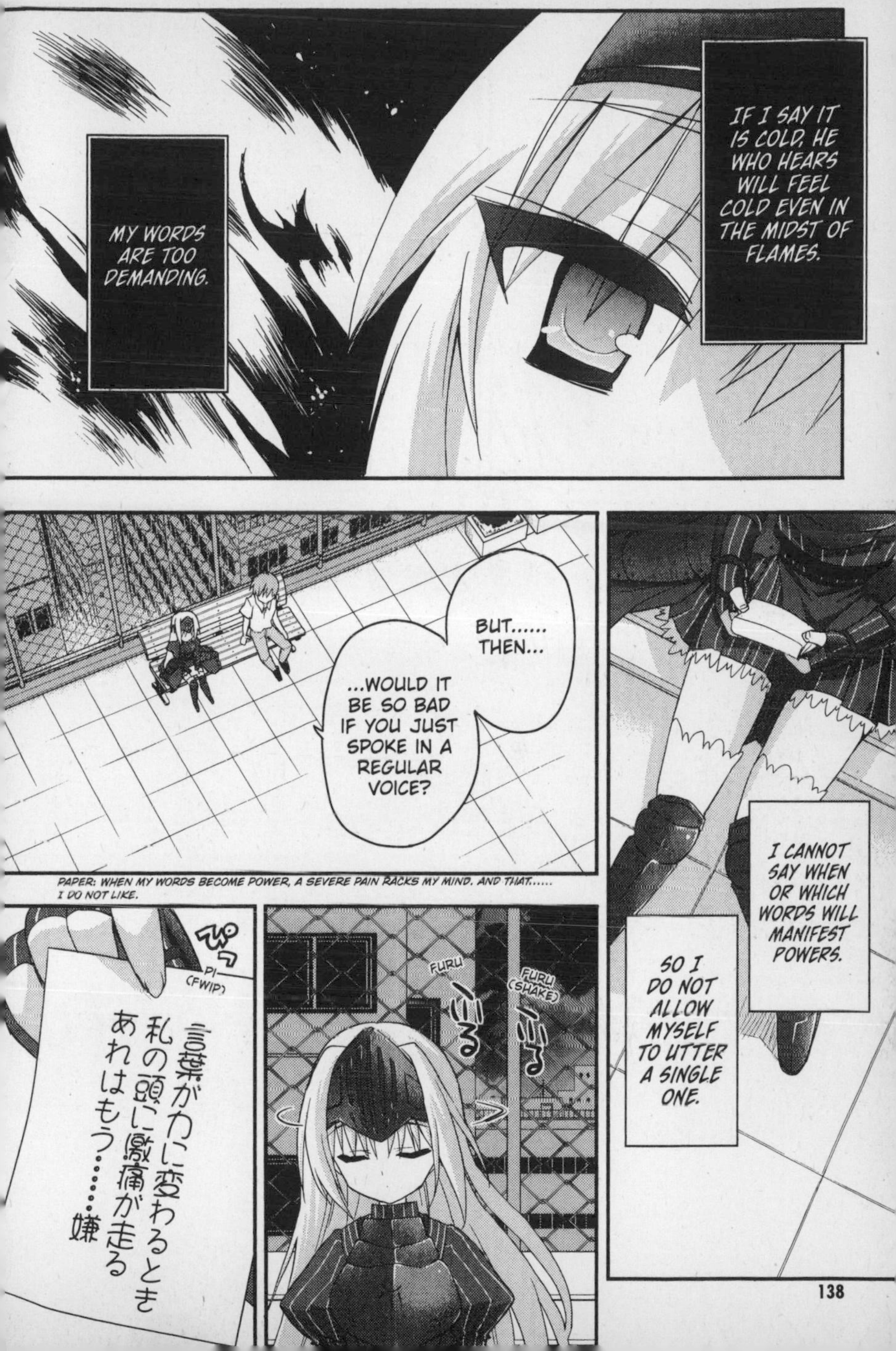
IF I SAY IT IS COLD, HE WHO HEARS WILL FEEL COLD EVEN IN THE MIDST OF FLAMES.
MY WORDS ARE TOO DEMANDING.
I CANNOT SAY WHEN OR WHICH WORDS WILL MANIFEST POWERS.
SO I DO NOT ALLOW MYSELF TO UTTER A SINGLE ONE.
BUT...... THEN...
...WOULD IT BE SO BAD IF YOU JUST SPOKE IN A REGULAR VOICE?
ふる FURU
ふる FURU (SHAKE)
ぴっ PI (FWIP)
言葉が力に変わるとき 私の頭に激痛が走る あれはもう……嫌
PAPER: WHEN MY WORDS BECOME POWER, A SEVERE PAIN RACKS MY MIND. AND THAT...... I DO NOT LIKE.

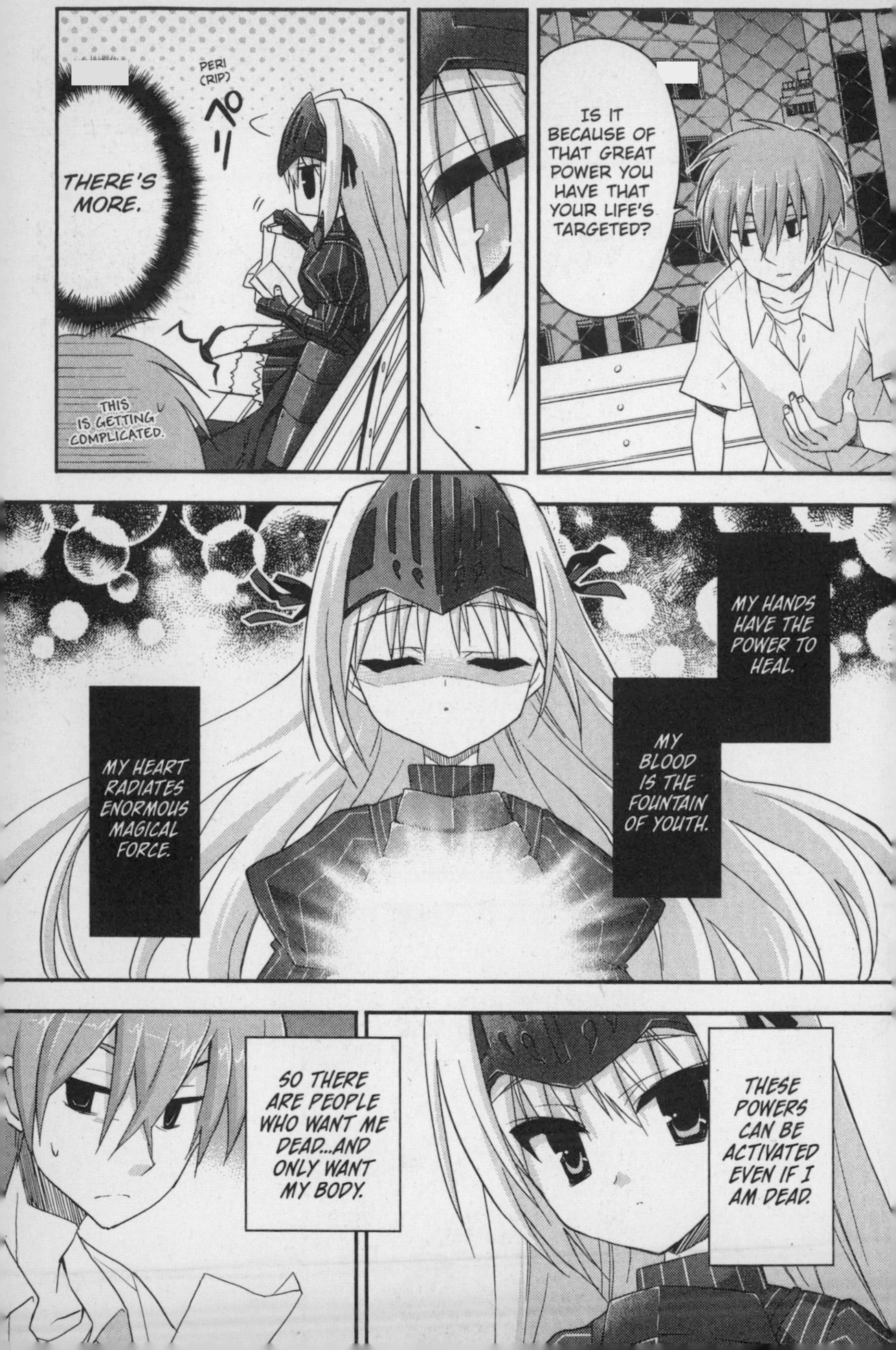
IS IT BECAUSE OF THAT GREAT POWER YOU HAVE THAT YOUR LIFE'S TARGETED?
PERI (RIP)
THERE'S MORE.
THIS IS GETTING COMPLICATED.
MY HANDS HAVE THE POWER TO HEAL.
MY BLOOD IS THE FOUNTAIN OF YOUTH.
MY HEART RADIATES ENORMOUS MAGICAL FORCE.
THESE POWERS CAN BE ACTIVATED EVEN IF I AM DEAD.
SO THERE ARE PEOPLE WHO WANT ME DEAD...AND ONLY WANT MY BODY.

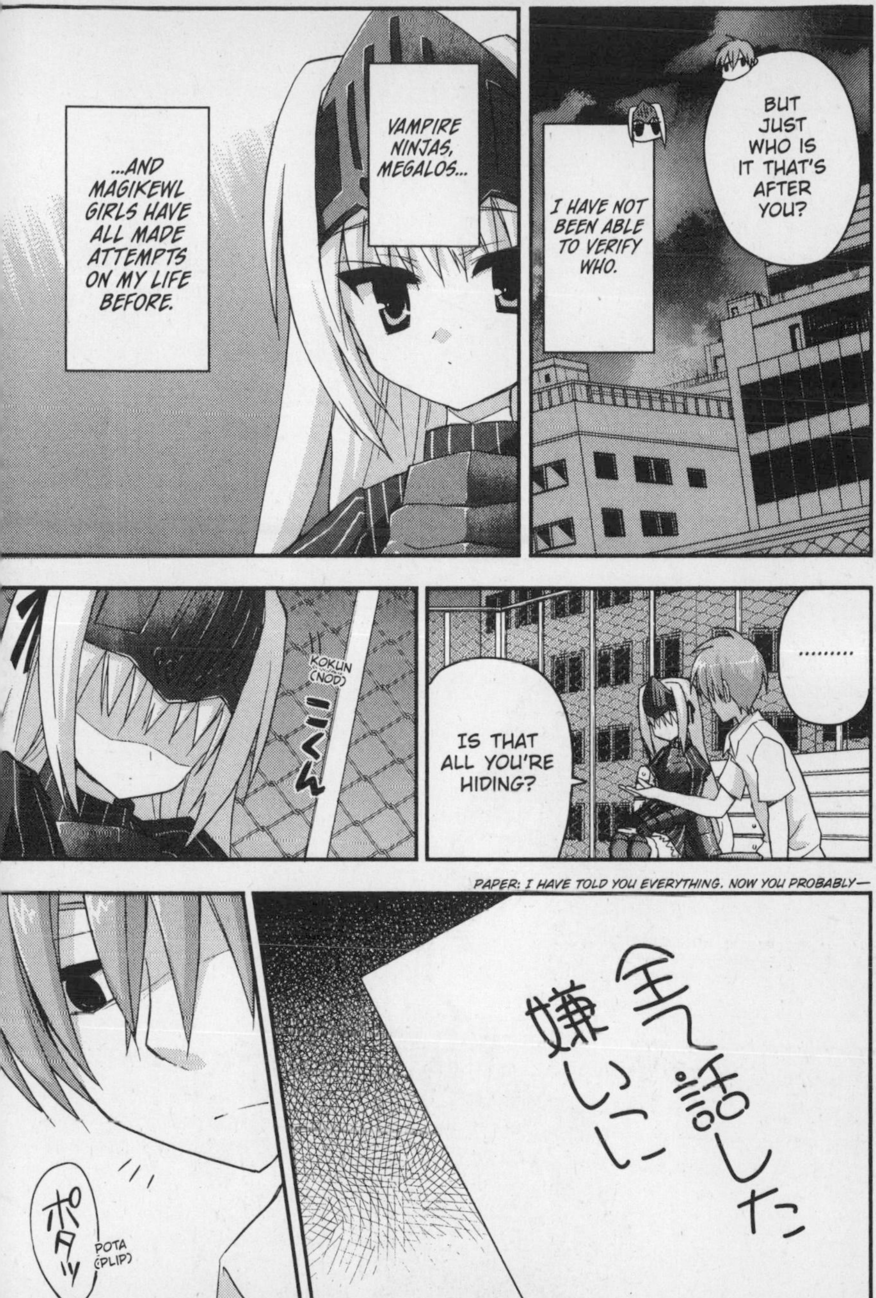
BUT JUST WHO IS IT THAT'S AFTER YOU?
I HAVE NOT BEEN ABLE TO VERIFY WHO.
VAMPIRE NINJAS, MEGALOS...
...AND MAGIKEWL GIRLS HAVE ALL MADE ATTEMPTS ON MY LIFE BEFORE.
....
IS THAT ALL YOU'RE HIDING?
こくん
KOKUN (NOD)
PAPER: I HAVE TOLD YOU EVERYTHING. NOW YOU PROBABLY—
全て話した
嫌いに
ポタッ
POTA (PLIP)

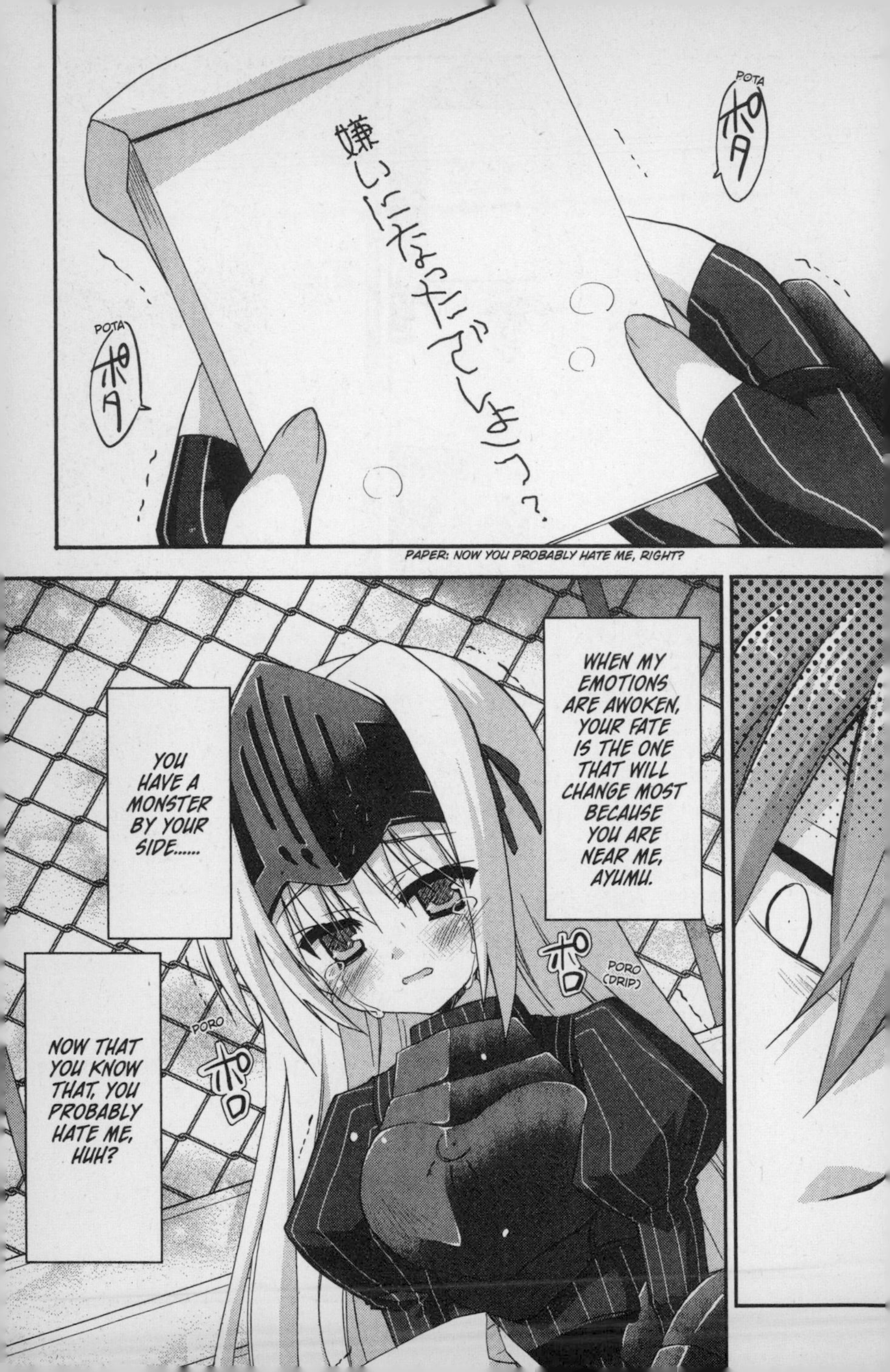
POTA
ポタ
嫌いになったでしょう?
POTA
ポタ
PAPER: NOW YOU PROBABLY HATE ME, RIGHT?
WHEN MY EMOTIONS ARE AWOKEN, YOUR FATE IS THE ONE THAT WILL CHANGE MOST BECAUSE YOU ARE NEAR ME, AYUMU.
YOU HAVE A MONSTER BY YOUR SIDE......
ポロ
PORO (DRIP)
NOW THAT YOU KNOW THAT, YOU PROBABLY HATE ME, HUH?
PORO
ポロ

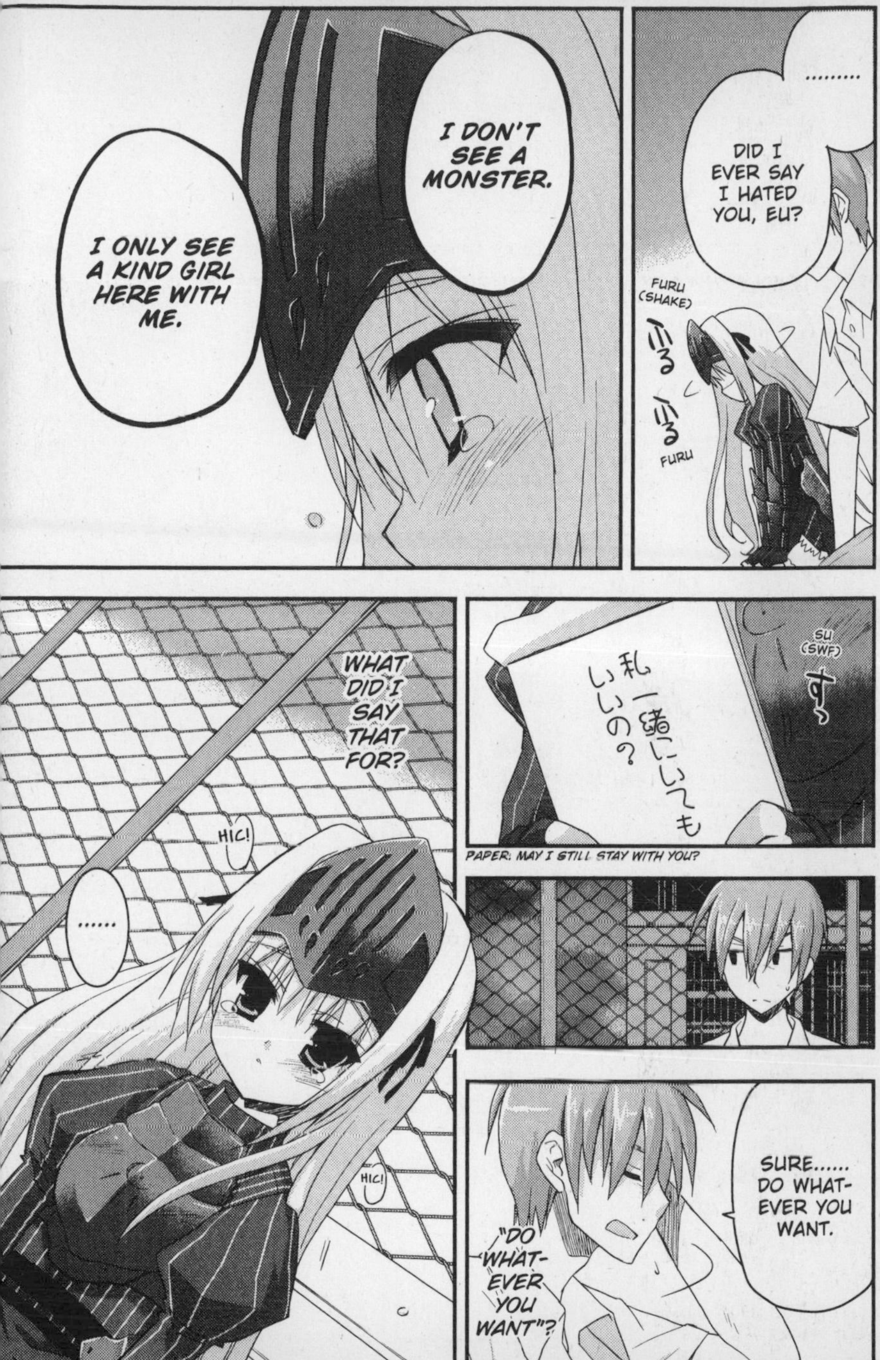
....
DID I EVER SAY I HATED YOU, EU?
FURU (SHAKE)
ふる
ふる
FURU
I DON'T SEE A MONSTER.
I ONLY SEE A KIND GIRL HERE WITH ME.
SU (SWF)
す
私一緒にいてもいいの？
PAPER: MAY I STILL STAY WITH YOU?
SURE...... DO WHAT-EVER YOU WANT.
"DO WHAT-EVER YOU WANT"?
WHAT DID I SAY THAT FOR?
HIC!
......
HIC!

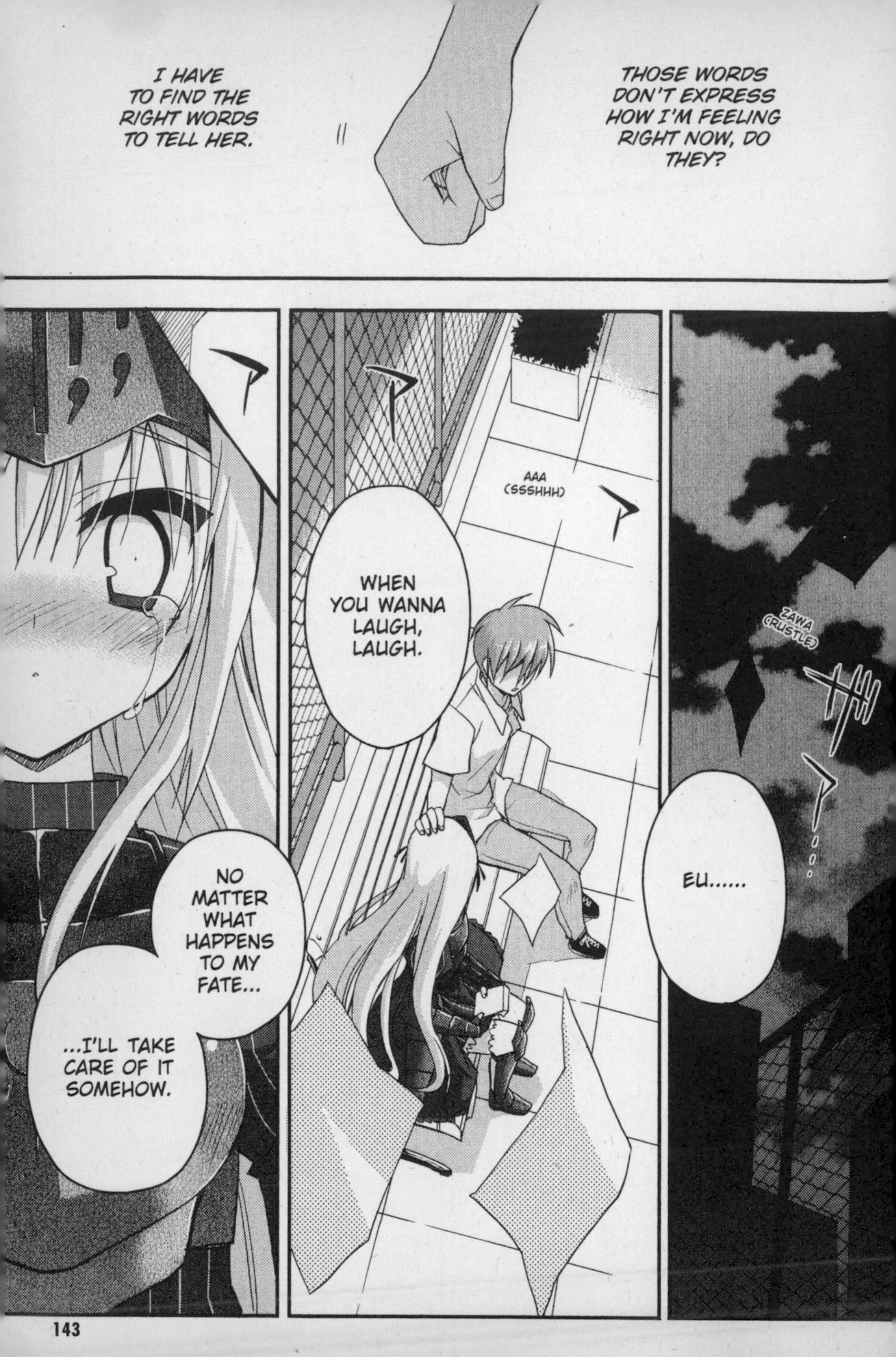
THOSE WORDS DON'T EXPRESS HOW I'M FEELING RIGHT NOW, DO THEY?
I HAVE TO FIND THE RIGHT WORDS TO TELL HER.
ZAWA (RUSTLE)
EU......
AAA (SSSHHH)
WHEN YOU WANNA LAUGH, LAUGH.
NO MATTER WHAT HAPPENS TO MY FATE...
...I'LL TAKE CARE OF IT SOMEHOW.

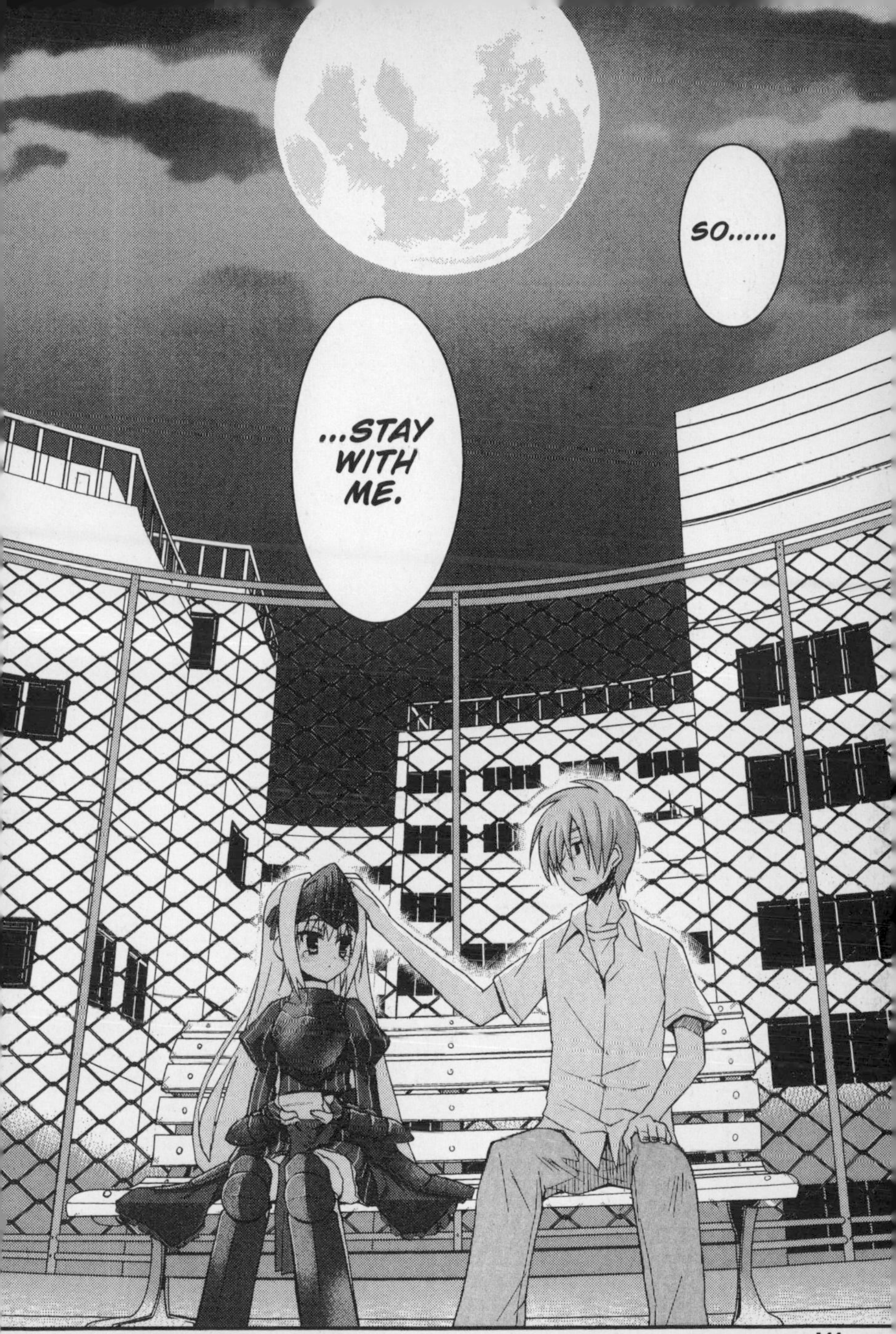
SO......
...STAY WITH ME.

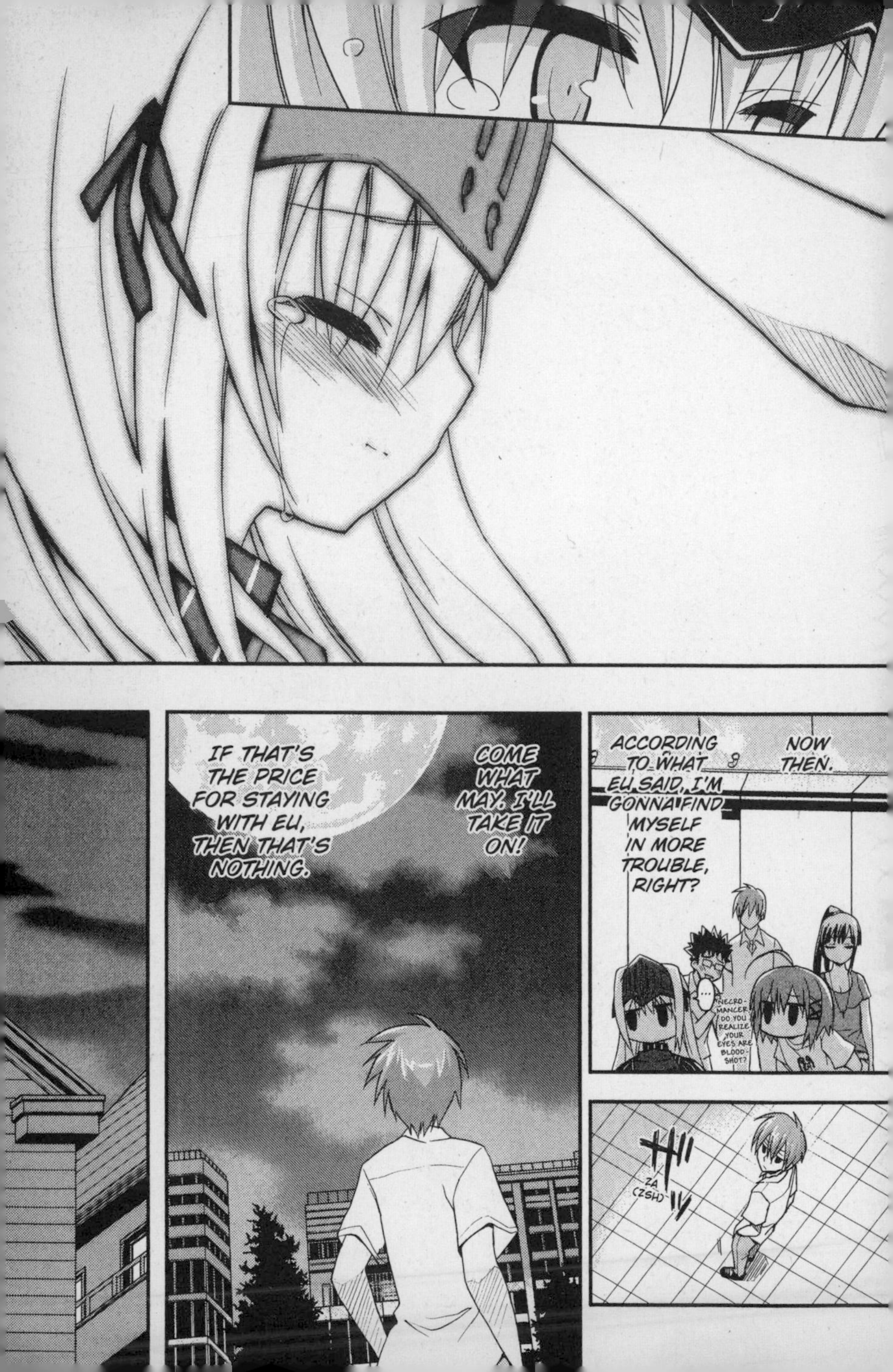

NOW THEN.
ACCORDING TO WHAT EU SAID, I'M GONNA FIND MYSELF IN MORE TROUBLE, RIGHT?
NECROMANCER, DO YOU REALIZE YOUR EYES ARE BLOODSHOT?
...
ZA (ZSH)
COME WHAT MAY. I'LL TAKE IT ON!
IF THAT'S THE PRICE FOR STAYING WITH EU, THEN THAT'S NOTHING.

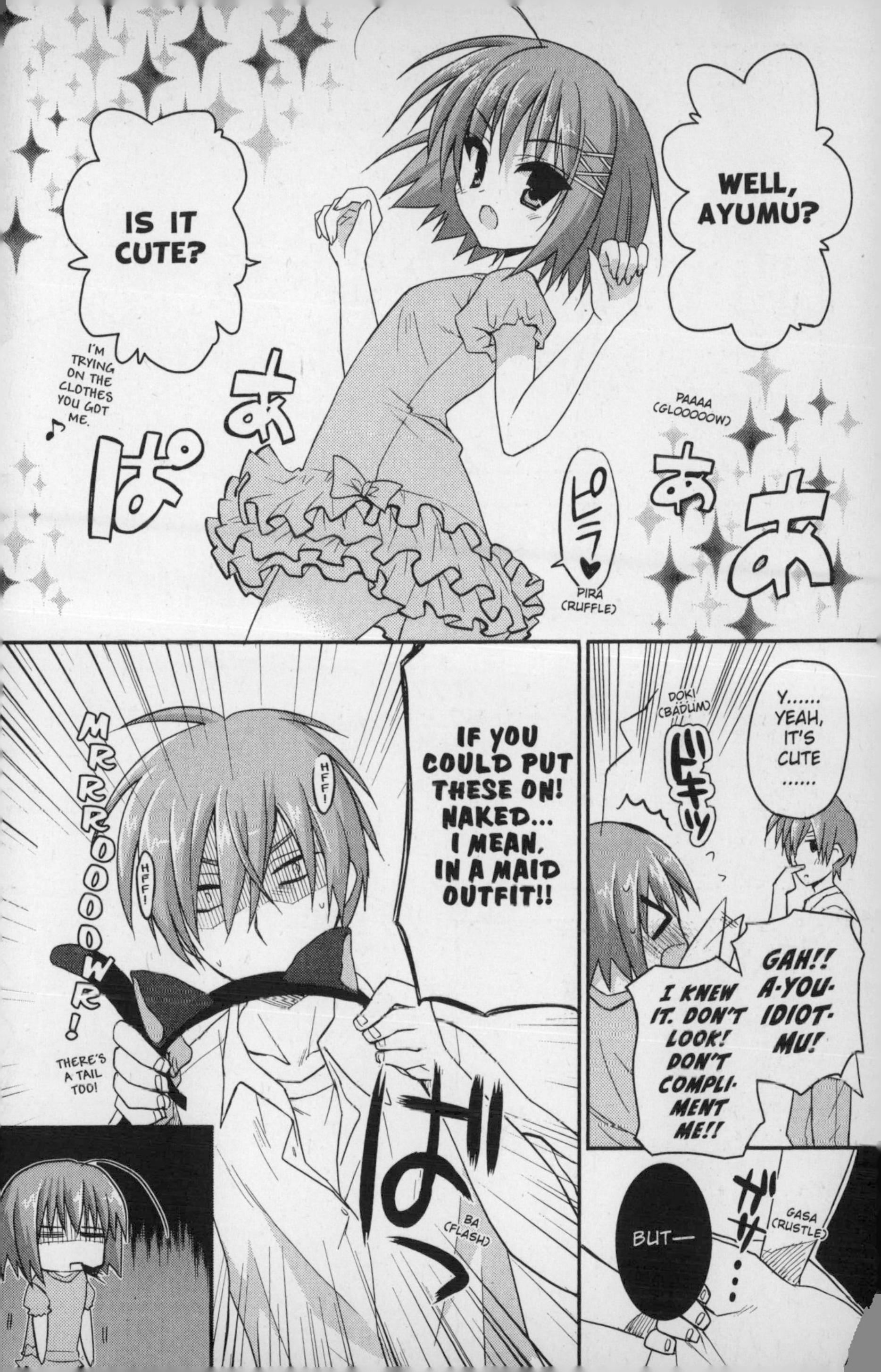
WELL, AYUMU?
PAAAA (GLOOOOOW)
ぱあああ
ピラ
PIRA (RUFFLE)
IS IT CUTE?
I'M TRYING ON THE CLOTHES YOU GOT ME. ♪
Y...... YEAH, IT'S CUTE ......
DOKI (BADUM)
ドキッ
GAH!! A-YOU-IDIOT-MU!
I KNEW IT. DON'T LOOK! DON'T COMPLI-MENT ME!!
BUT—
GASA (RUSTLE)
ガサ…
IF YOU COULD PUT THESE ON! NAKED... I MEAN, IN A MAID OUTFIT!!
HFF!
HFF!
MRRROOOOOWR!
THERE'S A TAIL TOO!
ばっ
BA (FLASH)

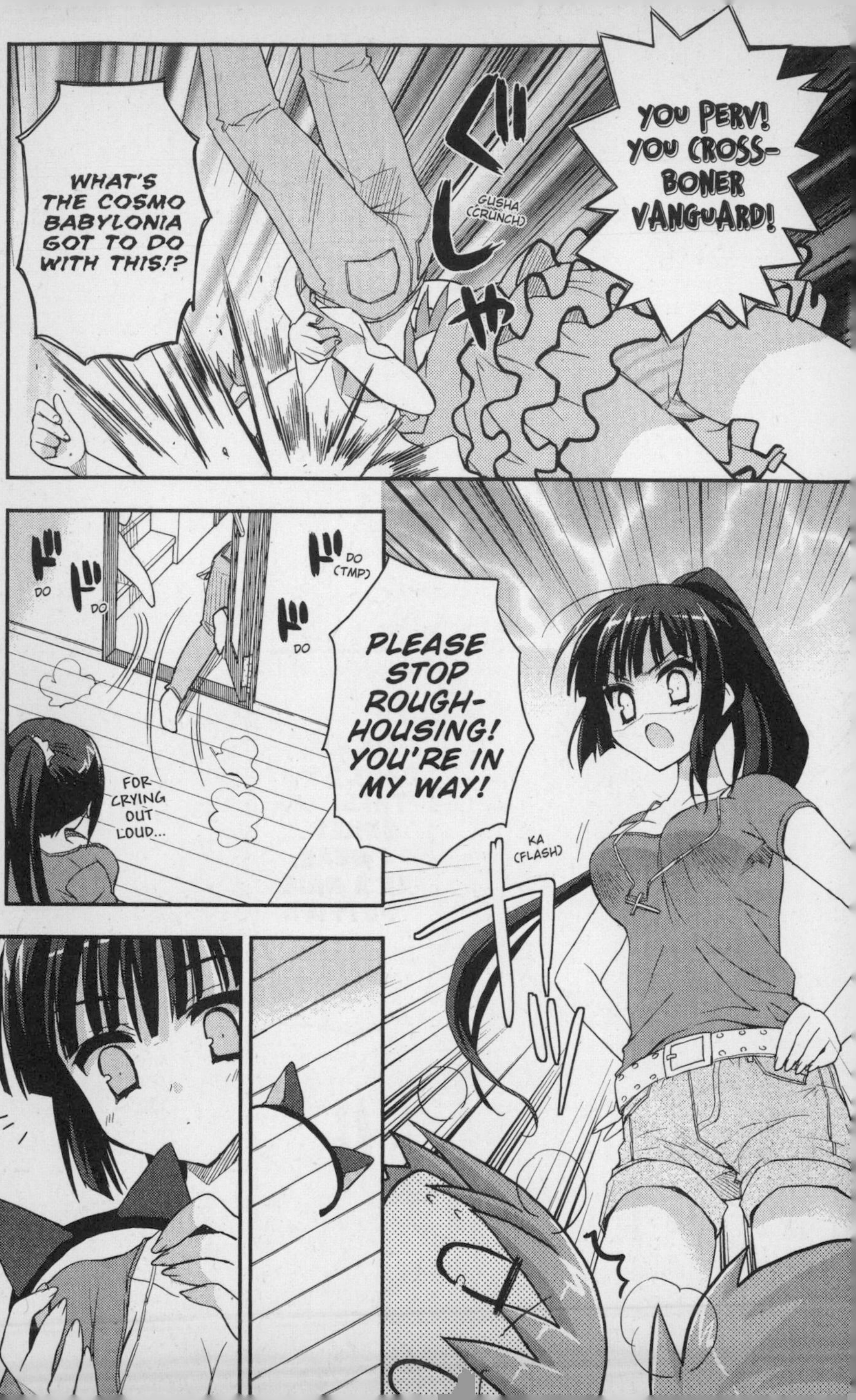
YOU PERV! YOU CROSS-BONER VANGUARD!
GUSHA (CRUNCH)
WHAT'S THE COSMO BABYLONIA GOT TO DO WITH THIS!?
PLEASE STOP ROUGH-HOUSING! YOU'RE IN MY WAY!
KA (FLASH)
DO (TMP)
DO
DO
DO
FOR CRYING OUT LOUD...

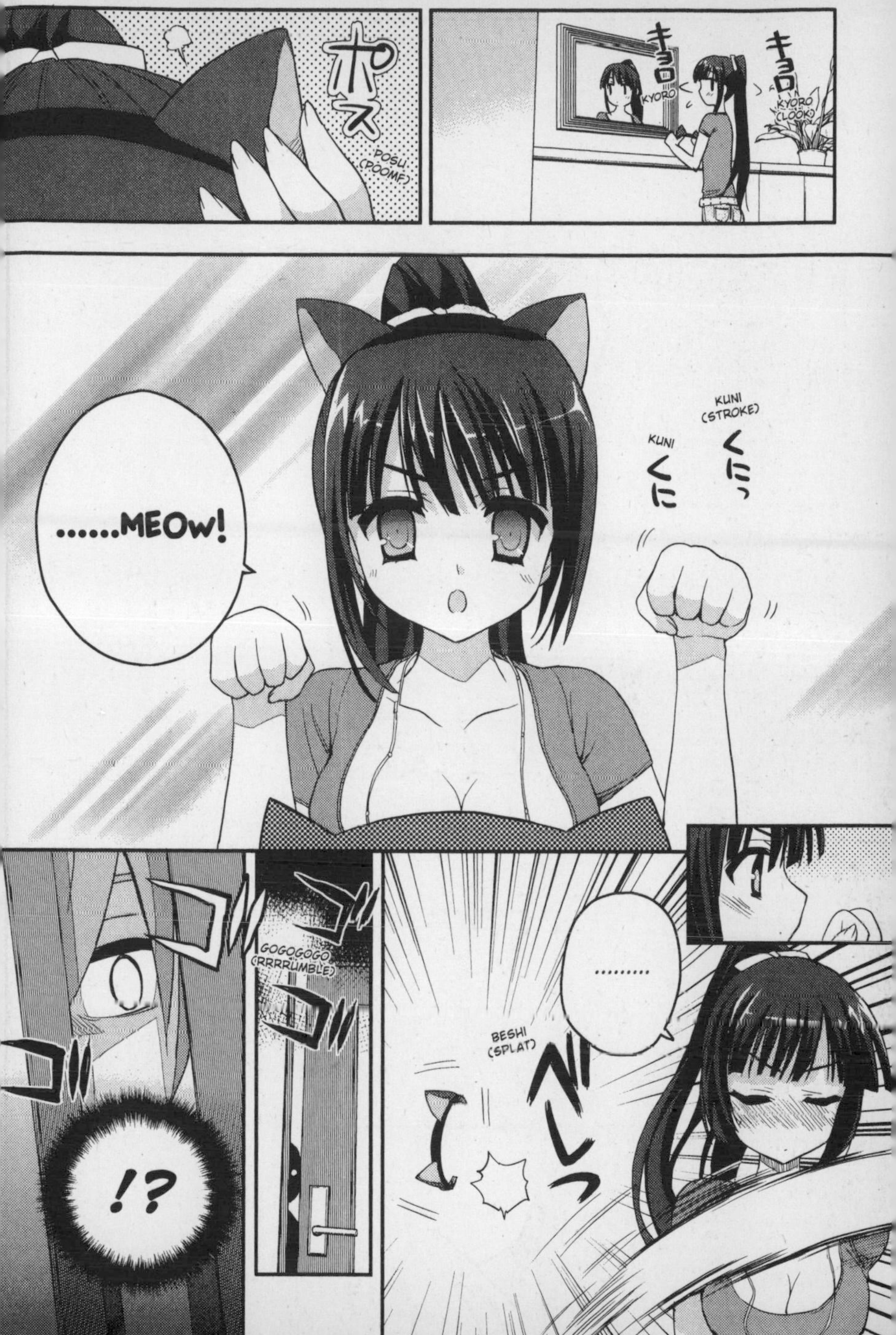

キョロ
KYORO (LOOK)
キョロ
KYORO
ポス
POSU (POOMF)
くにっ
KUNI (STROKE)
くに
KUNI
......MEOW!
....
べしっ
BESHI (SPLAT)
ゴゴゴゴ
GOGOGOGO (RRRRUMBLE)
!?

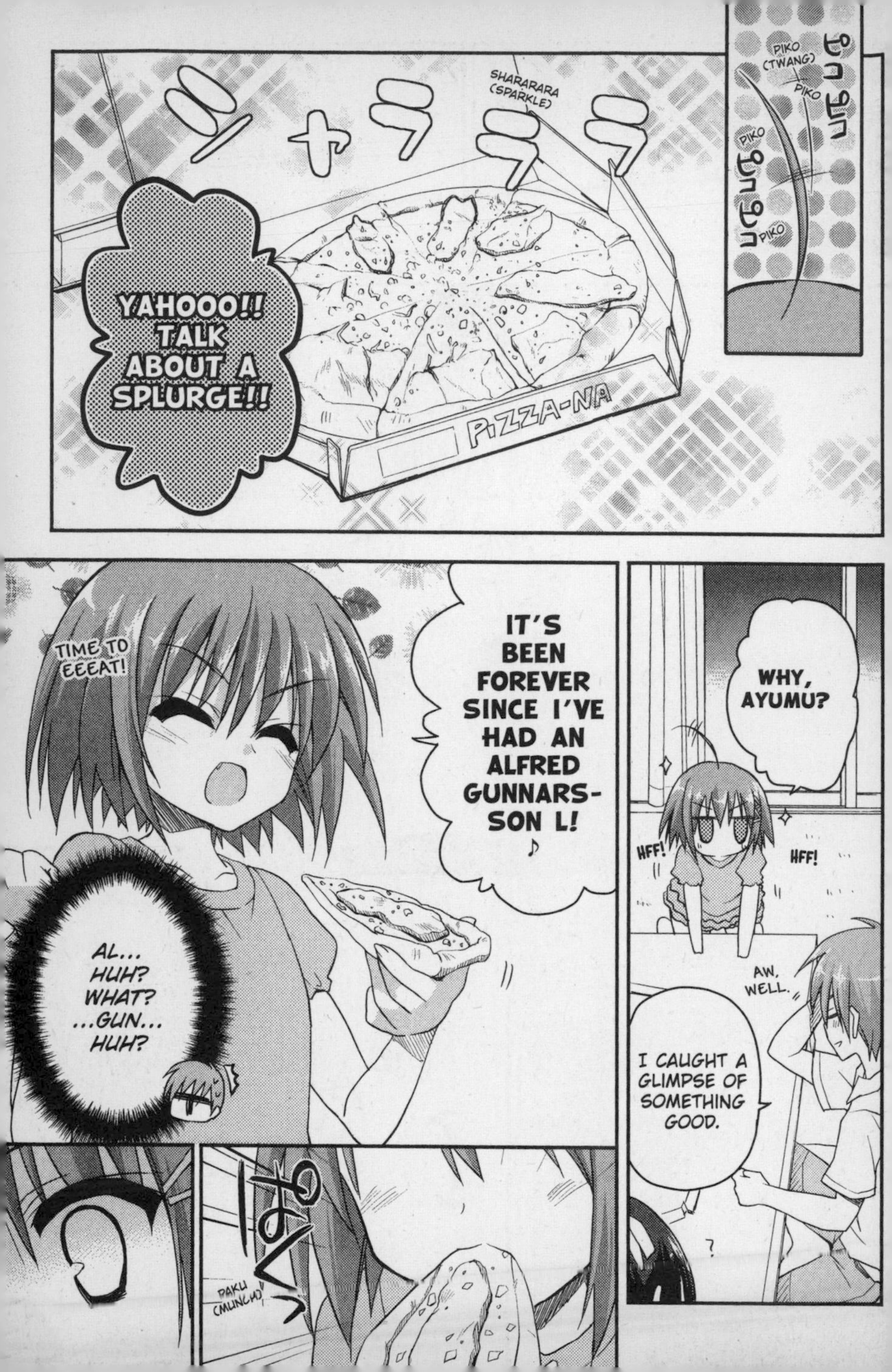
PIKO (TWANG)
PIKO
PIKO
PIKO
SHARARARA (SPARKLE)
YAHOOO!! TALK ABOUT A SPLURGE!!
PIZZA-NA
WHY, AYUMU?
HFF!
HFF!
AW, WELL.
I CAUGHT A GLIMPSE OF SOMETHING GOOD.
IT'S BEEN FOREVER SINCE I'VE HAD AN ALFRED GUNNARS-SON L! ♪
TIME TO EEEAT!
AL... HUH? WHAT? ...GUN... HUH?
PAKU (MUNCH)

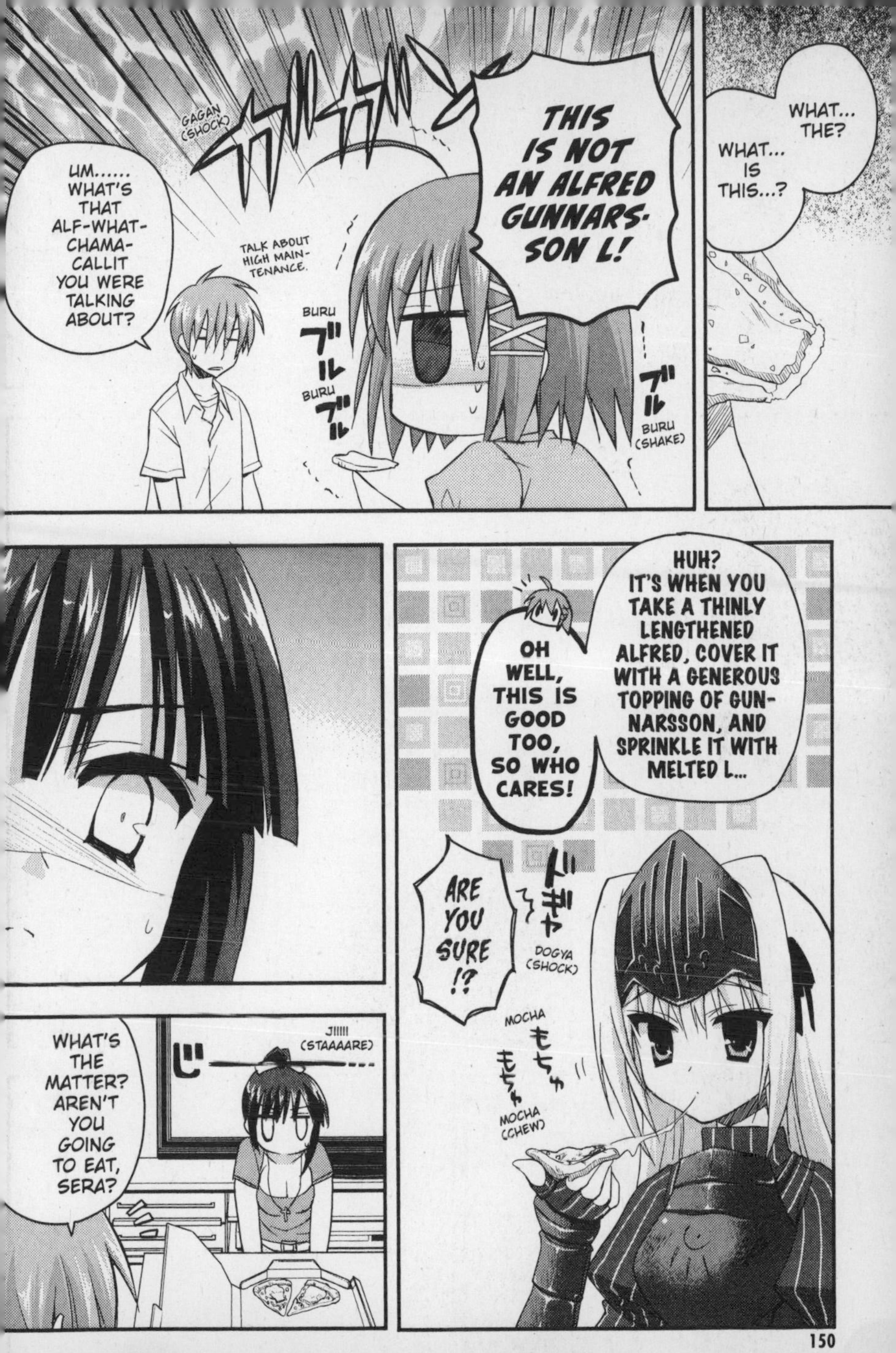
WHAT... THE?
WHAT... IS THIS...?
THIS IS NOT AN ALFRED GUNNARS-SON L!
GAGAN (SHOCK)
BURU (SHAKE)
BURU
BURU
TALK ABOUT HIGH MAIN-TENANCE.
UM...... WHAT'S THAT ALF-WHAT-CHAMA-CALLIT YOU WERE TALKING ABOUT?
HUH? IT'S WHEN YOU TAKE A THINLY LENGTHENED ALFRED, COVER IT WITH A GENEROUS TOPPING OF GUN-NARSSON, AND SPRINKLE IT WITH MELTED L...
OH WELL, THIS IS GOOD TOO, SO WHO CARES!
DOGYA (SHOCK)
ARE YOU SURE!?
MOCHA
MOCHA (CHEW)
JIIIII (STAAAARE)
WHAT'S THE MATTER? AREN'T YOU GOING TO EAT, SERA?

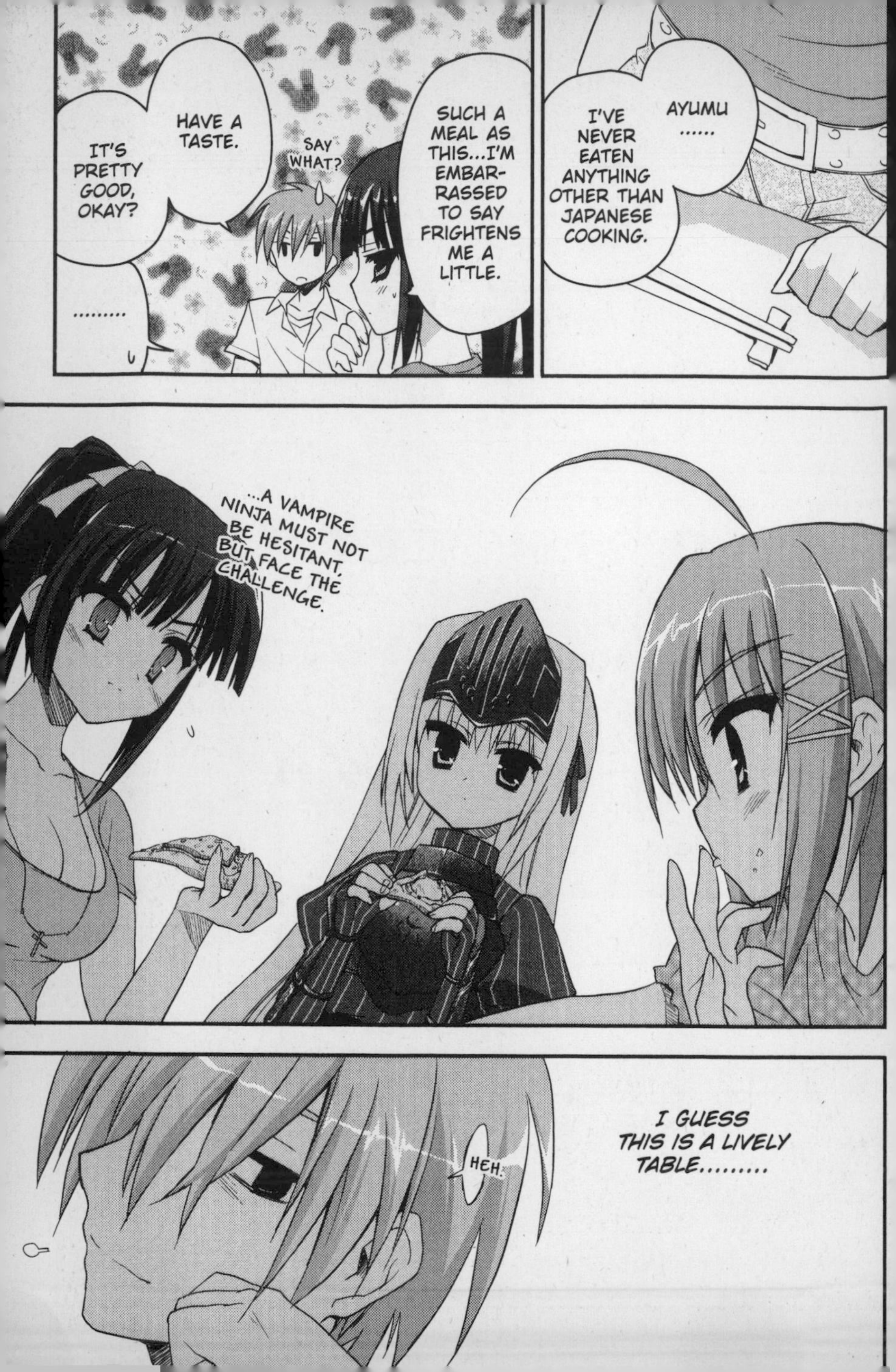
AYUMU......
I'VE NEVER EATEN ANYTHING OTHER THAN JAPANESE COOKING.
SUCH A MEAL AS THIS...I'M EMBARRASSED TO SAY FRIGHTENS ME A LITTLE.
SAY WHAT?
HAVE A TASTE.
IT'S PRETTY GOOD, OKAY?
....
...A VAMPIRE NINJA MUST NOT BE HESITANT, BUT FACE THE CHALLENGE.
I GUESS THIS IS A LIVELY TABLE.........
HEH.

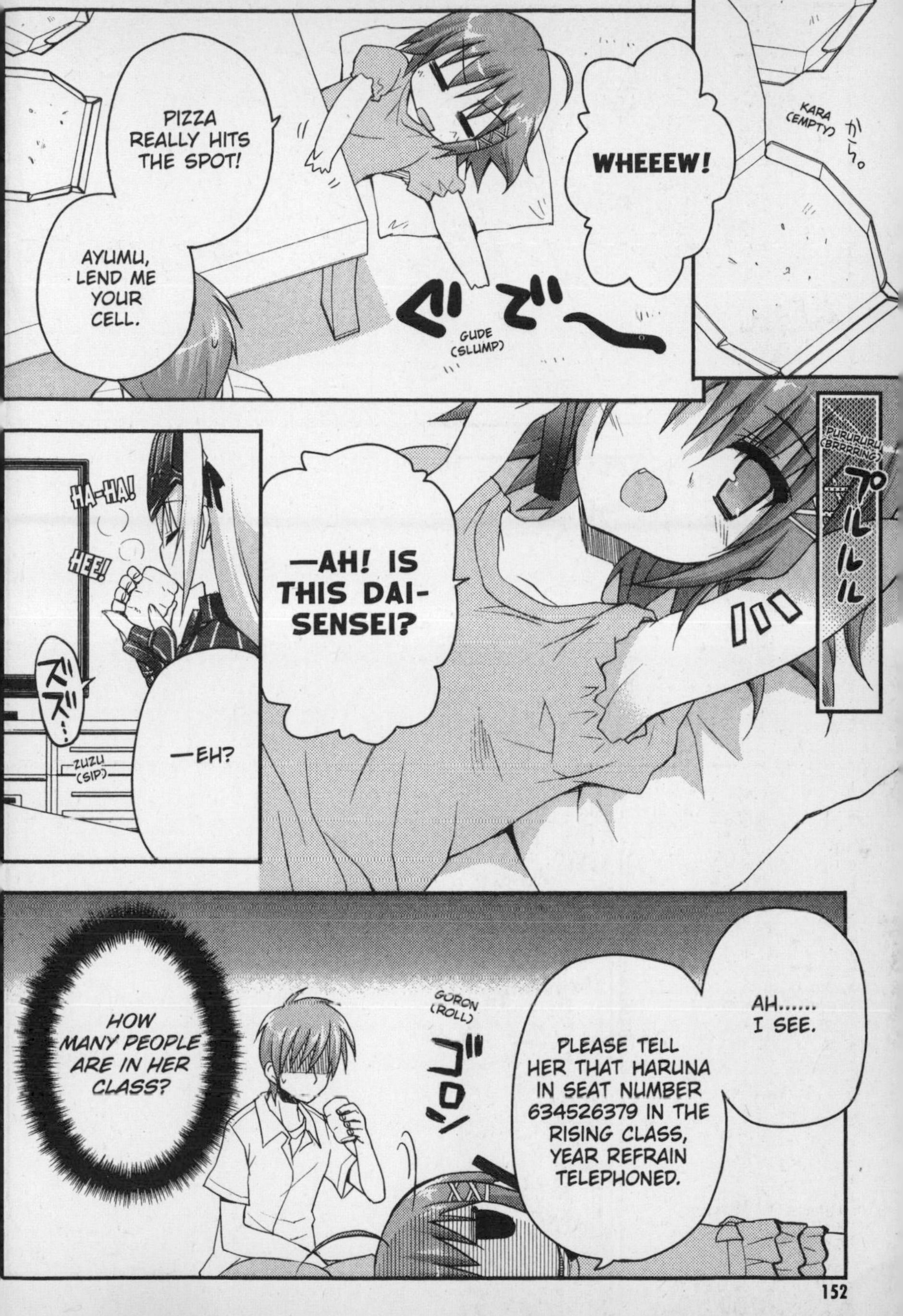
KARA (EMPTY)
から。
WHEEEW!
PIZZA REALLY HITS THE SPOT!
AYUMU, LEND ME YOUR CELL.
ぐで〜
GUDE (SLUMP)
PURURURU (BRRRRING)
プルルル
—AH! IS THIS DAI-SENSEI?
HA-HA!
HEE!
ズズ…
ZUZU (SIP)
—EH?
AH...... I SEE.
PLEASE TELL HER THAT HARUNA IN SEAT NUMBER 634526379 IN THE RISING CLASS, YEAR REFRAIN TELEPHONED.
GORON (ROLL)
ゴロ
HOW MANY PEOPLE ARE IN HER CLASS?

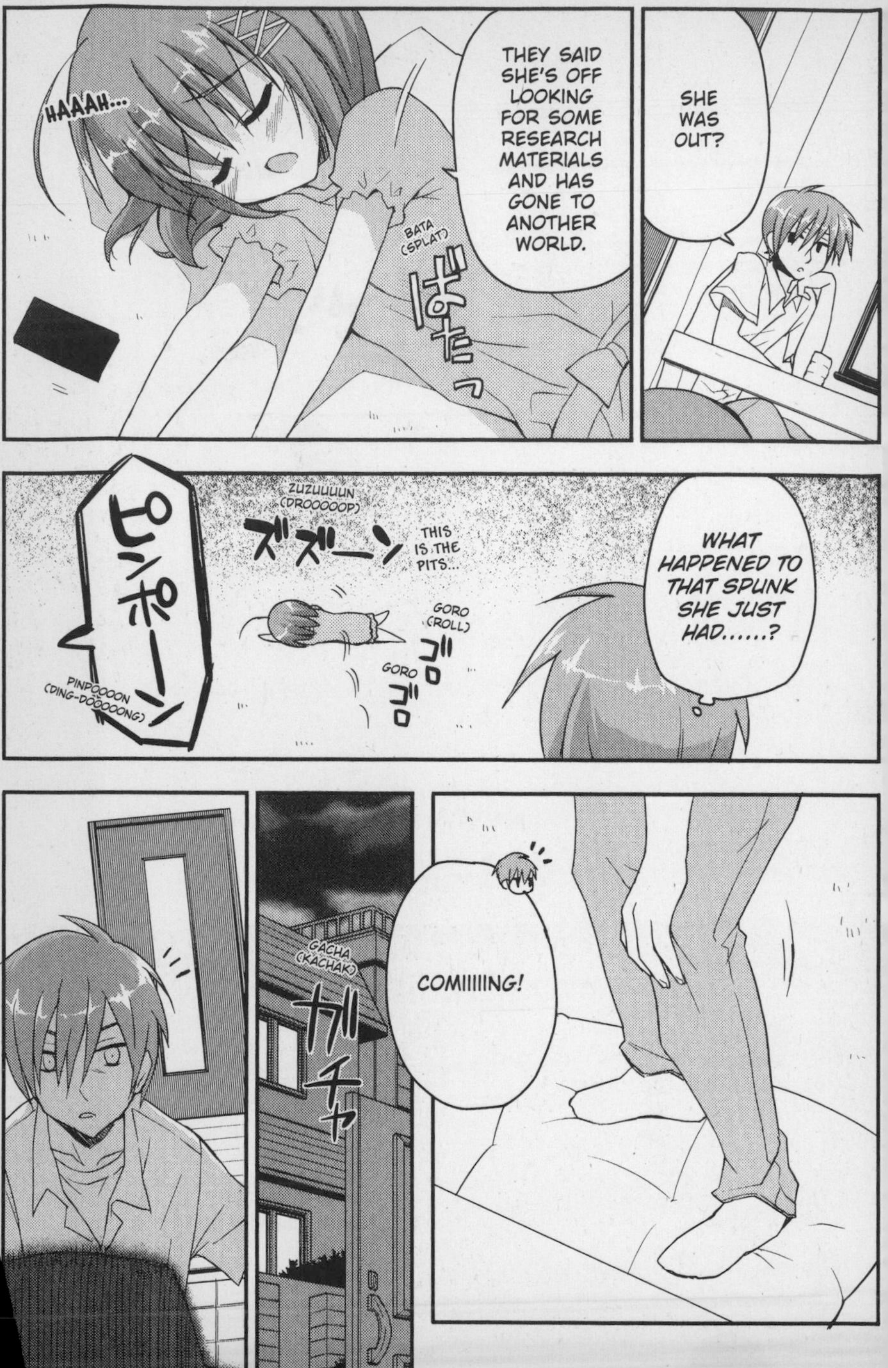
SHE WAS OUT?
THEY SAID SHE'S OFF LOOKING FOR SOME RESEARCH MATERIALS AND HAS GONE TO ANOTHER WORLD.
BATA (SPLAT)
ばたっ
HAAAH...
WHAT HAPPENED TO THAT SPUNK SHE JUST HAD......?
GORO (ROLL)
ゴロ
GORO
ゴロ
THIS IS THE PITS...
ZUZUUUUN (DROOOOOP)
ズズーン
ピンポーン
PINPOOOON (DING-DOOOOONG)
COMIIIIING!
GACHA (KACHAK)
ガチャ

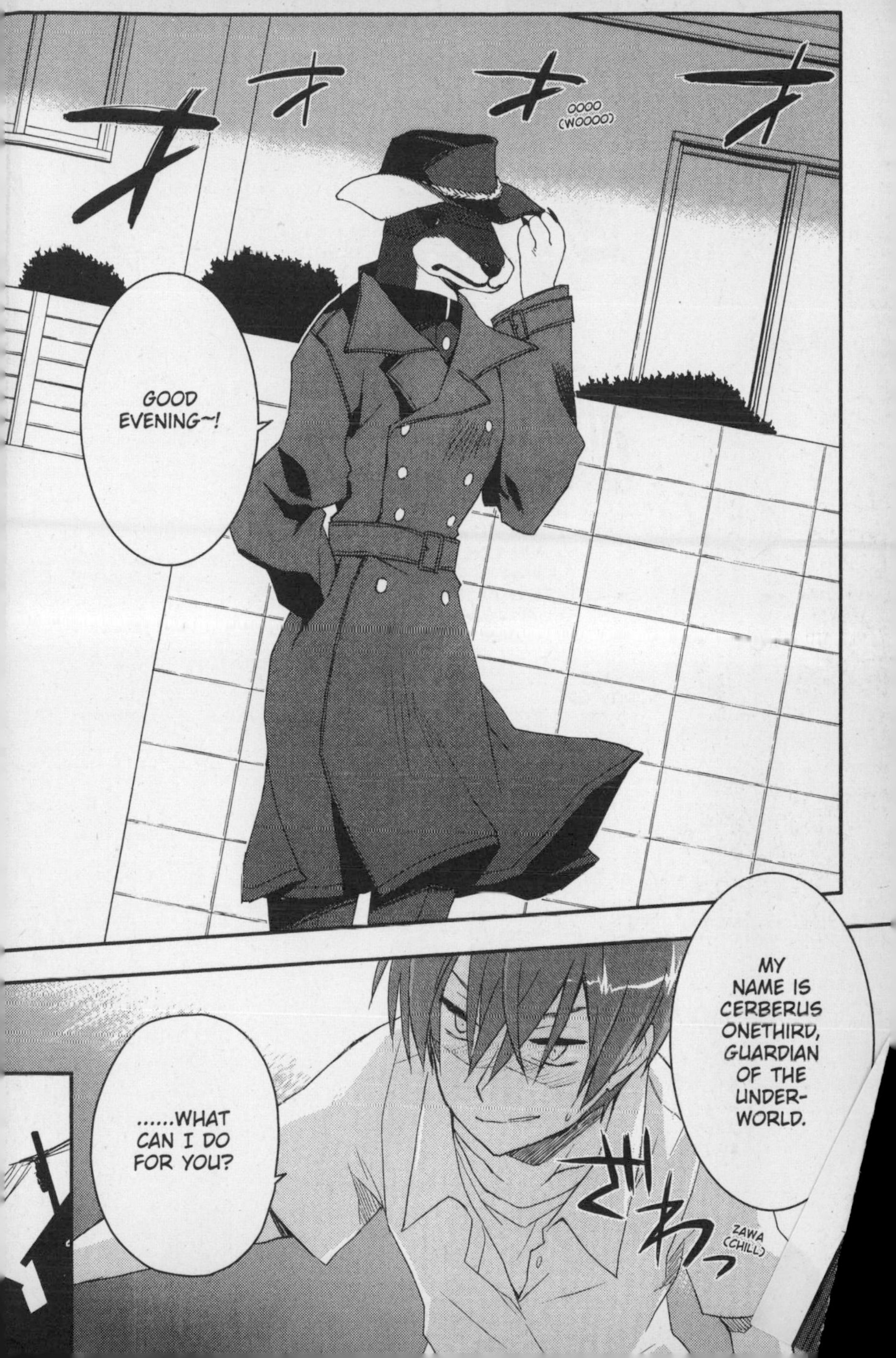
OOOO (WOOOO)
GOOD EVENING~!
MY NAME IS CERBERUS ONETHIRD, GUARDIAN OF THE UNDER-WORLD.
ZAWA (CHILL)
......WHAT CAN I DO FOR YOU?

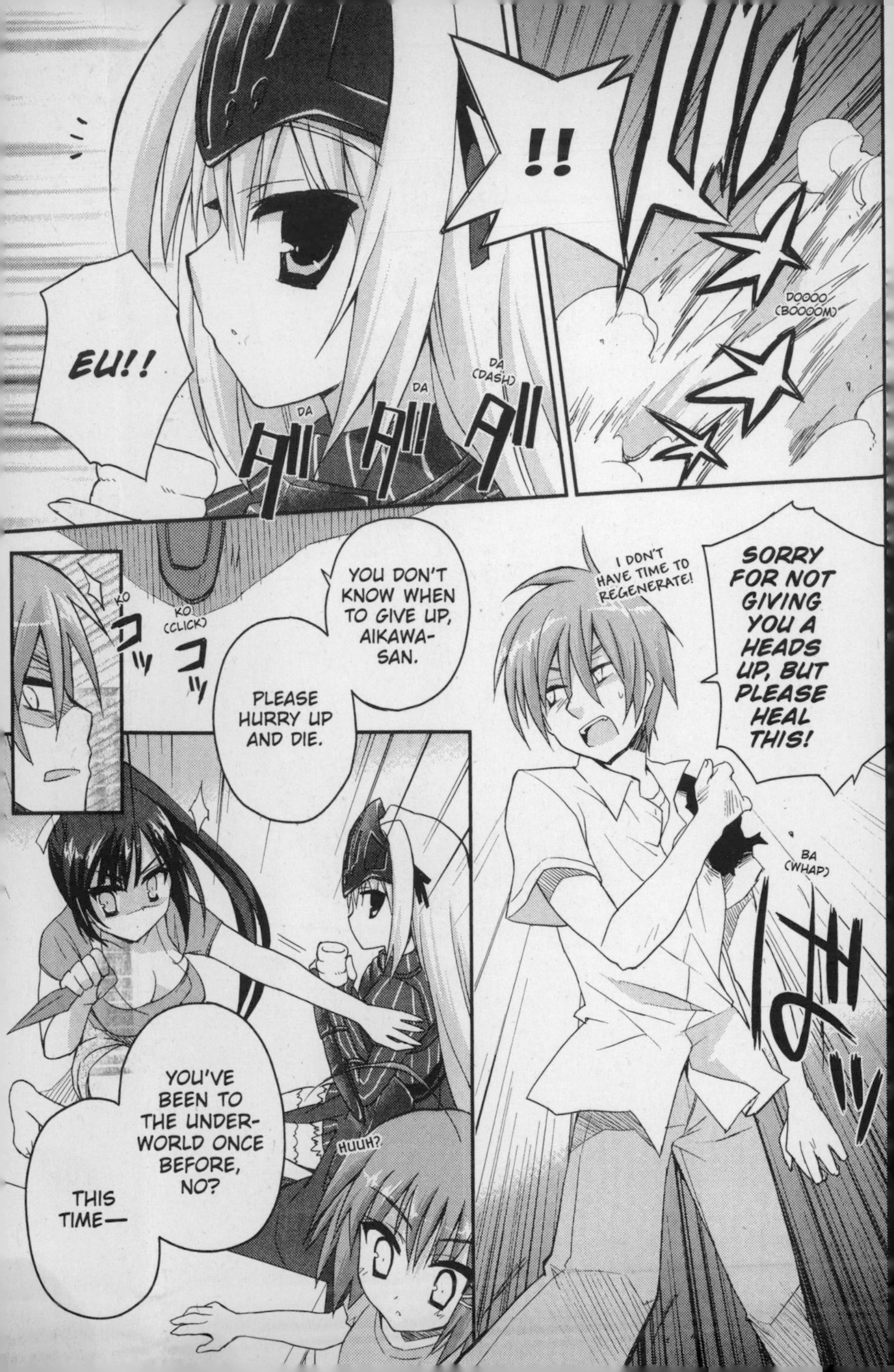
!!
DOOOO (BOOOOM)
EU!!
DA (DASH)
DA
DA
SORRY FOR NOT GIVING YOU A HEADS UP, BUT PLEASE HEAL THIS!
I DON'T HAVE TIME TO REGENERATE!
BA (WHAP)
KO (CLICK)
KO
YOU DON'T KNOW WHEN TO GIVE UP, AIKAWA-SAN.
PLEASE HURRY UP AND DIE.
HUUH?
YOU'VE BEEN TO THE UNDER-WORLD ONCE BEFORE, NO?
THIS TIME—

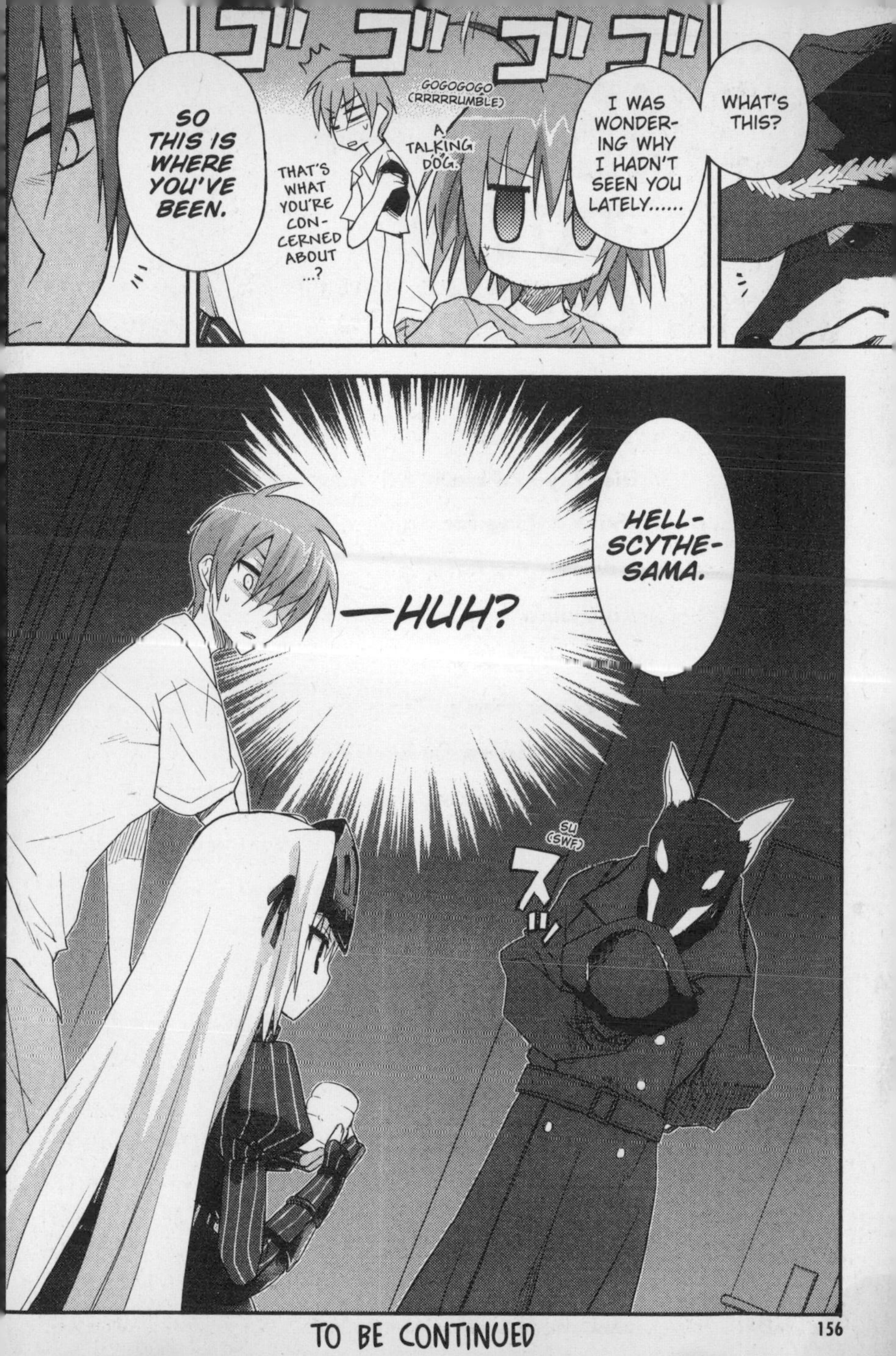
WHAT'S THIS?
I WAS WONDER-ING WHY I HADN'T SEEN YOU LATELY......
GOGOGOGO (RRRRRUMBLE)
A TALKING DOG.
THAT'S WHAT YOU'RE CON-CERNED ABOUT ...?
SO THIS IS WHERE YOU'VE BEEN.
HELL-SCYTHE-SAMA.
—HUH?
SU (SWF)

TO BE CONTINUED

ZOMBIE LOVEY-DOVEY LEVEL CHECKLIST

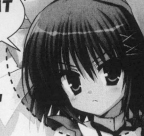

CHECK IT OUT!

☐ You decide to pull a Moon Somersault in front of the girl you like.

☐ You've become "Gross Ayumu."

☐ If you had a girlfriend, you'd make her wear armor.

☐ Even though you have a thing for big jugs, you like Haruna.

☐ You like leaf swords over the Revolcane.

☐ You don't believe a chainsaw is for cutting down trees.

☐ You can handle a household of smart asses.

☐ You've decided you're not even gonna worry about the story.

☐ You want Ayumu to bop you on the head for being a goof.

☐ You enjoy things other than Haruna's nudity.

☐ You laughed out loud reading this book! Or at least your knee did.

☐ Even when a girl is cold toward you, she's a doting little sister in your head.

☐ You want to Aikawa household's laundry.

☐ You've ordered a suit of armor off of Amaz•n.

☐ You follow Haruna-chan's Twitter account.

Score	Results
15	Eu "If you really mean it, then I am happy."
Other	Sera "That is highly revolting. That means you're already a zombie."
0	Haruna "Now you look here! You better start following now! You rotten natto beans!"

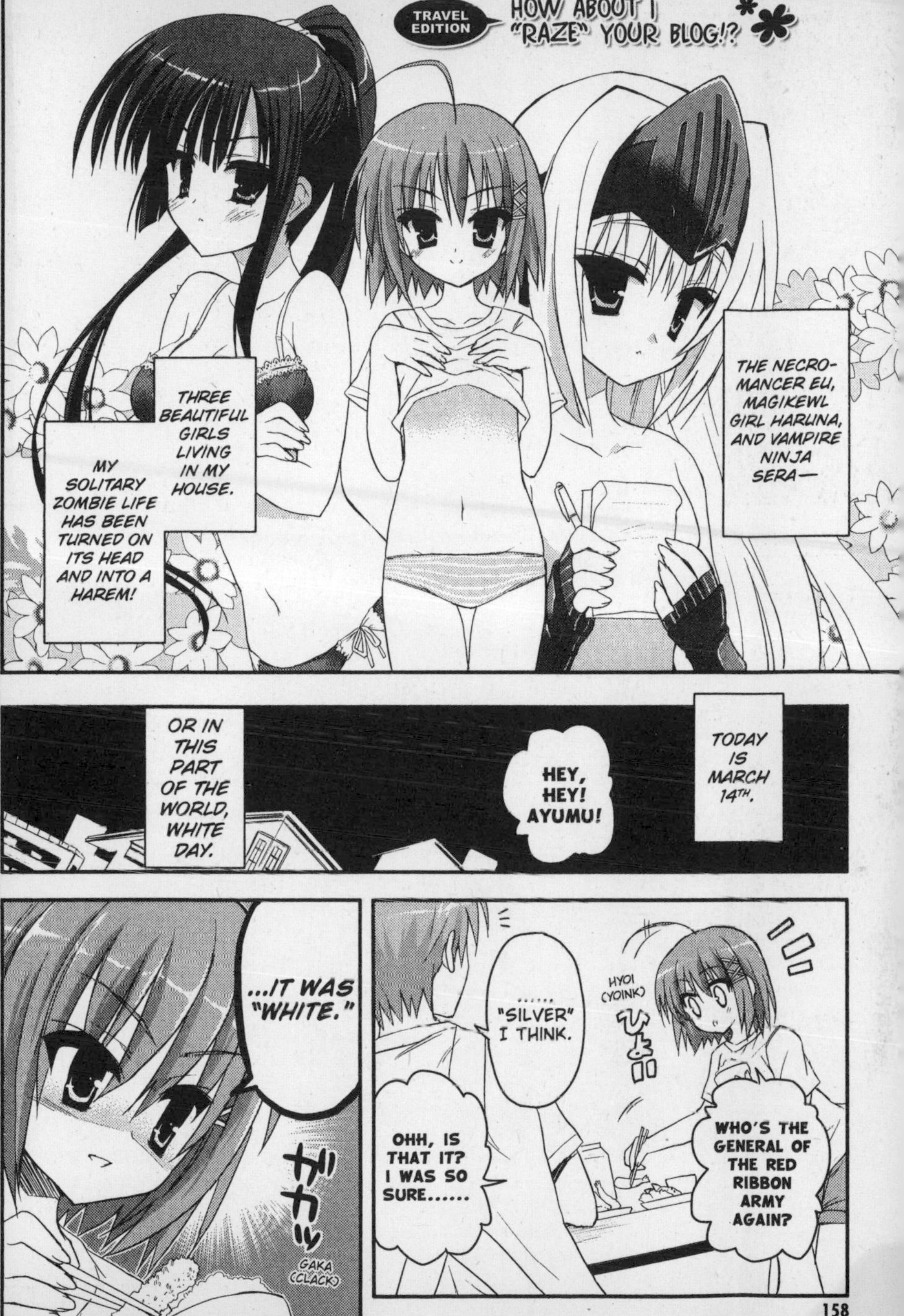
TRAVEL EDITION
HOW ABOUT I "RAZE" YOUR BLOG!?
THE NECROMANCER EU, MAGIKEWL GIRL HARUNA, AND VAMPIRE NINJA SERA—
THREE BEAUTIFUL GIRLS LIVING IN MY HOUSE.
MY SOLITARY ZOMBIE LIFE HAS BEEN TURNED ON ITS HEAD AND INTO A HAREM!
TODAY IS MARCH 14TH.
HEY, HEY! AYUMU!
OR IN THIS PART OF THE WORLD, WHITE DAY.
HYOI (YOINK)
WHO'S THE GENERAL OF THE RED RIBBON ARMY AGAIN?
......"SILVER" I THINK.
OHH, IS THAT IT? I WAS SO SURE......
...IT WAS "WHITE."
GAKA (CLACK)

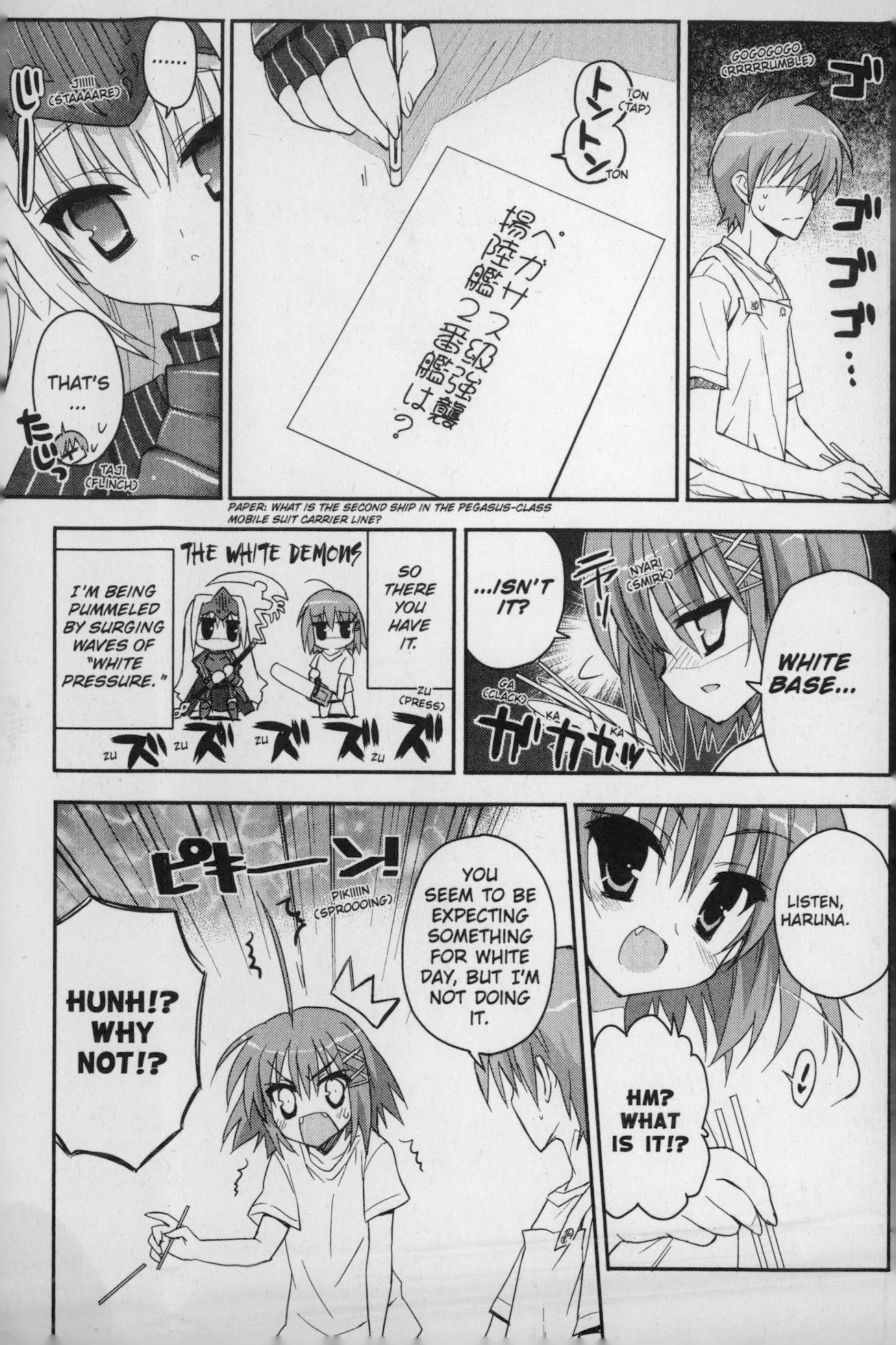
GOGOGOGO (RRRRRUMBLE)
ゴゴゴゴ…
トントン
TON (TAP)
TON
ペガサス級強襲揚陸艦2番艦は？
……
じ
JIIII (STAAAARE)
THAT'S …
たじっ
TAJI (FLINCH)
ニヤリ
NYARI (SMIRK)
WHITE BASE…
…ISN'T IT?
GA (CLACK)
KA
KA
SO THERE YOU HAVE IT.
THE WHITE DEMONS
I'M BEING PUMMELED BY SURGING WAVES OF "WHITE PRESSURE."
ZU (PRESS)
ZU
ZU
ZU
LISTEN, HARUNA.
!
HM? WHAT IS IT!?
YOU SEEM TO BE EXPECTING SOMETHING FOR WHITE DAY, BUT I'M NOT DOING IT.
ピキーン!
PIKIIIIN (SPROOOING)
HUNH!? WHY NOT!?
PAPER: WHAT IS THE SECOND SHIP IN THE PEGASUS-CLASS MOBILE SUIT CARRIER LINE?

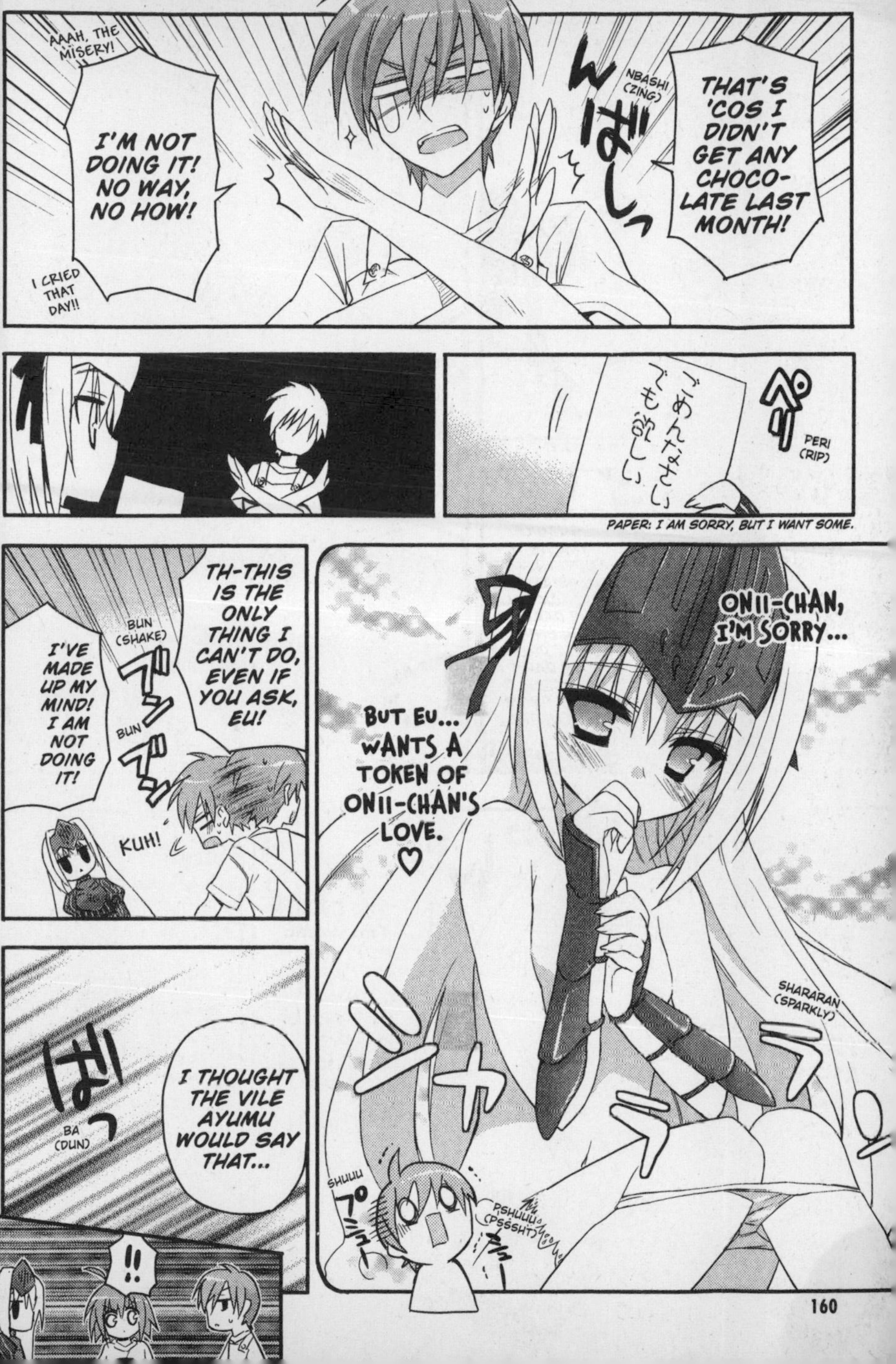
ばしっ
NBASHI (ZING)
THAT'S 'COS I DIDN'T GET ANY CHOCOLATE LAST MONTH!
AAAH, THE MISERY!
I'M NOT DOING IT! NO WAY, NO HOW!
I CRIED THAT DAY!!
ぺり
PERI (RIP)
ごめんなさい
でも欲しい
PAPER: I AM SORRY, BUT I WANT SOME.
ONII-CHAN, I'M SORRY...
BUT EU... WANTS A TOKEN OF ONII-CHAN'S LOVE. ♡
SHARARAN (SPARKLY)
SHUUU
PSHUUU (PSSSHT)
TH-THIS IS THE ONLY THING I CAN'T DO, EVEN IF YOU ASK, EU!
BUN (SHAKE)
BUN
I'VE MADE UP MY MIND! I AM NOT DOING IT!
KUH!
I THOUGHT THE VILE AYUMU WOULD SAY THAT...
ばっ
BA (DUN)
!!

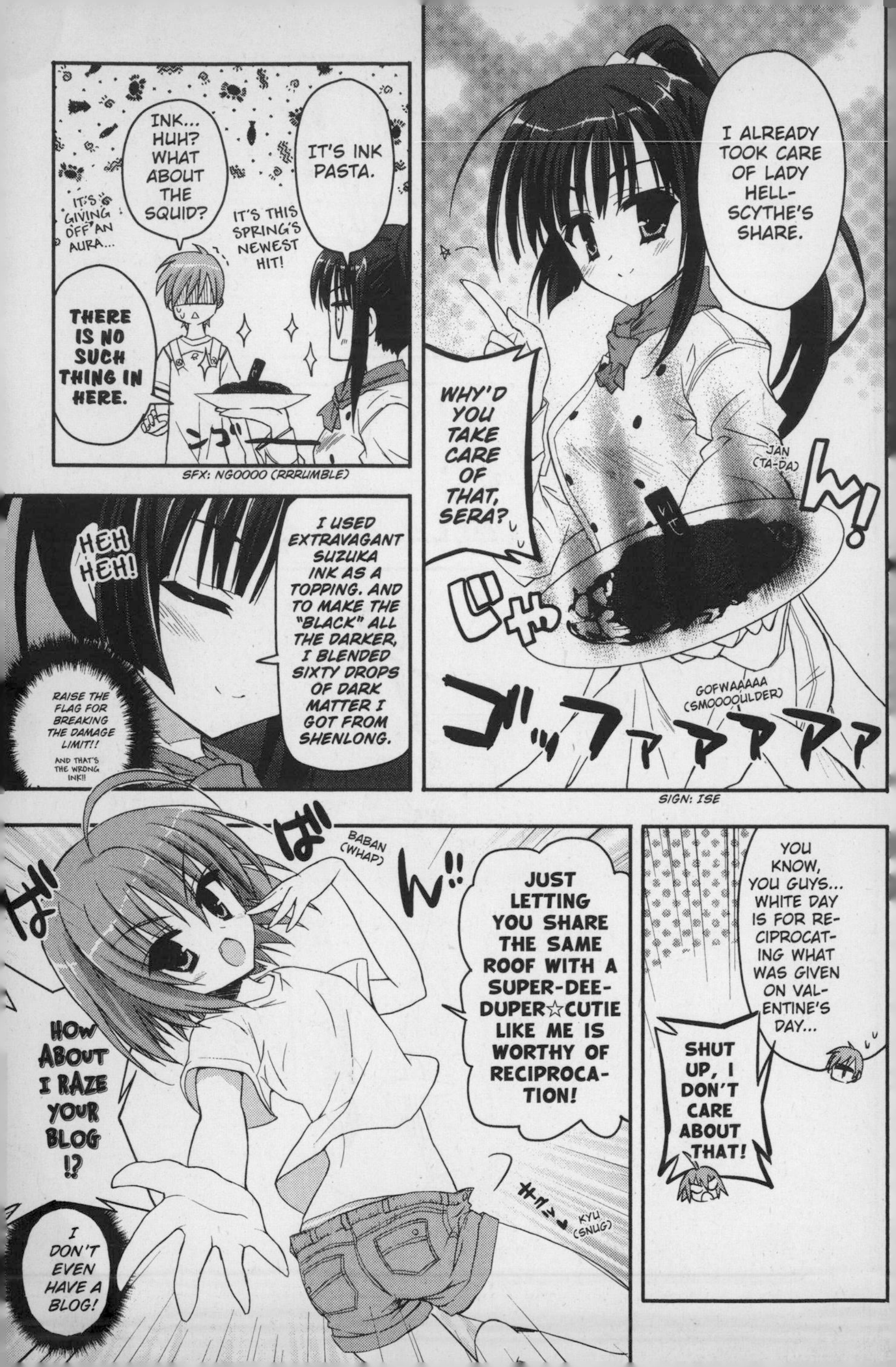
I ALREADY TOOK CARE OF LADY HELL-SCYTHE'S SHARE.
WHY'D YOU TAKE CARE OF THAT, SERA?
JAN (TA-DA)
GOFWAAAA (SMOOOOULDER)
SIGN: ISE
IT'S INK PASTA.
IT'S THIS SPRING'S NEWEST HIT!
INK... HUH? WHAT ABOUT THE SQUID?
IT'S GIVING OFF AN AURA...
THERE IS NO SUCH THING IN HERE.
SFX: NGOOOO (RRRUMBLE)
I USED EXTRAVAGANT SUZUKA INK AS A TOPPING. AND TO MAKE THE "BLACK" ALL THE DARKER, I BLENDED SIXTY DROPS OF DARK MATTER I GOT FROM SHENLONG.
HEH HEH!
RAISE THE FLAG FOR BREAKING THE DAMAGE LIMIT!!
AND THAT'S THE WRONG INK!!
YOU KNOW, YOU GUYS... WHITE DAY IS FOR RE-CIPROCAT-ING WHAT WAS GIVEN ON VAL-ENTINE'S DAY...
SHUT UP, I DON'T CARE ABOUT THAT!
BABAN (WHAP)
JUST LETTING YOU SHARE THE SAME ROOF WITH A SUPER-DEE-DUPER☆CUTIE LIKE ME IS WORTHY OF RECIPROCA-TION!
KYU (SNUG)
HOW ABOUT I RAZE YOUR BLOG!?
I DON'T EVEN HAVE A BLOG!

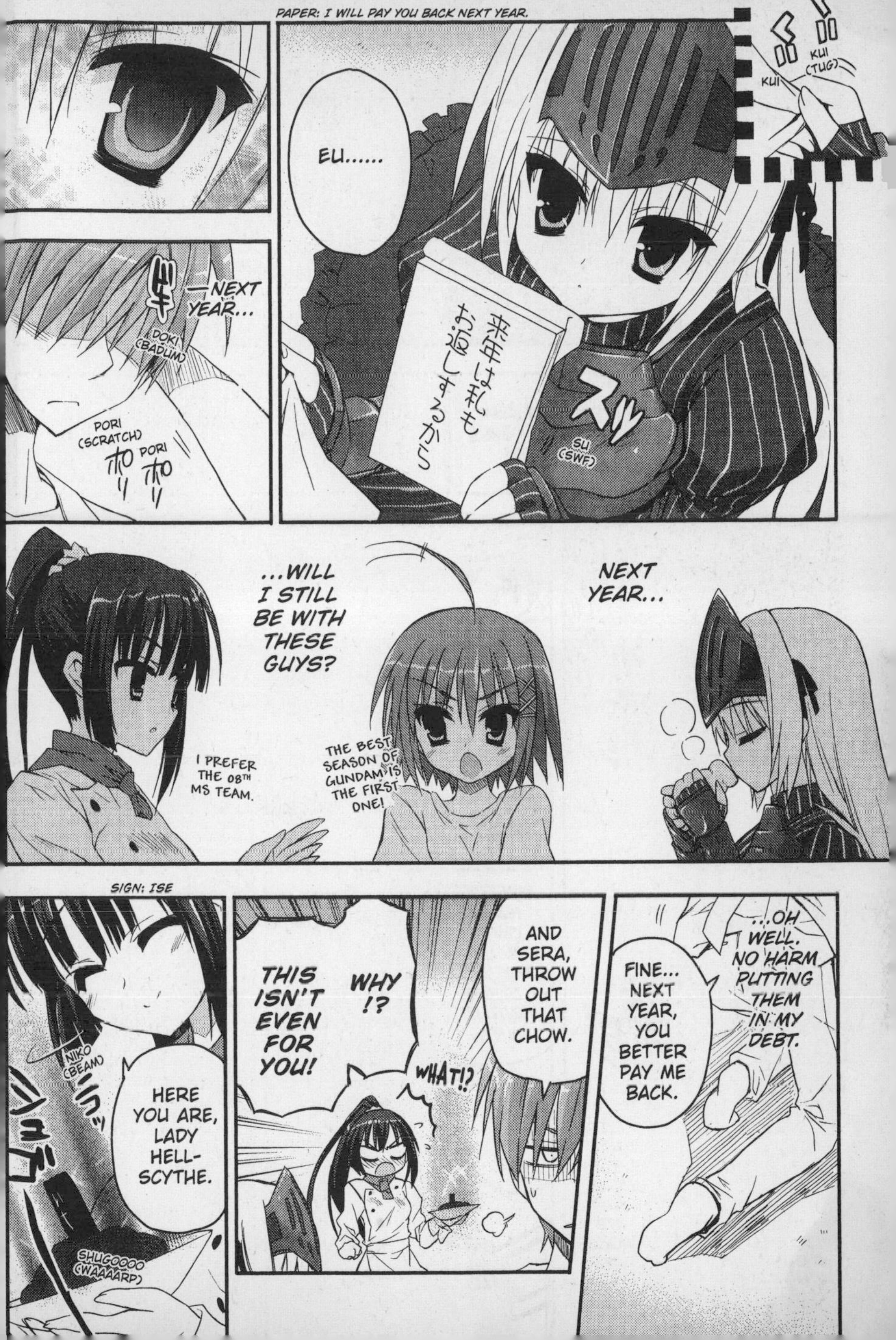
PAPER: I WILL PAY YOU BACK NEXT YEAR.
KUI
KUI (TUG)
EU......
SU (SWF)
来年は私もお返しするから
—NEXT YEAR...
DOKI (BADUM)
PORI (SCRATCH)
PORI
NEXT YEAR...
...WILL I STILL BE WITH THESE GUYS?
THE BEST SEASON OF GUNDAM IS THE FIRST ONE!
I PREFER THE 08TH MS TEAM.
...OH WELL. NO HARM PUTTING THEM IN MY DEBT.
FINE... NEXT YEAR, YOU BETTER PAY ME BACK.
AND SERA, THROW OUT THAT CHOW.
WHY!?
THIS ISN'T EVEN FOR YOU!
WHAT!?
SIGN: ISE
NIKO (BEAM)
HERE YOU ARE, LADY HELL-SCYTHE.
SHUGOOOO (WAAAARP)

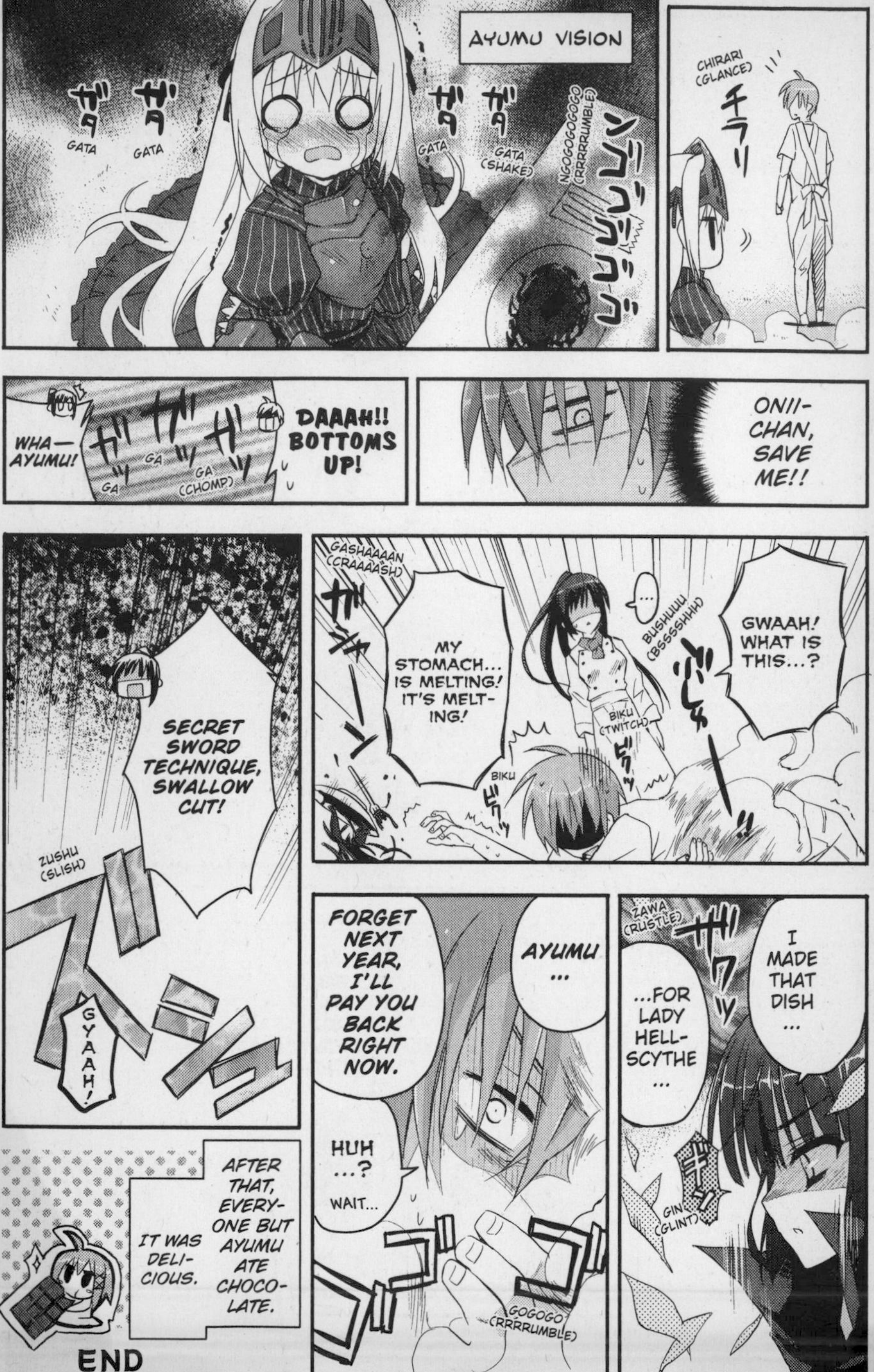
CHIRARI (GLANCE)
チラリ
AYUMU VISION
NGOGOGOGO (RRRRRUMBLE)
GATA (SHAKE)
GATA
GATA
GATA
ONII-CHAN, SAVE ME!!
DAAAH!! BOTTOMS UP!
GA (CHOMP)
GA
GA
WHA— AYUMU!
GWAAH! WHAT IS THIS...?
BUSHUUU (BSSSSHHH)
...
MY STOMACH... IS MELTING! IT'S MELTING!
BIKU (TWITCH)
BIKU
GASHAAAAAN (CRAAAASH)
I MADE THAT DISH...
ZAWA (RUSTLE)
...FOR LADY HELLSCYTHE...
GIN (GLINT)
AYUMU...
FORGET NEXT YEAR, I'LL PAY YOU BACK RIGHT NOW.
HUH...?
WAIT...
GOGOGO (RRRRUMBLE)
SECRET SWORD TECHNIQUE, SWALLOW CUT!
ZUSHU (SLISH)
GYAAAH!
AFTER THAT, EVERYONE BUT AYUMU ATE CHOCOLATE.
IT WAS DELICIOUS.
END

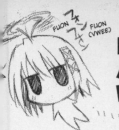

FUON
FUON
(VWEE)

IS THIS AN AFTER-WORD?

GENIUS.

INITIAL ROUGH OF HARUNA-CHAN

THANK YOU FOR PURCHASING VOLUME ONE OF THE *IS THIS A ZOMBIE?* MANGA!

I NEVER WOULD HAVE DREAMT I'D BE IN CHARGE OF THE MANGA ADAPTATION OF THIS SERIES!!

THAT WAS HOW I FELT WHEN THEY FIRST CONTACTED ME ABOUT THE JOB.

FIRST THING I DID WAS CATCH UP ON THE SERIES, AND THEN I QUICKLY FOUND MYSELF NECK DEEP IN THAT UNIQUE AND INTENSE STORY THAT KIMURA-SENSEI HAS WRITTEN AND THE WORLD OF "ZOMBIES" THAT KOBUICHI-SENSEI AND MURIRIN-SENSEI HAVE INTERWOVEN WITH THEIR ADORABLE CHARACTER DRAWINGS... (AND WHAT THE HECK IS AN ALFRED GUNNARSSON L!? HA!)

WHILE MARVELING AT HOW I EVER ENDED UP GETTING TO MAKE A MANGA OUT OF SUCH AN ENTERTAINING STORY, I FELT THE RESPONSIBILITY THAT COMES WHEN YOU'RE MIXING MEDIAS LIKE THIS AND HUMBLY TOOK THE JOB OF DRAWING IT TO BE AS FUNNY AS POSSIBLE.

DUE TO THE LIMITED NUMBER OF PAGES, THERE ARE LOTS OF PARTS THAT WE HAD TO EDIT OR CUT OUT, SO IT'D MAKE ME VERY HAPPY IF YOU FOLLOWED ALONG THROUGH THE NOVEL TOO.

IN VOLUME TWO, WE PLAN ON REVEALING THE TRUE IDENTITY OF THE CRIMINAL WHO KILLED AYUMU AND BRINGING IN A WHOLE LOT MORE NEW CHARACTERS!

LASTLY, I TRULY BELIEVE THAT I WAS ONLY ABLE TO COMPILE THIS BOOK THANKS TO ALL MY ASSISTANTS, THE EDITORIAL TEAM THAT GAVE ME FEEDBACK THROUGHOUT THE TIGHT PROCESS, KIMURA-SENSEI FOR CHECKING OVER THE ROUGHS, THE EDITORS OF THE LIBRARY COLLECTION, AND ALL YOU READERS WHO SUPPORT US ALONG THE WAY. THANK YOU VERY MUCH.

I HOPE YOU WILL CHEER US ON IN THE NEXT VOLUME TOO.

THANK YOU VERY MUCH!

SACCHI

★ASSISTANTS★ MIMIZU-SAN, TOMITA-SAN, KARAKU NISHIKI-SAN, EKAKIBITO-SAN, ANZU-SAN

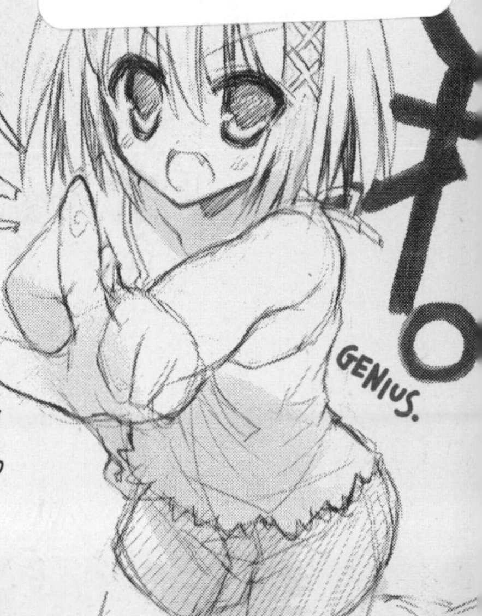